Counseling
& Helping Skills

Counseling & Helping Skills

Critical Techniques to Becoming a Counselor

Edward Neukrug

Old Dominion University

cognella® | ACADEMIC PUBLISHING

Bassim Hamadeh, CEO and Publisher
Amy Smith, Project Editor
Alia Bales, Production Editor
Jess Estrella, Senior Graphic Designer
Sara Schennum, Licensing Associate
Natalie Piccotti, Director of Marketing
Kassie Graves, Vice President of Editorial
Jamie Giganti, Director of Academic Publishing

Printed in the United States of America.

ISBN: 978-1-5165-3699-3 (pbk) / 978-1-5165-3700-6 (br) / 978-1-5165-9283-8 (al)

Dedicated to all the hard-working counselors

Brief Contents

Detailed Contents

Preface

Welcome to *Counseling & Helping Skills: Critical Techniques to Becoming a Counselor.* The book is divided into two sections, both of which are essential to being an effective counselor but focus on different areas of the counseling relationship. Section I: Attitudes, Skills, and Techniques provides you with knowledge and activities to learn and practice the majority of basic attitudes, techniques, and skills needed when working with clients. Section II: Treatment Issues provides you with a number of important activities related to the counseling relationship that are necessary to be effective with clients but are not directly related to the delivery of skills. As you go through both sections, you will find a large array of experiential and reflective exercises that will facilitate your learning, hopefully pique your interest, and add a bit of variety to the book. Let's look at the two sections in this text.

SECTION I: ATTITUDES, SKILLS, AND TECHNIQUES

Chapter 1: Characteristics of the Effective Counselor.

This chapter begins with a discussion of evidence-based and common factors of counseling, both of which are important to positive client outcomes. It then moves into a discussion of nine characteristics of the effective counselor important to working with clients. Six of these factors, *empathy, genuineness, acceptance, wellness, cultural sensitivity,* and your "*it factor,*" are all part of building a working alliance, while three of the factors, *competence, cognitive complexity,* and *belief in one's theory,* are aspects of delivering one's theoretical approach.

Chapter 2: Foundational Skills.

This chapter first reminds you of the characteristics of the effective counselor you just learned about in Chapter 1, then moves on to identify foundational nonverbal behaviors that can impact the counseling relationship, including office atmosphere, attire and dress, eye contact and facial expressions, body positioning and head nodding, proxemics (personal space), touch, and voice intonation. The second part of the chapter examines foundational skills related to creating an egalitarian and positive relationship, including honoring and respecting the client, showing caring curiosity, delimiting power and developing an equal relationship, being non-pathologizing, and being committed.

Chapter 3: Essential Skills.

Whereas the foundational skills discussed in Chapter 2 are critical to establishing the counseling relationship, the essential skills slowly nudge the client toward the self-examination process. Crucial near the beginning of the relationship, they are regularly revisited in the counseling relationship, especially when the counselor and client face an impasse or rupture in the helping relationship. They include silence and pause time, listening skills, reflecting feelings, reflecting content, paraphrasing, and basic empathy.

Although advanced empathy is briefly addressed, it is more fully highlighted in Chapter 4: Commonly Used Skills.

Chapter 4: Commonly Used Skills.

Skills in this chapter tend to be used after the working alliance has been formed, and they push the client toward increased awareness and identified goals. We first examine advanced empathy, which helps clients explore deeper feelings and fosters a more complex understanding of their situation. Next, we visit affirmation giving, encouragement, and support, all of which reinforce client behaviors and promote client movement toward goals. This is followed by offering alternatives, information giving, and advice giving, all of which provide ideas for attaining goals. Modeling, the next skill explored, helps clients find prototypes of new behaviors they can mirror in order to reach their goals, while self-disclosure is when the counselor provides personal examples of behaviors in an attempt to help the client develop new skills. The last skill, collaboration, ensures that clients are satisfied with their goal-seeking direction in the counseling relationship.

Chapter 5: Information-Gathering and Solution-Focused Questions.

Two kinds of questions are examined in this chapter: those that help gather information and those that help clients find solutions to problems. Information-gathering questions include closed questions, which limit client responses and are important when a counselor wants to obtain specific data; open questions, which allow clients to take the interview in myriad directions; tentative questions; and why questions. Solution-focused questions tend to be strength based and include preferred-goals questions, evaluative questions, coping questions, exception-seeking questions, solution-oriented questions (e.g., the miracle question), and scaling questions.

Chapter 6: Specialized Skills.

Although not used in every counseling relationship, most of the skills in this chapter are critical for some counseling relationships. Thus, in this chapter we explore advocacy; assessing for lethality (e.g., suicidality and homicidality); crisis, disaster, and trauma counseling; confrontation; challenge with support; cognitive-behavioral responses; interpretation; positive counseling; and coaching.

SECTION II: TREATMENT ISSUES

Chapter 7: Case Management.

A wide variety of tools that are important to the optimal management of clients are not directly related to attitudes, skills, and techniques and are broadly called "case management." Encompassing a broad range of activities, in this chapter we examine the process of providing informed consent and professional disclosure statements, conducting an assessment, developing client goals, monitoring psychotropic medications, writing notes and reports, maintaining confidentiality of records, ensuring security of client records, documenting client contact hours, terminating the counseling relationship and making referrals, conducting follow-up, and practicing time management.

Chapter 8: Case Conceptualization, Diagnosis, and Treatment Planning.

To develop effective treatment plans, counselors need to be able to effectively conceptualize their clients' situations and develop appropriate diagnoses. This chapter examines the case conceptualization process by exploring one model, the biopsychosocial model of assessment, in detail. It also reviews DSM-5, the process of making a diagnosis, and demonstrates how case conceptualization and diagnosis are used in the treatment planning process. It concludes with a section on how a counselor's theoretical orientation can help to drive, or give direction to, the treatment planning process.

Chapter 9: Culturally Competent Counseling.

Although touched on in Chapter 1 as a characteristic of the effective counselor, a more in-depth analysis of culturally competent counseling is offered in this chapter. Here, we underscore nine reasons why some diverse clients are wary of counseling, offer a definition of culturally competent counseling, describe three models that counselors can embrace to help them become culturally competent, and examine strategies for working with a number of select populations, including different ethnic and racial groups; people from diverse religious backgrounds; women; men; lesbian, gay, bisexual, transgender, and questioning (LGBTQ) individuals; those who are homeless and poor; children; older persons; individuals with serious mental disorders; individuals with disabilities; and substance users and abusers.

Chapter 10. Ethical, Legal, and Professional Issues.

This chapter examines a large array of ethical, legal, and professional issues. First, we examine the purpose of, and limitations to, ethical codes. Then, we explore four ethical decision-making models, including problem-solving, moral, developmental, and social constructivist models. Several important ethical concerns are addressed in this chapter, including informed consent, confidentiality, privileged communication, competence, maintaining boundaries and prohibited relationships, values in the counseling relationship, cross-cultural counseling, technology in counseling, supervision, and reporting ethical violations. The chapter also offers 26 best-practice behaviors and discusses the importance of malpractice insurance. This chapter is replete with vignettes and practice exercises related to ethical, legal, and professional issues in counseling.

Acknowledgments

I would like to thank a number of people who helped me in the development of *Counseling & Helping Skills: Critical Techniques to Becoming a Counselor.* Educators who took their time to review the book and provide me with ideas on how to elaborate, enhance, and strengthen concepts include: Dr. Lisa Brown, Lewis University; Dr. Melanie Hetzel-Riggin, Penn State Behrend; Dr. Darren H. Iwamoto, Chaminade University of Honolulu; and Dr. Jessica Waesche, University of Central Florida.

I would also like to thank Kassie Graves, editorial vice president of Cognella, who is simply amazing. A friend, a positive critic, a helper, and a wonderful person, she has assisted me in the development of this book and in other projects. Other individuals from Cognella who have been crucial in the development of this book include Jamie Giganti, director of academic publishing; Amy Smith, my project editor; Dani Skeen, marketing specialist; Jess Estrella, senior graphic designer (magnificent cover!); Alia Bales, production editor; and Michele Mitchel, copy editor. Thank you all for helping to put this project together. Finally, I'd like to thank my wife and children, Kristina, Hannah, and Emma, for loving me. They keep me going.

Section I

Attitudes, Skills, and Techniques

Section 1 of *Counseling & Helping Skills* contains six chapters and explores important attitudes, skills, and techniques needed to be an effective counselor. Chapter 1 offers an overview of nine critical characteristics of the effective counselor, parsed into two areas. The first area focuses on building the working alliance and includes empathy, genuineness, acceptance, wellness, cultural sensitivity, and something I call the "it factor." The second area has to do with delivering one's theoretical approach and includes competence, cognitive complexity, and belief in one's theory.

Chapter 2 presents foundational skills and includes the nonverbal behaviors of office atmosphere, attire and dress, eye contact and facial expressions, body positioning and head nodding, proxemics (personal space), touch, and voice intonation. The chapter also discusses egalitarian and positive skills, including honoring and respecting the client, showing caring curiosity, delimiting power and developing an equal relationship, non-pathologizing, and being committed.

Chapter 3 examines several essential skills, such as silence and pause time, listening, reflection of feelings, reflections of content, paraphrasing, and basic empathy.

Chapter 4 gives an overview of commonly used skills and includes advanced empathy; affirmation, encouragement, and support; offering alternatives, information giving, and advice giving; inadvertent and intentional modeling, content and process self-disclosure; and collaboration.

Chapter 5 focuses on two types of questions: information gathering and solution focused. Information-gathering questions include closed questions, open questions, tentative questions, and why questions. Solution-focused questions include preferred-goals questions, evaluative questions, coping questions, exception-seeking questions, solution-oriented questions, and scaling questions.

The last chapter in this section, Chapter 6, focuses on a number of specialized skills important to the work of the counselor and includes skills that may be critical in some, but not all, counseling relationships, including advocacy; assessing for lethality: suicidality and homicidality; crisis, disaster, and trauma counseling; confrontation: challenge with support; cognitive-behavioral responses; interpretation; positive counseling; and life coaching.

CHAPTER 1

Characteristics of the Effective Counselor

Learning Objectives

1. Identify toxic behaviors that can be detrimental to the counseling relationship
2. Understand evidenced-based practice (EBP) and common factors research and their impact on the counseling relationship
3. Explore nine characteristics critical to an effective counseling relationship, six of which are related to building the working alliance and three of which are associated with delivering one's theoretical approach:

    a. Building the working alliance
        i.   Empathy
        ii.   Genuineness
        iii. Acceptance
        iv.   Wellness
        v.   Cultural sensitivity
        vi.   The "it factor"

    b. Delivering one's theoretical approach
        i.   Competence
        ii.   Cognitive complexity
        iii. Belief in one's theory

Introduction

Learning specific skills to be effective with clients is, of course, critical to positive client outcomes. However, skills alone will not make for an effective counseling relationship. The attitudes that one embraces with clients will permeate the relationship and can positively or negatively affect the client's experiences and whether the client will be successful in the counseling relationship. For instance, we've all had friends or significant others be critical of us, dogmatic with us, moralistic to us, and perhaps even darn nasty. Called the toxins of the relationship, such attitudes can never foster a healthy counseling relationship. In contrast, there are certain attitudes and ways of being with clients that will result in a positive relationship and successful outcomes. This chapter will briefly outline toxic behaviors that can dampen a counseling relationship and then highlight the nine characteristics that will lend themselves to positive outcomes and clients leaving the relationship feeling good about having been in counseling. Specific skills of the counseling relationship will be highlighted in subsequent chapters of this section of the book.

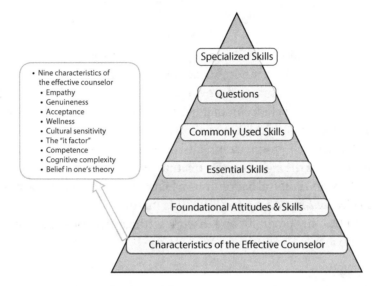

- Nine characteristics of the effective counselor
  - Empathy
  - Genuineness
  - Acceptance
  - Wellness
  - Cultural sensitivity
  - The "it factor"
  - Competence
  - Cognitive complexity
  - Belief in one's theory

FIGURE 1.1   Counseling and Helping Skills

Toxic Behaviors to Building a Counseling Relationship

We've all been exposed to people who have been critical, disapproving, disbelieving, scolding, threatening, discounting, ridiculing, or punishing. Or perhaps we have been around people who have been argumentative, accusatory, coercive, demeaning, condemning, rejecting, sexist, or racist. If truth be told, at some point in our lives we probably all have also acted in one or more of these toxic ways with others. As I'm sure you know, qualities like these do not lend themselves to healthy relationships or healthy development. And, if one is exposed to such behaviors over a long period of time, it will generally result in low self-esteem, reactive behaviors, and mental health problems. One of the most important habits that an effective counselor can learn is how to protect oneself from others' *toxic behaviors* and ensure that his or her own toxic habits are kept under wraps (Wubbolding, 2015). Exercise 1.1 asks you to identify times in your life when you have been exposed to toxic behaviors as well as the times when you may have used destructive responses. Finally, you will be asked what you can do when individuals are toxic to you and how you can monitor your toxic behaviors in all relationships, including the counseling relationship.

We can become cognizant of our toxic behaviors and, with a bit of restraint, prevent them from impacting our counseling relationships. In fact, it is probably easier to stop ourselves from being toxic with our clients than with our loved ones. With our loved ones, we have ongoing, close relationships with people who know how to "push our buttons," and those buttons sometimes lead to responses that include toxic behaviors. Although we should certainly focus on eliminating all toxic behaviors in our lives, it's usually easier to not exhibit them with our clients than with our loved ones. So perhaps we can see our relationships with our clients as a training ground for learning how not to be toxic with our loved ones. As we move ahead and examine those characteristics known to be important to developing healthy counseling relationships, remember that a voice in your head should always be monitoring and preventing you from exhibiting toxic behaviors. One too many times I've seen counselors acting irresponsibly toward a client. Don't let this be you.

Ensuring Counselor Effectiveness: Evidenced-Based Practice and Common Factors Research

As you might expect, a client's readiness for change, psychological resources, and access to social support are critical to successful outcomes (Beutler, 2014). In addition to what the client brings, the skills the counselor uses and the attitudes he or she embraces are closely related to positive change. Although confident that toxic behaviors should not be included in that list of attitudes and skills, some ways of being in the relationship have been shown to be critical to successful client outcomes. For instance, when a counselor (a) knows the best available research-proven treatments; (b) uses his or her clinical expertise to understand the client's situation and chooses the most effective treatments for it; and (c) takes into account the client's personal preferences, values, and cultural background when picking treatments, positive client outcomes are increased. Called *evidenced-based practice* (EBP), this manner of working with clients has quickly become commonplace in training programs and in work settings (American Psychological Association, 2005; Laska, Gurman, & Wampold, 2014).

REFLECTION EXERCISE 1.1

Toxic Behaviors Outside and Inside of You

First, identify toxic behaviors that you have experienced from others and consider what behaviors and feelings resulted from those behaviors. Then, in Part 2, identify toxic behaviors that you exhibited and the behavioral and emotional consequences to others. Write down ways that you can prevent toxic behavior by others and by yourself. Discuss your answers in small groups.

Part 1: Toxic Behaviors by Others

Identify the Behavior   *Behavioral and Emotional Consequences to You*

1. _____   _____
2. _____   _____
3. _____   _____
4. _____   _____
5. _____   _____

Identify steps you can take to prevent such toxic behaviors by others:

1. _____
2. _____
3. _____
4. _____
5. _____

REFLECTION EXERCISE 1.1—CONTINUED

Part 2: Toxic Behaviors by You

Identify the Behavior   *Behavioral and Emotional Consequences to Others*

1. _____   _____
2. _____   _____
3. _____   _____
4. _____   _____
5. _____   _____

Identify steps you can take to prevent such toxic behaviors by you:

1. _____
2. _____
3. _____
4. _____
5. _____

However, in addition to client resources and EBP, it has become clear that there are *common factors* underlying all therapeutic approaches that seem to be related to positive client outcomes. For instance, being able to develop a *working alliance* and the ability to *deliver one's theoretical approach* (regardless of the approach) both seem to be critical factors in positive client outcomes (Hilsenroth, 2014; Wampold, 2010a, 2010b; Wampold, & Budge, 2012; Wampold & Imel, 2015). In exploring these common factors, I have come up with nine characteristics important to developing an effective counseling relationship. Let's look at them.

Characteristics of Effective Counselors

When exploring the nine characteristics of effective counselors, I have found six fall into the realm of the working alliance and three fit nicely in the domain of delivering one's theoretical approach. As we see in Figure 1.2, *empathy, genuineness, acceptance, wellness, cultural sensitivity,* and your *"it factor"* are all part of building a working alliance, while *competence, cognitive complexity,* and *belief in one's theory* are aspects of delivering one's theoretical approach.

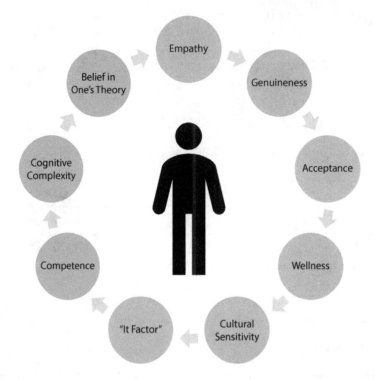

FIGURE 1.2   Nine characteristics of the effective counselor

When these qualities are not shown by the counselor, the likelihood of success is very small, if nonexistent. That is because the counselor who continually makes empathic failures cannot hear the client's problems, and the counselor who seems false, judgmental, dogmatic, and cross-culturally insensitive creates defensiveness. The physically, emotionally, or spiritually impaired counselor has a hard time taking care of someone else's needs, and the counselor who does not know his or her "it factor" flounders in the relationship as he or she tries to discover who he or she is. Also, the incompetent counselor does not know how to proceed in the relationship, and the counselor who lacks cognitive complexity has difficulty understanding and applying his or her theory. Finally, the counselor who does not believe in what he or she is doing lacks the enthusiasm to motivate the client Let's look at how we can embrace the qualities necessary for building the working alliance and delivering one's theoretical approach so we can become effective at what we do.

Being Empathic

Empathic individuals have a deep understanding of another person's point of view and can feel, sense, and taste the flavor of another person's experience (Bayne & Neukrug, 2017). These individuals know what it's like to be in another person's shoes and have a sense of what it is to be that person. Carl Rogers (1957) noted that the empathic person could sense the private world of the client as if it were his or her own, without losing the "as if" feeling. Empathic individuals accept and understand people in their differences and communicate this sense of acceptance to them. Today, being empathic is viewed as one of the most important qualities related to positive client outcomes (Elliot, Bohart, Watson, & Greenberg, 2011; Laska et al., 2014; Norcross, 2011).

While some of us are naturally empathic, most of us have to learn, develop, or at least refine this important tool. However, whether natural or learned, empathy enhances our relationships, whether they be with friends, colleagues, significant others, or clients. As a skill employed in the counseling relationship, empathy helps to both build the relationship and elicit information from the client—information that the client may not initially have felt comfortable sharing (Egan & Reese, 2019). Therefore, in Chapter 3 we will examine ways of enhancing our basic empathic skills with clients. Advanced empathy can further deepen the relationship and elicit feelings and thoughts of which the client was not aware. Such awareness helps clients gain great insight into their behaviors and nudges them toward the change process (Neukrug, 2017a; Neukrug, Bayne, Dean-Nganga, & Pusateri, 2012). Advanced empathy will be discussed in Chapter 4. To gain a sense of how empathic you are, do Reflection Exercise 1.2.

REFLECTION EXERCISE 1.2

Are You Empathic?

In class, your instructor will have you form triads and ask you to label each person as Number 1, Number 2, or Number 3. Number 1 begins by talking with Number 2 about an emotionally charged situation he or she has experienced. Number 1 should be as real as possible in relating the situation, while Number 2 is as empathic as possible. Number 3 will observe and record or take notes on the interaction. After about 10 minutes, review the notes or recording and, using the five-point scale, rate Number 2 on each of the six items. Then do the same, with Number 3 discussing an emotionally charged situation, Number 1 being empathic, and Number 2 being the observer. Finally, do it one last time, with Number 2 being the emotionally charged person, Number 3 being empathic, and Number 1 being the observer. After all triads have finished, find an average for the three triads. Discuss your results in your triads and in class.

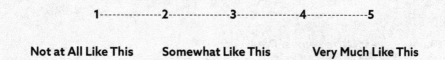

Not at All Like This   Somewhat Like This   Very Much Like This

1. *Talks minimally*: The empathic person will talk considerably less than the individual who is describing the situation.
2. *Asks few questions*: The empathic person will tend to ask few, if any, questions.
3. *Does not offer advice*: The empathic person will give little, if any, advice.
4. *Does not judge*: The empathic person will not judge the person he or she is listening to.
5. *Does not interpret*: The empathic person will not analyze or interpret the other person's situation.
6. *Does not cut off*: The empathic person will not cut off the other person and will allow him- or herself to be cut off by the person talking.

If, after scoring the responses, any individual or the group averages 3.0 or more (the ratings were mostly 3s, 4s, and 5s), you are doing well. If, however, your average is lower than 3.0 (the ratings were mostly 1s, 2s, or 3s), you have work to do. Chapters 3 and 4 examine the skill of empathy in more depth and offers the opportunity to fine-tune this important skill.

Genuineness

People can generally sense when a person is genuine or real with them versus someone who is acting in a false and deceptive manner. Genuine, or real, people are aware of their feelings and express them through their thoughts and actions, when appropriate. In contrast, those who are deceptive and fake tend to be out of touch with their feelings, and what they say does not reflect their inner world. Sometimes, such people can sense an internal tug that says "something's not right inside" or "I know I'm putting up a front with this person." Some individuals are so out of touch with their genuine side that they go through life unaware they are living dishonestly (see Reflection Exercise 1.3).

REFLECTION EXERCISE 1.3

Keeping Secrets

Keeping secrets is one way we prevent ourselves from being real with others. In the space provided, make a list of secrets you have kept from significant people in your life. Then, answer the questions given. Your instructor may have you gather in small groups to discuss what you discovered about your secrets (don't feel obligated to discuss specifics of your secrets, but do talk about your secrets without revealing details).

1. _____.
2. _____.
3. _____.
4. _____.
5. _____.

Questions

1. Was it relatively easy to remember five secrets?
2. Why have you kept these secrets?
3. Have you found it easier to keep these secrets than dialoguing with the person from whom you are holding the secret?
4. What might happen if the secrets were revealed?
5. What are the benefits of keeping the secret?
6. What are the drawbacks of keeping the secret?
7. Might the benefits of keeping your secret outweigh the drawbacks?
8. Might the drawbacks of keeping your secret outweigh the benefits?
9. What does keeping the secret do to the depth of the relationship?
10. Would you want someone to keep a secret from you?

Carl Rogers (1961, 1980) believed genuineness was a crucial element in all relationships, including the counseling relationship. He thus suggested that counselors must model realness but also pointed out that at times it might not be wise to immediately express one's true self. For instance, if a counselor initially has strong negative feelings about a client, if the counselor waits, the initial feelings will often dissipate as the counselor sees beyond the client's persona and is able to get to know the client in deeper ways. In addition, expressing strong negative feelings toward a client early on can cause a rupture in the counseling relationship. Monitoring one's emotions and waiting to see if a feeling persists or postponing the expression of a feeling to a more appropriate time is sometimes called *emotional intelligence* (Ciarrochi & Mayer, 2007). Emotional intelligence can increase the quality of the relationship; however, it does not mean ignoring one's feelings. Instead, those with high levels of emotional intelligence recognize their feelings and have the fortitude to be able to monitor them and express them at a later date if they persist. Like empathy, genuineness has been shown to be one more quality related to positive outcomes in the counseling relationship (Laska et al., 2014; Norcross, 2010; Zuroff, Kelly, Leybman, Blatt, & Wampold, 2010).

Some contend that every counseling relationship must address the important issue of *transparency* or *realness* (Gelso, 2009; Gelso et al., 2005). These individuals believe that counselors who do not reveal their genuine selves must somehow deal with how their clients perceive the walls they have put up. Of course, genuineness within a counseling relationship is always impacted by the boundaries of the relationship. For instance, it is rarely, if ever, wise to tell a client you are attracted to him or her. The bottom line, within the boundaries of the counseling relationship: one should be genuine, be able to monitor one's emotions, and be able to express one's feelings about the relationship at appropriate times.

Acceptance

Individuals who show acceptance feel comfortable allowing others to express their points of view, and they do not feel they need to change others to their way of understanding the world. Such *nonjudgmental* and *nondogmatic* individuals are open to understanding the views of others, open to feedback, and even open to changing their perception of the world after hearing other points of view. Such individuals are relatively free from biases and can accept people in their differences, regardless of dissimilar cultural heritage, values, or beliefs. In contrast, lack of acceptance can prevent one from listening effectively to another person. Non-accepting individuals are subtly, and sometimes not so subtly, expending energy trying to convince others to embrace beliefs they do not hold. That energy prevents them from hearing others effectively. In a helping relationship, an accepting counselor can hear about and understand a client's differences unconditionally, without "strings attached" to the relationship. Carl Rogers (1957) called such acceptance *unconditional positive regard*. Not surprisingly, research shows a relationship between the ability to be accepting and a being a good listener. As you might expect, acceptance leads to positive client outcomes (Laska et al., 2014; see Reflection Exercise 1.4).

Wellness

Wellness encompasses a wide range of activities that can be used to ensure self-care and provide optimal services to clients. The *American Counseling Association's Code of Ethics* (ACA, 2014) recognizes the importance of a counselor's wellness by noting that "counselors engage in self-care activities to maintain and promote their own emotional, physical, mental, and spiritual well-being to best meet their professional responsibilities" (Professional Responsibility section, Introduction). A few of the many self-care activities include support groups, eating healthy, meditation, prayer, exercise, hobbies, journaling, and reading. Reflection Exercise 1.5 addresses a number of factors to help you assess your level of wellness.

REFLECTION EXERCISE 1.4

Accepting Differences

Form triads, and using the list of situations that follow, assign one person to be pro and one person to be con. The third person is the moderator. Your task is to spend 5 to 10 minutes discussing the situation in the roles that were given to you. Try to go back and forth, presenting your point of view while listening to the other person's point of view. Regardless of how you actually feel about the role, take on the role given to you. During the exercise *or at any point afterward*, do not reveal how you actually felt about the situation. While the two individuals discuss the situation, the moderator should take notes and, after the discussion is completed, give feedback as to how each individual responded. After the first triad completes its discussion, repeat the situation, or do another situation, but this time the moderator takes on the role of pro or con and one of the other individuals is the moderator. Then do it a third time, ensuring that each person has had the opportunity to be a moderator. When you have finished, answer the questions listed under "points to consider."

Situations

1. Abortion
2. Increased taxes
3. Affirmative action
4. Opening an adult video store in your neighborhood
5. Capital punishment
6. Affordable Care Act (Obamacare)
7. Increased tuition
8. A database to monitor immigrants
9. Building a wall on our southern border to prevent illegal immigration
10. Increased gun control

Points to Consider

1. Did you become so emotionally charged that you had difficulty hearing the other person?
2. Did you think the other person was wrong?
3. Did you get tense while discussing the situation?
4. Did the individual with whom you were discussing the situation consider you open or closed to his or her point of view?
5. Did the moderator consider you to be open or closed?
6. Did you think you were open or closed?
7. Did you tend to cut off the other person from talking?
8. Were you preoccupied with coming up with a response in order to refute what the other person was saying?
9. Did the other person's point of view make sense to you?
10. Did you consider changing your point of view based on what you heard?

After considering points 1 through 10, reflect on ways that hindered you from hearing the other person. Discuss this in your small group and in class.

In addition to the methods just noted, another important way for counselors to address their own wellness is by attending counseling themselves. Counselors, like all people, have personal struggles and psychological issues that can be examined within the counseling relationship. In addition, due to the nature of their work, counselors may experience burnout, stress, *vicarious traumatization,* and *compassion fatigue* (Brownlee, 2016; Mayorga, Devries, & Wardle, 2015; Whitfield & Kanter, 2014). Participation in counseling can assist counselors in dealing with their personal difficulties, help them experience techniques firsthand, enable them to understand what it's like to sit in the client's seat, increase their cognitive complexity, and increase empathy, all of which can lead to more effective helping. Finally, personal counseling helps prevent countertransference, or the process of projecting one's issues onto clients (Murphy, 2013; Ponton & Sauerheber, 2014).

Perhaps not surprisingly, as much as 90% of practicing counselors have attended their own counseling (Kalkbrenner, Neukrug, & Griffith, in press). Although counselor trainees attend at lower rates than practicing counselors (Kalkbrenner & Neukrug, 2018a), they attend at higher rates than the 15% to 38% of the American public (Flynn, 2013; Hann, Hedden, Libari, Copello, & Kroutil, 2014; Kalkbrenner & Neukrug, 2018b). Despite the positive outcomes already noted about attendance in counseling, some counselors and counselor trainees resist counseling because they do not believe it is valuable enough, have difficulty finding a counselor with whom they feel comfortable, or are concerned about being stigmatized (Kalkbrenner & Neukrug 2018b). Counseling is certainly not the only road to increased emotional health; however, it can foster a very special relationship that is not achievable through friendships or other significant relationships. So if you have not been in counseling, consider finding a counselor with whom you feel comfortable.

Cultural Sensitivity

Even though close to 40% of Americans are from diverse ethnic and racial groups, compared to Whites, many clients from diverse backgrounds are fearful of seeking help from social service agencies, are more frequently misdiagnosed, and are more likely to discontinue services (Hatzenbuehler, Keyes, Narrow, Grant, & Hasin, 2008; Lo, Cheng, & Howell, 2013; National Alliance of Mental Illness, 2018b; U.S. Department of Health and Human Services, 2014). This may be because there continues to be a considerably higher percentage of Whites who administer and work in social service agencies, counseling theories have mostly been created by White males and may not be best when applied to non-Whites, implicit bias still exists in many people, and many other reasons. In fact, research has shown that if you're from a different ethnic or cultural group than your client, you are likely to have a harder time understanding him or her compared to someone from your own cultural or ethnic background (Nakash & Saguy, 2015).

With this knowledge, cultural sensitivity and cultural competence is more important than ever. A number of models and theories of how to work with clients who are different from ourselves have been developed, and some of these will be discussed in Chapter 9. For now, suffice it to say that all counselors should be sensitive to their clients and be willing to gain knowledge about their clients' cultures. One approach, the RESPECTFUL counseling model, highlights ten factors that counselors should consider when working with clients so that they can more readily understand and connect with their clients (see Reflection Exercise 1.5).

REFLECTION EXERCISE 1.5

Assessing Your Wellness

Myers and Sweeney (2008) developed the *indivisible self model,* which examines different aspects of self. What follows are abbreviated definitions of their five factors that constitute wellness. For each factor, rate yourself on a scale of 1 to 10, as noted:

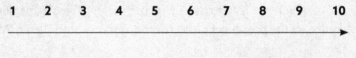

1   2   3   4   5   6   7   8   9   10

Needs Improvement   **Proficient/Competent**

Factor 1: *Creative self.* Being mentally aware. Allowing yourself to fully express your thoughts and feelings. Being positive and unique. Being who you truly are. Score:

Factor 2: *Coping self.* Having good self-esteem while knowing that humans are imperfect. Keeping stress at a reasonable level and being able to find solutions to life's problems. Being realistic about your problems. Score:

Factor 3: *Social self.* Feeling comfortable in social situations. Being able to feel a sense of connection with family and friends. Having friends and being able to love others. Score:

Factor 4: *Essential self.* Knowing and feeling comfortable with different aspects of self, such as our gender identity, cultural identity, placement in our families (e.g., father, first daughter), and spiritual self (however one defines that). Being comfortable with how you make meaning in life. Score:

Factor 5: *Physical self.* Eating healthy foods and being physically active. Not participating in restrictive eating or overeating. Being knowledgeable of your physical limits and positively addressing physical needs. Score:

Conclusion: After finishing your ratings, consider those factors on which you have scored lower (perhaps a score below 7). Then reflect on what you can do to increase your scores. Finally, if you had a total score below 35, you probably need to focus on your self-care in these areas a bit more.

R: religious/spiritual identity

E: economic class background

S: sexual identity

P: level of psychological development

E: ethnic/racial identity

C: chronological/developmental challenges

T: various forms of trauma and other threats to one's sense of well-being

F: family background and history

U: unique physical characteristics

L: location of residence and language differences

(Lewis, Lewis, Daniels, & D'Andrea, 2011, p. 54)

REFLECTION EXERCISE 1.6

Cultural Questionnaire

Using the scale that follows, write the number to the left of each statement that best represents your view. Your instructor might want to obtain a mean score from each item and then examine those items that seem to pique student interest. In class, discuss your varying responses. Allow different points of view to be expressed and heard.

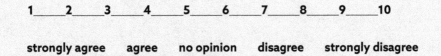

1____2____3____4____5____6____7____8____9____10

strongly agree   agree   no opinion   disagree   strongly disagree

1. Counseling theories have been created mostly by White men and therefore have inherent bias toward diverse clients.
2. Because all tests have inherent cultural bias, testing should be avoided in counseling.
3. Clients from some cultures are more difficult to work with.
4. Counselors should not have to adapt their theory based on the cultural background of clients.
5. The best client is one who is insightful and has good judgment.
6. Some cultural groups respond better to advice than others.
7. All clients need to be listened to empathically.
8. It is more important to show empathy and respect to female clients than male clients.
9. It is okay for counselors to focus on *only* working with special groups (e.g., women, men, certain diverse groups, etc.).
10. If a counselor knows little about a client's cultural background, he or she should refer that client to another counselor who is familiar with the client's background.
11. Diverse clients are more likely to be misunderstood and misdiagnosed.
12. It is best when a client sees a counselor from a similar cultural background.
13. All clients should be encouraged to seek autonomy.

REFLECTION EXERCISE 1.6—CONTINUED

14. Some acts that would normally be considered abhorrent in American culture should be tolerated, and maybe even affirmed, based on cultural background of the client (e.g., spanking, female genital mutilation).
15. If clients are gay or lesbian, they are more likely to have been abused than if they were heterosexual.
16. The past should always be discussed in counseling, as it impacts all clients.
17. All counselors carry unconscious bias, which can impact their work with clients.
18. Whenever we see cultural bias in the workplace from other counselors, we should confront them.
19. If a client has racist and discriminatory views, we should confront that client.
20. Clients from some cultural backgrounds are easier to work with.
21. Clients who are very religious may have a more difficult time with change.
22. Gender differences are more important than cultural differences when working with clients.
23. A client who is having difficulty accepting his or her same-sex attractions should be encouraged to change them.
24. A counselor has the absolute right to not see a client due to values differences.
25. All clients tend to struggle with very similar concerns.
26. When a counselor does not have the competence to work with a particular client, he or she should refer that client to someone else.

The "It Factor"

Can you imagine a crisis counselor joking with a suicidal client about ways to kill himself or herself, or an outpatient counselor taking scrupulous notes and barely looking up while a client talks? Or, what about a counselor who burns incense in the office, or another who suggests that each intake be followed up with a home visit to get a sense of the client's environment? Well, I've seen all these "techniques" used by various counselors over the years, and even though I would never recommend that you use them, they worked for these counselors. You see, these "ways of being" for these counselors were their "it factors." They were naturals at making jokes with clients (even suicidal clients), being a "scientist" with clients and taking those scrupulous notes, going on home visits to get a sense of the larger picture, and burning incense to help calm the office. It worked for them; it wouldn't have worked for me. Ask my friends if I'm empathic, and they'll say "kind of," but put me in a counseling relationship, and a switch gets turned on: this "it factor" in me is let go, and I'm one of the most empathic people there is. I'm not sure where it comes from, but it's there—almost naturally. So I suggest that each of you examine what makes you "you" and, over time, integrate that part of you into the counseling relationship. After all, just antiseptically making "correct" responses to clients, can, and will, get very boring.

We all need to understand our own it factor, which is reflective of who we are and how we act in relationships. After identifying our "it," it is incumbent on us to use "it" effectively with our clients. Don't ever forget your core skills, as they will ultimately provide the vehicle for positive client outcomes. But remember that you also have to be you. One word of advice, however: If your it factor is being a grouch, critical, mean, cynical, or nasty, you probably want to find another part of yourself that you can present to your clients. Presenting a toxic self is probably not your it factor—it's probably some leftover unfinished business that you need to work through. And one more word of advice—make sure your it factor is ethical. Unethical behaviors are not helping your clients and will eventually get you banished from the profession (see Reflection Exercise 1.7).

REFLECTION EXERCISE 1.7

Your "It Factor"

On your own, write down what you think your "it factor" is, and give some examples of how you might have expressed it in your life. Then, in small groups, share your various it factors and discuss how they might be used with clients. Discuss the possible pitfalls of using your "it factor" with clients as well as how your it factor may deepen your relationships with them.

Competence

Effective counselors have a thirst for knowledge and understand that the more they know, the better they become as counselors. They exhibit this quest for knowledge by joining professional associations, reading professional books and journals, participating in workshops and webinars, and more. Effective counselors understand that, for certain client populations, some techniques are more effective than others, and such professionals have a desire to learn what works best with varying types of clients (Baker, 2012). Competent counselors view education as a lifelong process, and they believe that counselors have both an ethical and a legal responsibility to be competent (Corey, Corey, & Corey, 2019).

ACA's ethical code (2014) has a whole series of standards on competence within Section C: Professional Responsibility. For instance, the code addresses the importance of only practicing within one's area of training and experience ("boundaries of competence"); to only practice new specialty areas if one has gained the appropriate education, training, and supervision; to not accept employment in areas in which one has not been properly trained; to monitor one's effectiveness and take appropriate steps when one realizes improvement is needed; to consult with others when one has ethical concerns; to participate in continuing education to keep up on current trends; to monitor oneself for physical and emotional problems and to stop counseling when one realizes he or she is seriously impaired; and to make appropriate plans for transfer of clients to a colleague in case of a "counselor's incapacitation, death, retirement, or termination of practice" (Section C.2.h).

How much do you value the acquisition of knowledge and the importance of being competent? Take the questionnaire in Reflection Exercise 1.8 to get a sense of how to rate your competence.

Cognitive Complexity

During the 1960s, William Perry (1970) studied the cognitive development of college students and found that they tended to be *dualistic*, or black-and-white thinkers, when they entered college and somewhat more *relativistic*, or complex thinkers, when they graduated college. Although times have

REFLECTION EXERCISE 1.8

How Much Do You Value Competence?

Take this inventory and see how much you embrace competence. If you do not embrace this characteristic, think about why you do not at this point in your career, if you believe you ever will, and how not embracing it can impact your work with clients.

For the 10 items that follow, place the number that best reflects your beliefs.

1. I very much disagree with this statement.
2. I disagree with this statement.
3. I neither agree nor disagree with this statement.
4. I agree with this statement.
5. I very much agree with this statement.

Items

1. ___I love the learning that takes place in school.
2. ___I often read books, journal articles, or related materials concerning subjects I want to learn more about.
3. ___I wish I did not have to take classes and someone could just give me a degree!
4. ___I view learning as a lifelong process.
5. ___I tend to be cynical in class.
6. ___I have joined, or plan to join, a professional association.
7. ___When I have a job in my profession, I plan on becoming active in one or more of my professional associations (e.g., be on a committee, run for office, etc.).
8. ___Research can add little to my knowledge of clients.
9. ___When I write research papers, I do an exhaustive search of the literature.
10. ___Consulting with other professionals is generally a waste of time.

Scoring the inventory: For items 1, 2, 4, 6, 7, and 9, give yourself the number of points that you wrote in for that item. For items 3, 5, 8, and 10, reverse score. That is, if you answered 1, give yourself 5 points; 2, give yourself 4 points; 3, give yourself 3 points; 4, give yourself 2 points; and 5, give yourself 1 point. The closer you scored to 50, the more you cherish the quality of competence.

changed and college students are certainly different than they used to be, much of his theory probably holds up today.

Perhaps with the knowledge gained from Perry's research, recent theorists who promote the *narrative therapy* approach to counseling suggest that people can have *thin descriptions* or *thick descriptions* of their lives (Neukrug, 2018). Somewhat like being dualistic, those with thin descriptions explain their lives simply. Those who have thick descriptions, on the other hand, can understand *multiple realities* people live by. For instance, one person with a thin description of his or her life may respond to the question "Why did you become a counselor?" with the following simple, but accurate, response: "Well, I entered the counseling profession to help people." In contrast, someone with a thick description of his or her life may state: "I entered the counseling profession for many reasons. I wanted to help people. I thought I would be good at it. I thought I could make money in the field. I was the middle child and was always a mediator in my family. My mother was nurturing, and I got that from her," and so on. These individuals can identify multiple origins that led them to where they are today, and such individuals can generally help others see different points of view within themselves. Or think of the client who is having a torrid affair and says, "I don't know what to do. I love my spouse." A counselor who is dualistic may judge and not understand this person, while a relativistic counselor can understand the multiple realities and complex lives we all have (see Reflection Exercise 1.9).

REFLECTION EXERCISE 1.9

Creating Multiple Narratives

Part 1: Jerome, a 48-year-old male, is married and has just lost his job at a print shop. He says, "I love my wife" but experiences his marriage as "depressing." He is concerned that he will not be able to find another job due to his age and the type of work he has done (print shop jobs are few and far between these days). He's worried he will not be able to support his two children, Maria, who is 19 and in college, and John, who is 17 and a junior in high school. He describes himself in the following manner:

1. "I'm too old to find another job."
2. "There are no print jobs available anymore—that's all I'm good at."
3. "My wife hates me; she's going to divorce me."
4. "I'm a horrible father 'cause I won't be able to support my kids through college."
5. "My lack of college means I can never move ahead."
6. "My wife's part-time job as a secretary will not be enough to help us out."

Jerome is thinking dualistically and describing his life using "thin" descriptions. In small groups, consider the responses that Jerome has made. Then help him think about the truth of his statements. See how you might devise responses to his statements that could help him rethink his responses—that is, help him see his responses in more complex ways. However, do this in ways that won't offend him. For instance, to the item "I'm too old to find another job," you might say, "Do you know any other people your age who have changed jobs at this point in their life?" Or, to his statement that "I'm a horrible father ... ," you might say: "Are there times in your relationship with your children when they have told you how much they love you or have shown you how much they appreciate you?" Make a list of some of the ways that you might respond to Jerome to encourage thick descriptions and share them in class.

Part 2: Reflect on a part of your life that has been difficult—perhaps a part that you see little hope in changing. Then consider alternate ways of viewing your situation and alternate narratives that might describe your life during that difficult time. Or consider how you can focus on other parts of self that were positive during that difficult time in your life. Are you able to develop new narratives or new ways of viewing and understanding the situation? If you feel comfortable, share them in small groups in class.

Counselors who are cognitively complex can generally be more helpful to clients and encourage deeper, more fruitful conversations (Granello, 2010; Jensen, McAuliffe, & Say, 2015). Cognitive complexity increases in a number of ways, such as through education, experience, being in counseling, placing oneself in situations that increase one's self-awareness, and allowing oneself to hear other points of view. Interestingly, there is some evidence that learning basic counseling skills will increase cognitive complexity. So enjoy this book and learn your skills!

Belief in One's Theory

> [Counselors] are attracted to therapies that they find comfortable, interesting, and, attractive. Comfort most likely derives from the similarity between the worldview of the theory and the attitudes and values of the therapist (Wampold, 2010a, p. 48)

The *Sage Encyclopedia of Theory in Counseling and Psychotherapy* lists approximately 300 counseling theories (Neukrug, 2015). With so many to choose from, which one is right for you? If you're using this book for a basic skills class, chances are you have not yet been exposed to a lot of theories, but at some point, you will be. So which do you use? For me, I feel some are too esoteric, some just don't make sense, some seem intuitively wrong, and some just simply turn me off. As Wampold (2010a) suggests in the quote, I drift toward those theories with which I feel comfortable and interested in learning more about.

Likely, your upbringing has more to do with the eventual theory you'll adhere to than you might believe. For instance, having a mother who was not particularly empathic (but loving in other ways) drew me toward person-centered counseling. And being a bit extroverted and perhaps a little theatrical led me to Gestalt therapy. On the other hand, as I've grown older, I've increasingly moved toward some of the complexities of the psychodynamic theories, such as psychoanalysis, Jungian therapy, and Adlerian therapy. More recently, I've become increasingly intrigued by some of the postmodern theories and their emphasis on sociocultural issues. Whatever theory you are drawn to, and for whatever reasons, you need to know it well and believe in it, as being facile with a theory and believing in the theory you apply appears to be related to positive client outcomes (Hilsenroth, 2014; Wampold & Imel, 2015).

REFLECTION EXERCISE 1.10

What Theory Are You Drawn To?

The following website contains a 72-item survey, with each item reflecting a particular view of human nature drawn from one of 12 classic counseling theories. You'll be asked to determine how strongly you agree with each item. When you finish the survey, you will receive a score that reflects how strongly your responses match each of the 12 theories. A second score will reflect your preference for each of four schools of therapy from which the theories align (psychodynamic, existential-humanistic, cognitive-behavioral, and postmodern). Examine your results and consider which of the theories and the schools are most like you. This is the beginning of your journey toward developing a theoretical approach. As a side note, most of the skills you will learn and practice in this book can be useful in many of the schools.

Link to survey: www.odu.edu/~eneukrug/therapists/booksurvey.html

After finishing the survey, form small groups and share your results. Your instructor might want to place students who scored similarly together or develop small groups that reflect a mixture of the different theories. In either case, in your small groups, discuss what it was it about your upbringing that may have resulted in the scores that you received.

It may be a bit early for you to pick a theory, but it's always good to think about the different theories. So complete Reflection Exercise 1.10 and reflect on those theories with which you obtained your highest score. Then consider why you are drawn to those. Finally, whatever theory you end up using, know it and believe in it—that will increase your chances of having success with clients. And if you're finding you are bored with your theory, find a different one to use, and know and believe in that theory.

Bringing It All Together

This chapter examined nine characteristics that seem to empirically or theoretically relate to effectiveness as a counselor: empathy, genuineness, acceptance, wellness, cultural sensitivity, it factor, competence, cognitive complexity, and belief in one's theory. Few, if any of us, have embraced all these characteristics fully. More likely, as we travel the road of our professional lives, we should periodically pause and take a personal inventory that focuses on how fully we embrace each of these qualities. Experiential Exercise 1.1 gives you an opportunity to review all the characteristics examined in the chapter.

Summary

We began this chapter with a discussion about the importance of avoiding toxic behaviors as a counselor. We then went on to define evidence-based practice (EBP) and common factors research, noting that both are important in providing positive outcomes for clients. Focusing on common factors research, we noted two broad areas that seem to underlie all theoretical approaches and are likely related to positive client outcomes: the working alliance and delivering one's theoretical approach. For the working alliance, we identified six important characteristics: empathy, genuineness, acceptance, wellness, cultural sensitivity, and one's it factor. Under delivering one's theoretical perspective, we identified three important characteristics: competence, cognitive complexity, and belief in one's theory. The rest of the chapter examined each of these nine characteristics.

Highlighted first was the importance of being empathic, or the professional's ability to understand another person's experience of the world. Made popular by Carl Rogers, we noted that being empathic was a way of being in the world as well as a skill that can be taught.

Next, we discussed the importance of genuineness and knowing how and when to be real or transparent with clients. Along these lines, we discussed emotional intelligence, or the ability of the counselor to manage his or her emotions in reference to knowing when, and how, to reveal an aspect of self within

EXPERIENTIAL EXERCISE 1.1

A Self-Inventory of the Nine Characteristics

Using the scale that follows, place the appropriate number next to each characteristic based on the importance you place on it (I consider them all critical). Then, using the same scale, rate yourself on each characteristic. After you have finished, find two or three persons who know you well, ask them to rate you, and place their ratings in the appropriate box. Then make a note of when you last exhibited that quality and what you can do to enhance that characteristic, if need be. This exercise should give you an overview of how well you display each of the nine characteristics.

1	2	3	4	5	6	7	8	9	10
An Extremely Low Rating							**An Extremely High Rating**		

	Importance	Self-rating	Other-rating	Last exhibited?	How can you improve?
Empathy					
Genuineness					
Acceptance					
Wellness					
Cultural Sensitivity					
Your "It Factor"					
Competence					
Cognitive Complexity					
Belief in One's Theory					

the counseling relationship. We noted that it has been suggested that realness is an issue that all helpers must deal with at some point in a counseling relationship.

Acceptance, or being nonjudgmental, was the third quality discussed, and we noted that this characteristic allows a client to feel understood and safe in the counseling relationship. Also called "unconditional positive regard" by Carl Rogers, this quality ensures that there are no "strings attached" to the relationship.

Wellness, the next characteristic, was viewed as important because it can moderate burnout, stress, vicarious traumatization, and compassion fatigue. Also, being well can help prevent countertransference. We pointed out how the ACA Code of Ethics highlights the importance of addressing impairment as a counselor and maintaining wellness. Many ways of developing a wellness focus were noted, including being in one's own counseling, attending support groups, eating healthy, meditation, prayer, exercise, journaling, reading, and more. We summarized the indivisible self model and suggested you examine your own wellness relating to each of its five factors: the creative self, the coping self, the social self, the essential self, and the physical self.

We noted that cultural sensitivity was another characteristic counselors should embrace. This characteristic is particularly important, as clients from nondominant groups have historically not been served well by many so-called helpers. We offered the respectful model, which highlights a number of areas to examine when working with diverse clients and noted that this important area will be discussed in more depth in Chapter 9.

We defined the it factor and noted that this quality is different for each person and has to do with how one brings oneself into the counseling relationship. It was suggested that we all need to know how we can use our unique personalities to foster positive counseling relationships.

Being competent was the next quality highlighted, and we pointed out the importance of ensuring that one continues to have a thirst for knowledge throughout one's career. We suggested that competence was an ethical issue and a legal concern and highlighted the many ways that competence is focused upon in the ACA Code of Ethics.

The quality of cognitive complexity was next highlighted. We pointed out that William Perry discussed this characteristic in light of being a dualistic or relativistic thinker and that the postmodernists, such as narrative therapists, suggested that those with thicker descriptions of their lives have deeper and more complex narratives. We suggested that the best helpers see the world from multiple angles and can help a client move from thin, dualistic narratives to thick or complex narratives.

The last quality, belief in one's theory, suggests that it is important that we have a theoretical perspective from which to work when counseling clients. We noted that early in one's training, students are just beginning to identify their theoretical perspective, and we suggested taking a survey to begin to understand what theory you might feel most akin to. We pointed out that one must be competent and believe in one's theory, regardless of the theory, if one is to see positive client outcomes.

Key Words and Terms

ACA Code of Ethics	multiple realities
acceptance	narrative therapy
belief in one's theory	nondogmatic
characteristics of the effective counselor	nonjudgmental
cognitive complexity	Perry, William
common factors	realness
compassion fatigue	relativistic
competence	RESPECTFUL counseling model
countertransference	Rogers, Carl
cultural sensitivity	thick descriptions
delivering one's theoretical approach	thin descriptions
dualistic	toxic behaviors
emotional intelligence	transparency
empathy	unconditional positive regard
evidence-based practice (EBP)	vicarious traumatization
genuineness	wellness
indivisible self model	working alliance
it factor	

CHAPTER 2

Foundational Skills

Learning Objectives

1. To explore a number of basic common-sense, foundational skills that each counselor should exhibit throughout his or her career regardless of theoretical orientation
2. To quickly review the nine characteristics of the effective counselor, as they are foundational to the work of the counselor
3. To review nonverbal behaviors foundational to building an effective counseling relationship:
    a. Office atmosphere
    b. Attire and dress
    c. Eye contact and facial expressions
    d. Body positioning and head nodding
    e. Proxemics (personal space)
    f. Touch
    g. Voice intonation
4. To examine egalitarian and positive foundational skills:
    a. Honoring and respecting the client
    b. Showing caring curiosity
    c. Delimiting power and developing an equal relationship
    d. Non-pathologizing
    e. Being committed
5. To discuss how foundational skills can be mediated by cross-cultural differences

Introduction

A number of important foundational skills exist that all counselors should demonstrate if they are to be effective. These skills are fairly universal; that is, they tend to be used regardless of one's theoretical orientation and should be applied throughout the counseling relationship. Thus, in this chapter, we first remind you of the nine characteristics of the effective counselor, as they too are foundational. Then we go on to describe a number of foundational nonverbal behaviors that can impact the counseling relationship. They include the office atmosphere, attire or dress, eye contact and facial expressions, body positioning and head nodding, proxemics (personal space), touch, and voice intonation. Finally, we examine foundational skills related to creating an egalitarian and positive relationship. Having become increasingly popular in recent years, these include honoring and respecting the client, showing caring curiosity, delimiting power and developing an equal relationship, being non-pathologizing, and being committed (see Figure

2.1). Unfortunately, I've seen many counselors ignore or forget to use these skills—perhaps because they became burnt out. So make a copy of Box 2.1, cut it out, and keep it with you in a prominent place when you do counseling. It will remind you of the importance of these skills throughout your practice.

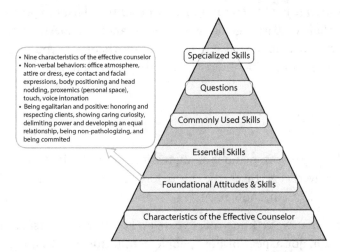

FIGURE 2.1 Counseling and helping skills

BOX 2.1

Foundational Skills to Remember

The nine characteristics of the counselor

- Empathy
- Genuineness
- Acceptance
- Wellness
- Cultural sensitivity
- "It factor"
- Competence
- Cognitive complexity
- Belief in one's theory

Nonverbal behaviors of the counselor
- Office atmosphere
- Attire and dress
- Eye contact and facial expressions
- Body positioning and head nodding
- Proxemics (personal space)
- Touch
- Voice intonation

Egalitarian and positive skills
- Honoring and respecting the client
- Showing caring curiosity
- Delimiting power and developing an equal relationship
- Being non-pathologizing
- Being committed

Copy these skills, cut them out, place them on your wall, and don't forget them!

Nine Characteristics of the Effective Counselor

As you remember from Chapter 1, toxic counselors who are critical, scolding, judgmental, nasty, cynical, and so forth, are not helpful to clients and can lower the self-esteem of some clients and raise the wrath of others. On the other hand, the *nine characteristics of the effective counselor* highlighted in Chapter 1 will tend to strengthen the counseling relationship and lead to positive client outcomes. If you remember, they include empathy, genuineness, acceptance, wellness, cultural sensitivity, your it factor, competence, cognitive complexity, and belief in one's theory. As you read through this chapter, always remember that these nine characteristics are the bedrock of a positive working relationship with clients.

Nonverbal Behaviors

> "[C]lients may develop predispositions or impressions on the basis of the counselor's attire, the counselor's nonverbal gestures, the counselor's greeting, the office environment, and the reception staff. ..." (Bedi, 2006, p. 33)

This quote epitomizes what we've known for years and what recent research continues to show: nonverbal behavior is a major aspect of how people communicate (Knapp, Hall, & Horgan, 2014; Matsumoto, Frank, & Hwang, 2013). In fact, although nonverbal behavior is often out of a person's consciousness, with a little bit of focused self-awareness, we can begin to be more intentional about our nonverbals. This is critical, as nonverbals that communicate "Don't open up to me" will obviously affect clients very differently from those that communicate "I'm open to hearing what you have to say." Some nonverbal behaviors that are particularly important include *office atmosphere, attire or dress, eye contact and facial expressions, body positioning and head nodding, proxemics (personal space), touch, and voice intonation.*

Office Atmosphere

Building a trusting relationship begins with the client's initial contact with the counselor's setting. Such contacts, whether through e-mail, phone, walk-in, or other ways, should be followed up expeditiously. Also, when clients come to an agency or office, the receptionist and staff should be courteous and kind with them. In addition, since the client will have an immediate reaction to the counselor's office (Knapp et al., 2014), ensuring that one's office is a quiet, comfortable, and safe place where confidentiality can be ensured is crucial to successful helping relationships.

How a helper arranges his or her office can be important in eliciting positive attitudes from clients (Bedi, 2006; Nassar & Devlin, 2011), and most agree that it should be relatively soundproof, have soft lighting, be uncluttered, have client records electronically and/or physically secured, be free from distractions such as a phone ringing or knocks on the door, and have comfortable seating. Large pieces of furniture, such as a desk, should generally not be between the counselor and the client, although this might vary as a function of the helper's counseling style, personality, and the particular situation (e.g., I've worked with volatile clients when I felt it would be wise to have a desk between me and them). As the counselor creates his or her office, each will try to find a balance between how the office reflects his or her taste while ensuring that the office is appealing to the majority of clients (see Experiential Exercise 2.1).

EXPERIENTIAL EXERCISE 2.1

Arranging Your Office

From the list that follows, draw the items that appeal to you on a piece of paper, or cut out pictures of the items from a magazine and glue them to the paper. Create your office space! Share your office arrangement with others and describe what makes your office special. Discuss what makes your office conducive to a positive helping relationship.

Desk	Plant	End tables
File cabinet	Wicker basket	Printer
Couch	Bookcase	Pictures
Desk chair	Coffee table	Large lamp
Chair	Radio/CD player	Small lamp
Computer	Magazine rack	Rocking chair
Other items		

How the counselor arranges furniture is not the only thing that will affect whether a client will be emotionally available during an interview. Often, the kind of literature or other items on display can greatly affect a client's willingness to be open. To highlight this point, complete Reflection Exercise 2.1. Of course, no matter how a counselor arranges his or her office, some people will be offended by something. In addition, it may be that you will want to attract certain clientele who would feel comfortable with a particular ambiance. For instance, a highly religious counselor might include articles of a religious nature in his or her office, while a person dealing with mostly gay and lesbian issues might include LGBTQ literature.

REFLECTION EXERCISE 2.1

Selecting Items to Place in Your Office

After examining the items in the list that follows, decide whether any of them would be offensive to you if you walked into a counselor's office and saw them. Then think about the most liberal and the most conservative people you know and imagine how those people might feel if they walked into a counselor's office and saw any of the items. In class, discuss whether you think the items listed should be included in a counselor's office.

- Feminist literature
- A compulsively clean desk
- A bear rug
- An AIDS pin
- Information on transgender issues
- A desk between counselor and client

- Fundamentalist religious literature
- Information on human sexuality
- A cluttered desk
- A Christian cross
- Information on abortion
- An American flag

- Leather furniture
- Buddhist meditation material
- LGBTQ literature
- A Confederate flag

Attire or Dress

How the counselor dresses can project whether the counselor is ready listen to and assist the client, or it can shut the client down (Segal et al., 2011). Should jeans be worn at work? What about an expensive suit? Are the counselor's clothes revealing? What does jewelry or hairstyle say about the counselor? Are shoes nicely polished or scuffed? Are sneakers okay to wear? Are clothes tucked in neatly or falling out all over the place? Is it okay to have piercings, tattoos, tattered clothes, and so forth?

Consciousness about, and sensitivity to, how a client reacts to a counselor's attire is critical. The counselor should always be considering the following questions: "What is my appearance saying to my client?," "Do I need to change how I dress for my clients?," "Should I have a discussion with my clients about my appearance?," and "How much does my dress feed my own ego?" (see Reflection Exercise 2.2).

REFLECTION EXERCISE 2.2

What Are You Wearing?

Have each student stand in front of the class and all the other students write, anonymously, what they believe each student's appearance says about him or her. If possible, make specific remarks about tattoos, piercings, type of clothes, hairstyle, etc. Each student should receive the other students' comments and read them to himself or herself. Then the student who stood in front of the class can remark on the comments made by other students.

Alternative exercise: Instead of having students stand in front of the room, the instructor can find pictures of people online in various attire, and students can discuss their ideas about how each picture would elicit positive or negative responses from clients.

Eye Contact and Facial Expressions

How counselors and clients look at one another says much about each of them (Howes, 2012; Knapp et al., 2014). Is the counselor maintaining eye contact in a way that invites the client to talk? Does the client show a willingness and desire to work with the counselor? Is the counselor excited, curious, and desirous of working with the client? And is the client excited, fearful, or wary of working with the counselor? Counselors need to be tuned into what they are saying to their clients with their eyes and also be sensitive to clients' feelings as expressed by clients' eyes—their windows to their soul.

Although intense eye contact (e.g., staring) will certainly turn off almost any client, the counselor who has difficulty maintaining any eye contact will not have an easy time building a trusting relationship. Thus, finding the "correct" amount of eye contact tells a client the counselor is ready to listen and should be one goal of the counseling relationship. Sometimes, cross-cultural differences in tolerance for eye contact makes determining the amount of eye contact a difficult task (Ratts, Singh, Nassar-McMillan, Butler, & McCullough, 2015, 2016). Thus, counselors should be trained, as best as possible, in difference in eye contact tolerance as a function of culture. In addition to eye contact, the counselor's facial expressions will also telegraph how a counselor experiences a client (Matsumoto & Hwang, 2013a). Often, it is important for facial expression to match the client's affect (e.g., sadness, anxiety, concern, joy; see Box 2.2).

BOX 2.2

Reflecting You/Reflecting Me

The first time I was in counseling, I had a wonderfully empathic counselor who seemed to always be "with me." One day, he was looking at me and seemed particularly sad. I'll never forgot when I said to him, "How come you look so sad?" and he replied, "I'm reflecting back what I'm sensing from you." At that moment, I realized how sad I was and began to sob. That was the beginning of some important self-realizations.

For many counselors, finding the right amount of eye contact comes naturally; however, some will have difficulty. You may want to explore your ability at maintaining eye contact (see Experiential Exercise 2.2).

EXPERIENTIAL EXERCISE 2.2

How Comfortable Are You With Eye Contact?

People's ability to tolerate eye contact can vary greatly and may be related to cross-cultural differences. To test this out, your instructor will randomly divide the class into groups of four to six students. Have one person be the counselor while others take turns being the client. The counselor should be comfortable with eye contact and offer a reasonable amount to each person in the group, one at a time, as the group members share a small issue or problem in their lives. When finished, discuss whether the participants' level of comfort with eye contact varied considerably, and if so, why. Share your responses with the larger group.

Body Positioning and Head Nodding

Whether it be in a counseling relationship or a personal relationship, we are constantly communicating with others nonverbally (Knapp et al., 2014; Matsumoto & Hwang, 2013b). And the longer and better we know a person, the more capable we are at reading each others' body language. In the counseling relationship, our body positioning, including head nodding, is particularly important in communicating with our client. Optimally, the counselor should have his or her feet on the ground, body leaning forward slightly and arms positioned in an open manner, all of which suggests the counselor is ready to listen. In addition, appropriate head nods tell the client, "Keep going" and "I'm here for you." To see how important body language can be, complete Reflection Exercise 2.3.

REFLECTION EXERCISE 2.3

Body Positions, Head Motions, and Facial Expressions

In small groups, have one person role-play a counselor and another a client. The rest of the group should observe. The client should talk about an emotionally charged situation, and the counselor should only respond through body positioning, head nods, and facial expressions. The rest of the group observes, and after the counselor and client role-play for a few minutes, give feedback to the counselor. Then allow others to take on the role of the counselor. If time allows, everyone in the group can be the counselor.

Proxemics (Personal Space)

Mediated by such factors as culture, age, gender, and personal histories, individuals vary greatly in their level of comfort with personal space (Knapp et al., 2014; Sommer, 2007). Therefore, counselors must be sensitive to the amount of distance between themselves and their clients. Too much space, and the client will experience the counselor as distant, aloof, and disinterested. Too little space, and the client will feel as if his or her boundaries have been violated and be less likely to share. Although this will generally happen in subtle ways, optimally, the counselor should take the lead in creating an appropriate distance by having awareness of what might be the "right" amount of space for any particular client. Reflection Exercise 2.4 examines your own comfort level regarding personal space.

REFLECTION EXERCISE 2.4

Your Comfort With Personal Space

Your instructor will have the class stand in two lines, five feet apart, with each student facing another student. Then the instructor will direct each student in one line to move a comfortable distance closer to or further away from the student he or she is facing, based on the first student's level of comfort with personal space. Then, after 15 seconds, reverse the exercise and have students in the line that didn't move step closer or further away from students in the other line, based on their level of comfort with the current amount of personal space. The instructor will facilitate a discussion about various levels of comfort students had with personal space.

Touch

Touch, one of the most important things we can do to show affection and caring, is critical in all relationships, including the counseling relationship (Calmes, Piazza, & Laux, 2013). For instance, when someone is expressing deep pain, it is not unusual to hold the person's hand or to lightly embrace the person while he or she sobs. Or when a person is coming to or leaving a session, many counselors may find it natural to place a hand on a shoulder or give a hug. However, in today's litigious society, touch has become a delicate subject, and it is important for all counselors to be sensitive to their clients' boundaries, their own boundaries, and the limits of touch as suggested by one's professional codes of ethics. Physical contact with a client should be based on (a) the counselor's assessment of the client's needs, (b) the counselor's awareness of his or her own needs, (c) an awareness of  what is appropriate within the cultural context of the client's world, (d) a sense of how the client will interpret touch, and (e) knowledge of agency policies and customs as well as ethical codes and the law (see Reflection Exercise 2.5).

Voice Intonation

Human communication is complex, perhaps more so than we sometimes would like to admit, and how the counselor responds can sometimes hold multiple meanings (Watzlawick, Beavin, & Jackson, 1967). Relative to one's tone of voice, counselors must be aware that what they say may not always match how they're saying it. Saying "I like you" in an angry tone gives a mixed message and can greatly impact the client's experience of the counselor (Frank, Maroulis, & Griffin, 2013; Knapp et al., 2014; Sommer, 2007). Of course, being aware of the meaning of a client's voice intonation is equally as important. In addition, all counselors will make a number of short responses to clients during a session, such as "uh huh," that can go a long way in telling clients whether they are being attended to (see Reflection Exercise 2.6).

A Cross-Cultural Perspective on Nonverbal Behaviors

Although counselors have been taught to lean forward, have good eye contact, speak in a voice that meets the client's affect, and rarely touch their clients, research suggests that cross-cultural differences exist in the ways that clients perceive and respond to nonverbal behaviors exhibited by counselors (Knapp et al., 2014; Matsumoto & Hwang, 2013c). Therefore, it is suggested that counselors be acutely sensitive to client nonverbal differences while being knowledgeable and skilled in culturally appropriate responses (Ratts et al., 2015, 2016).

Some nonverbal behaviors are out of bounds in the counseling relationship, regardless of the cultural background of the client (e.g., seductive looks, inappropriate touch, harshly critical facial expressions). However, culturally skilled counselors are also aware of how *their* nonverbal behaviors could have a negative impact on their clients. In addition, they are knowledgeable of differences in nonverbal behaviors as a function of their client's cultural background. This knowledge helps them understand their clients in deep and meaningful ways.

Effective cross-cultural counselors must understand that some clients will expect to be looked at, while others will be offended by eye contact; that some clients will expect the counselor to lean forward, while others will see this as intrusive; that some clients will want a hug when they leave, while others will see this as crossing a boundary and inappropriate. Effective counselors keep in mind that what works for many will not work for all, and they are sensitive to the individual needs and responses of all their clients (see Box 2.3).

BOX 2.3

Your Level of Comfort With Touch

I was in counseling with a therapist for a number of years. One day, I had a particularly poignant and insightful session with him. At the end of the session, I stood up and went to give him a hug. He seemed embarrassed and quickly and nicely said, "I'm just not a touchy person." Of course, during our next session, we then had to process the fact that he wouldn't hug. Go figure. So I guess we need to be aware of our client's level of comfort as well as our own!

Conclusion

In this section, we touched on a number of nonverbal aspects of the counseling relationship important to positive client outcomes. One acronym I sometimes use to remember these is: *CHASE LOVE:* **C**ross-cultural concerns, **H**ead nodding, **A**ttire, personal **S**pace (proxemics), **E**ye contact, **L**eaning forward and open body posture, **O**ffice atmosphere, **V**oice intonation, and facial **E**xpression. Now that you learned about various types of nonverbal behaviors, do Experiential Exercise 2.3 to review your understanding of them.

Egalitarian and Positive Attitudes and Skills

The recent popularity of *postmodern approaches* to counseling have underscored a number of attitudes and skills that are widely used by many counselors today. These strength-based approaches assume we should treat clients as equals—with respect and with the belief that they can increasingly see their lives in a more positive manner (Neukrug, 2018; Rice, 2015). Some specific attitudes and skills that are in line with this thinking include *honoring and respecting* clients, showing *caring curiosity* toward clients, *delimiting power and forming equal relationships* with clients, *non-pathologizing* clients, and *being committed* to clients. Let's look at each of these.

EXPERIENTIAL EXERCISE 2.3

Practice Nonverbal Behaviors

Using groups of four or five students, have one student role-play a counselor while another student role plays a client for 3 or 4 minutes. The other students should observe the role-play and, using the chart that follows, write comments about the nonverbal behaviors of the counselor. Be specific. After you finish each role-play, give the counselor feedback. Take turns being the counselor and the observers.

	Positive qualities	Needs improvement
Cross-cultural concerns		
Head nodding		
Attire		
Proxemics (personal) space		
Eye contact		
Leaning forward		
Open body posture		
Voice intonation		
Facial expression		

Honoring and Respecting the Client

The primary responsibility of counselors is to respect the dignity and promote the welfare of clients (American Counseling Association, 2014, Section A.1.a).

Honoring and respecting clients acknowledges and affirms the unique paths clients have taken and will take in their lives (Sung & Dunkle, 2009). Such honor and respect often starts with a *professional disclosure statement* that reflects important values of the helping relationship, which are also upheld in ethical codes (e.g., ACA, 2014; Jansson, 2016). Such a written statement is given to clients when we first meet them and often includes the 10 items listed in Experiential Exercise 2.4 (Corey, Corey, & Corey, 2019; Remley & Herlihy, 2016).

EXPERIENTIAL EXERCISE 2.4

Writing a Professional Disclosure Statement

A professional disclosure statement ensures that clients feel welcomed in the helping relationship, are knowledgeable about what is to occur, and understand the process of the counseling relationship. It should delineate what is to occur in the relationship and any boundaries of the relationship. It should be written in a manner that is accepting and honoring of the client. Using the 10 items that follow, write your own professional disclosure statement. Students can share their statements in class. A more involved discussion of professional disclosure statements can be found in Chapter 7.

1. Information about credentials
2. Purpose of the helping relationship
3. Support of the client's unique diversity
4. Statement about keeping promises to clients
5. Statement about being committed to the client
6. Synopsis of a counselor's theoretical orientation
7. Statement about the importance of the client's self-determination
8. Information about limits to and boundaries of the helping relationship
9. Statement about agency rules and legal issues that might impact the relationship
10. Statement about the confidential nature of the relationship under all but certain circumstance (e.g., danger to self or others)

In addition to the professional disclosure statement, honoring and respecting a client means that the counselor is appreciative of the client and demonstrates unconditional acceptance of where the client is in his or her life (Gold, 2008; Jansson, 2016). In that sense, the resistant client is honored as the counselor tries to understand the reasons for the defiance. In this context, the client is not labeled as a "difficult" client but a client who has faced some challenging circumstances that have led to resistance. Similarly, the depressed client's sadness is acknowledged and seen as a message to the client about his or her life, not a sign that there is something inherently wrong or that he or she can never get better. Or the cynical client is seen as a person who has a reason for having a skeptical attitude, and the counselor's goal is to understand this attitude. Honoring the client is accepting the client in all his or her feelings and attitudes, understanding the context in which the client has come to be, and having a desire to help (see Reflection Exercise 2.7).

REFLECTION EXERCISE 2.7

Honoring Resistance

Years ago, I went to a workshop entitled "Working With Resistant Adolescents." Since adolescents are known to be a difficult population with which to work, I was interested in how this workshop leader would help us understand resistant adolescents who seem to not want our help. I was initially startled, and then enlightened, at the beginning of the workshop when I heard the workshop leader say, "There are no resistant adolescents. There are only resistant helpers." The point he was making was that it's not the adolescent's job to not be resistant. Instead, it is the counselor's responsibility to understand and honor the resistant adolescent as well as to understand and respect how he or she has come to show such behavior. He suggested that helpers should not play the "blame game" by making the resistant adolescent be the person with the problem. The problem is with the counselor who cannot reach the adolescent.

Think about times when you have had friends, clients, or acquaintances you were quick to label—perhaps you saw them as resistant to change, depressed, or even "crazy" or psychotic. Would you be able to change that attitude and replace it with honor and respect instead? Would you be able to understand them? Discuss your experiences in small groups.

Although the attitude of acceptance we talked about in Chapter 1 is closely related to honoring and respecting your client, one difference is that honor and respect is often shown through the types of questions and statements made to the client, especially early on in the relationship. The following are a few examples:

- Tell me what brings you here today.
- I'm so glad you were able to come here today, and I hope you feel comfortable here.
- So, it seems like you've had a difficult time. I hope I can help in some way.
- I can tell you really don't want to be here, but maybe there's some way that I can help make your time worthwhile.
- What do you think would be most helpful for you during your time here?
- How can I best help you?
- I really want to understand how you have come to feel the way you feel.
- I want to be helpful in the best ways possible. Let me know if what I'm doing is working for you.

Many questions or statements can be used to show clients you honor and respect them and want to understand their predicament. Using the theme of acceptance of all the client's feelings and attitudes, understanding the context in which clients have come to be, and having a desire to help the client, write in additional questions or statements that can be used to honor and respect clients. Try to formulate questions that show the client the counselor is a positive force in the client's life and honors the client. Then do Experiential Exercise 2.5.

1. _____
2. _____
3. _____
4. _____
5. _____

EXPERIENTIAL EXERCISE 2.5

Honoring and Respecting Clients

The following statements are from two clients who are having a difficult time in their lives. Using some of the responses we made previously or coming up with some new responses, show how you might respond to Jillian and Simeon in ways that demonstrate honor and respect.

Example 1: Jillian is new to your practice and is depressed and anxious. During her initial interview, she says the following:

I've been depressed for years. I can barely do my work and keep up things at home. I've been in counseling before, and it really didn't help. I doubt you can help me.

Have one person role-play Jillian and someone else role-play the counselor. How might the counselor respond in a way that honors and respects Jillian?

Example 2: Simeon just broke up with his partner and feels alone in the world. During his first interview, he says the following:

I loved Rafael, but I know the relationship wasn't working. Yet I was surprised when he left. Now, I feel alone and have this constant sense of anxiety. I'm not sure what to do, and I certainly don't feel like dating at this point.

Have one person role-play Simeon and the other role-play a counselor. How might the counselor respond in a way that honors and respects Simeon?

Possible Responses: After you have made some possible responses to Jillian and Simeon, examine some of the examples at the end of the chapter. In small groups or as a class, discuss how your responses compare to mine.

Showing Caring Curiosity

Successful counselors are naturally curious about others (Rice, 2015). How did he happen to end up like this? What made her react like that? What tragedies has he faced? What childhood traumas did she go

through? How did she feel when that happened? These are just a few of the many questions that go through the mind of a curious helper. However, successful counselors are not just thinking about these questions; they are also willing and wanting to ask their clients questions about their lives—they are naturally interested in the lives of others. As you might imagine, successful counselors are comfortable inquiring about clients' lives while simultaneously honoring and respecting them.

Curious and effective counselors do not avoid subjects because they know that inquiring about clients' lives can be the initial path to helping clients resolve important life concerns. Such inquiry is never demeaning; it is always from a place of curiosity and caring. Some of the types of statements and questions that can be used when showing curiosity include the following:

- I'm curious to know more about that.
- How do you feel about sharing more about that?
- Can you tell me how that happened?
- That is so interesting; please, go on.
- Tell me more, if you can.
- You lived an amazing life; tell me more.
- I'm really interested in what you are saying!
- What you're saying intrigues me. Keep going.

Obviously, these represent just a few of the questions or statements that can be asked by a counselor who is interested in his or her client and curious to know more. Experiential Exercise 2.6 helps you practice this important skill. See if you are willing to encourage the role-play client to reveal aspects of himself or herself beyond what might normally be uncovered in a conversation.

EXPERIENTIAL EXERCISE 2.6

Practicing Being Curious

Pair up with two other people in class. One will be the counselor, the second a client, and the third an observer. The counselor's job is to demonstrate to your client a sense of curiosity in a caring, honoring, and respectful manner. The observer will take notes and provide feedback to the counselor regarding whether the counselor is being curious, honoring, caring, and respectful. In class, the observers can share some of the responses made by the counselors.

Delimiting Power and Forming an Equal Relationship

> Most counselors, of course, probably experience themselves as partners with their clients in the treatment process, not as "truth bullies" who beat down clients' perspectives with their superior views. (Hansen, 2006, p. 295)

In the past, the counseling relationship was seen as one in which the counselor was the expert who had some knowledge to reveal to the client. This created a power dynamic in which one person had "the answer" and the other was in the relationship to gain knowledge about his or her disorder or problem. Although counselors do have legitimate skills that can assist clients, in recent years it has been increasingly common for counselors to see themselves as partners in the relationship—partners who have some skills to assist clients in their life's journey (Harrison, 2013). No longer are they separate, objective, prescriptive experts who stand apart from their clients and tell them what to do (see Reflection Exercise 2.8).

REFLECTION EXERCISE 2.8

Differentiating Equal From Power Relationships

If you were like me, when growing up, you learned that helping people involved giving advice. Although advice giving has its time and place (see Chapter 4), if provided too frequently and if offered authoritatively, it can lead to power disparities in the helping relationship, a dependent relationship, and feelings of disempowerment (Egan & Reese, 2019; Neukrug, 2018).

Think about the different relationships you have had in your life. Which ones would you consider power relationships and which might you put into the category of equal relationships? Write down some of the attributes that predominated these different types of relationships. Discuss your list in a small group and make a master list in class that differentiates between equal and power relationships.

How does the counselor build an equal relationship with shared power? It begins with honoring and respecting the client, but it also entails monitoring one's responses so they do not appear overly authoritative, prescriptive, or bossy. For instance, look at the two responses to a young mother trying to decide whether to stay home with her children or work.

Counselor 1: Stay-at-home moms tend to not have a sense of identity and will often have lower self-esteem. Moms who work often feel as if they are missing out on an important aspect of their lives—motherhood. I think I know you pretty well and can tell what might be best for you.

Counselor 2: I'm really wanting to hear the pros and cons that you have come up with for working versus motherhood, or some combination thereof. Do you feel comfortable sharing that with me? I want you to take the path that seems best for you.

Clearly, Counselor 1 is considerably more authoritarian and prescriptive than Counselor 2, who views the relationship on a more equal basis. You can imagine the different types of dynamics that would occur due to a Counselor 1 response in contrast to a Counselor 2 response. From this example, you can see that there are some ingredients generally seen in an equal relationship that delimits power. These include the following:

1. *Being a good listener:* Using good nonverbal behaviors, you are ready and wanting to listen to your client.
2. *Honoring and respecting your client:* Showing these attributes as your client tells his or her story (problem).
3. *Being curious:* Showing caring curiosity about your client's story (problem).
4. *Being humble:* Believing your client has the ability to empower himself or herself and seeing yourself as a person who can facilitate that empowerment. You show this by not rushing in to give advice or prescribing answers.
5. *Using questions:* Using questions that are honoring and respectful, show curiosity, and are asked with a sense of humility (see Experiential Exercise 2.7).

EXPERIENTIAL EXERCISE 2.7

Developing Equal Relationships

Developing an equal relationship with clients starts with honoring and respecting your client, being curious about your client, and not acting haughty or like an expert with your client. Pair up with a student in class and have one play a counselor and the other play a client. A third observer can later offer feedback to the counselor. The counselor should try to develop an equal relationship by:

1. listening to your client;
2. honoring and respecting your client;
3. being curious about your client;
4. not being prescriptive or advice giving; and
5. being humble.

After the first role-play is complete, switch roles. Then switch roles again, allowing all three students to be the counselor. Then, in class, discuss how successful each counselor was in developing an equal relationship.

Non-Pathologizing

Pathologizing others is not unusual. Ever call a person a name—either to his or her face or under your breath? Ever been in a relationship in which you "diagnosed" the other person? Oh, that "blankity blank" person is a depressive, or "OCD," or a "borderline personality," or simply "crazy." When people are not happy with others, they sometimes diagnose them in an effort to dismiss what they are saying and uplift their own sense of self-righteousness. Unfortunately, a diagnosis can dehumanize a person, and if it occurs within the counseling relationship, it can negatively impact the working alliance (Glasser, 2013; Pickersgill, 2013; see Reflection Exercise 2.9).

When clients come in for counseling, they often feel marginalized or less than or experience low self-esteem (Gallagher & Street, 2012). When a counselor sees a client and treats that person as if he or she has a problem, is defined by a diagnosis, or is less than human, the counselor is often feeding into an already existing worldview of the client. Such an attitude detracts from the client's humanness, sets the counselor up as a judge of others, and lessens opportunities for client growth. Although a diagnosis can help with treatment planning and medication determination and can help a client understand himself or herself better, it is important to not define the person as the diagnosis. "Ed Neukrug is a depressive" is how we set up a person to be the diagnosis. "Ed Neukrug is a person who sometimes struggles with depression" is much more hopeful, and Ed is no longer defined as a diagnosis.

REFLECTION EXERCISE 2.9

Pathologizing Others

We've all done it: thought that another person was—or told another person that he or she was—"diagnosable" in some way. Think back on your relationships and consider when you may have diagnosed a person—that is, tried to define him or her with a particular formal or informal mental disorder ("crazy," "stupid," "overly anxious," "clinically depressed," "bipolar," etc.). Write down times you may have done this and discuss your list with other students in your class. Did you have positive outcomes when you did this? What were some of the negative consequences of your responses? How did such responses on your part make the other person feel? How did it make you feel? If you were to do it again, might you have a better way of responding?

In line with honoring and respecting the client and not setting oneself up as the expert, when one depathologizes the helping relationship, the client increasingly becomes an equal to the counselor and is more likely to feel comfortable, safe, and trusting within the relationship. William Glasser, who developed *reality therapy* and *choice theory*, suggested that counselors should develop *caring habits* by using language that is supportive, encouraging, accepting, trusting, and respectful and not use language that will pathologize, diagnose, blame, or criticize the client (Glasser & Glasser, 2007; van Nuys, 2007; see Experiential Exercise 2.8).

Having, not BEING, a Diagnosis

Today, the *Diagnostic and Statistical Manual, 5th edition (DSM-5)* is used to help mental health professionals find diagnoses for mental disorders (American Psychiatric Association, 2013). Although the DSM-5 can be helpful in conceptualizing client problems, planning treatment, making decisions about medication, and more, it sometimes results in the client feeling as if he or she is the diagnosis, as opposed to a person who has some qualities *of* the diagnosis (Corey et al., 2019; Pickersgill, 2013). Although using DSM-5 may be important at times, it is equally important that when clients are diagnosed they are not treated as if they *are* the diagnosis.

In class, with the help of your instructor and using the DSM-5, choose two or three diagnoses. Then, using one of these diagnoses, have one individual role-play a counselor who treats the client with dignity, honor, and respect and does not attempt to pathologize the client despite the fact that the client acts as if he or she *is* the diagnosis—that is, acts like his or her identity is defined by the diagnosis. In other words, the counselor should treat the client as if he or she is a worthy human being who is *not* defined by the diagnosis. After role-playing with the first client, you may want to do this a couple more times, using one or two additional diagnoses.

After role-playing for 10 to 15 minutes, discuss the positive results of treating a person as if his or her identity is not defined by a diagnosis. Do you think you can do this with clients? If time allows, each person in the class should practice such role-plays with others.

Being Committed

Being committed means that you follow up on promises that you make to clients, that you remember what you said to them during their last appointments, and that they have a sense that you are there for them. Commitment does not mean you are at your clients' beck and call. However, it does mean that you are willing to put in the time that it takes to work with them and are vigilant about following through with clients on their treatment plans. It means when they are low, you are their advocate and when they are doing well, you are their cheerleader. It means that when they don't show up for appointments, you contact them and encourage them to come in. It is a never-ending dedication you have to the well-being of your clients—even when they might not have it themselves. It shows them that you are a rock in their sometimes shaky lives (Wubbolding, 2015; see Experiential Exercise 2.9).

EXPERIENTIAL EXERCISE 2.9

Practicing Egalitarian and Positive Attitudes and Skills

In class, break up into groups of three. Have one student role-play a counselor and another role-play a client for 10 minutes. The third student is an observer who should write comments about how effectively each counselor was able to demonstrate egalitarian and positive attitudes and skills. The counselor should also remember to demonstrate appropriate nonverbal behaviors. When the role-play is complete, the observer should share his or her feedback. Switch roles so every student gets to be a counselor.

	How demonstrated	Ways to improve
Honoring and respecting		
Caring curiosity		
Delimiting power/ Developing equal relationship		
Non-pathologizing		
Being committed		
Nonverbal behaviors		

Conclusion

Being egalitarian and positive by honoring and respecting clients, showing caring curiosity, delimiting power and developing an equal relationship, being non-pathologizing, and being committed have become increasingly important to the counseling relationship in recent years. Along with the nonverbal behaviors, counselors should attempt to demonstrate all these attitudes and skills throughout the counseling relationship. Often, those who do not will end up having ruptures in their counseling relationships and find it less likely to build a positive working alliance.

Summary

This chapter reviewed a number of foundational skills that can influence the overall atmosphere of the counseling relationship. First, we reminded you that the nine characteristics of the effective counselor were foundational and should always be adhered to within the counseling relationship. We also reminded you to stay away from toxic skills that will rupture the counseling relationship. Next, we identified a number of nonverbal behaviors critical to developing a strong counseling relationship. These included office atmosphere, attire or dress, eye contact and facial expressions, body positioning and head nodding, proxemics (personal space), touch, and voice intonation. We highlighted the notion that nonverbal behaviors are impacted by cross-cultural differences and that counselors should become aware of how individuals might respond differently to various nonverbal behaviors. We identified the acronym CHASE LOVE as one way of remembering some of the nonverbal behaviors: **C**ross-cultural concerns, **H**ead nodding, **A**ttire, personal **S**pace (proxemic), **E**ye contact, **L**eaning forward and open body posture, **O**ffice atmosphere, **V**oice intonation, and facial **E**xpression.

The next part of the chapter examined a number of egalitarian and positive attitudes and skills that counselors should embody if they are to have positive client outcomes. These attitudes and skills have been an outgrowth of the recent popularity of the postmodern therapies that view the counselor as more of an equal in the counseling relationship. The skills we explored included honoring and respecting clients, showing caring curiosity toward clients, delimiting power and forming an equal relationship with clients, non-pathologizing clients, and being committed to clients. The chapter concludes by giving you a chance to practice the egalitarian and positive attitudes and skills as well as your nonverbal skills.

Possible Responses to Jillian and Simeon in Experiential Exercise 2.5

Example 1 (Jillian): I 've been depressed for years. I can barely do my work and keep up things at home. I've been in counseling before, and it really didn't help. I doubt you can help me.

> *Counselor*: Well, I think I hear how you doubt counseling will be helpful, but I want you to know that I am here to help in any way.

> *Counselor*: I'm really committed to helping you, if I can. It sounds like it's been a really difficult time for you.

> *Counselor*: Counseling didn't work for you before—I hear that. I'm really hoping I can help you and want you to know that I'm here to help.

Example 2 (Simeon): I loved Rafael, but I know the relationship wasn't working. Yet I was surprised when he left. Now, I feel alone and have this constant sense of anxiety. I'm not sure what to do, and I certainly don't feel like dating at this point.

> *Counselor*: That must have been really disappointing. I'm here to help you get through this depression and anxiety.

> *Counselor*: You've been through a lot; let's see what we can do to make things a bit better for you.

> *Counselor*: I guess I hear how important that relationship was and how it has impacted you now. I'm hoping to do my best to help you feel better.

Key Words and Terms

attire or dress

being committed

body positioning

caring curiosity

caring habits

CHASE LOVE

choice theory

cross-cultural issues and nonverbal behavior

delimiting power/forming equal relationship

eye contact

facial expressions

Glasser, William

head nodding

honoring and respecting

nine characteristics of the effective counselor

nonverbal behaviors

non-pathologizing

office atmosphere

personal space

postmodern therapies

professional disclosure statement

proxemics

reality therapy

touch

voice intonation

Credits

CHAPTER 3

Essential Skills

Learning Objectives

1. Understand the importance of essential skills in establishing the relationship, building trust and rapport, and starting the client's process of self-examination

2. Examine how to respond to clients using the following essential skills:

   a. Silence and pause time
   b. Listening
   c. Reflection of feelings
   d. Reflection of content
   e. Paraphrasing
   f. Basic empathy

3. Briefly discuss the role of advanced empathy in the counseling relationship

Introduction

The foundational skills just described in Chapter 2 are critical to establishing the counseling relationship. However, the essential skills slowly nudge the client toward the self-examination process. Although important throughout the helping relationship, these skills are most crucial near the beginning of the relationship. Often revisited in the counseling relationship, essential skills are especially useful when the counselor and client face an impasse or rupture in the relationship, as they tend to bring the relationship back to its calm, neutral state. The essential skills include *silence and pause time, listening skills, reflecting feelings, reflecting content, paraphrasing, and basic empathy* (see Figure 3.1). In addition, we will briefly address *advanced empathy*, although advanced empathy will be discussed more fully in Chapter 4: Commonly Used Skills.

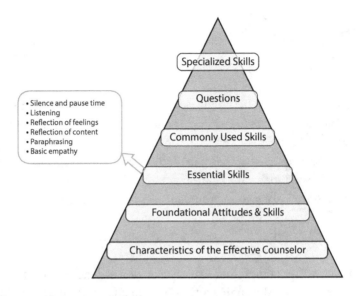

FIGURE 3.1 Counseling and helping skills

Silence and Pause Time

When is empty space facilitative, and when does it become a bit much?

Silence is a powerful tool in the helping relationship that can be used for the client's benefit (Kenny, 2011; Little, 2018). It allows the client to reflect on what he or she has been saying, enables the counselor to process the session and formulate his or her next response, says to the client that communication is not always verbal, and gives the client an opportunity to examine how words can sometimes be used to divert the client from his or her feelings. Silence is powerful. It will sometimes cause the client to feel anxious, which could push the client to delve deeper

into a topic or could drive the client out of the counseling relationship. It can allow a client to hear his or her depression and help facilitate a client's examination of deep pains and hurts. Or it can cause a client to become defensive as the client attempts to avoid his or her deep feelings.

To be an effective listener, one must be able to maintain the amount of silence that can be facilitative, not destructive. And for each client, that amount will vary. I once had a professor who suggested waiting 30 seconds before responding to a client. Thirty seconds is a *really* long time. Complete Experiential Exercise 3.1 and explore how much silence might feel comfortable to you.

How Much Silence Is Right for You?

Pair up with another student. One should be the client and the other should be the counselor. The client should begin to role-play a counseling situation and continue talking for about 1 minute, at which point the instructor should say "stop." At that point, the counselor should formulate a response to the client but not say it until the instructor says "go" 30 seconds later. After making the response, the counselor and client should discuss how it felt to wait this relatively short amount of time. You may want to do this a few times with varied pause times. Also, make sure each student gets to be the counselor.

I'm pretty confident that after completing Exercise 3.1, you will agree that 30 seconds is a long time to wait before making a response. Although waiting that long is unusual, you probably found that such a pause allowed the counselor to formulate his or her response, gave the client the opportunity to think about what he or she said, and allowed the client to consider what to say next. How long a pause works best for you? Do you think it would be helpful to work on making your pauses longer?

Cultural background may influence an individual's use and interpretation of silence, as research has found that silence manifests differently among various cultures (Mariska & Harrawood, 2013; Zur, 2007). For instance, Native Americans have sometimes been labeled as withdrawn or even resistant to treatment because they are simply more comfortable with longer pauses than other cultural groups. As a counselor, you may want to consider your pause time to discover your comfort level while recognizing that your client's pause time might vary as a function of his or her culture.

Listening

First there is the hearing with the ear, which we all know; and the hearing with the non-ear, which is a state like that of a tranquil pond, a lake that is completely quiet and when you drop a stone into it, it makes little waves that disappear. I think that [insight] is the hearing with the non-ear, a state where there is absolute quietness of the mind; and when the question is put into the mind, the response is the wave, the little wave. (Krishnamurti, cited in Jayakar, 2003, p. 328)

Before talking about the importance of listening and how to listen effectively, let's take a quick quiz to see what kind of listener you are. Complete Experiential Exercise 3.2.

Listening Quiz

Place a "U" next to the response if you think a person "usually" should respond in that manner, an "S" if you think a person "sometimes" should respond in that manner, and an "R" if you think a person should "rarely" respond in that manner. Compare your answers to the answers that can be found at the end of this chapter.

____1. When listening, I try to determine what should be talked about during the interview.
____2. When listening to someone, I prepare myself physically by sitting in a way in which I can make sure I hear what is being said.
____3. I try to be "in charge" and lead the conversation.
____4. I usually clear my mind and take on a nonjudgmental attitude when listening to another.
____5. When listening to another, I try to tell that person my opinion of what he or she is doing.
____6. I try to decide from the other's appearance if what he or she is saying is worthwhile.
____7. I attempt to ask questions if I need further clarification.
____8. I try to judge from the person's opening statement if I know what is going to be said.
____9. I try to listen intently to feelings.
____10. I try to listen intently to content.
____11. I try to tell the other person what is "right" about what he or she is saying.
____12. I try to "analyze" the situation and give interpretations.
____13. I try to use my experiences to best understand the other person's feelings.
____14. I try to convince the other person of the "correct" way to view the situation.
____15. I try to have the last word.

Although easy to define, *listening* is one of the most difficult skills for Americans to learn, as we are rarely taught how to hear another person. In fact, ask an untrained adult to listen to another, and usually, he or she will end up interrupting and giving advice (see Reflection Poem 3.1). Effective listening, however, helps to build trust, convinces the client that he or she is being understood, encourages the client to reflect on what he or she has said, ensures the counselor that he or she is on the right track, and is an effective way of collecting information from a client without the potentially negative side effects of using questions (Nichols, 2009).

Listen to Me

When I ask you to listen to me and you start giving me advice, you have not done what I asked.

When I ask you to listen to me and you begin to tell me why I shouldn't feel that way, you are trampling on my feelings.

When I ask you to listen to me and you feel you have to do something to solve my problem, you have failed me, strange as that may seem. Listen: All that I ask is that you listen, not talk or do—just hear me.

When you do something for me that I can and need to do for myself, you contribute to my fear and inadequacy.

But when you accept as a simple fact that I do feel what I feel, no matter how irrational, then I can quit trying to convince you and get about this business of understanding what's behind these feelings. So, please listen and just hear me.

And, if you want to talk, wait a minute for your turn—and I'll listen to you.

(Different versions of this poem have been attributed to psychiatrist Dr. Ralph Roughton.)

Hindrances to Effective Listening

Even when one knows how to listen, many factors can prevent a person from listening effectively. In class, you'll have the opportunity to work through Experiential Exercise 3.3 and explore some of the *hindrances to listening.* I suspect your list of hindrances to listening will be similar to some of the ones listed:

1. *Preconceived notions*: Having preconceived ideas about the person based on how he or she is dressed (or other factors) leads you to make assumptions about what the person has said—sometimes incorrect assumptions.
2. *Anticipatory reaction*: Anticipating what the person is about to say prevents you from hearing what he or she has said.
3. *Cognitive distractions*: Thinking about what you are going to say blocks you from hearing what the person is saying.
4. *Personal issues*: Having your own unfinished business or personal issues preoccupies your mind and inhibits your ability to listen.
5. *Emotional response*: Having a strong emotional reaction to the content of what the person says prevents you from being able to hear the person accurately.
6. *Distractions*: Being distracted by such things as noises, room temperature, hunger pangs, and so forth makes your mind wander.

EXPERIENTIAL EXERCISE 3.3

Hindrances to Listening

Form groups of three students each. Each person take a number: 1, 2, or 3. Number 1 chooses any of the topics listed and starts presenting the pro side of the situation while Number 2 listens. Then, when Number 1 has presented his or her side, Number 2 presents the con side while Number 1 listens. Keep going back and forth for a few minutes. Number 3 is the objective observer who helps as needed and takes notes concerning each person's ability to reflect accurately. The observer should also note any important body language. Number 3 should also offer feedback when the role-play is completed. When you have finished the first situation, have Numbers 2 and 3 role-play a second situation, and then have Numbers 3 and 1 role-play a third situation while the other person is the objective observer.

When all role-plays are completed, the instructor will ask for feedback regarding what prevented any of you from hearing the other person. Make a list of these hindrances to listening and compare them to the ones listed.

Possible topics: Abortion, torturing of suspected terrorists to gain information, gun control, racial profiling by police, capital punishment, national health care (Obamacare), free college tuition, or other topics of your choosing.

Good Listening

Good listening is an active process, is intimately related to client outcomes, and involves the following (Egan & Reese, 2019; Ivey, Ivey, & Zalaquett, 2016):

1. Talking minimally
2. Concentrating on what is being said
3. Not interrupting
4. Not giving advice
5. Not expecting to get something from the relationship
6. Hearing the speaker's content
7. Hearing the speaker's affect
8. Using good nonverbals to show you are hearing the person, such as having good and appropriate eye contact, using head nods, saying "uh-huh," and so forth
9. Asking clarifying questions such as "I didn't hear all of that, can you say it again?" or "Can you explain that in another way so I'm sure I understand you?"
10. Not asking questions (other than clarifying questions)

Preparing for Listening

When you are ready to listen, the following practical suggestions should assist you in your ability to hear a client effectively (Egan & Reese, 2019; Ivey et al., 2016).

1. *Calm yourself down.* Prior to meeting with your client, calm yourself down: meditate, pray, jog, or take deep breaths.
2. *Stop talking and don't interrupt.* You cannot listen while you are talking.
3. *Show interest.* With your body language and tone of voice, show the person that you're interested in what he or she is saying.
4. *Don't jump to conclusions.* Take in all of what the person says, and don't assume you understand the person more than he or she understands himself or herself.
5. *Actively listen.* Deeply concentrate. Focus on what the person is saying. If your mind is wandering, you are not listening.
6. *Concentrate on feelings.* Identify and acknowledge what the person is feeling.
7. *Concentrate on content.* Identify and acknowledge what the person is saying.
8. *Maintain appropriate eye contact.* With your eyes, show the person you are listening; however, be sensitive to cultural differences in the amount of eye contact given.
9. *Have an open body posture.* Face the person and show the person you are ready to listen through your body language, but be sensitive to cultural differences.
10. *Be sensitive to personal space.* Be close enough to the client to show him or her that you are ready to listen, but have a sense of the amount of personal space that is comfortable for your client.
11. *Don't ask questions.* Questions are often an indication that you are not listening (you have an agenda). Try to avoid questions unless they are clarifying ones (e.g., "Can you tell me more about that?").

Listening comes with practice. Experiential Exercise 3.4 is a good beginning point.

EXPERIENTIAL EXERCISE 3.4

Practicing Listening

Form groups of three to practice your listening skills. Have one person role-play a client while the other listens. The third person will observe and give feedback regarding how well the listener heard what the client said. The listener should first prepare for listening, as just noted. Then he or she should make sure that there are as few hindrances to listening as possible. Next, this person should try to listen actively by paraphrasing what his or her partner has said. After the first role-play, have different students play the client, listener, and observer. Then do a third role-play, giving the last student an opportunity to be the listener.

Reflection of Feelings, Reflection of Content, and Paraphrasing

Reflection of feelings, reflection of content, and *paraphrasing* are three important skills that are essential at the beginning of the helping relationship. However, use them too much, and the client will think you're a novice who can only parrot back what he or she has said. Used judiciously, however, they can be very helpful in ensuring that the client will keep talking.

Reflection of Feelings

As the term implies, reflection of feelings relies on concentrating on client feelings and repeating the feelings back to the client with the same feeling word the client used or a word that is similar to the one the client used (e.g., the client says "sad" and you respond with "down"). Generally, such reflections use statements such as the following:

I think you might be feeling …

It sounds like you're feeling …

… is the feeling I'm hearing from you.

Your ability to discern a feeling is critical to being able to reflect feelings accurately and be empathic (discussed later; see Experiential Exercise 3.5).

EXPERIENTIAL EXERCISE 3.5

Practicing Reflection of Feelings

Pair up with two other students. Have one be the counselor, one the client, and one an observer. The client should discuss a problem or situation, and the counselor should only reflect feelings, using the framework just discussed. The observer monitors the effectiveness of the reflections and gives feedback to the counselor when the role-play is over. Do this for a few minutes. Then switch roles. Make sure each person has a chance to be the counselor.

Appendix A offers a list of feeling words. If you need practice discerning feelings, go through the list and make sure you understand each word's meaning. Then spend some time talking about each of these words with individuals so you are clear on the different feeling words. Practice reflection of feelings with friends and classmates on your own, using this list.

Reflection of Content

Like reflection of feelings, reflection of content focuses on repeating back to the client specific statements the client has made, but instead, it focuses on the meaning of what the client said. Similar sentence stems highlighted in the section on reflection of feelings can be used when one is reflecting content; however, instead of using the word "feeling," use the words "saying," "suggesting," etc. (e.g., I think that you're saying … ; It sounds like you're saying …). Here are some examples of stems that can be used when reflecting content (these stems can also be used for reflection of feelings, but use the word "feeling" rather than "saying," "suggesting," or "stated that"):

I hear you saying that …

I think you're suggesting that …

What most stands out for me is when you stated that … (see Experiential Exercise 3.6).

EXPERIENTIAL EXERCISE 3.6

Practicing Reflection of Content

Pair up with two other students: have one be the counselor, one the client, and one an observer. The client should start discussing a problem situation, and the counselor should only reflect content, using the previous examples or other similar types of responses. The observer monitors the effectiveness of the reflections and gives feedback when the role-play is over. Do this for a few minutes and then switch roles. Have each person be the counselor.

Paraphrasing

In a sense, paraphrasing is combining the reflection of feeling and content. It is the ability to reflect back the general feelings and information expressed by the client. This can be done by parroting the client's actual statements; however, if you repeat back verbatim to clients too often, they may get annoyed with the repetition. Therefore, it is usually suggested that one take the general meanings and feelings of clients' statements and reflect them back to them. This can be especially difficult if the client has made a rather long statement. Obviously, you can't reflect back everything. Here are some rules you might consider when paraphrasing what a client has said:

1. Listen for the feelings.
2. Listen for the content.
3. If the client talks for a relatively long time, zero in on the feelings and content that seem most poignant and reflect back only those items.
4. Use words and feelings that are synonyms or similar to what the client said rather than the exact words and feelings the client used (see Experiential Exercise 3.7).

EXPERIENTIAL EXERCISE 3.7

Practicing Paraphrasing

Pair up with two other students: have one person be a counselor, one a client, and one an observer. The client should start discussing a problem situation, and the counselor should practice paraphrasing. The observer monitors how effective the paraphrasing has been and gives feedback to the counselor when the role-play is over. Do this for a few minutes and then switch roles. Make sure each person has an opportunity to be the counselor.

Basic Empathy

Listed as one of the important counselor qualities in Chapter 1, empathy is also an important skill in the helping relationship. Highlighted for centuries as an important quality to embrace (Gompertz, 1960), it wasn't until the 20th century that empathy was formally incorporated into the counseling relationship. Probably the person who has had the greatest impact on our modern understanding and use of empathy is Carl Rogers.

> The state of empathy, or being empathic, is to perceive the internal frame of reference of another with accuracy and with the emotional components and meanings which pertain thereto as if one were the person, but without ever losing the "as if" condition. (Rogers, 1959, pp. 210–211)

Empathy is the act of showing the client that he or she has been heard, and numerous research studies have shown it's important in building a working alliance and in positive client outcomes (Elliot, Bohart, Watson, & Murphy, 2018). Showing empathy can be done in many ways, including the use of reflective listening techniques and paraphrasing, like we just discussed. The popularity of Rogers's work during the 20th century eventually led to the development of a number of scales to measure empathy. One such scale, the *Carkhuff scale,* is a widely used instrument in the training of helpers (Carkhuff, 2009; Cormier, Nurius, & Osborn, 2013; Neukrug, 2017b).

The Carkhuff scale ranges from a low of 1.0 to a high of 5.0, with .5 increments. Any responses below a 3.0 are considered *subtractive* or nonempathic, while responses of 3.0 or higher are considered empathic. Empathic responses that are around a level 3 are often called *basic empathy*, and responses over 3.0 are called *additive* or advanced empathic responses (see Figure 3.2). *Advanced empathy* will be examined in Chapter 4: Commonly Used Skills.

	1.5		2.5		3.5		4.5	
1		2		3		4		5
Very Much Off The Mark. Inaccurate Reflections		Slightly Off The Mark		Accurate Reflections of Feelings and Content		Reflections Slightly Beyond Client Awareness Leads to New Insights		Connection With Client in Deepest Moments of Pain/Joy

FIGURE 3.2 The Carkhuff scale

As is obvious in Figure 3.2, the Carkhuff scale defines level 1 and level 2 responses as detracting from what the person is saying (e.g., advice giving, reflecting inaccurate feelings or content), with a level 1 response being way off the mark and a level 2 only slightly off. For instance, suppose a client said, "I don't know what's wrong with me. I'm anxious all the time, have heart palpitations, am becoming a recluse, and am scared of talking with almost anyone. I'm a mess." A level 1 response might be "Well, you best get your life in order so you can get through this" (advice giving and being judgmental). A level 2 response might be "Sounds like you're having a bad time right now" (does not reflect the intensity of the feeling and is not specific enough about the content). On the other hand, a level 3 response accurately reflects the affect and meaning of what the client has said. Using the same example, a level 3 response might be "You are really going through a lot right now. You're feeling intense anxiety, and I hear what a struggle it has been to even talk with people."

Level 4 and level 5 responses, sometimes called advanced empathy, often reflect feelings beyond what the person is saying and add meaning to what the person has said (Neukrug, 2017a). For instance, in the previous example, a level 4 response might be "It sounds like you're really distressed and increasingly finding yourself isolating from everyone else." This expresses a new feeling—"isolated"—which the client didn't outwardly state but is indeed feeling. And as soon as the counselor reflects this feeling, the client becomes aware of it. This is not a hypothesis or a guess; it is a feeling that the helper experiences from the client and one which the client is on the verge of experiencing himself or herself. Level 5 responses are usually made in long-term therapeutic relationships with expert helpers. They express to the client a deep understanding of the emotions (e.g., intense pain or joy) he or she feels as well as recognition of the complexity of the situation.

Usually, in the training of helpers, it is recommended that they attempt to make basic, or level 3, empathic responses. A large body of evidence suggests that such responses can be learned in a relatively short amount of time and are beneficial to clients (Carkhuff, 2009; Cormier, et al., 2013; Elliot et al., 2018). Basic empathic responses need to be mastered prior to the advanced empathic responses, which are considered value-added responses—that is, although not critical to the helping relationship, they can lend depth and breadth to client understanding of self.

For effective empathic responding, it is not only crucial to "be on target" with the feelings and the content but also to reflect these feelings at the moment when the client can absorb the helper's reflections. For instance, you might sense a deep sadness or anger in a client and reflect this back to him or her. However, if the client is not ready to accept these feelings, then the timing is off and the response is considered subtractive. Fact Sheet 3.1 provides some guidelines for making an effective basic empathic, or level 3, response.

FACT SHEET 3.1

Keys to Making Basic (Level 3) Empathic Responses

1. Reflect back feelings accurately.
2. Reflect back content accurately.
3. If a client talks for a lengthy amount of time, reflect back the most poignant feelings and content only.
4. Use paraphrasing and similar words as the client.
5. Use language attuned to the client's level of understanding.
6. Do not add new feelings or new content.
7. Do not respond with a question (e.g., "Sounds like you're feeling bad about the situation?").
8. Do not make the response too lengthy (keep it to about one sentence or two short sentences).
9. Do not hypothesize or make guesses about what the client is saying.
10. If the client verbally or nonverbally says your response is "off," assume it is and move on.
11. Do not ask, "Is this correct?" (or something akin to that) at the end of your sentence. (However, listen to the client's response; you'll know if it's correct.)
12. Don't get caught up thinking about the next response—you'll have trouble listening to the client.

Making Formulaic Empathic Responses

When beginning counselors first practice empathic responding, it is often suggested that they make a formulaic response to client statements, which starts with reflecting the feeling the client has expressed, followed by paraphrasing the client's content. In fact, helpers often call these *reflections of feelings* or *active listening* responses. In the following example, note how the words "you feel" precede the feelings the client is expressing and how the word "because" precedes the content of what the client is saying. After looking at the example, do Experiential Exercise 3.8.

Client: My boyfriend has left me, and I just can't stop crying. I'm so depressed.

Counselor: You feel depressed *because* your boyfriend has left you.

EXPERIENTIAL EXERCISE 3.8

Making Formulaic Responses

Use a formulaic response to the scenarios that follow. In the first few scenarios, use the feeling words given to you by the client. However, as the scenarios continue, you will have to imply what the individual is feeling. Try to imply what is obvious; that is, don't try to read too much into the individual's feeling state. Use Appendix A if you need some help identifying feeling words.

1. Young adult to counselor:
   Client: My girlfriend split up with me, and I'm feeling anxious all the time—I don't know what to do with myself.
   Counselor: You feel _____ because _____
   _____.

2. Individual with a disability to counselor:
   Client: I still can't believe I am paralyzed. It happened so quickly.
   Counselor: You feel _____ because _____
   _____.

3. Pregnant teenager to counselor:
   Client: OMG. What am I going to do? I should tell my parents, but I'm afraid how they will react.
   Counselor: You feel _____ because _____
   _____.

4. Husband to counselor:
   Client: I thought we had such a good relationship. Suddenly, she was gone. Just left me with the kids and everything. I just feel like I have nothing in my life.
   Counselor: You feel _____ because _____
   _____.

5. Eight-year-old to counselor:
   Client: Those other kids keep making fun of me. I try to stay away from them, but they're always laughing at me. Makes me want to hit them.
   Counselor: You feel _____ because _____
   _____.

6. Prisoner to counselor:
   Client: I didn't do nothing. Those charges are trumped up. They just want to get me because they know I've been in trouble before!

EXPERIENTIAL EXERCISE 3.8—CONTINUED

Counselor: You feel _____ because _____
_____.

7. Workaholic to counselor:
    Client: I work really hard ... maybe too hard. I'm really tired at the end of the day, and I know that impacts my relationship with my wife and kids.
    Counselor: You feel _____ because _____
    _____.

8. Mother to counselor:
    Client: I want to work, and I want to be a mother. How can I do both? What should I do?
    Counselor: You feel _____ because _____
    _____.

9. Female upset with brother to counselor:
    Client: He treats me really poorly—curses at me, yells at me, ignores me, and never listens to me at all.
    Counselor: You feel _____ because _____
    _____.

10. Alcoholic to counselor:
    Client: I've been drinking for 30 years. Why should I stop now? My health is good, and I can handle it.
    Counselor: You feel _____ because _____
    _____.

Making Natural Empathic Responses

As counselors become more facile with formulaic responses, they can move toward making empathic responses using more natural conversational tones. These natural responses maintain the reflection of feeling and the paraphrasing of content but aren't as stilted as the formulaic responses. For instance, in the following example, look at the natural response made to the client.

Client: I can't believe how bad things are. I keep trying to make changes, but nothing seems to work. I even changed my job and tried to work on my marriage. Then I saw that psychiatrist for meds, but I'm still depressed. Nothing seems to work.

Counselor: You have really tried to make changes, yet I hear that despite all your efforts, things are still really bad and you are pretty down.

Here, you can see how the feeling word is still reflected and the basic content is still included; however, it is said in a more conversational tone. Now, using the same scenarios you used earlier, make natural responses to the situations in Experiential Exercise 3.9.

EXPERIENTIAL EXERCISE 3.9

Making Natural Responses

In contrast to formulaic responses, natural responses are more conversational; however, they still have the basic elements of reflection of clients' feelings and content. See if you can make natural responses to the same situations in which you earlier made formulaic responses:

1. Young adult to counselor:
   Client: My girlfriend split up with me, and I'm feeling anxious all the time—I don't know what to do with myself.
   Counselor: You feel _____ because _____
   _____.

2. Individual with a disability to counselor:
   Client: I still can't believe I am paralyzed. It happened so quickly.
   Counselor: You feel _____ because _____
   _____.

3. Pregnant teenager to counselor:
   Client: OMG. What am I going to do? I should tell my parents, but I'm afraid how they will react.
   Counselor: You feel _____ because _____
   _____.

4. Husband to counselor:
   Client: I thought we had such a good relationship. Suddenly, she was gone. Just left me with the kids and everything. I just feel like I have nothing in my life.
   Counselor: You feel _____ because _____
   _____.

5. Eight-year-old to counselor:
   Client: Those other kids keep making fun of me. I try to stay away from them, but they're always laughing at me. Makes me want to hit them.
   Counselor: You feel _____ because _____
   _____.

6. Prisoner to counselor:
   Client: I didn't do nothing. Those charges are trumped up. They just want to get me because they know I've been in trouble before!
   Counselor: You feel _____ because _____
   _____.

7. Workaholic to counselor:
   Client: I work really hard ... maybe too hard. I'm really tired at the end of the day, and I know that impacts my relationship with my wife and kids.
   Counselor: You feel _____ because _____
   _____.

8. Mother to counselor:

Client: I want to work, and I want to be a mother. How can I do both? What should I do?

Counselor: You feel _____ because _____

_____.

9. Female upset with brother to counselor:

Client: He treats me really poorly—curses at me, yells at me, ignores me, and never listens to me at all.

Counselor: You feel _____ because _____

_____.

10. Alcoholic to counselor:

Client: I've been drinking for 30 years. Why should I stop now? My health is good, and I can handle it.

Counselor: You feel _____ because _____

_____.

Practicing Empathic Responses

Appendix B gives you information about the Miller family: Jake, Angela, Luke, and Celia. The family is struggling, and you have the opportunity to make empathic responses to each member. After reading about the Miller family, respond to each member in Experiential Exercises 3.10–3.13 using first a formulaic response and then a natural response. When you have finished practicing empathy, go to Box 3.1.

Practicing Empathic Responding: Jake

It is important that you first read Appendix B prior to making your responses. That will give you background on the four members of the Miller family, to whom these responses are made. First, we start with Jake.

1. *Jake:* I don't know really where to begin. I feel like everything was going well until Luke messed around with the car. It so reminded me of myself when I got into the accident with Justine. Well, the bottom line is that I've been a nervous wreck since then.

Formulaic response: You feel _____ because _____.

Natural response: _____

_____.

2. *Jake:* You know, when I was a kid, I felt responsible for the car accident that Justine and I got into. It's my fault that she is the way she is.

Formulaic response: You feel _____ because _____.

Natural response: _____

_____.

3. *Jake:* I'm just freaked out that if I don't have control over the kids and the house, something bad will happen. Look, something bad almost did happen with Luke and Celia.

   Formulaic response: You feel _____ because _____.

   Natural response: _____

   _____.

4. *Jake:* Until the incident with Luke and Celia, our family was doing pretty good, but I think I was just putting my head in the sand. I now know that I should have been more in charge of things. More in control so bad things won't happen.

   Formulaic response: You feel _____ because _____.

   Natural response: _____

   _____.

5. *Jake:* I know that Angela is upset with me. She now just sees me as a controlling husband, but I think I'm doing the best I can under the circumstances.

   Formulaic response: You feel _____ because _____.

   Natural response: _____

   _____.

6. *Jake:* I know Luke's acting out at school, and Celia's stomach issues are partly my responsibility. But if they could just come around and listen to me, we all would be better off.

   Formulaic response: You feel _____ because _____.

   Natural response: _____

   _____.

7. *Jake:* Okay, okay. Maybe I'm looking at this backwards. Maybe I need to back off and deal with my anxiety. Maybe I'm the cause of all of this. If not, I'm afraid Angela will leave me and the kids, and they'll hate me forever.

   Formulaic response: You feel _____ because _____.

   Natural response: _____

   _____.

8. *Jake:* So what do you think I need to do to get things calmed down in my house? Be nicer? Lay off of everyone? Family counseling? I really love my family, and I don't want to lose them.

   Formulaic response: You feel _____ because _____.

   Natural response: _____

   _____.

EXPERIENTIAL EXERCISE 3.11

Practicing Empathic Responding: Angela

Now that you've had some practice counseling Jake, let's see how you do with Angela. You might want to review Appendix B again and then respond to the following items.

1. *Angela:* Well, I know I've struggled with my own identity over the years. When I lived in Nigeria, I was seen as White, and in the states, well, definitely Black. And am I a caretaker of my family or a working woman? Who am I?
   Formulaic response: You feel _____ because _____.
   Natural response: _____
   _____.

2. *Angela:* I'm very concerned about Jake's controlling attitude lately. He seems to be causing a general uproar in the family. I'm convinced that everything he has done has caused the kids to be upset, and well, frankly, I'm not exactly his biggest admirer lately.
   Formulaic response: You feel _____ because _____.
   Natural response: _____
   _____.

3. *Angela:* Maybe if I had a bit more guts I'd stand up to Jake and none of this would have happened. Maybe, in a sense, I'm to blame.
   Formulaic response: You feel _____ because _____.
   Natural response: _____
   _____.

4. *Angela:* Instead of standing up to Jake, I've just gone into my usual caretaker role. So easy for me to do that, but maybe it's not the best thing for everyone.
   Formulaic response: You feel _____ because _____.
   Natural response: _____
   _____.

5. *Angela:* You know, maybe Jake needs a wake-up call. I should go take the kids and leave for a while. Maybe go up to Philly and visit my sister. That will teach him.
   Formulaic response: You feel_____ because _____.
   Natural response: _____
   _____.

6. *Angela:* On the other hand, if I really had guts, I wouldn't have to go visit my sister. I'd just stand up to Jake right here. Tell him what I really think and give him an ultimatum.
   Formulaic response: You feel _____ because _____.
   Natural response: _____
   _____.

7. *Angela:* You know, I think I am going to stand up to him. I can do it nicely—I don't have to be mean, but he needs to back off and become "nice Jake" again. Otherwise, we aren't going to make it.
   Formulaic response: You feel _____ because _____.

EXPERIENTIAL EXERCISE 3.11—CONTINUED

Natural response: _____

_____.

8. *Angela:* Maybe I can do that on my own, but also, maybe some couples or family counseling would be helpful. That would help us all see what parts we play in this. What do you think?
   Formulaic response: You feel _____ because _____.
   Natural response: _____

_____.

EXPERIENTIAL EXERCISE 3.12

Practice with Empathy: Luke

Now that you've had some practice counseling Jake and Angela, let's see how you do with Luke. You might want to review Appendix B again and then respond to the following items.

1. *Luke:* Daddy was really angry with me when I was playing in the car. It wasn't my fault it rolled in the street.
   Formulaic response: You feel _____ because _____.
   Natural response: _____

_____.

2. *Luke:* Since that time, things have been really different. He's just no fun anymore.
   Formulaic response: You feel _____ because _____.
   Natural response: _____

_____.

3. *Luke:* Mommy and Daddy just seem to argue all the time. No wonder everyone is upset—even little Celia.
   Formulaic response: You feel _____ because _____.
   Natural response: _____

_____.

4. *Luke:* At least Mommy is good to me. She always loves me no matter what I do. I can count on her. My dad used to be fun, but now, Mommy is the only one I really love.
   Formulaic response: You feel _____ because _____.
   Natural response: _____

_____.

5. *Luke:* I just wish things could be back to the way they were. Can you help us? I hate our family now.
   Formulaic response: You feel _____ because _____.
   Natural response: _____

_____.

Practice with Empathy: Celia

Now that you've had some practice counseling Jake, Angela, and Luke, let's see how you do with Celia. You might want to review Appendix B again and then respond to the following items.

1. *Celia:* My tummy always hurts.
   Formulaic response: You feel _____ because _____.
   Natural response: _____
   _____.

2. *Celia:* I never want to go to school anymore. When I do, my stomachache just comes back. I just want to be home with Mommy.
   Formulaic response: You feel _____ because _____.
   Natural response: _____
   _____.

3. *Celia:* I think things got really bad when Luke and I got in trouble with the car. We shouldn't have done that. We were bad.
   Formulaic response: You feel _____ because _____.
   Natural response: _____
   _____.

4. *Celia:* Luke and Daddy are in bad moods all the time lately. Daddy's always yelling, and Luke gets in trouble all the time. It makes me feel bad.
   Formulaic response: You feel _____ because _____.
   Natural response: _____
   _____.

5. *Celia:* Can you help us get better? I want my family back the way it was.
   Formulaic response: You feel _____ because _____.
   Natural response: _____
   _____.

BOX 3.1

Watching Dr. Austin With Tiara

Your instructor may want to show you a video of Dr. Jude Austin working with Tiara. In this video, he uses a person-centered counseling approach, which largely relies on empathic responding. As you watch Dr. Austin, consider the following:

1. Did Dr. Austin use appropriate nonverbal responses?
2. Can you rate each of Dr. Austin's responses on the Carkhuff scale?
3. When Dr. Austin did not make an empathic response, what did he do instead?
4. Were Dr. Austin's nonempathic responses more facilitative than if he had made empathic responses? Why or why not?
5. How comfortable would you be working with a client in this manner?
6. Other thoughts?

More Practice With Empathy

The best way to become expert at making empathic responses is to practice, practice, and practice. Thus, in class or at home, your instructor will encourage you to practice making formulaic and natural empathic responses. It is important that you, or a fellow student, rate each of your responses on the Carkhuff scale so you can gain general feedback as to how you are doing. In addition, your instructor may ask you to submit video and/or audio files of role-play sessions or, in some cases, real sessions. This way, the instructor can listen to your responses and give you additional feedback.

In addition to practicing with fellow students, I encourage you to practice making empathic responses with important people in your life. You will know if you're on target if they keep talking, want to talk more, seem eager to speak to you, and if they don't say to you, "Are you practicing your counseling skills with me?" If they do make a statement like that, don't get discouraged—this is how you learn. It's better to learn from people you care about than to have a client drop out of counseling because he or she felt like you were a novice because you seemed to be practicing empathy rather than being an expert at empathy. Practice, practice, and practice; you'll be amazed at how much people will tell you about themselves when you get really good at making empathic responses.

Conclusion

Empathy is critical in the development of a strong working relationship and crucial for maintaining a bond with the client, and it can help the client understand deeper parts of himself or herself. Probably the most important skill a counselor can use, basic empathy can be learned rather quickly and, if applied well, can quickly help clients in the helping process. Although advanced empathy can deepen the relationship even further and add breadth to the counseling relationship, it is not considered an essential skill. Instead, advanced empathy is a value-added skill; that is, it's not essential but can add deeply to the relationship. Advanced empathy is discussed in Chapter 4: Commonly Used Skills.

Summary

This chapter examined the important foundational skills of silence and pause time, listening, reflection of feelings, reflection of content, paraphrasing, and basic empathy. We also touched very briefly on advanced empathy, although this skill will be discussed in more detail in Chapter 4: Commonly Used Skills.

We began by noting that silence is a very powerful skill that allows the client and the counselor to review what has been said in an interview. When the counselor allows silence, the client sometimes fills the void with important information about his or her life. Too much silence, however, could push a client out of the helping relationship. We highlighted the point that talking is not silence, and it is important for counselors to learn how to be comfortable with silence. Pause time, which is closely related to silence, is the amount of time a counselor allows between responses. It was pointed out that the length of pause time with which a client feels comfortable may depend on his or her cultural background. Therefore, counselors should be sensitive to the amount of pause time with which clients are comfortable.

Listening, one of the most important helping skills, does not come easily to many individuals. A number of hindrances to listening were highlighted in the chapter, including preconceived notions, anticipatory reactions, cognitive distractions, personal issues, emotional responses, and distractions. Practical suggestions for listening were noted, including talking minimally, concentrating on what is being said, not interrupting, not giving advice, being able to give without expecting to get, accurately hearing content and feelings, using good nonverbal communication to show attentiveness, asking for clarification when necessary, and not asking questions. A number of suggestions were also made for preparing for listening, including calming yourself down, not talking and not interrupting, showing interest, not jumping to conclusions, actively listening, concentrating on feelings, concentrating on content, maintaining eye contact, having an open body posture, being sensitive to personal space, and not asking questions.

Next in the chapter, three forms of basic responding were highlighted, including reflection of feeling, reflection of content, and paraphrasing. Specific ways to reflect feelings and content were noted and practiced. Paraphrasing—which, in many ways, is the combination of the reflection of feeling and reflection of content—was defined and practiced in the chapter.

Empathy, the ability to perceive the internal world of the client as if one were that person "without losing the 'as if' feeling," is probably the counselor's most important skill and was the next focus of the chapter. Although empathy has been discussed for centuries, during the 20th century it was popularized for helping professionals by Carl Rogers and was operationalized by Carkhuff and others. Cakrhuff's five-point scale became particularly popular in the learning of empathy and was highlighted in this chapter. It was noted that helpers who make a level 3 or higher empathic response are generally helpful to clients, and those who consistently make less than a level 3 response may be harmful. A level 3, or basic, empathy response was defined as one that accurately reflects the affect and content of what the client is saying. Level 1 or 2 responses are judgmental, or off the mark, in reflecting affect and meaning. At the other end of the scale, advanced empathic responses are level 4 or level 5 responses. Level 4 reflects feelings and meaning beyond what the client is aware of, and level 5 responses express deep understanding of a client's emotions as well as recognition of the complexity of the client's situation. Although we did not discuss advanced empathic skills in detail within this chapter, we noted that it will be focused upon more fully in the next chapter: Commonly Used Skills.

We noted that usually, in the training of counselors, it is recommended that they make basic or level 3 empathic responses. We pointed out that a large body of evidence suggests that such responses can be learned in a relatively short amount of time, help to build the working alliance, and result in positive client outcomes. Basic empathic responses need to be mastered prior to advanced empathic responses, which are considered value-added skills; that is, although not critical to the helping relationship, they can lend depth and breadth to client understanding of self.

Answers to Experiential Exercise 3.2

Usually: 2, 4, 9, 10; Sometimes: 7, 13; Rarely: 1, 3, 5, 6, 8, 11, 12, 14, 15

Key Words and Terms

active listening

advanced empathy

additive empathy

basic empathy

Carkhuff, Robert

Carkhuff scale

empathy

formula empathic responses

good listening

hindrances to effective listening

listening

natural empathic responses

silence and pause time

subtractive empathy

paraphrasing

preparing for listening

reflecting deeper feelings

reflection of content

reflection of feeling

Rogers, Carl

Credits

Photo 3.1: Source: https://pixabay.com/en/man-art-face-people-cartoon-3077831/.
Photo 3.2: Source: https://pixabay.com/en/sculpture-bronze-the-listening-3365574/.
Photo 3.3: Source: https://pixabay.com/en/sunset-lighthouse-dawn-dusk-sun-3120484/.
Photo 3.4: Source: https://pixabay.com/en/face-head-empathy-meet-sensitivity-985976/.

CHAPTER 4

Commonly Used Skills

Learning Objectives

1. Highlight the more commonly used skills in the helping relationship
2. Learn the important role that the following commonly used skills play in the helping relationship:
   a. Advanced empathy
   b. Affirmation, encouragement, and support
   c. Offering alternatives, information giving, and advice giving
   d. Inadvertent and intentional modeling
   e. Content and process self-disclosure
   f. Collaboration

Introduction

Whereas the nine characteristics of the effective counselor, the essential skills, and the foundational skills are all critical to building a working alliance in a nondirective, client-centered manner, the commonly used skills examined in this chapter gently push the client toward increased awareness and client-identified goals. *Advanced empathy,* the least helper-centered of the skills in this chapter, offers a mechanism for clients to become in touch with feelings beyond their awareness and provides them a new way of seeing the complexity of their situation. *Affirmation giving, encouragement,* and *support* reinforce client behaviors and promote client movement toward their goals. *Offering alternatives, information giving, and advice giving* provide ideas for attaining client goals. *Modeling* and counselor self-disclosure help clients generate new behaviors as they attempt to reach their goals. Finally, *collaboration* ensures that clients are satisfied with their goal-seeking direction in the counseling relationship. All these skills are integral to the counseling relationship and tend to emerge soon after the working alliance has been established (see Figure 4.1).

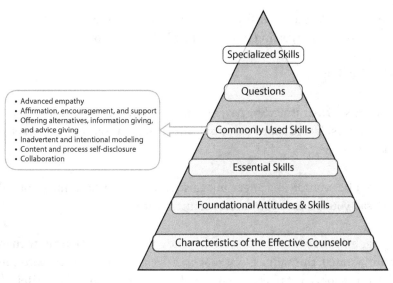

FIGURE 4.1 Counseling and helping skills

Advanced Empathy

Now that you've gained a handle on *basic empathy*, you're ready to tackle *advanced empathy*. If you remember from Chapter 3: Essential Skills, basic empathy is one of the most important skills a counselor can use when working with clients. Advanced empathy takes off from where basic skills end, as it facilitates client awareness of underlying feelings and can help clients

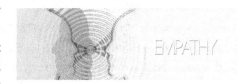

understand new ways to conceptualize their situations. These *additive empathy* responses give clients new ways of examining their situations and are often the precursor to new goals.

There are many ways of showing understanding through the use of advanced empathy, including (a) reflecting nonverbal behaviors, (b) reflecting deeper feelings, (c) pointing out conflictual feelings or thoughts, (d) using visual imagery, (e) using analogies, (f) using metaphors, (g) using targeted self-disclosure, (h) reflecting tactile responses, (i) using media, and (j) using discursive responses (Bayne & Neukrug, 2017; Neukrug, 2017a; Neukrug et al., 2012). On the Carkhuff scale, advanced empathic responses can range anywhere from a level 3.0 or higher, although it's not unusual to find them in the 3.5 to 4.0 range. Here are some examples:

Reflecting Nonverbal Behaviors

Client: Client walks into the office, bent over, moving slowly, and eyes are moist. He sits in the chair and look down.

Counselor: Boy, I can see from your body language that things are not going well. Seems like you're feeling pretty depressed.

When you know a person well, you can easily pick up on his or her body language. This example demonstrates this and is a way of quickly getting into "the meat" of the session.

Reflecting Deeper Feelings

Client: My daughter is so frustrating. She never listens to anything I say, she acts like a know-it-all, and it just seems like she doesn't care about me or anything. She's in college, and sometimes I just feel like giving her a good spanking.

Counselor: I hear your frustration and anger, but I also think I know how much you value a relationship with her and how sad you feel that you cannot connect with her.

In this example, look at how the counselor first reflects the client's frustration but then moves on to reflect sadness. Not outwardly stated, this sadness was *subceived* ("felt/experienced": a word coined by Rogers) by the counselor. If the counselor is on target, the client will respond accordingly (see Reflection Exercise 4.1).

REFLECTION EXERCISE 4.1

Reflecting Deeper Feelings Nonverbally

One time while seeing a client who was furious at her husband, I reflected to her, "You seem really sad and disappointed that the relationship has not worked out." She began to sob.

Consider whether responses such as the one I made to my client are interpretations or reflections of my experience of my client. It's important for advanced empathic responses to be reflections, not interpretations.

Can you come up with ways of reflecting deep feelings a client is experiencing without using similar words or paraphrasing what the client said? Some of the following examples will show some additional ways of doing this.

Pointing Out Conflicting Feelings or Thoughts

Client: I love my wife. We've been married for 25 years, and there is nothing I wouldn't do for her. She means everything to me, and I can't see living without her.

Ten minutes later:

Client: The affair has been going on for 3 months. It is so passionate. It livens up my life and makes me feel alive!

Counselor: On the one hand, your love for your wife is deep and lasting; on the other hand, you feel this passion in your life that you haven't had for a long time. It must be hard reconciling those different feelings.

We all live with conflicting feelings or thoughts about different aspects of our lives. Sometimes we tend to compartmentalize them—put them in their own little box, which offers the temporary fix of avoiding a dilemma. In counseling, however, sometimes it's important for a counselor to underscore these conflicting feelings and thoughts so the client can face them head-on and make some decisions about where to move in his or her life. Imagine how the conversation might go if this client faced his current dilemma.

Visual Imagery

Client: I can't believe how well I'm doing. I feel good, my life has moved in a positive direction, and my relationships—well, they just seem to be better than ever. I'm kind of flying.

Counselor: I have this picture in my head of you being picked up by your friends and loved ones as they hold you over their heads. Everyone is happy, but you have the biggest smile.

Sometimes when we sit with clients, visual images of their lives that reflect their experience float into our consciousness. This example shows just that. Responses like these are processed by the brain through different neural pathways than basic empathy responses and thus bring understanding to clients in new and deeper ways.

Using Analogies

Client: I'm nobody. At work, I sit in my cubicle, just one of a thousand people. We all do the same thing for the "greater good." And at home, I don't feel special. Nothing sets me apart from everyone else. I'm just the same.

Counselor: It's kind of like you're just a worker ant. You're one of many and don't know how to become a queen bee.

With analogies, the counselor compares the client's situation to a similar situation, sometimes in nature, that the client is experiencing. Like visual images, the brain takes in analogies through different neural pathways than the basic empathic response and thus brings understanding to clients in new and deeper ways.

Using Metaphors

Client: Since I lost my wife, I don't feel like living any longer. I'm just depressed all the time and don't want to do anything. I have little energy and sleep all day long. I don't want to be with people.
Counselor: Sounds like your drowning in a sea of grief.

Similar to analogies, metaphors offer a comparison, but in this case, the comparison is of a more abstract nature. Like visual images and analogies, the brain processes metaphors in different ways than it does basic responses, thus embedding them in the client's consciousness in deep ways.

Targeted Self-Disclosure

Client: The depression I feel seems bottomless. I don't see how I can ever get through this. No amount of counseling or medication will likely help. What do you think?

Counselor: I've got to say, I had a time in my life when I was pretty low myself and questioned whether I'd ever make it through. However, I did get through that rough time. Your situation reminds me of that time in my life.

Sometimes a personal revelation by a counselor can be an empathic response and also be a hopeful model for the client. In this example, the counselor sharing about a low time in her life shows that she understood the client and can give the client hope that he can get through. However, also note how the counselor does not reveal specifics about her low time. After all, this session is about the client, not the counselor, and the counselor should not share too much. Self-disclosure should be done carefully and conducted in a manner that shows the client that he or she is being heard—not as a catharsis for the counselor (see Chapter 5 for more on self-disclosure).

Tactile Responses

Client: The way he broke up with me was wrenching. It made me so depressed I didn't know what to do. I couldn't imagine he could be so hurtful. And he wouldn't stop harassing me … (client goes on and on about the harassment).

Counselor: Your description of the breakup sounds horrible; I felt physically sickened when you described it. I'm thinking this must have been how you felt.

Here, the description of a physical reaction by the counselor to the client's statement demonstrates that the counselor has heard him or her deeply. These responses, although rare, can go far in demonstrating understanding of a client's situation.

Using Media

Client: You know, I didn't think I had it in me. But I reached deep down inside and found my inner strength. Then I went up to my husband and told him my concerns. I was really brave, and you know what? I think he heard me—probably because I felt so strong. I then even spoke up to my boss—in a nice way, but I said what I was thinking. I'm so proud of myself!

Counselor: You know, you remind me of the Cowardly Lion in the *Wizard of Oz*, who clearly was not cowardly. He had the courage in him all the time; he just had to recognize it. And that he did—just like you did. I'm so proud of you, too!

Here we see how an allusion to the *Wizard of Oz* captures what the client is experiencing. This empathic response, like so many others we talked about, is a creative way of responding to clients without relying on the same old reflection-of-feeling-and-content response. It also leaves the client with a visual image that can stay with her. Notice how I also decided to use some affirmation here (to be discussed shortly).

Using Discursive Responses

Client: I just felt like my life was so oppressed. My husband was just pushing me around, my boss was constantly telling me what to do, and then I was stopped by the cops for no reason.

Counselor: I almost get a sense that you felt "shackled." Kind of like being enslaved, like your ancestors were. You have no escape.

Discursive empathic responses take the cultural history of a person and connect them with the person's current-day feelings and behaviors. In this example, this African American client is reminded of her family's history of slavery and how remnants of feelings passed down through generations may remain with her and impact her daily living.

Conclusions

Although beginning counselors are generally encouraged to make formulaic or natural empathic responses, as they become more proficient at these basic empathic responses, they can slowly begin to practice making the advanced responses. As with basic empathy, you will find the more you practice, the more natural these kinds of responses will become. Experiential Exercises 4.1 and 4.2 will give you the opportunity to formulate some additional advanced empathic responses. At this point, your instructor might want to show you a role-play of me working with a client named John using an existential-humanistic approach. Also, a second video of me with Jake (from "The Millers" in Appendix B), also using an existential-humanistic approach, can be viewed. As you view either of these videos, consider which skills I am using that we covered in the book. Finally, as you watch these videos, rate my responses on the Carkhuff scale.

EXPERIENTIAL EXERCISE 4.1

Making Advanced Empathic Responses

Form groups of four or five in your class. As a group, come up with advanced empathic responses to the same scenarios that were used in making basic empathic responses in Chapter 3. Use any of the 10 kinds of advanced empathic responses you want: reflecting nonverbal behaviors, reflecting deeper feelings, pointing out conflictual feelings or thoughts, using visual imagery, using analogies, using metaphors, using targeted self-disclosure, reflecting tactile responses, using media, and using discursive responses.

1. Young adult to counselor:

   Client: My girlfriend split up with me, and I'm feeling anxious all the time—I don't know what to do with myself.

   Advanced response: _____

   _____.

2. Individual with a disability to counselor.

   Client: I still can't believe I am paralyzed. It happened so quickly.

   Advanced response: _____

   _____.

3. Pregnant teenager to counselor:

   Client: OMG. What am I going to do? I should tell my parents, but I'm afraid how they will react.

   Advanced response: _____

   _____.

4. Husband to counselor:

   Client: I thought we had such a good relationship. Suddenly, she was gone. Just left me with the kids and everything. I just feel like I have nothing in my life.

   Advanced response: _____

   _____.

5. Eight-year-old to counselor:

   Client: Those other kids keep making fun of me. I try to stay away from them, but they're always laughing at me. Makes me want to hit them.

   Advanced response: _____

   _____.

6. Prisoner to counselor:

   Client: I didn't do nothing. Those charges are trumped up. They just want to get me because they know I've been in trouble before!

   Advanced response: _____

   _____.

EXPERIENTIAL EXERCISE 4.1—CONTINUED

7. Workaholic to counselor:

   Client: I work really hard ... maybe too hard. I'm really tired at the end of the day, and I know that impacts my relationship with my wife and kids

   Advanced response: _____

   _____.

8. Mother to counselor:

   Client: I want to work, and I want to be a mother. How can I do both? What should I do?

   Advanced response: _____

   _____.

9. Female upset with brother to counselor:

   Client: He treats me really poorly—curses at me, yells at me, ignores me, and never listens to me at all.

   Advanced response: _____

   _____.

10. Alcoholic to counselor:

    Client: I've been drinking for 30 years. Why should I stop now? My health is good, and I can handle it.

    Advanced response: _____

    _____.

EXPERIENTIAL EXERCISE 4.2

Making Advanced Empathic Responses

Form groups of three: a counselor, client, and observer. Record your session. The client should talk about a real or made-up issue, and the counselor should reply by using basic and advanced empathic responses. Try your best. Stay to the basic responses as much as you need to, but if you think of an advanced response, throw that in. Remember, however, even if you do not come up with any advanced responses, basic responses are great and result in positive client outcomes. Advanced empathic responses will come in time. Good luck! The observer can give feedback, and, if time allows, listen to your recording and rate yourself on the Carkhuff scale.

Affirmation, Encouragement, and Support

Affirmations, encouragement, and support all build client self-esteem and begin the slight push toward client self-identified goals (Dean, 2015; Lively, 2014; Wong, 2015). Thus, these skills begin the gentle tug clients may experience toward making change and by their nature tend to be delivered slightly after the client-centered essential and foundational skills. Let's examine these important skills in the counseling relationship.

Affirmation

Whether called "reinforcement" or a "genuine positive response," affirmations are an important aspect of acknowledging a client's actions and a positive move toward change and, if done well and at the correct moment, can be a significant tool for raising a client's self-esteem. Statements such as "Good job," "You are lovable and capable," or "You are a good person" help the client feel supported and worthwhile. Other statements and behaviors, such as saying, "Well done," or "I'm happy for you" and giving caring handshakes, warm hugs, and approving smiles are other effective ways of communicating affirmation. Affirmations are a natural part of all healthy relationships and are ways that individuals acknowledge positive aspects of others or, sometimes, positive aspects of self.

Although affirmation given by the counselor can be a critical skill in helping to raise a client's self-esteem and subtly reinforce client change, helping clients learn how to be self-affirming can be even more powerful as clients integrate this skill into their repertoire of behaviors. Therefore, it is important to teach clients how to self-affirm so they can inspire themselves and begin the process of "positive and sustained self-change" (Lively, 2014, para. 6). When teaching clients to affirm themselves, instruct them to

1. address themselves in the first person ("I am loving and capable");
2. be positive and joyful about self;

3. have an emotional component (instead of "I spend time with my spouse," say, "I appreciate myself so much more now that I make time to spend with my spouse"); and

4. state in the present, not the past or future (not "I will be loving and capable" but "I am loving and capable").

If you did not grow up in an affirming environment, then you may have difficulty affirming others and will almost assuredly have a hard time affirming yourself. Reflection Exercise 4.2 and Experiential Exercise 4.3 can help you look at how you have been affirmed and who has affirmed you in your life. It will also provide ways of practicing affirming others and affirming yourself.

REFLECTION EXERCISE 4.2

Have You Been Affirmed? *

Part 1: On the left side of a piece of paper, write down five things you are good at. Then, on the right side, write down who, if anyone, has affirmed you for what you wrote down. If you have not been affirmed for a particular activity on the left side of the paper, then write "No one" on the right side (see my example). When you have finished, form groups of four to eight students and move on to Part 2.

Things I'm Good At	People Who Have Affirmed Me
Writing	My students, colleagues, my wife
Running	No one
Discussing issues	Friends
Being a dad	My wife, my daughters, my mother-in-law
Being an administrator	My dean, my colleagues

Part 2: Pick one of the items you listed in Part 1 (if there was any item for which you were not affirmed, pick that one). Now, sit in the middle of your group and tell your fellow group members how you are good at that item. Then have each group member go around and affirm you in that area. When each member of your group has finished, join the rest of the class to discuss the following.

1. How did it feel to be affirmed by others?
2. Did you have an easy or difficult time affirming others? Why or why not?
3. Do you find that you are often affirmed in life?
4. Do you think that affirming others, especially clients, would feel genuine?
5. Do you believe that affirmations can really raise a person's self-esteem?
6. Do you think you can increase the number of affirmations you give?

REFLECTION EXERCISE 4.2—CONTINUED

Part 3: Using the item picked in Part 1 (or another item, if you prefer) practice self-affirming using the four steps listed earlier. For example, for "running," I might say the following:

1. I am a good runner.
2. Running has given me so much in my life: a sense of freedom, joy, and centeredness.
3. I feel so much better about myself when I am involved with running or, for that matter, other active sports activities.
4. I like myself as a runner.

*Note: Part 1 and Part 3 may be used with clients if you are seeing them individually. Parts 1 and 2 may be used with clients if you are running a group.

EXPERIENTIAL EXERCISE 4.3

Giving and Getting Affirmations

Part 1: In small groups or as a class, students may be given the opportunity to tell others something positive to raise others' self-esteem. Statements could be in the form of an acknowledgement of the way one interacts in class, how one dresses, how one presents oneself, and so forth. See how it feels to offer other people an affirmation. After you've done this for a few minutes, talk about how it felt to give and receive affirmations. *Part 2:* The instructor may develop some mechanism for students to give anonymous affirmations through- out the semester. For instance, each student's name could be written on an envelope and posted on the classroom wall so students can leave affirmations for one another. Or students could visit a website where they are able to share affirming posts with one another. There is no harm in allowing students to identify who wrote their affirmations, although this is not necessary, and it's sometimes interesting, and even more revealing, to not know. One important rule is that the statement must be positive. Periodically, the instructor can process the kinds of affirmations students are receiving and how they feel about receiving (or not receiving) affirmations.

Encouragement

Wong (2015) suggests that encouragement is "the expression of affirmation through language or other symbolic representations [e.g., nonverbal gestures] to instill courage, perseverance, confidence, inspiration, or hope in a person(s) within the context of addressing a challenging situation or realizing a potential" (p. 183). Thus, encouragement takes affirmation a step further by helping a client achieve a specific goal. You can see why encouragement can also be a vital tool for raising a client's self-esteem. Encouragement includes statements such as "I know you can do it," "Just keep trying," "You've made a great start," and so forth. Within the helping relationship, encouragement is generally focused on being a cheerleader for a client while he or she attempts to reach identified goals. Experiential Exercise 4.4 gives you practice in using encouragement.

Support

Somewhat more allusive than affirmation and encouragement, "offering support" is a general term acknowledging that one role of the counselor is to help the client feel as if there is someone in his or her corner. Support comes in many forms. For instance, a client may feel supported by a counselor emotionally, may know that the counselor is available if he or she is in crisis, may know that the counselor may advocate for the client, and more. Although support is an important part of the counseling relationship, there may be ethical concerns depending on the type of support one is offering. Read the following ethical standard and then complete Reflection Exercise 4.3. Consider which, if any, types of support might be crossing ethical boundaries.

> Counselors consider the risks and benefits of extending current counseling relationships beyond conventional parameters. Examples include attending a client's formal ceremony (e.g., a wedding/commitment ceremony or graduation), purchasing a service or product provided by a client (excepting unrestricted bartering), and visiting a client's ill family member in the hospital. In extending these boundaries, counselors take appropriate professional precautions such as informed consent, consultation, supervision, and documentation to ensure that judgment is not impaired and no harm occurs. (ACA, 2014, Section A.6.a. Previous Relationships)

EXPERIENTIAL EXERCISE 4.4

Encouraging Encouragement

Part 1: Get together in pairs and have one student be the counselor and the other be the client. The client should discuss a personal goal he or she is having difficulty accomplishing (e.g., losing weight, finding a job, communicating more with a loved one). The counselor should encourage the client by saying things such as "I know you can do it," "You have the inner strength to accomplish this," "Keep trying and I know you'll accomplish this," and so forth. After a few minutes, switch roles. After you have completed the exercise, form groups of six to eight students and discuss how it felt to be encouraged by another person.

Part 2: Remaining in your groups, have one student agree to share a current problem he or she is facing. That person should sit in the middle of the group and share how he or she has been working toward solving the problem. When appropriate, any group member can practice giving affirmations and encouragements. Students should only say something if it feels genuine. If time allows, other members of the group can sit in the middle and share their personal issues. After the exercise is completed, any individual who sat in the middle of the class should discuss how it felt to be affirmed and encouraged.

REFLECTION EXERCISE 4.3

The Limits of Support

In small groups, discuss whether you think each of the following counselor behaviors would be ethically acceptable as a means of supporting your client:

1. Lending money to your financially strapped client
2. Finding extra time for your client when he or she is in crisis
3. Driving your client to work because your client's car was stolen
4. Attending your client's wedding
5. Calling the school of your client's child to ensure the child gets needed services
6. Paying your client to do a small job (e.g., fix your car)
7. Giving your client extra time during a session when he or she is dealing with an emotionally charged situation
8. Spending extra time with your client to teach him or her good parenting skills
9. Providing after-school space in an empty office for your client's children because your client has to work and cannot afford child care
10. Having a cup of coffee, off hours, with a client to ensure he or she is doing okay

Final Thoughts

Some have warned that too much affirmation, encouragement, and support could cause the client to become dependent on the counselor (Kinnier, Hofsess, Pongratz, & Lambert, 2009). However, as counseling relationships have taken on an increasingly humanistic and interpersonal focus compared to the somewhat antiseptic, objective focus many helpers have used in the past, responses such as these have increasingly become part of the counselor's repertoire of skills. By offering such responses, the counselor hopes that clients will realize that affirmation, encouragement, and support have been lacking in their lives. Such insight can be the predecessor for clients taking their first steps in developing an increased self-affirming approach to life—one in which they are open to finding new relationships that are more affirming, encouraging, and supportive.

Offering Alternatives, Information Giving, and Advice Giving

Common to the skills of offering alternatives, information giving, and advice giving are their helper-centered focus; that is, such responses originate from the counselor, with their purpose being to assist the client in solving problems (Anderson, 2012; Ivey, Ivey, & Zalaquett, 2016; Kirschenbaum, 2015). Although helpful in many cases, they have the potential of creating a dependent relationship if the client believes that the counselor has the answer for most of the client's problems. In addition, a client can easily feel judged when a counselor uses these skills. Although all three of these skills have the potential to damage the counseling relationship, some are more likely to cause more problems than others (see Figure 4.2). Despite their drawbacks, such skills can help clients find solutions, when used appropriately.

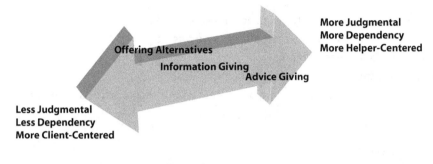

FIGURE 4.2   Potential damaging effects of skills

Offering Alternatives

Offering alternatives suggests to the client that there may be a number of ways to tackle a problem and provides the client with a variety of options from which to choose (Neukrug, 2017b). Compared to information giving and advice giving, offering alternatives has the least potential for harm. This is because it does not presume there is one solution to the problem, it has the least potential for setting up the counselor as the final expert, and, to some degree, it allows the client to pursue various options while maintaining a sense that he or she is directing the session (see Figure 4.2). See Experiential Exercise 4.5 to learn about offering alternatives.

Information Giving

Information giving offers the client important "objective" information (Ivey et al., 2016; Neukrug, 2017b). Since clients often know more than counselors might suspect, the key to making a successful information-giving response is to offer information of which the client is truly unaware. Thus, information offered should be seen as useful and likely to be used by the client. However, since information-giving responses assume the counselor has some valuable information the client needs, such responses tend to set up the counselor as the expert, increasing the potential for the client to become dependent on the relationship. Experiential Exercise 4.6 can help you see the pitfalls of information giving.

EXPERIENTIAL EXERCISE 4.5

Practicing Offering Alternatives

Form small groups of three and have one student be a counselor, one a client, and the third an observer who will assist the counselor. The client should talk for a few minutes about a real or made-up problem, and the counselor is to offer possible alternatives. It is probably best if you first use your basic listening and empathy skills in an effort to understand the problem fully. After listening, offer alternatives.

   If the counselor is having difficulty coming up with alternatives, the observer can make suggestions. After a few minutes, switch roles. If even more time allows, you can switch roles again. After you have finished, discuss in your triad the questions listed. Students in each triad may want to share their responses with the whole class.

1. Was it easy for the counselor to come up with alternatives?
2. Did the client already know the alternatives being offered?
3. Was offering alternatives helpful?
4. How did the client react to being offered alternatives?
5. Do you think another skill would have been more helpful than offering alternatives?

Giving Unnecessary Information

Pair up with another student and have one role-play the counselor and the other the client. The counselor should give the client information of which the client is already aware. You can use one of the scenarios listed or come up with one of your own (make sure the client is already familiar with the chosen topic and has information that may be given by the counselor). The client may respond in any way he or she wishes. For example, some clients might respond politely but think to themselves that they are already aware of the information being offered. Other clients might become belligerent and tell the counselor, "I already know about that; you're not helping me." After you've role-played for a few minutes, switch roles. When you are finished role-playing, form small groups to discuss how it felt to be offered alternatives on a topic you already knew thoroughly.

Possible Scenarios:

1. A client is concerned about becoming HIV-positive. Thus, the counselor decides to give information on how one can acquire HIV.
2. A client is concerned about becoming pregnant. Therefore, the counselor decides to give information on different kinds of birth control.
3. A client is worried about saving money for his children, and the counselor gives information on how to budget money.
4. A client is interested in obtaining a master's degree in counseling (or psychology, sociology, etc.), and the counselor gives information on what that entails.
5. "Other" scenario of your choice.

Advice Giving

When advice giving, the counselor offers expert opinions and hopes the client will follow through on the suggestions. This kind of response has the potential for developing a dependent relationship, as the client could end up relying on the counselor for problem-solving. In addition, advice giving may mimic control issues from the client's family of origin (e.g., parents giving advice) and thus can be seen as a value-laden response (Duan, Knox, & Hill, 2018).

Because of the potential pitfalls of advice giving, some consider it a response that should be avoided (Anderson, 2012; Ivey et al., 2016). For instance, it is not unusual for parents of teenagers to tell their children a wide range of ways to live in the world (e.g., how to study, who to date, what to do with their future). However, many teenagers will be highly offended by such advice.

Although our clients may not be teenagers, there is a little bit of teenager in all of us, and most people look askew at advice giving—especially when the advice given has already been considered. However, if given gently, and if the advice is something the client has not already thought of, this response can assist a client in finding solutions quickly. Remember, there are many ways to give advice, and a counselor need not act like a tyrant while doing so (see Experiential Exercise 4.7).

EXPERIENTIAL EXERCISE 4.7

Levels of Advice Giving

Have one student sit in the middle of three concentric circles. The student in the middle is to role-play a client problem. The innermost circle is to offer advice in a gruff, authoritarian manner. For instance, students in this circle might start responses with statements like "You should … !" or "It's imperative that you … !" The middle circle is to offer advice in a milder form, but still with a dogmatic tone. Some examples of how these students might start responses include "Why don't you … " or "You might want to …" The outermost circle is to offer advice in a mild, tentative way while attempting to not be authoritarian. Students in this circle might start their responses with statements such as "I've been wondering if you ever thought about … " or "Have you ever given thought to … "

You may want to have a few students take turns sitting in the middle of the circles. After you have done this exercise for 10 or 15 minutes, the students who sat in the middle should share how they experienced each of the circles. Also, individuals in the circles might want to share how they experienced the exercise. In the future, when you are in the role of an advice giver, consider the different ways that you might offer advice.

Final Thoughts

Offering alternatives, information giving, and advice giving—three valuable ways of helping clients problem solve. However, they also have potential for being destructive to the counseling relationship. Thus, the helpfulness of these responses needs to be balanced with their potential to cause harm. By carefully evaluating a client's needs and considering whether an alternative response could be more effective, a counselor must judge whether these responses will be helpful to the client. When the helping relationship is most effective, clients are more likely to brainstorm alternatives independently or ask the counselor for advice prior to the helper offering it.

Modeling

Counselors will act as models for their clients *whether or not they want to be* (Bussey, 2015; Martin & Pear, 2015). Modeling is sometimes called *social learning, imitation,* or *behavioral rehearsal,* and counselors constantly model for their clients in a variety of ways. For instance, when helpers are empathic, clients may learn how to listen to loved ones more effectively. When helpers model assertiveness, clients may learn how to positively confront someone in their lives, and when helpers model being effective mediators, clients may learn new ways of dealing with conflict. Counselors are change agents when they model for clients, which may occur either *inadvertently* or *intentionally.*

Inadvertent Modeling

Clients tend to look up to counselors and even idealize them (Neukrug, 2016). Such admiration creates the perfect condition for the development of inadvertent modeling, or the process of unconsciously taking on the qualities and attributes of another person after viewing that person. This process has the potential to powerfully affect and dramatically influence the client's change process (Bussey, 2015; Zur, 2016).

When counselors model inadvertently, they do not purposefully set out to change specific client behaviors (Bussey, 2015). Instead, the counselor acts as a powerful model because he or she is seen as an important person in the client's life and uses helpful skills within the relationship. Whether it is using good nonverbal behaviors, showing empathy, being a good listener, being genuine, or offering alternatives, clients will often pick up on the manner in which the counselor is working and copy it. Inadvertent modeling occurs in all helping relationships and should never be underestimated! Reflection Exercise 4.4 helps you look at how others have inadvertently modeled for you.

Intentional Modeling

Many counselors use intentional modeling as an important tool in their arsenal of change methods. By providing multiple ways of helping clients change targeted behavior (Ivey et al., 2016; Neukrug, 2016), intentional modeling can occur (a) through deliberate displays of specific behaviors on the part of the counselor (e.g., deliberately expressing empathy, being nonjudgmental, or being assertive and hoping the client will pick up such traits), (b) through role-playing with the client and displaying models of specific behaviors (e.g., the counselor might role-play job interviewing skills), and (c) through teaching the concept of modeling to clients and encouraging them to identify individuals who have positive characteristics they would like to emulate in their everyday lives (e.g., a person who has a fear of public speaking might choose an orator he or she admires and view the person live, on YouTube, etc.).

Intentional modeling involves a two-part process that includes first observing a targeted behavior and then practicing it. Thus, clients need to have appropriate models to imitate and practice the desired behavior inside and/or outside the session. With intentional modeling, any targeted behaviors the client wishes to acquire need to have a high probability of being adopted. For instance, an individual who has a fear of making speeches would first need to find a model to emulate. After observing this model, a hierarchy could be devised whereby the client would first make a speech to his or her counselor, then to some trusted friends, then to a small group, and so forth, perhaps asking for feedback along the way to sharpen his or her performance. Using these baby steps helps to assure a high probability that targeted behaviors will be adopted by the client (in this case, making speeches).

Intentional modeling is a powerful tool that may be used by counselors to effectively change client behavior. While inadvertent modeling occurs throughout the helping relationship regardless of whether the counselor and client realize it, intentional modeling requires the client to make a deliberate attempt to practice new behaviors with the consultation of the counselor. This kind of modeling requires a trusting relationship, should be carefully and deliberately planned, and demands a thorough assessment of the client's needs to ensure the appropriate choice of targeted behaviors. Therefore, intentional modeling does not generally take place at the beginning of the helping relationship. It requires the counselor to first take time to build rapport with the client and establish an accurate assessment of the client and his or her situation. Work through Reflection Exercise 4.4, followed by Experiential Exercise 4.8, for practice with intentional modeling.

REFLECTION EXERCISE 4.4

Models That Influenced You

On the top row of the table that follows are the names of individuals whom I have modeled or would like to model. In the second row, I have filled in qualities I have adopted from these significant others in my life. In the third row are qualities I have observed in others that I would like to adopt in my own life. See how I completed the table, and in the second table, fill in the appropriate spaces. If you have additional names you would like to add, create a new table on a blank piece of paper.

NAME OF PERSON YOU MODELED

	My father	Roger: My first counselor	Wife	My Sister
Qualities you modeled from that person	Integrity: My father was always honest and thoughtful. I have always tried to show integrity to others and see my father in my mind's eye when I do.	Empathy: Roger was great at exhibiting empathy, and I learned how to be empathic by experiencing it from him.	Patience: I watched my wife with my children and learned how to be patient with them when they did not do what I wanted them to do.	My sister is a strong, assertive person who is direct with her communication. As a younger sibling, I feel like she modeled this for me, and I adopted many of these qualities.
Qualities you viewed and would like to adopt	Thoughtfulness: My father always took time before making major decisions or responding to others' opinions. I would like to be more thoughtful at times.	Pausing: Roger had a great ability at pausing prior to responding to people.	My wife has the ability to not worry about things. I would like to worry less about some things, such as my health and the health of my children.	Nothing else comes to mind.

REFLECTION EXERCISE 4.4—CONTINUED

NAME OF PERSON YOU MODELED

Qualities you modeled from that person

Qualities you viewed and would like to adopt

EXPERIENTIAL EXERCISE 4.8

Intentional Modeling

List the qualities you would like to adopt from Reflection Exercise 4.4. Then write specific ways you could practice acquiring them. In small groups, discuss the qualities you would like to adopt and the specific plans you have developed to acquire them. Some groups might want to meet on an ongoing basis to encourage the acquisition of the qualities. How might these qualities work positively for you as a counselor?

Qualities you would like to acquire	*Mechanism for acquiring the qualities listed*
1.	1. 2. 3.
2.	1. 2. 3.
3.	1. 2. 3.
4.	1. 2. 3.

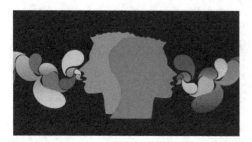

Self-Disclosure

Self-disclosure occurs when counselors reveal something about themselves to the client unwittingly or purposefully (Bloomgarden & Mennuti, 2009; Ivey et al., 2016). However, self-disclosure is often seen as a mixed bag. On the one hand, it can lead to increased client self-disclosure, can be a way of expressing empathy by demonstrating that the counselor understands the client's experience due to having been in similar situations, and can be a method of demonstrating new skills, such as when the counselor describes behaviors that were beneficial in his or her life, hoping that the client may try similar behaviors. On the other hand, self-disclosure can make a client feel uncomfortable, as some clients will feel it is inappropriate for the counselor to share information about his or her life. In extreme cases, it can be considered an unethical practice, especially when the counselor is focusing more on his or her own needs instead of the needs of the client (see Reflection Exercise 4.5).

REFLECTION EXERCISE 4.5

Self-Disclosure Gone Awry

One of my former students was in therapy with a psychiatrist who, over time, increasingly began to disclose his problems to her. One day, she heard that he had hanged himself. Following his death, she revealed to me her feelings of intense guilt for not having saved his life. What a legacy to leave this student! Clearly, the psychiatrist's self-disclosure was unhealthy and unethical. Ironically, the comedian Sarah Silverman appears to have seen the same psychiatrist and also experienced the negative results of his suicide! (Week Staff, 2010)

Despite the situation described, there are circumstances where self-disclosure may be appropriately used to help a client open up and may also serve as a model of positive behavior. What do you think is the appropriate amount of self-disclosure in the helping relationship?

Generally, two types of self-disclosure have been identified: *content self-disclosure,* in which counselors reveal personal information about themselves; and *process self-disclosure,* sometimes called *immediacy,* in which counselors reveal moment-to-moment information about their experience in the relationship with their clients (Conason, 2017; Simonds & Spokes, 2017).

Content Self-Disclosure

The revelation of personal information on the part of the counselor is called content self-disclosure. Done well, such revelations can enhance the counseling relationship by showing the client that the counselor is "real" and by building a stronger working alliance. Content self-disclosure can also add deeper intimacy to the relationship, which ultimately could foster increased self-disclosure by the client. Sometimes, this kind of self-disclosure is akin to an empathic response, such as when it is used to show a client that a counselor is listening and understanding:

> *Counselor:* When I went through my divorce, I felt sad and depressed. I think I'm hearing that's how you're feeling.

Finally, content self-disclosure can sometimes offer a new model for the client to emulate:

> *Counselor:* After my divorce, when I was ready, I decided to get back into the dating scene, which upped my spirits some. Do you think you might be ready for that?

In these examples, notice how the counselor keeps the disclosures to a minimum and immediately focuses back on the client. After all, the intent of this kind of self-disclosure is to enhance the client's experience of rapport and trust, be empathic, or offer a solution for the client. It should not be used as an opportunity for counselors to talk about themselves. Even if self-disclosure is being used to benefit the client, some may feel put off by self-disclosure and think that counselors should keep their life stories out of the relationship or feel that the counselor's revelation of his or her own struggle is an indication of weakness. Thus, using content self-disclosure should be done with great care, and only after consideration of the client's needs.

Process Self-Disclosure

In contrast to content self-disclosure, process self-disclosure, sometimes called immediacy, involves sharing the counselor's moment-to-moment experience of self in relation to the client (Ivey et al., 2016; Sackett, Lawson, & Burge, 2012; Simonds & Spokes, 2017). Process comments can help clients see the impact they have on a counselor and make connections between how this impact is similar to the way they affect others in their lives. Also, clients may learn how moment-to-moment communication can enhance relationships. For instance, a counselor might say the following to a client:

> Counselor: You know, I really feel connected with you right now. You seem to be more open and willing to be yourself.

This "immediate" sharing of one's feelings models how to share feelings and thoughts in a relationship and will hopefully be followed up by an "immediate" response from the client. Practicing these new forms of communication can sometimes be generalized to others in the client's life. Similar to the Rogerian concept of genuineness, process self-disclosure allows the counselor to be real with his or her feelings toward the client. However, counselors should not confuse such disclosure with the unethical practice of sharing their feelings with a client in an effort to work through their own issues or to achieve catharsis (Rogers, 1957).

Some counselors suggest using care in sharing moment-to-moment feelings with clients. Rogers (1957) points out that clients are rapidly changing as they share deeper parts of themselves, and as they change, the counselor's feelings toward them will quickly change as well. Instead of sharing moment-to-moment feelings, Rogers suggests that it is often more important to share persistent feelings, as these are more meaningful to the relationship. If you remember from Chapter 1, the ability to monitor one's emotions and share feelings at intentional and meaningful times is sometimes called *emotional intelligence*.

When to Use Self-Disclosure

> I try not to make a fetish out of not talking about myself. If a client, on the way out the door, asks in a friendly and casual way, "Where are you going on your vacation?" I tell where I'm going. If the client were then to probe, however ("Who are you going with? Are you married?"), I would be likely to respond, "Ah … maybe we'd better talk about that next time." (Kahn, 2001, p. 150)

Self-disclosure needs to be done sparingly, at the right time, and as a means of promoting client growth rather than satisfying the counselor's needs (Harrison, 2013). A general rule of thumb that I use is if it feels good to self-disclose, don't. If it feels good, you're probably meeting more of your needs than the needs of your client. Some general guidelines for the use of self-disclosure include the following:

1. Use self-disclosure sparingly and only if the client seems comfortable with it.
2. Use self-disclosure to build the relationship, to reveal new possible avenues of behavior for clients, or to show empathy.
3. Don't self-disclose to have one's own needs met.
4. Never self-disclose when it leads to blurred boundaries, and particularly don't self-disclose on personal topics, such as sexual issues and intimacy.
5. Consider if other responses might be more effective (see Experiential Exercise 4.9).

EXPERIENTIAL EXERCISE 4.9

Self-Disclosure

First, students should pair up based on whether they have had one of the following problem situations in their lives (or other common problems):

1. Divorce
2. Getting fired
3. Being dumped by a significant other
4. Problem pregnancy
5. Trust with friend
6. Financial problems
7. Marital problems
8. Disliking parent(s)

In your dyad, have one person be the counselor while the other plays the client. The client should talk about the chosen situation for 5 to 10 minutes, during which the counselor should attempt to make at least one self-disclosing response that relates to the situation. If possible, the response should be given in a manner that would facilitate the client's exploration of self. After you have finished, if time allows, switch roles. In class, address the following questions:

1. Was the counselor's self-disclosure helpful to the client?
2. Did the client and counselor develop a greater alliance as a result of self-disclosure?
3. Did the self-disclosure change the focus of the session in any manner?
4. Were there better possible responses than self-disclosure?

Collaboration

Collaboration is the intentional practice of discussing, with clients, the opinions about the types of techniques that might be applied as well as checking in with them regarding their perceptions of the amount and type of progress that has been made in the counseling relationship (Meyers, 2014a; Sommers-Flanagan & Sommers-Flanagan, 2017). Collaboration suggests that the counselor is able and willing to hear the voice of the client, even if the feedback is negative, and shows a willingness on the part of the counselor to change strategies if clients are not content with what has occurred or are not happy with specific techniques that will be used. Collaboration should be deliberate and occur at multiple times during the counseling relationship. Although there is no set limit on the number of times a counselor should collaborate with clients, some counselors like to ask clients for feedback every time a new technique is applied, and many counselors will ask clients, at the end of each session, their perceptions of how each session has gone. Some general ways of collaborating with clients and asking for feedback from them include the following:

1. The use of basic listening and empathy skills to offer a summary of what has occurred and provide time for the client to respond.

   Counselor: So, it seems like thus far, you believe that the helping relationship has been beneficial to you and that you are looking forward to making more progress in the future.

2. Using questions about upcoming techniques to be applied.

   Counselor: Well, we've been talking quite a bit about some of the panic attacks you have. I was thinking that we might try some relaxation techniques, which I can first explain to you in detail. What do you think?

3. Using questions to ask clients their thoughts on progress to date.

   Counselor: What are your thoughts about how things are going thus far?

4. Using questions to ask clients about new directions they would like to take.

   Counselor: So, what ideas do you have about where you would like to take these discussions in the future?

5. Using counselor self-disclosure to reveal what progress the helper believes has occurred so far, followed by a request for feedback.

   Counselor: You know, overall you have made some significant changes, although it does seem like you're somewhat stuck in resolving some issues regarding your wife. What do you think?

6. Using counselor self-disclosure and a request for feedback to provide ideas for future direction.

   Counselor: My sense is that you have made some good progress, and I'm now wondering if you would like to try some new ideas on working through some of your concerns. For instance ...

7. Encouraging an honest discussion concerning discrepancies between clients' and counselors' beliefs about current progress and direction in the future.

    Counselor: It seems like I'm seeing some progress being made in your relationship with your children, but you do not. Let's talk about that. For instance, I think you have really been able to work on how you discipline them. What are your thoughts on that?

    Client: Well, yes, I have made some progress, but it seems like it's just too little too late. I'm wondering if we can maybe find some other things that might work more quickly.

Collaboration is a powerful tool that can only occur if the counselor has the willingness to hear constructive feedback from the client. If counselors are too fragile and defensive about their skills, then they may have a difficult time using this skill. On the other hand, if the counselor is open to feedback, willing to adjust his or her style of counseling, and wanting to work with the client toward goals, collaboration can go far in improving client outcomes (see Experiential Exercise 4.10).

EXPERIENTIAL EXERCISE 4.10

Practicing Collaboration

Find a partner and role-play a counselor-client situation for a few minutes. After the session has gained some momentum, practice using one or more of the collaboration techniques just listed. A third person should be an observer and list each time a collaboration technique is applied. When the role-play is complete, discuss the collaboration technique using the following questions:

1. What technique(s) did you apply?
2. Did it seem natural to ask for feedback?
3. How did the client respond to the request for feedback?
4. Would other ways of asking for feedback have been beneficial?
5. Overall, what are the positive and negative effects of collaboration?

Conclusion

A variety of skills have been highlighted in this chapter and the preceding two chapters. To a large degree, they were discussed in the order generally displayed in the helping relationship; that is, one usually starts with the foundational skills, moves on to the essential skills, and then moves on to the commonly used skills. Keeping this in mind, Experiential Exercise 4.11 is your chance to practice many of these skills. Remember to keep your use of questions to a minimum, if used at all (remember, we have not even discussed questions yet).

EXPERIENTIAL EXERCISE 4.11

Practicing Skills

This chapter and the previous chapters offered a number of helping skills that should be beneficial in the helping relationship. Here's your chance to practice what you've learned thus far. Find a partner and record a 30- to 60-minute session. Try using a variety of the skills you have learned from the chapters during that session. At the end of the session, make sure that you conclude with collaboration and ask your client how the session went. Then, at home, write out each of your responses, identify what kind of skill you used, and make a note about whether you think you used the appropriate skill and whether you could have been sharper in the manner in which you used the skill. Your instructor may want you to hand in the recording and your responses or talk about your responses in class. Keep in mind that the next chapter focuses on questions, so do your best to *not* ask any questions at this point. Questions are often easily used by students and it's good to practice *not* using them.

Summary

Chapter 4 focused on some of the more commonly used helping skills of counselors. We started where we left off in Chapter 3, with empathy, but this time focused on advanced empathy. We noted that these responses facilitate client awareness of underlying feelings and can help clients understand new ways to conceptualize their situations. These additive empathy responses give clients new ways of examining their situations and are often the precursor to new goals. We highlighted ten ways of showing advanced empathy, including reflecting nonverbal behaviors, reflecting deeper feelings, pointing out conflictual feelings or thoughts, using visual imagery, using analogies, using metaphors, using targeted self-disclosure, reflecting tactile responses, using media, and using discursive responses.

Next, we discussed affirmation giving, encouragement, and support and noted their importance to raising a client's self-esteem. We pointed out that affirmations are general positive responses that can help raise a client's self-esteem, encouragement reinforces a client's efforts toward established goals, and support is a general term that means the counselor shows, in various ways, that he or she is "in the client's corner."

Moving on to offering alternatives, information giving, and advice giving, we stressed that all three skills can result in the client feeling judged by the counselor or creating a dependent relationship. However, we noted that offering alternatives is less likely to do this than information giving, and information giving is less likely to do this than advice giving. We then demonstrated ways these skills may be used so they are more likely to be useful and accepted by the client.

Modeling, we noted, can be conducted in two ways. Inadvertent modeling occurs as a by-product of the helping relationship and takes place when the client, due to the importance of the helping relationship, unconsciously picks up important skills that the counselor is exhibiting. In contrast, intentional modeling involves the deliberate display of specific behaviors by the counselor in hopes that clients will emulate those skills. This can happen by identifying new behaviors with clients so they can practice the new skills during the session or by teaching clients about the modeling process so they can find models to emulate outside of the helping relationship.

Self-disclosure, or the revelation of something about the counselor's life to the client, can be conducted purposefully or unwittingly. We noted that content self-disclosure, or the sharing of information about the counselor, can be conducted in many ways and has a number of purposes. For instance, it can involve discussing personal information about the counselor in an effort to build the relationship, be used to show the client that the counselor understands him or her, be a manner of fostering deeper self-disclosure on the part of the client, and be used as a model for the development of new behaviors. Process self-disclosure, sometimes called immediacy, is the sharing of the counselor's moment-to-moment experience of self in relation to the client. This type of self-disclosure is a model for how clients can be more genuine within their relationships. It was stressed that self-disclosure is a skill that should be used sparingly. A number of guidelines to using self-disclosure were provided.

The last commonly used skill we reviewed was collaboration, which focuses on checking in with the client to ensure that the client is satisfied with the direction of the helping relationship. Collaboration shows respect for client feedback and can be used throughout all of the sessions. A number of different ways to be collaborative were noted.

Key Words and Terms

additive empathy	pointing out conflictual feelings or thoughts
advanced empathy	process self-disclosure
advice giving	reflecting deeper feelings
affirmation	reflecting nonverbal behaviors
basic empathy	reflecting tactile responses
behavioral rehearsal	self-disclosure
collaboration	social learning
content self-disclosure	support
encouragement	using analogies
imitation	using discursive responses
immediacy	using media
inadvertent modeling	using metaphors
information giving	using targeted self-disclosure
intentional modeling	using visual imagery
modeling	
offering alternatives	

Credits

CHAPTER 5

Information-Gathering and Solution-Focused Questions

Learning Objectives

1. Understand the purpose and use of questions
2. Learn the differences between information-gathering and solution-focused questions
3. Learn how to use the following information-gathering questions in the helping relationship:
    a. Closed questions that delimit content and affect
    b. Open questions that delimit content and affect
    c. Tentative questions
    d. Why questions
4. Understand when it is best to use closed, open, tentative and why questions
5. Learn how to use the following solution-focused questions:
    a. Preferred-goals questions
    b. Evaluative questions
    c. Coping questions
    d. Exception-seeking questions
    e. Solution-oriented questions
    f. Scaling questions

Introduction

Questions can play an important role in the counseling relationship; however, used too frequently or inappropriately, they can cause ruptures in the relationship and prevent the building of the working alliance. This chapter examines the use of questions and is divided into two sections: *information-gathering questions* and *solution-focused questions*. First, here are a few questions to ponder, then examine Figure 5.1.

- What purpose do questions serve in the counseling relationship?
- Can questions gather information quickly?
- Can questions increase client insight?
- Can questions help clients reach their goals?
- Might questions interfere with the helping process?
- Can questions make a person defensive?

- Might it be better to use other techniques in lieu of questions?
- At what point should one use questions?

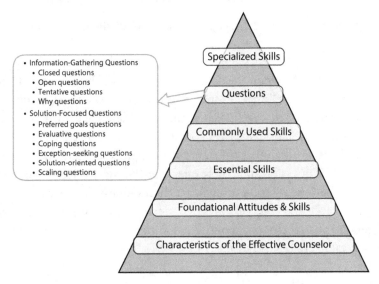

FIGURE 5.1   Counseling and helping skills

Information-Gathering Questions

Considered *helper-centered* because they are developed from what the helper believes is important, not necessarily what the client views as critical, information-gathering questions are particularly useful at the beginning of a relationship to gather a full picture of the client. In fact, they are often used during intake interviews or early assessment of client  needs in order to develop treatment plans. However, they can be used at any point during counseling if the counselor wants to delve further into a particular area of interest. They include *closed questions, open questions, tentative questions,* and *why questions.*

Closed Questions

Closed questions are important when the counselor wants to limit (close) the types of responses clients are likely to make in an effort to gather very specific information quickly. They are often asked using a *yes/no, forced-choice,* or *focused question* format, such as in the following examples (Egan & Reese, 2019; Hill, 2014; Ivey, Ivey, & Zalaquett, 2016; Neukrug, 2017b):

> Yes/No format: "Do you think your mom was an angry person?"
>
> Forced-choice format: "Who do you think was angrier, your mom or dad?"
>
> Focused question format: "Tell me how anger was shown in your family."

Closed questions can delimit content or affect. For instance, the previous examples focus on content. In contrast, the examples that follow delimit affect:

Yes/No format: "Do you feel sad about the loss of your pet?"

Forced-choice format: "Do you feel sad or angry about the loss of your pet?"

Focused question format: "What feelings do you have about the loss of your pet?"

Closed questions are particularly helpful when the counselor needs to obtain information quickly from a client, as in an intake interview, or when the counselor is pressured by time constraints. They should be used gingerly in a long-term counseling relationship, as they tend to set up the counselor as the expert authoritarian, or even interrogator, and can make the client feel defensive. Although such questions can be helpful in gathering information quickly, they sometimes lend themselves to choices that may not accurately represent the client. For instance, in the first example, the client may have a more nuanced answer than "yes" or "no" to the question about his or her mom being angry, or in the second set of examples, perhaps the client is experiencing something other than sadness or anger about the loss of the pet. Clients often have more involved and complex ways of understanding their situations, and forced-choice or focused questions tend to push them to respond in a manner that might not truly reflect how they see themselves (see Experiential Exercise 5.1 then 5.2).

Closed Questions Bombardment

Break up into small groups of five to eight students and have one person sit in the middle who acts as a client and shares a real or made-up problem. The rest of the students, except one, should sit in a circle around the client, and the last student (the "observer") should sit outside of the circle. As the client talks, those in the circle should respond with closed questions. The observer should write down the kinds of responses made. After a few minutes, discuss the following:

1. The kinds of closed questions that were asked
2. Whether the closed questions seemed helpful (ask the client)
3. If other kinds of responses would have been more helpful

Practicing Closed Questions

Break up into groups of three. One person role-play a client, the second a counselor, and the third should be an observer. The client should role-play a person with a problem, and the helper should try to respond only with closed questions. The observer should make a note of the different kinds of closed questions that were asked. After you have role-played for about 5 or 10 minutes, switch roles, and then switch roles a third time so that everyone gets to practice. After each role-play, have the observer share the different kinds of closed questions made by the helper. Finally, as a group, discuss how effective the closed questions were in eliciting information from the client.

Open Questions

In contrast to closed questions, open questions enable the client to have a wide range of responses to the question being posed (Egan & Reese, 2019; Hill, 2014; Ivey et al., 2016). Like closed questions, open questions can be focused on content or on affect. For instance, a client could be asked a content-focused open question such as "How did you decide what career to focus on?" or "What makes your marriage so unique?" Or, a client might be asked an affect-focused open question such as "So, how did you feel about that?" or "What were you feeling after the incident?"

Open questions can be powerful, as they allow clients the freedom to respond in a multitude of ways. This creates an environment in which the client has more leeway in directing the focus of the session. Thus, this type of question is seen as less helper-centered (more *client-centered*) than a closed question (see Experiential Exercises 5.3 and 5.4. Then complete Experiential Exercise 5.5).

EXPERIENTIAL EXERCISE 5.3

Open Questions Bombardment

Break up into small groups of five to eight students and have one person sit in the middle who acts as a client who is sharing a real or made-up problem. The rest of the students, except one, should sit in a circle around the client, and the last student should sit outside of the circle. As the client talks, those in the circle should respond with open questions. The observer should write down the kinds of responses made. After a few minutes, discuss the following:

1. The kinds of open questions that were asked
2. Whether the open questions seemed helpful (ask the client)
3. If other kinds of responses would have been more helpful

EXPERIENTIAL EXERCISE 5.4

Practice With Open Questions

Your instructor should break the class into groups of three. Within your triad, identify a helper, a client, and an observer. The client should discuss a real or made-up problem, and the helper should respond by asking only open questions. The observer is there to assist the helper should she or he have difficulty with the task. Also, if the observer believes the helper did not respond with an open question, he or she should stop the interview, and the three students should discuss what open questions could be asked. Then resume the exercise. After doing this for 5 to 10 minutes, change roles and have the client be the helper, the observer be the client, and the helper be the observer. Then, after another 5 to 10 minutes, do the exercise one last time, changing roles again. In class, discuss the relative ease or difficulty of asking open questions.

EXPERIENTIAL EXERCISE 5.5

Contrasting Closed Questions and Open Questions With Empathic Responses

Have a student volunteer talk about a topic of his or her choice that involves some kind of dilemma or difficulty. The rest of the class should create two circles around the student. The first circle should only ask closed questions, and the second circle should only ask open questions. Have the student discuss the dilemma or difficulty for about 5 minutes while the first circle only responds with closed questions. Then, for the next 5 minutes, the second circle should only respond with open questions. Finally, for 5 more minutes, anyone should respond with only empathic responses. When you have finished, discuss the following questions as a group:

1. How did the student experience the first part of the exercise?
2. How did the student experience the second part of the exercise?
3. How did the student experience the last part of the exercise?
4. Was it easier for the helpers to ask closed questions, open questions, or to make empathic responses?
5. Did questions need to be asked at all?
6. Do you think it would be better to ask a good question or to make a good empathic response?

Open or Closed Questions—Which to Use?

If a counselor wants to facilitate a deeper counseling relationship, he or she should generally rely more on open questions than closed ones. For instance, when asking a client about his or her family, a simple open question, such as "Can you tell me more about your family?" can be quite useful and lead to a wide range of responses. In contrast, the use of a closed question is important when the counselor wants to gather specific information quickly, such as when the counselor wants to know the relative positions of various members in a family. In that case, quick questions such as "Who is in your family and what are their ages?" could be important. Or, if a counselor wants to quickly assess a client's feelings about his or her family, the counselor might ask a closed question, such as "Overall, do you think your family was dysfunctional or functional?" The downside to questions like these is that they may direct the session in a manner that is not particularly relevant to what the client wishes to discuss and can limit the range of discussion. A counselor should always remember that sometimes one type of question will be more effective in eliciting certain responses, and sometimes not using a question at all might be the best route. Counselors need to consider the purpose of the question—is it to gain information quickly through the use of a closed question, to allow the client to discuss a topic broadly through the use of open questions, or to simply listen and reflect and not use any questions at all?

Tentative Questions

Questions can be asked tentatively, suggesting that the counselor is testing the waters. For instance, rather than asking "What are the names and ages of the people in your family?" one could ask, "Would you mind telling me about your family members, their names and ages?" Or, rather than asking the question "How sad do you feel about your divorce?" a counselor could ask the tentative question "I'm wondering if you might be feeling sad right now about your divorce?" Or, rather than saying "How are you feeling about the divorce?" one could say "I would guess that you might have some feelings about the divorce?" Sometimes counselors will add a small question, such as "Is that true?" at the end of a sentence to make a question sound more tentative. Tentative questions lessen the harshness sometimes found with the use of closed and even open questions and give the client an easier opportunity to back out of responding to the question if feeling uncomfortable.

Sometimes, tentative questions are very similar to empathic responses. For instance, in the previous example, rather than saying "I would guess that you might have some feelings about the divorce?" the counselor could say "It seems like you're having some feelings about the divorce." Tentative questions tend to sit well with clients. They're easier to hear, help the session flow smoothly, help to create a nonjudgmental and open atmosphere, and are generally responded to positively by clients. Experiential Exercise 5.6 helps to identify how you can ask tentative questions, and Experiential Exercise 5.7 helps you practice your skills with tentative questions.

EXPERIENTIAL EXERCISE 5.6

Developing Tentative Questions

In class, come up with different beginning phrases that might start a tentative question. For instance, in the previous examples, I began the responses by stating "I wonder if you … " and with "I would guess that you … "

Think of a number of different ways one might begin a tentative question. Write them in the space provided and share your various responses in class.

1. _____.
2. _____.
3. _____.
4. _____.
5. _____.
6. _____.

EXPERIENTIAL EXERCISE 5.7

Making Responses Using Tentative Questions

In this exercise, use the responses made in Experiential Exercise 5.6 or other tentative responses you may come up with. Break into groups of threes. One person role-play a client, the second a counselor, and the third the observer. The observer should help when needed. The client should role-play a person with

Why Questions

"Why do you feel that way?" "Why do you think you responded like that?" "Why did you do that?" "Why" questions would be the best questions in the world if they didn't make one feel defensive, self-protective, suspicious, cautious, or distrustful. Their intent is good—to get to the root of the problem. Unfortunately, they tend to put clients on the spot. Because of this, it is generally recommended that rather than using why questions, counselors use other kinds of questions or make empathic responses (De Jong & Berg, 2013; Ivey et al., 2016; Nevid, 2015). If one could honestly answer why, why questions would be the most powerful question used in the helping relationship. However, clients use the helping relationship to find the answer to why. If they knew, they wouldn't be in the counselor's office. I have found that after I've formed an alliance with a client, I might periodically slip in a soft why question and say something such as "Why do you think that is?" However, if I use this type of question at all during a session, I use it sparingly.

When to Use Closed, Open, Tentative, and Why Questions

Questions tend to come easy to people, while empathic responses take work. However, questions are not always the best route to take when working with clients. Although questions can be helpful in uncovering patterns, inducing self-exploration, and challenging the client to change, their overuse can set up a demeaning atmosphere—one in which the client feels humiliated and put on the spot, as the counselor acts as the superior expert. Some also note that the use of questions can lead to dependence on the counselor, as the client increasingly assumes the helper is taking the lead in the helping relationship (Cormier, Nurius, & Osborn, 2013). Therefore, some suggest that the empathic response should often be considered as an alternative to the question (Neukrug, 2017a; Neukrug et al., 2012; Rogers, 1942). For instance, suppose a client said the following:

Client: My kids just seem to hate me, and they are just out of control. I'm not sure what's wrong with them.

A counselor could respond with this question:

Counselor: What's going on with your kids to make you feel that way?

Although this response might be made from a sincere and thoughtful place, it could make the client feel defensive and can even lead the client to think the counselor believes there is something wrong with the children. However, look at the following response:

Counselor: It seems like you feel unloved and are not sure what's going on with your kids.

Generally, if one is *not* needing to quickly gather information and not particularly worried about time, an effective response that can lead to a deepening working alliance is to make an empathic response. You may want to consider how much time you have with clients and if you are relying too much on using questions. Although much more can be said about the different uses of questions in the interviewing process, remember to be careful whenever you ask questions. Some guidelines for the use of questions include the following:

1. Are you aware that you are asking a question?
2. Under the current situation, is asking a question the best response you can make?
3. Are you using the type of question most amenable to the situation at hand?
4. Have you considered alternatives to asking questions?
5. Will the question you are about to ask inhibit the flow of the interview? If so, do the benefits of using it (e.g., gathering specific information quickly) outweigh the drawbacks of not using it?

After reviewing Fact Sheet 5.1, complete Experiential Exercise 5.8 so you can practice the use of questions thus far examined in the chapter.

FACT SHEET 5.1

Information-Gathering Questions

Type of question	Definition	Examples	Advantages/ Disadvantages
Closed questions delimiting content	Questions that focus on a particular topic or point of view and force the client to pick between yes-or-no answers or forced-choice answers, or direct the client in a manner that limits his or her response.	"Do you think you will live with your parents or on your own after the child is born?"	Useful when needing to gather information quickly. They can set up an atmosphere in which the counselor is seen as an authoritarian figure, which, in turn, can lead to feelings of client dependency. Client elaboration is limited.
Closed questions delimiting affect	Questions that force the client to pick between yes-or-no or forced-choice feeling choices.	"Did you feel happy or sad when you found out that you were pregnant?"	Useful when needing to gather information quickly. They can set up an atmosphere in which the counselor is seen as an authoritarian figure, which, in turn, can lead to feelings of client dependency. Client elaboration is limited.
Open questions	Questions that allow the client to respond in a myriad of ways.	"How do you feel about being pregnant?"	Less repressive than closed questions and allow the client to respond in a wide range of ways. Not as client-centered as tentative questions or empathic responses.

FACT SHEET 5.1—CONTINUED

Tentative questions	Questions asked in a gentle manner that often allow for a large range of responses from the client.	"Is it that you have a lot of mixed feelings about being pregnant?"	The least helper-centered (most client-centered) of the different types of questions, although the content of what is being talked about is still picked by the counselor.
Why questions	A question that seeks a deep, thoughtful response but often results in defensiveness on the part of the client.	"Why do you think your parents were so mean to you?"	The most potentially damaging question, as individuals tend to respond to such questions defensively. However, if asked at the right moment and time, they could be facilitative of deep exploration.

EXPERIENTIAL EXERCISE 5.8

Asking Effective Questions

Examine the following and see if they tend to be closed, open, tentative, or why questions. Also, consider whether some questions could be a combination of these. Finally, decide if an alternative, better response (e.g., an empathic response) can be made in its place.

Type of Question

Example: "Did you feel more sad or angry about your divorce?"   Closed
Alternative response: "Sounds like you had some strong feelings about your divorce."

Question 1: "Did you feel good or bad about the breakup?"   _____
Alternative response: _____.

Question 2: "How did you feel about the loss of your pet?"   _____
Alternative response: _____.

Question 3: "How surprised were you at your friend's engagement?"   _____
Alternative response: _____.

Question 4: "What's your role in your family dynamics?"   _____
Alternative response: _____.

Question 5: "Were you angry or distrustful toward your friend for lying to you?"   _____
Alternative response: _____.

Question 6: "Were you were mildly, moderately, or greatly upset at your breakup?"   _____
Alternative response: _____.

Question 7: "I wonder if you can tell me more about that situation."   _____
Alternative response: _____.
Question 8: "Might you have some strong feelings about the accident?"   _____
Alternative response: _____.
Question 9: "I'm wondering if it might take two or three months to get over this."   _____
Alternative response: _____.
Question 10: "How often have you been in counseling, and who were your counselors?"   _____
Alternative response: _____.
Question 11: "Why do you think your parents divorced?"   _____
Alternative response: _____.

Solution-Focused Questions

Suppose that one night, while you were asleep, there was a miracle and this problem was solved. How would you know? What would be different? (de Shazer, 1988, p. 5)

Like de Shazer's famous *miracle question* just quoted, solution-focused questions have become a staple for many counselors in recent years. Focused on identifying what behaviors have worked in a client's life and where the client wants to be in the future as well as helping clients reach their desired goals, these types of questions have been an important addition to the repertoire of counselor responses (Bannink, 2015; De Jong & Berg, 2013; de Shazer et al., 2007; Trepper et al., 2014). A strength-based approach to counseling, solution-focused questions focus on positive qualities of clients, not problems; are non-pathologizing; and help clients move toward finding solutions instead of rehashing past concerns and issues. Such questions can generally be classified into one of six areas:

1. *Preferred-goals questions,* which examine what the client is hoping his or her future will look like
2. *Evaluative questions,* which involve an assessment of whether or not client behaviors have been productive toward reaching client goals
3. *Coping questions,* which are used to identify behaviors the client has successfully used to deal with his or her problems
4. *Exception-seeking questions,* which identify times in the client's life when he or she has not had the problem and which focus on what the client was doing during those times
5. *Solution-oriented questions,* which broadly ask the client how his or her life would be different if the problem did not exist
6. *Scaling questions,* which are used to assess how the client is feeling and to measure progress in counseling

Vignette 5.1 offers a scenario concerning Jeannette, who has sought counseling due to ongoing depression and anxiety. This scenario will be used to exemplify how different kinds of questions might be used.

Jeanette

Jeanette, a 33-year-old married female, is severely depressed and has suffered with anxiety most of her adult life. She reports having trouble sleeping and has lost weight in recent months. The youngest of four sisters, she describes growing up in a family with rigid rules. She states that her mom was always "checking in on her and her three older sisters." She describes the family home as a "nunnery" and says that everyone always needed to be on their best behavior. She noted that all the girls were expected to do well in school, ensure that the house was clean, help with cooking, and "act caring and loving even if we hated someone." Jeanette describes her father as supporting the rigidity of the household but more on the periphery of the home and not that involved with her and her sisters.

Jeanette notes that she was married when she was 24, "just like she was supposed to be." She has one child, a boy who is 4 years old. She states her husband is "nice" but confides in her counselor that she has always had attractions toward women. She feels "guilty and sinful" about her attractions. She is hoping that you, her counselor, can help her feel better and decide what to do in her life. She states that today she has a "close but fake" relationship with her parents—she feels like she really can't talk with her mom or dad. Jeannette has been in counseling before, is currently taking an antidepressant medication that also has some anti-anxiety features, has tried talking with her priest, and has recently started an exercise regime.

Preferred-Goals Questions

Preferred-goals questions are future oriented and help clients identify how their lives would look if identified goals were to be reached (de Shazer, 2007; Trepper et al., 2014). Some preferred-goals questions that we could apply to Jeanette's situation include the following:

- Jeanette, if this were to be the best helping session you ever had, can you imagine what goals you would identify to focus on and how you might try to reach them?
- How would you act differently in the future, Jeanette, if coming here has been worthwhile for you?
- If your life was better in 1 month, 6 months, or a year, what would be happening? What might you be doing differently, Jeanette?
- Jeanette, if you were getting closer to reaching your goals and things were getting better, how might you be acting differently?

You can see that you can replace Jeanette's name with anyone's name and use the exact same preferred-goals questions.

Evaluative Questions

The purpose of evaluative questions is to identify what behaviors have worked so clients can do more of them and to identify what has not worked so clients will not spend endless amounts of energy focusing on less productive behaviors (De Jong & Berg, 2013; Franklin et al., 2012). For instance, in Jeanette's case, the following questions might be asked:

- Jeanette, what has worked for you in trying to alleviate your depression?
- How helpful was the use of antidepressants, Jeanette?
- What aspects of counseling were most helpful to you, Jeanette?
- Jeanette, you've mentioned that you have been exercising a lot lately. How has that worked for you in helping you feel better?
- Was talking to your priest helpful? What aspects were most helpful?
- Out of all the ways you've tried, what was the most effective in alleviating your anxiety and depression, Jeanette?
- What has worked best for you in dealing with your relationship with your parents, Jeanette?

Notice how evaluative questions are almost exclusively focused on what has worked. Focusing on what has not worked would be a waste of time and energy and considered a useless rehash of past failures. For instance, if Jeanette says, "Counseling made me feel worse," then a discussion about it should be limited, although it would be okay to ask a question such as "Although overall, counseling was not helpful, were there any aspects of it that were helpful for you?" This question has the assumption that although counseling was not productive overall, a small aspect may have been helpful, and if you can identify what was helpful, you can do more of it. Overall, the counselor should focus on those behaviors that have worked so those behaviors can be used in solution building.

Coping Questions

In contrast to evaluative questions, which focus on actual behaviors that have been attempted, coping questions have a broad focus and assume there have been times in a client's life when he or she was able to deal successfully with his or her problems (De Jong & Berg, 2013; Franklin, Trepper, Gingeric, & McCollum, 2012). Thus, rather than asking questions such as "Have there been times when you were able to cope with (the problem)?" counselors ask "What ways have you found to cope with (the problem)?" In contrast to the first question, the second question assumes the client did have some successful coping times in his or her life. In Jeanette's case, a counselor might ask some of the following coping questions:

- So Jeanette, tell me about times when you have been successful in coping with your depression. What about the anxiety?
- Jeanette, what was going on with you when you were able to sleep?
- Jeanette, when you felt really good about eating or having a meal, what was different or going on with you then?
- Jeanette, when you think back on your life, what things helped to alleviate your depression and anxiety?
- Jeannette, when you were feeling good about your sexuality, what were you doing or thinking then?

- What kinds of things were you doing, Jeanette, when you were able to feel good about your relationship with your parents?

Exception-Seeking Questions

Exception-seeking questions, one of the most well-known types of solution-focused questions, explore what is going on in a client's life when the client is *not* experiencing the problem (Bannink, 2015; De Jong & Berg, 2013; Franklin et al., 2012). This type of question helps to quickly focus on the task at hand—finding a solution. As with coping questions, rather than asking if the client has exceptions, there is an assumption that the client has had exceptions in his or her life. In Jeanette's case, the following questions could be used:

- I bet there have been times in your life, Jeanette, when you have not felt depressed or anxious. Can you describe them for me?
- What was going on in your life, Jeanette, when you did not feel anxious?
- When undergoing hardships, people often have moments when they feel good. Jeanette, can you describe times like that for me? What was or is going on with you during those times?
- Jeanette, it seems like you were less depressed and less anxious a couple of years ago. What was going on in your life then that seemed to ward off your depression and anxiety?
- Jeanette, I bet there were times in your life when you felt good about your sexuality. Can you describe those times for me?
- When you were feeling good about your relationship with your parents, Jeanette, what was going on then?

Solution-Oriented Questions

Similar to preferred-goals questions, solution-oriented questions also look at the client's future but have a broader focus, as they don't zero in on specific behaviors (Bannink, 2015; De Jong & Berg, 2013; Franklin et al., 2012). However, both types of questions look at how things are different in the future. One kind of solution-oriented question, the miracle question, was noted at the start of this section. Here are some additional solution-oriented questions, applied to Jeanette's situation:

- Jeanette, how would your life look different if you were not depressed or anxious?
- Jeanette, if you were given a magic pill that would somehow make everything better, how would your life look?
- If you could change anything in your life so you would feel better, Jeanette, how would things be different?
- Jeanette, if there was some deity that could suddenly make your life better, what would your life look like?

Scaling Questions

Often used when first starting counseling and at the beginning of each session, scaling questions are simply a rating of how the client is feeling to see if the client has made progress (Bannink, 2015). This enables the counselor to assess whether counseling is moving in a positive direction. There are a number of ways to ask scaling questions, and sometimes a simple assessment instrument can be given to the client (see Figure 5.2). Here are a few, using Jeanette as an example:

- Jeanette, if you were to rate how you were feeling on a scale from 1 to 10, with 1 being horrible and 10 being great, where do you think you would fall?
- Here's a question for you, Jeanette, to see if we have made some progress. Using the same scale we used last week, with 1 being horrible and 10 being great, how are you doing this week?
- Jeanette, on a scale from 1 to 10, with 1 being the worst you ever felt and 10 being the best you ever felt, where would you put yourself?

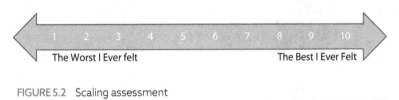

FIGURE 5.2   Scaling assessment

Final Thoughts About Solution-Focused Questions

Solution-focused questions are steeped in the *positive counseling* tradition (McAuliffe, 2019; Terni, 2015). This means that they don't spend an inordinate amount of time talking about the past, avoid focusing on pathology, concentrate on those aspects of a person's life that bring contentment, and assume that clients have strengths that can help them overcome their current dilemmas. In Jeanette's situation, you can see how there was a limited focus on her upbringing and the problems in her family. Instead, there was a focus on her future goals, ways that she's been able to cope with her problems, and new behaviors she might be able to adopt that will help her ensure a positive outlook on life. Review Fact Sheet 5.2, then do Experiential Exercises 5.9 and 5.10.

FACT SHEET 5.2

Summarizing Different Types of Solution-Focused Questions

Type of question		Definition	Examples
Preferred-goals questions	➡	Questions that assess specific behaviors the client will be doing in the future if his or her life becomes better	"If the helping relationship was successful, what would you be doing differently?"
Evaluative questions	➡	Questions that involve an assessment of whether client behaviors have been productive or not.	"Has your new exercise regime helped you feel better, Jeanette?"
Coping questions	➡	Questions that are used to identify behaviors the client has successfully used in the past to deal with his or her problems	"When you felt this way in the past, what worked best for you?"

Exception-seeking questions	➡	Questions that identify times in the client's life when he or she has not had the problem and that focus on what the client was doing during those times	"Although you have felt badly in the past, there were there moments when things were going well. What were you doing during those moments?"
Solution-oriented questions	➡	Questions that broadly ask how the client's life would be if the problem did not exist	"If you suddenly walked out this door and everything was better, what would your life look like?"
Scaling questions	➡	Questions that assess how the person is feeling and see how much progress has been made	"From a scale of 1 to 10, with 1 feeling horrible and 10 feeling great, where do you think you fall this week?"

EXPERIENTIAL EXERCISE 5.9

Helping Jeanette

Form groups of seven students. Have one student role-play Jeanette while the other students each pick one of the six types of solution-focused questions. As Jeanette talks about her life, take turns asking a type of question falling under the category you chose. You can use the questions identified in the book, but better yet, try to come up with your own questions that match the category.

EXPERIENTIAL EXERCISE 5.10

Practicing Solution-Focused Questions

Pair up with another person in class and either role-play a made-up situation or share a personal life problem with your partner. The helper should try his or her best to mostly respond with solution-focused questions. However, to keep the dialogue moving, the helper may want to be a good listener and also respond empathically to his or her role-playing client. A third person, an observer, can note the different responses the helper is making and review them when the role-play is over.

Integrating Questions Into the Counseling Relationship

So far in the text, you have reviewed a number of critical skills useful in conducting an interview with a client. Here's your chance to practice them. To some degree, the sequencing of these skills occurs in the order in which they have been presented. Thus, the foundational skills are generally delivered first, followed by the essential skills, commonly used skills, and the use of questions. However, there are times when this is not the case, such as when it is critical for the counselor to gather initial information from the client when he or she first enters an agency. In this case, the use of questions may parallel or even precede the use of the essential skills and commonly used skills (we hope the foundational skills always come first).

So, while keeping the basic structure in mind, here is your chance to practice these skills. Using Log Sheet 5.1 to help you remember the many skills you've learned and the basic sequencing of them, role-play with another student in class. As usual, a third student can be an observer. Spend between 30 and 60 minutes role-playing with the student so you can practice as many skills as possible. The observer will make notes of the counselor's responses on the log sheet. When you have finished, the three of you can discuss the counselor's various responses, their efficacy, and whether they were made at an appropriate time. This assignment can also be done outside of class, as long as there is an observer to complete the log. Don't forget to embrace the nine characteristics of the effective counselor. When the role-play is complete, you can make some general comments regarding how effectively the counselor embraced the nine characteristics (see end of log).

LOG SHEET 5.1

Assessing Skill Usage

Time: Write down the approximate time the response was made (e.g., "5" means 5 minutes into role-play).
Key words or behaviors: Make a note of key words or behaviors so you can talk about the response that was made.
Effectiveness: Quickly write "Good," "Okay," "Poor," or any words you wish to give some quick feedback about response.

Type of skills	Tracking responses		
Foundational Skills	Time	Key Words or Behaviors in Response	Effectiveness
Nonverbal Behaviors			
Office atmosphere			
Attire and dress			
Eye contact/facial expressions			
Body positioning/head nodding			
Proxemics (personal space)			
Touch			
Voice intonation			
Egalitarian and Positive Attitude and Skills			
Honoring and respecting			
Caring curiosity			
Delimiting power/being equal			

LOG SHEET 5.1—CONTINUED

    Non-pathologizing

    Being committed

Essential Skills

    Silence and pause time

    Listening

    Reflection of feelings

    Reflection of content

    Paraphrasing

    Basic empathy

Commonly Used Skills

    Advanced empathy

    Affirmation giving

    Encouragement

    Support

    Offering alternatives

    Information giving

    Advice giving

    Modeling

    Self-disclosure (inadvertent or intentional)

    Collaboration (content or process)

Questions

    Information-gathering questions

    Closed

    Open

    Tentative

    Why

    Solution-focused questions

    Preferred Goals

    Evaluative

    Coping

    Exception-seeking

    Solution-oriented

    Scaling

Characteristics of The Effective Counselor: empathy, genu-ineness, acceptance, wellness, cultural sensitivity, "it factor," competence, cognitive complexity, and belief in one's theory

General comments:

Summary

This chapter examined various types of questions often used in the helping relationship. Starting with information-gathering questions, we noted that these responses are helpful when one is concerned about gathering information to help solve the client's problems or address the client's concerns. These questions tend to be helper-centered, as they are developed from what the counselor believes is important, not necessarily what the client sees as critical. We noted that there were four types of such questions, including closed questions, open questions, tentative questions, and why questions. Closed questions are usually asked when a counselor needs to gather information quickly and generally require a yes-or-no or forced-choice response by the client or a specific answer to a direct question. They can focus on the content or affect that the client is presenting. Open questions allow a wide range of responses to questions and are generally used when wanting a client to expand on the content or affect that the client is presenting. Tentative questions are used when one is wanting to make the question a bit more inviting and client-centered. In contrast to the other types of questions, it was suggested that why questions be rarely used because they can often make a client feel defensive. If a counselor has developed a strong alliance, however, a why question might be slipped in periodically.

In addition to information-gathering questions, in this chapter we focused on solution-focused questions. These types of questions are goal oriented and non-pathologizing and focus on client strengths. They examine what behaviors have worked in a client's life, identify where the client wants to be in the future, and assist in the development of ways of helping the client achieve his or her goals. We focused on six types of solution-focused questions: (a) preferred-goals questions, which examine what the client is hoping his or her future will look like; (b) evaluative questions, which involve an assessment of whether client behaviors have been productive toward reaching client goals; (c) coping questions, which identify behaviors the client has successfully used in the past to deal with his or her problems; (d) exception-seeking questions, which identify times in the client's life when he or she has not had the problem and focus on what the client was doing during those times; (e) solution-oriented questions, which broadly ask the client how the client's life would be if the problem did not exist; and (f) scaling questions, which assess how the person is feeling and evaluate how much progress has been made. This section of the chapter concluded with a look at how questions are integrated into all the skills talked about thus far in the book. The chapter concluded with a log sheet to help you examine how well you are doing at producing the various skills examined.

Key Words and Terms

client-centered	open questions
closed questions	positive counseling
coping questions	preferred-goals questions
evaluative questions	scaling questions
exception-seeking questions	solution-focused questions
focused-question closed format	solution-oriented questions
forced-choice closed questions	tentative questions
helper-centered	why questions
information-gathering questions	yes/no closed questions
miracle question	

Credits

Photo 5.1: Source: https://pixabay.com/en/man-woman-question-mark-problems-2814937/.

Photo 5.2: Source: https://pixabay.com/en/questions-font-who-what-how-why-2245264/.

Photo 5.3: Source: https://pixabay.com/en/question-questions-man-head-2519654/.

CHAPTER 6

Specialized Skills

Learning Objectives

1. To examine a number of specialized skills often used in the counseling relationship, including the following:

    a. Advocacy
    b. Assessing for lethality: suicidality and homicidality
    c. Crisis, disaster, and trauma counseling
    d. Confrontation: challenge with support
    e. Cognitive-behavioral responses
    f. Interpretation
    g. Positive counseling
    h. Life coaching

Introduction

When recently editing an encyclopedia, I found nearly 300 theories of counseling and psychotherapy, each with its own unique skills (Neukrug, 2015). With so many theories, one has to ask "Which skills do we embrace and apply?" Thus far, we have explored some of the more important and commonly used skills that tend to be cross-theoretical. In this chapter, we explore some additional skills that are generally not used with all clients but may be critical with some clients. Thus, in this chapter we explore advocacy; assessing for lethality; crisis, disaster, and trauma counseling; confrontation: challenge with support; cognitive-behavioral responses; interpretation; positive counseling; and coaching (see Figure 6.1).

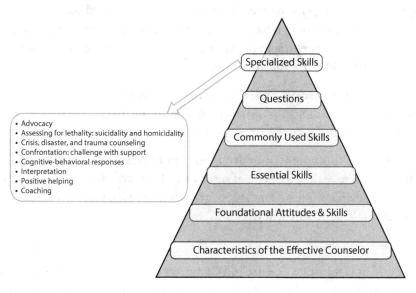

FIGURE 6.1 Counseling and helping skills

Advocacy

First they came for the Socialists, and I did not speak out—

because I was not a Socialist.

Then they came for the Trade Unionists, and I did not speak out—

because I was not a Trade Unionist.

Then they came for the Jews, and I did not speak out—

because I was not a Jew.

Then they came for me—and there was no one left to speak

for me.

(Niemöeller, as cited by Littell, 1986, p. viii)

Considered part of a *social justice* focus, *advocacy* has become an increasingly critical aspect of the counseling relationship. In fact, advocacy has become so important that the Multicultural Counseling Competencies were expanded to include a large section on advocacy and were renamed the Multicultural and Social Justice Counseling Competencies (Ratts, Singh, Nassar-McMillan, Butler, & McCullough, 2015, 2016). Endorsed by the ACA Governing Council in 2015, advocacy work is focused on taking active steps at an "individual, group, institutional, and societal level" to heal societal wounds that have created "potential barriers and obstacles that inhibit access and/or the growth and development of clients" (ACA, 2014, Section A.7.a., Advocacy; Simpson, Abadie, & Seyler, 2016).

Although a critical aspect of what a counselor might do, for some beginning counselors, advocacy can become a mechanism to avoid doing the tough personal work that is needed within the counseling relationship. On the other hand, counselors can rely too much on maintaining the sanctity of the counseling relationship.

I felt that we were creating kind of a revolving door where we would see clients, they would feel better, and then leave and go back in their world and get exposed to whatever issues or injustices that were happening to them, and their pain and difficulties would just come back. (Chung, cited in Meyers, 2014b, para. 6)

Thus, it is important that counselors find the right balance between the sanctity of applying the traditional tools in the counseling relationship and the need to advocate for clients outside of that relationship. In addition, it is critical that counselors obtain permission from clients prior to engaging in advocacy efforts:

Counselors obtain client consent prior to engaging in advocacy efforts on behalf of an identifiable client to improve the provision of services and to work toward removal of systemic barriers or obstacles that inhibit client access, growth, and development. (ACA, 2014, Section A.7.b., Confidentiality and Advocacy)

Levels and Types of Advocacy Interventions

The Multicultural and Social Justice Counseling Competencies identify six *levels and types of advocacy interventions* where counselors should intervene for, or on behalf of, clients. Box 6.1 gives a summary of these areas. The full Multicultural and Social Justice Counseling Competencies are discussed more fully in Chapter 9.

BOX 6.1

Levels and Types of Advocacy Interventions

Levels of counselor intervention	Brief description of intervention
Intrapersonal: "The individual characteristics of a person such as knowledge, attitudes, behavior, self-concept, skills, and developmental history."	Helping clients understand the kinds of internalized oppression or internalized privilege that permeates their lives.
Interpersonal: "The interpersonal processes and/or groups that provide individuals with identity and support (i.e., family, friends, and peers)."	Assisting clients in examining how their relationships maintain certain views of the world and, in some cases, foster privilege or oppression due to the types of communication and actions in which they participate.
Institutional: "Represents the social institutions in society such as schools, churches, community organizations."	Having counselors examine whether social institutions are preventing clients from moving forward in their lives and employ techniques to remove barriers within those institutions.
Community: "The community as a whole represents the spoken and unspoken norms, value, and regulations that are embedded in society. The norms, values, and regulations of a community may either be empowering or oppressive to human growth and development."	Having counselors examine the norms, values, and regulations in communities to determine whether they promote privilege and hinder marginalized clients so that such irregularities can be addressed.
Public Policy: "Public policy reflects the local, state, and federal laws and policies that regulate or influence client human growth and development."	Having counselors examine local, state, and federal laws and policies and promote changes in such laws and policies if they hinder marginalized clients and promote privilege.
International and Global Affairs: "International and global concerns reflect the events, affairs, and policies that influence psychological health and well-being."	Ensuring that counselors have knowledge of international politics, laws, and policies and promote changes in laws and policies if they hinder marginalized clients and promote privilege.

Source: Ratts et al., 2015

The practice of advocacy includes a wide variety of skills and attitudes, many of which we have already discussed. The following gives examples of each of the six areas. As you read them, consider how advocacy plays a role and what tools and skills are needed to be an advocate in a particular situation. After reading the example, do Experiential Exercise 6.1, then Experiential Exercise 6.2.

Intrapersonal example: A female client of yours has low self-esteem and feels as if she can never get a word in with her husband. He always insists he is right and generally treats her as if she knows little. Over time, in counseling, she begins to find her voice and stands up to her husband. After a while, she decides to find a job, which increases her sense of self. Eventually, she joins a group of women who reinforce each other's newfound sense of self. Your client eventually finds that she can stand up to her husband and have a strong voice with others when she needs to. Eventually, her husband seeks marital counseling with her, and her newfound sense of self results in a more equal and, eventually, loving relationship with her husband.

Interpersonal example: Your client, a White upper-middle-class male, is proud of all the wealth he has acquired, supports segregating schools based on grades, believes that some people are just "ignorant," and believes the Black Lives Movement is a racist political association. He is in counseling due to feelings of anger and stress, partly related to the fact that others don't see the world as he does. While supporting how proud he is of all the accomplishments he has made, he is eventually able to see how the relationships in his life all reinforce one view of the world. Over time, in counseling, he begins to see the complexity of views that make up the world, and he becomes more accepting of others' perspectives. His anger dissipates.

Institutional example: You notice that within your agency there is "back talk" about certain clients. Some of the counselors insinuate that some of their clients will never change due to their ethnic and cultural backgrounds. You decide to talk with your supervisor, who concurs with your beliefs, and the two of you arrange multicultural training. Your hope, at the very least, is that other counselors will not express these negative beliefs and, eventually, will change their beliefs altogether.

Community example: After the United States Attorney General's office declares that there has been embedded racism in your local police department, your agency reaches out to the police department to conduct training with them on how they can utilize community policing, become more aware of their own prejudices and biases, and work more closely with the community.

Public policy example: You work for a mental health clinic, and as an agency, the staff decides to support national legislation that would fund free and low-cost access to mental health centers for the poor. Literature is handed out at the agency in support of this legislation, and the staff commits to contacting their legislators to encourage them to pass this bill.

International and global affairs: You realize that in wealthier countries, there is one mental health worker per 2,000 people; however, in poorer countries, this drops to one in 100,000 (World Health Organization, 2018). Concerned about this, you decide to advocate for an international division of ACA that would support counseling and mental health services throughout the world, particularly in poorer countries.

These present a number of different ways you can advocate for clients and individuals. Certainly, some of them have a certain political perspective, and if you do not agree with them, then consider what types of advocacy with which you might feel comfortable. Advocacy is the responsibility of all counselors, and you should consider those types of advocacy efforts with which you think you could make the most change. (See Experiential Exercise 6.1, then Experiential Exercise 6.2).

EXPERIENTIAL EXERCISE 6.1

Advocacy Skills and Tools

First, on your own, make a list of skills and tools you think you might need to accomplish the different advocacy tasks listed for each of the situations previously described. Then form small groups of four or five and discuss your list. What skills are most necessary? Which skills have not been addressed in this book thus far? Each group can pick a spokesperson and discuss what they found with the class.

EXPERIENTIAL EXERCISE 6.2

Advocating for Clients

In small groups, discuss the following:

1. Situations where you might want to help clients advocate for themselves
2. Situations where you might want to advocate for clients
3. Situations where you might want to advocate within your agency
4. Situations where you might want to advocate for changes in your community
5. Situations where you might want to become politically active toward changes nationally
6. Situations where you might want to become politically active globally/internationally

How might advocacy look in these situations? Do you think taking an advocacy position in any of these situations might cause you problems at work? Would you be willing to be an advocate?

Assessing for Lethality: Suicidality and Homicidality

Regardless of where he or she works, at some point in his or her career, every counselor will be faced with a client who is suicidal or homicidal. Since there are high stakes involved with suicidal or homicidal thoughts and actions, it is important to assess for lethality whenever a counselor suspects a client may be at risk. *However, a word of warning: there are few assessment instruments or ways of clinically interviewing a client that can be 100% accurate in assessing lethality* (Giddens, Sheehan, & Sheehan, 2014). However, the following offers an overview of what helpers typically look for when assessing for suicidality and homicidality.

Assessing for Suicidality

Traditionally, when counselors assess for suicidality, they examine clients on a continuum ranging from ideation (thinking about it), developing a plan, having a means to carry out the plan, preparing to implement the plan, rehearsing the plan, and finally, acting on the plan (Poa & Kass, 2015; Resnick, 2011; Scott & Resnick, 2005; see Figure 6.2).

Establishing the client's placement on the continuum by asking pointed, information-gathering types of questions is helpful in determining risk level for harming self. Although not all individuals who are suicidal follow this path, many will. In addition to determining where

No Suicidal Thoughts

Having Suicidal Ideation

Developing a Plan

Having the Means

Preparing

Rehearsing

Acting

FIGURE 6.2 Assessing for suicide

in Figure 6.2 the person falls, there are a wide range of risk factors that can help counselors assess the likelihood of a person committing suicide (see Fact Sheet 6.1). Although by no means an exhaustive list, this fact sheet identifies many of these risk factors.

FACT SHEET 6.1

Risk Factors for Suicide

- Depression
- Making a will
- Prior attempts
- Problems at work
- Giving things away
- Financial problems
- Giving verbal hints
- Relationship breakup
- History of being abused
- Family history of suicide
- Medication incompliance
- Alcohol/substance abuse
- Preoccupation with death
- Feeling a burden to others
- Chronic disease or disability
- Withdrawing from activities
- Extreme anxiety or agitation
- Suddenly giving things away

FACT SHEET 6.1—CONTINUED

- Feeling angry and aggressive
- Recent loss of someone close
- Impulsivity/lack of self-control
- History of significant problems
- History of psychiatric treatment
- Feeling trapped by current situation
- Problems eating or eating too much
- Dramatic shift of mood or feeling states
- Problems sleeping or sleeping too much
- Stress from prejudice and discrimination
- Talking about wanting to die or killing oneself
- Hopeless or lack of purpose or meaning in life
- Sudden poor performance in school or on the job
- Engaging in risky or impulsive behaviors without care of consequences
- Suddenly recovering from depressive symptoms or sudden positive outlook
- Having access to a lethal means (the more lethal, the more serious [e.g., having a gun])

Sources: ACA, 2011a; Centers for Disease Control and Prevention, 2017, 2018; Hoff, Hallisey, & Hoff, 2009; Juhnke, Granello, & Lebron-Striker, 2007; Substance Abuse and Mental Health Services Administration, 2017.

In contrast to *risk factors*, there are a number of *protective factors* that seem to guard against the likelihood of a person committing suicide or homicide. Some of these are highlighted in Fact Sheet 6.2.

FACT SHEET 6.2

Protective Factors for Suicide and Homicide

The following represent factors that may mediate against suicidal or homicidal behaviors. Although certainly not always the case, they can be taken into account when considering the probability of a client harming self or others.

- Pregnancy
- Stable employment
- Medication compliance
- Children living at home
- Safe and stable home life
- Connected with a therapist
- Children under the age of 18
- Firearms locked and unloaded
- Strong religious or spiritual beliefs

FACT SHEET 6.2—CONTINUED

- Easy access to clinical interventions
- Sense of meaning and purpose in life
- Strong family or community supports
- No evidence of alcohol/substance abuse
- Positive coping and problem-solving skills
- Ability to communicate with people to get needs met
- Connected to friends, family, and community institutions

Sources: ACA, 2011a; CDC, 2015; Juhnke, Granello, & Lebron-Striker, 2007; Kanel, 2018; Suicide Prevention Resource Center, 2018; U.S. Department of Veteran Affairs, n.d.

A Model for Working With Suicidal Clients

Assessing for suicide risk is not an exact science (Pisani, Murrie, & Silverman, 2015), and Figure 6.2, along with the risk and protective factors, gives you a quick sense of how to evaluate for suicidality. Different models have been developed to work with suicidal clients, and they tend to incorporate these assessment areas into a broader counseling strategy to help ensure clients do not act on their suicidal urges (Montague, Cassidy, & Liles, 2016). Integrating some of these models, we find the following steps important in conducting a suicidal assessment and counseling regime with such clients:

Step 1: Establish rapport
Step 2: Conduct a clinical interview
Step 3: Listen to client's story
Step 4: Use Fact Sheet 6.1 to assess for risk factors
Step 5: Use Fact Sheet 6.2 to assess for protective factors
Step 6: Use Figure 6.2 to assess for lethality
Step 7: Help client manage feelings
Step 8: Explore alternatives
Step 9: Develop behavioral strategies
Step 10: Follow up with client

Finally, whenever assessing for suicidality, it is critical that counselors know their local laws and adhere to ACA's ethics code to ensure that clients do not harm self or others:

> The general requirement that counselors keep information confidential does not apply when disclosure is required to protect clients or identified others from serious and foreseeable harm or when legal requirements demand that confidential information must be revealed. Counselors consult with other professionals when in doubt as to the validity of an exception. Additional considerations apply when addressing end-of-life issues. (ACA, 2014, Section B.2.a., Serious and Foreseeable Harm and Legal Requirements; see Experiential Exercise 6.3)

Assessing for Suicidality

Your instructor will ask students to form groups of four or five. From each group, one student will volunteer to be a role-play client who is at some amount of risk for suicide. The instructor will privately give each of the role-play clients a description of the client's situation. The role-play clients will go back to their group, and the group should collectively use the 10-step model just described to work with the client. Group members might want to sit in a circle around the client. After the role-play is completed, answer the following questions:

1. What risk factors were identified?
2. What protective factors were identified?
3. Where in Figure 6.2 did the client fall?
4. Was rapport built with the client? How?
5. Was the client's story heard?
6. Were feelings managed, alternatives explored, and behavioral strategies determined? Identify them.
7. Was a follow-up plan designed?
8. Did you leave assured that the client would not kill himself or herself? If not, what did you do?

Assessing for Homicidality

Like assessment for suicide, assessment for homicide is not an exact science. However, as with suicidal clients, a number of risk factors have been identified that may predict assault and homicidal behavior (see Fact Sheet 6.3). In addition, Hoff (2015) has developed the *assault and homicidal danger assessment tool*, which can help counselors determine if a client is likely to be at risk for assault or homicidal behaviors (see Assessment Tool 6.1).

FACT SHEET 6.3

Risk Factors for Homicide

- Feeling rejected
- Feeling humiliated
- Giving verbal hints
- History of violence
- Poor impulse control
- Loss of reality testing
- Wanting to seek revenge
- Medication incompliance
- History of abusing others

FACT SHEET 6.3—CONTINUED

- Alcohol/substance abuse
- Preoccupation with death
- Extreme anxiety or agitation
- Antisocial personality disorder
- Thoughts of committing harm
- History of significant problems
- Impulsivity/lack of self-control
- Feeling trapped by current situation
- Some forms of traumatic brain injury
- Talking about wanting to kill someone
- Thoughts that people want to harm you
- Dramatic shift of mood or feeling states
- Having feelings of anger, aggression, and rage
- Engaging in risky or impulsive behaviors without care of consequences
- Having access to lethal means (the more lethal, the more serious [e.g., having a gun]).

Sources: ACA, 2011a; Centers for Disease Control and Prevention, 2017; Hoff, Hallisey, & Hoff, 2009; Juhnke, Granello, & Lebron-Striker, 2007; Substance Abuse and Mental Health Services Administration, 2017.

ASSESSMENT TOOL 6.1

Assault and Homicidal Danger Assessment

Assault & Homicidal Danger Assessment Tool

Key to Danger	Immediate Dangerousness to Others	Typical Indicators
1	No predictable risk of assault or homicide	Has no assaultive or homicidal ideation, urges, or history of same; basically satisfactory support system; social drinker only
2	Low risk of assault or homicide	Has occasional assault or homicidal ideation (including paranoid ideas) with some urges to kill; no history of impulsive acts or homicidal attempts; occasional drinking bouts and angry verbal outbursts; basically satisfactory support system
3	Moderate risk of assault or homicide but	Has frequent homicidal ideation and urges to kill but no specific plan; history of impulsive acting out and verbal outbursts while drinking, on other drugs, or otherwise; stormy relationship with significant others with periodic high-tension arguments
4	High risk of homicide	Has homicidal plan; obtainable means; history of substance abuse; frequent acting out against others but no homicide attempts; stormy relationships and much verbal fighting with significant others, with occasional assaults
5	Very high risk of homicide	Has current high-lethal plan; available means; history of homicide attempts or impulsive acting out, plus feels a strong urge to control and "get even" with a significant other; history of serious substance abuse; also with possible high-lethal suicide risk

Source: L. A. Hoff, B. J. Hallisey, and M. Hoff, "Assault and Homicidal Danger Assessment," *People in Crisis: Clinical and Diversity Perspectives*, p. 439. Copyright © 2009 by Taylor & Francis Group.

A Model for Working With Homicidal Clients

When counseling clients for possible acting out by assault or homicide, we have a similar model to the one just described for suicide. It includes the following 10 steps. After examining the steps, do Experiential Exercise 6.4.

Step 1: Establish rapport
Step 2: Conduct a clinical interview
Step 3: Listen to client's story
Step 4: Use Fact Sheet 6.3 to assess for risk factors
Step 5: Use Fact Sheet 6.2 to assess for protective factors
Step 6: Use Assessment Tool 6.1 to assess for lethality
Step 7: Help client manage feelings
Step 8: Explore alternatives
Step 9: Develop behavioral strategies
Step 10: Follow up with client

EXPERIENTIAL EXERCISE 6.1

Assessing for Assault and Homicidality

Your instructor will ask students to form groups of four or five. From each group, one student will volunteer to role-play a client who is at some amount of risk for assault or homicide. The instructor will privately give each of the role-play clients a description of the client's situation. The role-play clients will go back to their group, and the group should collectively use the 10-step model just described to work with the client. Group members might want to sit in a circle around the client. After the role-play is completed, answer the following questions:

1. What risk factors were identified?
2. What protective factors were identified?
3. Where in Assessment Tool 6.1 did the client fall?
4. Was rapport built with the client? How?
5. Was the client's story heard?
6. Were feelings managed, alternatives explored, and behavioral strategies determined? Identify them.
7. Was a follow-up plan designed?
8. Did you leave assured that the client would not harm or kill another person? If not, what did you do?

Crisis, Trauma, and Disaster Counseling

As a result of Hurricane Katrina, the 9/11 attacks, and thousands of soldiers coming home from the Middle East with *post-traumatic stress disorder* (PTSD), counselors realized that their training in *crisis, trauma, and disaster counseling* was limited (Meyers, 2017; Phillips, 2018). Thus, in recent years, counselors and other helpers have become better trained in crisis counseling, are better able to understand and help those who have experienced trauma, and are better able to work with people experiencing disasters. As a result, models of how to respond to crises, traumatic events, and disasters have been developed.

In general, crisis, disaster, and single-event trauma counseling is seen as short-term, anonymous in that records are often not kept on people, built on client strengths, non-diagnostic oriented, and provided in nontraditional settings (e.g., homes or settings where the crisis occurred; Federal Emergency Management Agency, 2015). Counselors who work with individuals who have experienced a crisis, disaster, or trauma often build on and refer to community resources. Although there is much overlap between those who have experienced a crisis, trauma, or a disaster, there are some important differences among the three terms (ACA, 2011b; James & Gilliland, 2013):

Crisis: A crisis is when an event or situation is perceived as so intolerable that it prevents the person from being able to use his or her usual coping mechanisms and resources to effectively deal with the problem, resulting in cognitive, affective, and behavioral problems. It is often a onetime event, and most people are able to regain some semblance of balance within 6–8 weeks following the crisis. Examples of crises include the sudden death of a loved one, the loss of a job, and the aftermath of a disaster.

Trauma: Originating from the Greek word for "wound," a trauma is an injury to the body that cannot heal without some type of medical or counseling intervention. Often, trauma leads to a diminished sense of self, loss of dignity, and cognitive, affective, and behavioral problems. The person's usual way of dealing with stress does not work effectively. Trauma can be a onetime event, which usually leaves detailed memories, or an ongoing series of events that may lead to dissociation, denial, and internal rage. Examples of trauma include rape, assault, abuse, being a witness to a horrendous event, and more.

Disaster: With its early origins meaning unfavorable ("dis") position of the stars ("astrum"), a disaster is the result of some type of major social disruption that often results in injury and death as well as property destruction throughout a community. Disasters can be human generated or natural. Some examples of human-generated unintentional disasters include plane crashes, oil spills, and other environmental disasters. Examples of human-generated intentional disasters include wars, ethnic conflicts, and terrorism. Examples of natural disasters include earthquakes, hurricanes, tornadoes, wildfires, famines, floods, and so forth. Disasters can lead to crises or trauma.

Although there is overlap between crisis counseling, responses to trauma, and disaster assistance, there are differences in how one generally responds. Let's look at some ways of dealing with crises, trauma, and disasters.

Dealing With A Client in Crisis

ACA suggests that the goals of crisis counseling are to (a) ensure safety, (b) make sure the individual is stable following the crisis, and (c) make sure individuals have formal or informal resources and support available to them. When in crisis, individuals generally meet one to three times with the counselor, and crisis counseling can range from 15 minutes to 2 hours. ACA (2011c) suggests the following *eight steps when dealing with a person in crisis*:

Step 1.	Establish rapport
Step 2.	Let individuals tell the story
Step 3.	Identify major problem(s)
Step 4.	Assess for safety issues
Step 5.	Help individuals deal with their feelings
Step 6.	Explore alternatives with individuals
Step 7.	Develop an action plan
Step 8.	Make referrals if ongoing services are needed

Dealing With A Client Who Has Experienced a Disaster

The National Child Traumatic Stress Network and National Center for Post-Traumatic Stress Disorder (PTSD) (Brymer et al., 2006) delineate *eight steps when responding to a disaster* (although they also suggest this can apply to many crisis situations):

Step 1.   *Contact and engagement:* Initiating caring, helpful, and compassionate contact with those in need.

Step 2.   *Safety and comfort:* Ensuring that there are no further safety issues and providing psychological and physical comfort to those involved.

Step 3.   *Stabilization (if needed):* Helping orient survivors, providing a peaceful environment, and helping calm those who are emotionally overwhelmed.

Step 4.   *Information gathering:* Understanding immediate concerns and needs by gathering information from the individual(s) and devising helping interventions based on the information gathered.

Step 5.   *Practical assistance:* Addressing immediate concerns and needs through practical help to survivors.

Step 6.   *Connection with social supports:* Developing brief or ongoing contact with family members, friends, and community resources.

Step 7.   *Information on coping:* Reducing distress and encouraging healthy functioning by making available information on stress reactions to crisis and disaster situations.

Step 8.   *Linkage with collaborative services:* Ensuring that individuals faced with crisis and disaster situations have needed services now and in the future.

Dealing With A Client Who Has Experienced a Traumatic Event

When a person experiences a traumatic event, it can often leave scars that can stay with the person for years. In fact, it is not unusual for individuals who have experienced ongoing trauma to have PTSD. Thus, those who have experienced trauma often need long-term counseling with counselors who have expertise in working with trauma. There are a number of cognitive-behavioral and neurotherapeutic techniques that have shown promise in working with those suffering from PTSD (Neukrug, 2015). In contrast, some who have experienced a onetime traumatic event often (but not always) have an easier time working through the situation. In this case, counselors would work with individuals in a fashion similar to the way one would work with a client who has experienced a crisis (see "Dealing With A Client In Crisis").

Conclusion

Although crisis, disaster, and trauma counseling have different origins than the more traditional counseling generally conducted with clients, most of the foundational, essential, and commonly used skills noted in this text are critical to the work of the crisis, disaster, and trauma counselor. However, sometimes other, more advanced skills are also needed. This is especially true in the case of the person who has experienced ongoing trauma. Although generally short term, some clients who have undergone a crisis, disaster, or trauma will require more long-term counseling and will need to address long-term affective, cognitive, and behavioral issues.

EXPERIENTIAL EXERCISE 6.5

Working With Clients Who Have Experienced A Crisis, Trauma, or Disaster

Your instructor will ask students to form three groups: a crisis group, a trauma group, and a disaster group. From each group, one student will volunteer to be a role-play client who is in crisis, experiencing a one-time traumatic event, or has just lived through a disaster, depending on the group's focus. The instructor will privately give each of the role-play clients a description of the client's situation. The role-play clients will go back to their group, and the group should collectively apply the crisis model described earlier if the client is experiencing a crisis or one-time traumatic event, or the disaster model if the client is experiencing a disaster. When the role-play is finished, answer the following questions:

1. Was the group successful in completing the protocol?
2. What decisions were made based on the protocol?
3. Does the client need to follow up with you? If yes, why? If no, why not?
4. Do you believe you successfully dealt with the crisis, trauma, or disaster?
5. What counseling skills did you use to help the client work through his or her crisis, trauma, or disaster?

When all groups are finished, have a spokesperson from each group give a summary of how the role-play went and describe what skills were successful and if any seemed harmful or unsuccessful.

Confrontation: Challenge With Support

Within the context of the helping relationship, confrontation is thought of as a soft challenge to the client's understanding of the world and offers the client an invitation to discuss *discrepancies between*

a client's values and behaviors, feelings and behaviors, idealized self and real self, and *expressed feelings and underlying feelings* (Neukrug, Bayne, Dean-Nganga, & Pusateri, 2012; Strong & Zeman, 2010; Thompson, 2016).

To be effective, confrontation within the helping relationship first involves the building of a trusting and caring relationship, often through one's listening skills and empathy. This is then followed by an invitation, on the part of the counselor, to discuss the discrepancy (Egan & Reese, 2019; Strong & Zeman, 2010). This process of support, followed by an invitation for dialogue and conversation, offers the best potential to change the client's perception of reality (Neukrug, 2017a).

Four Types of Client Discrepancies

Ever get baited into a conversation with a friend and end up in an argument because the two of you saw things differently? This certainly has happened to me and, unfortunately, has even happened with some of my clients on occasion. Sometimes, clients simply "hook" me, and I start bickering with them about discrepancies I view in their lives. As you have probably learned from your own confrontations with friends, this type of confrontation is rarely helpful and almost always a result of unfinished business. Effective counselors, however, can disengage from these emotional entanglements and build relationships that offer the potential to challenge clients through honest and thoughtful conversations concerning discrepancies in clients' lives. As noted, four types of discrepancies include those between a client's values and behaviors, feelings and behaviors, idealized self and real self, and expressed feelings and underlying feelings.

1. **Discrepancy between a client's values and behavior**

    When a client expresses a certain value and then his or her actions do not match that expressed value, there is incongruity in the client's life. For instance, suppose a client has been a staunch anti-gun advocate and then, after getting robbed, decides to purchase a gun. Pointing out the discrepancy to the client might assist him or her in either reformulating his or her values or changing his or her behavior. However, how the incongruity is presented to the client is important. For instance, one counselor could say "I thought you were against having guns. Why are you doing this?" Such a confrontation might make a client defensive (notice the why question!). However, another counselor could say "That's interesting. I was under the impression that you did not feel comfortable owning a gun. Help me understand how you came to make sense of that now."

2. **Discrepancy between a client's feelings and behaviors**

    Asserting certain feelings and then acting in a manner that seems to indicate the client feels otherwise demonstrates a second type of discrepancy. For instance, suppose a mother tells a counselor that she loves her teenage daughter but then goes on to note how often she yells at her, criticizes her, and tries to control her. As with discrepancies between values and behaviors, the counselor can further client self-realization by noting such inconsistency.

Counselor: So, I clearly hear your love for your daughter, yet I'm confused by the yelling, the criticizing, and the attempts to control her. Do you have some thoughts on that?

Confronting the client in this manner is an invitation for a discussion—*not* an invitation for an argument.

3. **Discrepancy between idealized self and real self**
   It is not unusual for clients, and indeed most individuals, to experience a difference between how they believe they should act (their idealized selves) and how they actually act (their real selves). For instance, a client might state he wants to live a gentler, more loving life:

   Client: I'm going to buy myself a ring to remind myself that I want to be nicer and more loving in my life—especially with my wife, kids, and colleagues. Every time I see or feel it, I'll be reminded.

   Now, imagine the client comes back the following week and starts telling the counselor how angry he's been at his wife, kids, and colleagues. The counselor could respond with the following:

   Counselor: So, the last time you were here, you talked about the importance of being more loving and kind in many of your relationships and even talked about purchasing a ring to remind you to be that way. So what happened to that thought?

4. **Discrepancy between expressed and underlying feelings**
   Discrepancies between a client's verbal expression of feelings and the underlying feelings that are often just below the surface are common. For instance, as the client states the following, she seems to be holding back tears:

   Client: My relationship with my mom is good, despite her recent health problems. I just feel so loving toward her.

   In this case, the counselor makes the following response:

   Counselor: I certainly hear the love for your mom, and I think I also hear some sadness—perhaps about her failing health.

   This empathic response by the counselor invites the client to talk about the underlying feelings. If you remember from the discussion on advanced empathy in Chapter 4, this would be considered an advanced empathic response (above level 3), as it brings out feelings not outwardly expressed by the client.

Five Ways to Challenge Client Discrepancies

After building a strong foundation to the counseling relationship, invitations to discuss a client's discrepancy can occur in a number of ways, including you/but statements, inviting the client to justify the discrepancy, reframing, using satire, and using higher-level empathy.

1. **You/but statements**
   Here, the counselor verbally identifies the incongruence through the use of a "you said/but" statement and follows this with an invitation for a discussion. For instance, for the client from Example 1 who said he was against owning guns but then purchased one, the counselor might say the following:

Counselor: You say that you were against gun ownership, but I see now that you decided to purchase one. How do you make sense of that?

2. **Asking the client to justify the discrepancy**

   A second way of highlighting discrepancy is to invite a client to discuss the contradiction so the counselor can better understand how the client makes sense of it and so the client can begin to wrestle with his or her inconsistency. From Example 2, for the mom who says she loves her daughter yet yells at her, criticizes her, and tries to control her, a counselor might say the following:

   Counselor: Okay, I'm clearly hearing how you say you love your daughter, but I think you also spend a lot of time yelling at her, criticizing her, and trying to control her. Let's try to make sense of all of this.

3. **Reframing**

   This way of highlighting the discrepancy offers the client an alternative way of viewing his or her situation, followed by a discussion of this new reality. This is an invitation to discuss the discrepancy from a new frame of reference. From Example 3, for the person whose idealized and real selves are not the same, a counselor might say the following:

   Counselor: You are a person who sets high goals for himself. I admire that. But I also wonder if it's working for you. What do you think?

4. **Using satire**

   A fourth way a counselor could point out a discrepancy is through satire. Highlighting the contradiction in this way can be more confrontational than the other techniques and should be done carefully, if at all. With satire, the absurdity of the discrepancy is confronted. For instance, for a client who says he wants to be honest with his wife but is having an affair, the counselor could say the following:

   Counselor: Well, I guess in this instance it's okay to be dishonest. After all, you're saving your wife from those painful feelings. Want to discuss this?

5. **Higher-level empathy**

   The final way of challenging a client's discrepancy is through advanced empathic responses. Any of the advanced empathic responses discussed in Chapter 4 can be used to help bring new awareness to the client about discrepancies in his or her life. For instance, reflecting deeper feelings or pointing out conflicting feelings and thoughts exposes the client to deeper parts of himself or herself. For the same example just used (the client who wants to be honest with his wife but is having an affair), the following responses could be made:

   Reflecting deeper feelings and pointing out conflicts:

   Counselor: As you are talking, I think I hear the guilt you're feeling about the affair—on the one hand, guilt, and on the other hand, exhilaration about this other person. That must be a difficult place to be.

   Pointing out conflicting feelings and thoughts:

   Counselor: You must be feeling quite conflicted. On the one hand, you say you believe in honesty; on the other hand, you are hiding an affair. I guess I sense there is more to this story for you.

Now that we've discussed discrepancies and ways to confront them, use Experiential Exercise 6.6 to practice the art of confronting discrepancies in your helping relationships.

EXPERIENTIAL EXERCISE 6.6

Confronting Violet

Violet is a client who is struggling with a number of issues. In small groups of three to five, consider the different kinds of discrepancies in Violet's life. Have one person role-play Violet, and, using one or more of the previously described methods, confront Violet about the discrepancies you found. When you are done, switch roles, and the other students can role-play Violet. Observers can make note of the types of responses used. Discuss how it was to confront Violet using the techniques described earlier.

Violet

Violet, a 26-year-old White single female, makes minimum wage at her grocery store job and has two children, ages 8 and 5, with two different fathers. She receives food stamps. She has never been married. She abuses marijuana—smoking daily, usually in the morning and evening, often in front of her children. She has a live-in boyfriend, Jorad, who does not work. She states Jorad is "loving but lazy" and that he is not looking for a job. He sometimes helps with child care. He is living off her meager salary. She practices unprotected sex, even though she doesn't want to have any additional children. Violet came into counseling at your agency because she stated she wanted to "change her life."

You have been seeing Violet for approximately 2 months and have gained her trust. She readily opens up to you and has identified a number of goals, which include the following: (a) obtaining her GED, (b) going to community college to obtain a degree and training as a phlebotomist (person who draws blood), (c) stopping her smoking marijuana, and (d) having a stable love relationship (with Jorad or someone else who works). Despite identifying some specific goals, she has made no progress toward reaching them. You have decided to gently confront Violet in the hopes that she can begin to move toward some of her self-identified goals.

Cognitive-Behavioral Responses

During the 1950s and 1960s, Aaron Beck and Albert Ellis independently developed approaches to therapy that focused on cognitions (Neukrug, 2018; Neukrug & Ellis, 2015; Weishaar, 2015). Later called cognitive-behavioral therapies because they also focused on behavioral change, their theories had much in common and greatly impacted the way many helpers conduct counseling. For instance, Beck believed we have *core beliefs* (e.g., "I am powerless," "I am helpless") that impact our *intermediate beliefs* (attitudes, rules, and assumptions we make based on our core beliefs), which are responsible for developing our *automatic thoughts* (Rice, 2015). Automatic thoughts are ongoing fleeting thoughts we have about our interactions during the day (e.g., "I shouldn't have said that," "Why did I do that?," "I'm not smart enough," "That was a pretty good response," etc.). We all can become aware of our automatic thoughts, although some of us need a little practice to access them. Beck stated that our automatic thoughts affect how we feel and act as well as our physiological responses (e.g., increase in stress hormones). So, if a person's core belief is one of "I am powerless," a resulting attitude might be "Life sucks, as I have no control over it," and a possible assumption could be "I assume that things will more or less stay the way they are." These intermediate beliefs affect the person's reactions, so a person might feel sad (feelings), stay at home all day and do nothing (behaviors), and have increased cortisol levels (physiology), which increase stress levels.

If a counselor can assist a client in accessing his or her automatic thoughts, the client can work backwards and get a pretty good sense of his or her intermediate thoughts and, eventually, his or her core beliefs. Then, the counselor can assist the person in changing those core beliefs (and, by default, the intermediate beliefs, the automatic thoughts, and the feelings, behaviors, and physiology). Like Beck, Ellis also focused on cognitions, but he stated there are three *irrational thoughts* and that many of us abide by some of them (Ellis, 2015). They include the following:

1. "I *absolutely must* under all conditions do important tasks well and be approved by significant others or else I am an inadequate and unlovable person!"
2. "Other people *absolutely must* under all conditions treat me fairly and justly or else they are rotten, damnable persons!"
3. "Conditions under which I live *absolutely must* always be the way I want them to be, give me almost immediate gratification, and not require me to work too hard to change or improve them; or else it is *awful*, I *can't stand* them, and it is impossible for me to be happy *at all!*" (Ellis & MacLaren, 2005, pp. 32–33)

Ellis strongly noted that it is not an event that makes us feel and behave the way we do; it is our thoughts about the event. He called this the "*A, B, and Cs*," where A is the *activating event*, B is the *belief about the event*, and C is the *consequential feelings and behaviors*. If you know your B (which is being impacted by one of the three irrational thoughts), then you can guess what your C will be. So, if my partner breaks up with me and I become depressed, it's not because she left me. Rather, it's because of what I believe about her leaving—which is related to one or more of the three irrational beliefs.

Of course, Beck's and Ellis's theories are much more involved than the short descriptions I just offered. However, their basic ideas are these:

1. Our thinking impacts our feelings, behaviors, and physiology, sometimes in ways that are out of awareness.
2. It is relatively easy to gain awareness of the types of thoughts we are having that impact our feelings, behaviors, and physiology.
3. By sharing our thoughts (e.g., automatic thoughts, irrational beliefs) with someone else, we can begin to see which thoughts are making us feel badly and behave in maladaptive ways.
4. After we identify which thoughts are making us feel and behave poorly, we can dispute those thoughts and eventually develop new ones that result in good feelings, behaviors, and physiological responses.
5. In addition to identifying and changing our negative thoughts to positive ones, we can develop behaviors that reinforce new ways of thinking.

Although I don't expect beginning counselors to be full-fledged cognitive therapists, I do think this general approach can be used by the counselor in working with many clients. Thus, when a counselor has a client who is feeling down, anxious, or worried, he or she might consider a modified cognitive approach by asking the client to examine automatic or irrational thoughts. If the client can identify how his or her thinking makes the situation worse, the counselor can help him or her work on developing new, more positive ways of thinking and, at the same time, work on changing some behaviors that would be in line with a more positive approach to living (see Reflection Exercise 6.1).

REFLECTION EXERCISE 6.1

Practicing Cognitive Disputations

Part I: Use the example that follows of a client who just experienced the activating event of "my lover has left me." Then examine the automatic thought, irrational belief(s), and possible consequences. Then go on to Part II.

Activating event (A): My lover has left me.

Automatic thought: I can't live in this world without her (or him).

Irrational belief (iB): Conditions under which I live *absolutely must* always be the way I want them to be, give me almost immediate gratification, and not require me to work too hard to change or improve them or else it is *awful*, I *can't stand* them, and it is impossible for me to be happy *at all!*

Possible consequence (C): *Feelings consequence:* Depression, panic, isolation

Behavioral consequence: Need to immediately seek out another person, even if the relationship may not be healthy or positive. Or isolation, if depression is particularly bad.

Part II: Consider how you can dispute the client's irrational thoughts and help him (or her) develop new rational thoughts as well as new behaviors that would result in a healthier way of living. When you are finished, discuss your responses with others in small groups and talk about the possibility of using this approach with clients.

Cognitive disputations (disputing the irrational belief):

New, rational belief:

Behaviors to support new, rational belief:

It is likely that you will get additional training in cognitive-behavioral therapy in your program, probably in a counseling theories class, a practicum, an internship, or elsewhere. Also, if your instructor wishes, you can view a quick role-play of me working with Jake Miller (see Appendix B) in a cognitive-behavioral manner. Meanwhile, you can begin to consider how cognitions impact yourself, your loved ones, and your clients. The following gives you a bit more practice in cognitive-behavioral therapy (see Experiential Exercise 6.7).

EXPERIENTIAL EXERCISE 6.7

Practicing Cognitive-Behavioral Therapy Approaches to Counseling

Using either Beck's or Ellis's approach to cognitive-behavioral therapy, find two other students with whom you can role-play. One person role-plays the counselor, the second the client, and the third is an observer. The client should come up with some emotionally laden situation, and, after initially practicing some basic listening, the counselor should try a cognitive intervention by either addressing the person's irrational beliefs or by identifying automatic thoughts that may be impacting how the person responds affectively, behaviorally, and physiologically. See if you can get the person to change his or her irrational beliefs or automatic thoughts. When you are finished, switch roles. Make sure everyone gets to role-play the counselor.

This role-play gives you a quick taste of cognitive-behavioral therapy. However, please note that the actual application is much more involved than this. Good luck!

Interpretation

SIGMUND FREUD

A client explains the difficulty he has connecting with his son. He describes his son as aloof, disconnected, and rebellious. He goes on to state that he believes his son has some serious mental problems. As he continues in counseling, he details his relationship with his parents. He describes his mother as loving but critical and his father as "nonexistent." After further discussion, he says, "My dad was never in my life; he always seemed so distant and hard to talk to." After hearing these stories about the client's life, the counselor states, "It sounds like there are some similar patterns occurring between you and your son that occurred between you and your dad." The client says, "Oh my God, that is really interesting." Is the counselor's response interpretation, or is this empathy? Although some may consider this interpretation, this could very well be a high-level empathic response (Carkhuff scale, above level 3.0) for a number of reasons. First, it is a result of deep listening and concentration by the counselor. Second, it is based on a deep understanding of the client's framework of reality. Third, the counselor has reflected an understanding of the client's predicament without adding material not produced by the client and without jumping to conclusions or making assumptions. And finally, the client agrees with the counselor's assessment. The counselor is on target with the response. This type of response is profound, reaches deep inside the client's soul, and speaks to the imaginary line between facilitating and leading a client (Neukrug, 2017a; Neukrug et al., 2012).

In contrast, compare this counselor with the counselor who states, "I believe your relationship with your son is the result of an unresolved Oedipal complex in that you never fully identified with you father." This kind of interpretation is based on a preset model of counseling and psychotherapy that makes assumptions about how a person would react under certain circumstances and is often used in psychodynamic approaches to counseling (Neukrug, 2018).

Psychoanalysis, one type of psychodynamic approach, uses interpretation as a major therapeutic intervention. For instance, psychoanalysts believe that dreams hold symbols to unresolved conflicts from our psychosexual development and can provide the client with understanding into his or her development (Bishop, 2015). A dream about a goat being a person's pet in an immaculately clean apartment could represent an underlying need to rebel against a repressive upbringing, with the goat representing the archetypal oppositional animal. Similarly, some cognitive therapists assume that individuals with specific diagnoses would be expected to have certain kinds of underlying cognitive structures (ways of thinking) that can be interpreted to the client (Neukrug, 2018). For example, it could be assumed that a person with an anxiety disorder has an underlying belief that the world is a fearful and dangerous place and underestimates his or her ability to deal with anxiety. This, too, is an interpretation of behaviors based on a preset model of behavior.

Whether one is psychodynamically oriented, cognitively oriented, or relying on some other theoretical approach, the timing of the interpretation is crucial. If all goes well, the interpretation will provide a deep understanding of why the client responds the way he or she does. The hope is that when this new understanding about the client is offered, it will lead to client change.

Interpretations can help clients make giant leaps in therapy; however, there are risks involved. For instance, interpretation sets the counselor up as the expert and lessens the likelihood of a genuine relationship occurring between the counselor and client (Daniels, 2015). In addition, it lessens the here-and-now quality of the therapeutic relationship while increasing the amount of intellectualizing that occurs during the session, as both the counselor and client discuss the interpretive material (Resnick, 2015). Finally, because it is difficult to measure the efficacy of interpretation and other psychoanalytic techniques, questions arise about their use (Gaskin, 2014; Kernberg, 2006). It is for these reasons that Carl Rogers (1970) and others vehemently opposed the use of interpretation.

> To me, an interpretation as to the cause of individual behavior can never be anything but a high-level guess. The only way it can carry weight is when an authority puts his experience behind it. But I do not want to get involved in this kind of authoritativeness. "I think it's because you feel inadequate as a man that you engage in this blustering behavior," is not the kind of statement I would ever make. (Rogers, 1970, pp. 57–58)

When to Use and Not Use Interpretation

Your opinion regarding the use of interpretation most likely depends on your view of human nature. If you align yourself with a model of counseling that makes assumptions about human behavior external to the client's understanding of reality, then interpretation of client material will become an important tool for you. On the other hand, if you assume that client growth is based on clients obtaining a fuller understanding of themselves from their own view of reality, then interpretation is likely to be a useless tool for you in the helping process. Finally, if you believe interpretation can be a valuable tool in the counselor's repertoire, then clearly it should be used only after a trusting relationship has been established and with a sound knowledge of the theoretical approach you follow. Now that you know what interpretation is and how it can be used incorrectly, examine how effective you think interpretation might be (see Experiential Exercise 6.8).

Unlike many of the skills discussed in this text, if you use interpretation, I suggest you use it *very carefully*, if at all. This is because the efficacy of interpretation is questionable, and to use interpretation effectively, counselors must have a thorough knowledge of the theoretical model on which the interpretation is based—knowledge usually not obtained at this point in your program. Also, interpretation takes a lot of practice, and I often find that counselors use interpretation in a haphazard manner, making up their own interpretations as they go.

EXPERIENTIAL EXERCISE 6.8

Practicing Interpretations

Break up into groups of four that include a counselor, a client, and two observers. The client is to discuss a real or made-up problem situation. The counselor is to first listen to the client carefully and then try to make an interpretive response. So, if the client says, "I'm having trouble with my girlfriend, she never wants to listen to me," you might say, "I'm thinking your parents may not have listened to you either." Make as many interpretive responses as possible. Meanwhile, observers should be writing down the different interpretations. When you are finished, respond to the following questions. If time allows, switch roles.

1. How easy was it to make an interpretive response?
2. Were the interpretations mostly on target or not?
3. If the interpretation was on target, was it helpful for the client?
4. If the interpretation was not on target, how harmful was it for the relationship?
5. Do you think interpretation is something that would be helpful in your work as a counselor?

Positive Counseling

If you remember, a large section of Chapter 5 focused on solution-focused questions. These questions are the bedrock of what some have called positive counseling, or the positive psychology movement, which has emerged over the past 25 years (Lopez, Pedrotti, & Snyder, 2015; McAuliffe, 2019). Positive counseling assumes that we have choices in our lives relative to our mental, physical, and spiritual states; that we are not determined by early childhood or other factors; and that we need to be careful when labeling or diagnosing a person, as such labels can result in negative attributions or self-statements by professionals or by the clients themselves. Researchers suggest that a positive focus can lead to greater resilience, a longer life, a decrease in health problems, and an increase in creativity, engagement in life, and a personal sense of meaning (Bolier et al., 2013; Rankin, 2013; see Reflection Exercise 6.2).

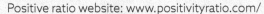

REFLECTION EXERCISE 6.2

Your Positivity Ratio

Some research indicates that a healthy positivity ratio is 3 to 1, which means that positive thoughts and actions outweigh negative ones to that degree. If you go to the Web address provided, you can assess your positivity ratio. After completing the instrument, consider if you need to do some things in your life to become more positive. Also, reflect on how you might be able to use an instrument like this with your clients.

Positive ratio website: www.positivityratio.com/

McAuliffe (2019) suggests that counselors should be guided by three principles when using positive counseling: (a) increasing positive emotion about the past, present, and future; (b) increasing engagement and absorption in "love, work, and leisure"; and (c) promoting a meaningful life. He goes on to offer activities that could be integrated into practice, including *strength exercises, gratitude exercises, hope and optimism exercises, drawing positives out of negatives,* and *other positive counseling interventions.*

Strength Exercises

Highlighting existing strengths is a critical mechanism for helping clients stay positive. Such strengths should be experience-based and become part of a person's daily routine so they can become socially reinforced.

Gratitude Exercises

Gratitude comes in many forms, including appreciating self, appreciation of others, being thankful for life and nature, and more. These exercises help to identify, highlight, and show appreciation for those positive aspects of clients' lives they take for granted.

Hope and Optimism Exercises

Noting that humans are sometimes inclined to focus on the negative, these exercises shift clients' attention to the positives in their lives. They entail focusing on past, present, and potentially future positive aspects of clients' lives, noting exceptions to negative events in clients' lives, helping clients learn how to shift their attention to the positive, and projecting a positive future.

Drawing Positives Out of Negatives

Rather than focusing on negatives, here the counselor helps the client find positives (making lemonade out of lemons). For instance, for the client who suggests she is always depressed and never wants to do anything, the counselor can ask the exception-seeking question "With your depression, how was it that you were able to get out of bed and go to work?" And the counselor might go on to say: "So, I hear how depressed you were the last week, but maybe you can identify some moments when you laughed or at least felt a bit uplifted. What was different about those moments?" You can see how important solution-focused questions are to drawing out positives.

Other Positive Counseling Interventions

McAuliffe identifies a number of other activities that can also be used to draw out positive aspects of the person, and a creative counselor can come up with dozens of ways to help a client look at life in a more positive manner. Although some psychotherapeutic approaches to positive counseling have been developed (see Ruini, 2017), many psychotherapeutic theories can integrate positive counseling into their existing approach (see Experiential Exercise 6.9). Finally, your instructor might want to show you a role-play of me working with Angela Miller (see Appendix B) using a positive, postmodern approach.

EXPERIENTIAL EXERCISE 6.9

Integrating Positive Counseling Into Your Approach

Have two volunteers role-play a counselor-client situation in the middle of the class. The rest of the class can form a circle around these two students. As the counselor uses the traditional tools discussed in the first five chapters of the book, periodically, a student in the circle can shout out a positive counseling question or statement. Consider using one of McAuliffe's techniques just discussed (strength exercises, gratitude exercises, hope and optimism exercises, drawing positive out of negatives, and so forth). After the role-play is completed, discuss, as a group, how effective the positive questions or statements were. If you like, you can try doing the same role-play in dyads or in triads (with an observer for feedback).

Life Coaching

Life coaching (sometimes just called *coaching*) has become another mechanism for clients to develop healthy habits and fits nicely into the model of positive counseling just discussed (Labardee, Williams, & Hodges, 2012). In contrast to traditional counseling, coaching spends little time examining the past or focusing on problems. Rather, coaching relies on a short-term-focused helping relationship in which the coach uses solution-focused questions to identify one or more issues on which to concentrate, collaboratively sets goals, affirms and encourages the client to work on goals, and helps to ensure continued follow-up after goals have been reached to ensure maintenance of goals (Shallcross, 2011; Sheff, 2016). A whole host of concerns that tend to be short-term and not based on deeply held problems or deep client wounds can be focused on in this process, such as weight loss, finding a job, communication skills, developing an exercise regime, managing one's budget, and so forth.

Coaching eschews diagnosis, does not generally rely on third-party (insurance) payments, and is viewed as less stigmatizing than the more traditional helping relationship. Life coaching will not likely replace counseling and therapy but does offer an additional venue in which some clients can participate.

Drawbacks to coaching include the fact that it is not conducive to digging up underlying core issues and the fact that health insurance companies tend not to cover coaching services (Shallcross, 2011; Sheff, 2016). In addition, because coaching sacrifices depth in favor of efficiency, it probably has limited efficacy in treating more serious mental health issues (Ley, 2014). Today, coaching has become its own specialty area, and a counselor can become a *board-certified coach* (BCC) through the Center for Credentialing and Education (CCE, 2016). In coming years, we will have a better sense of the popularity of life coaching and whether coaching will move into the mainstream of helping services (see Experiential Exercise 6.10).

EXPERIENTIAL EXERCISE 6.10

Coaching a Partner

Pair up with another student and, using the helping skills you learned in chapters one through five, assist that person with a life problem or issue. However, because coaching is not therapy, make sure this is not a long-term emotional or psychological problem but a life problem that the client can more easily tackle (e.g., reducing stress, increasing physical health, talking more effectively with one's spouse or children, etc.). While coaching, the coach may want to focus on the following:

1. Using foundational and essential skills to build the relationship
2. Using information-gathering questions to determine what to focus on
3. Using solution-focused questions to help the person identify goals and strategies for change
4. Using commonly used skills to support clients and suggest solutions
5. Highlighting identified goals and strategies and setting dates for change
6. Encouraging and affirming your client along the way
7. Having a positive focus, building on your client's strengths, being committed, being encouraging and affirming, and gently nudging your client to work on identified goals and strategies for change

After role-playing for 20 to 30 minutes, discuss the coaching process with each other. Was it helpful? Do you think that coaching could be beneficial long-term? What are some of the positive and negative aspects of coaching?

Summary

This chapter explored a number of specialized skills counselors sometimes use in their work with clients, including advocacy; assessing for lethality; crisis, disaster, and trauma counseling; confrontation: challenge with support; cognitive-behavioral responses; interpretation; positive counseling; and coaching.

We started the chapter by noting that advocacy is part of a social justice focus and is now addressed in the Multicultural and Social Justice Counseling Competencies, which have been endorsed by ACA. We noted that advocacy can be conducted at six levels: intrapersonal, interpersonal, institutional, community, public policy, and international and global affairs. We defined each of these levels and gave some examples to highlight how a counselor might advocate at each level.

Assessing for lethality was the next special skill we examined. For the assessment of suicide, we offered a continuum that ran from no suicidal thoughts to having suicidal ideation, to developing a plan, to having the means, to preparing, to rehearsing, to acting. We identified a number of risk factors and protective factors for suicidal behavior. We also offered a 10-step model for how to work with a suicidal client.

For the assessment of assaultive and homicidal potential, we presented the assault and homicidal assessment tool, which has five levels, from no predictable risk of assault or homicide to a very high risk of homicide. Like suicide, we identified a number of risk and protective factors that tend to be at play with individuals who are potentially assaultive or homicidal. We offered a 10-step model for working with assaultive and homicidal clients.

The next important skill we looked at was how to do crisis, trauma, and disaster counseling. We first defined crisis, trauma, and disaster and then offered steps on how to deal with a client in crisis, a client who has experienced a disaster, and a client who has experienced a traumatic event. We noted that those who have experienced ongoing trauma often have PTSD and that ongoing counseling may be critical in those cases. We noted that crisis, disaster, and single-event trauma counseling is generally short-term, anonymous in that records are generally not keep, built on client strengths, non-diagnostic oriented, and provided in nontraditional settings (e.g., homes or settings where the crisis occurred).

The next skill we examined was confrontation: challenge with support. We noted that confrontation begins with building a trusting and caring relationship, followed by an invitation to discuss discrepancies. Four types of discrepancies we outlined included those between a client's values and behaviors, feelings and behaviors, idealized self and real self, and expressed feelings and underlying feelings. Five ways of inviting discussions about discrepancies included you/but statements, asking the client to justify the discrepancy, reframing, using satire, and using higher-level empathy. Examples of how to invite discussions regarding discrepancies were given.

Cognitive-behavioral responses to clients were the next skills we examined. We noted that Aaron Beck and Albert Ellis developed two different theories that both spoke to how cognitions impact affect, behaviors, and physiological responses. Whereas Beck talked about the relationship between core beliefs, intermediate beliefs, automatic thoughts and the resulting feelings, behaviors, and physiological responses, Ellis talked about the A, B, and Cs of thinking, noting that it is not the activating event (A) that causes consequences (C), such as negative feelings or maladaptive behaviors; it is the beliefs (B) about the activating event that impact consequences (C). Irrational thoughts, said Ellis, cause negative consequences. We suggested that counselors could use cognitive-behavioral responses when working with clients by helping them change cognitions and adopt behaviors that match the new, healthier ways of thinking.

Interpretation was the next skill we looked at. Interpretation is the analysis of a client's understanding of the world from the perspective of the counselor and is based on a preset model of counseling. It should be used cautiously but has the potential of offering large movement in the counseling relationship. However, if off base, it can damage the relationship. Psychodynamic-oriented helpers use interpretations to make leaps about a person's behaviors, and cognitively oriented counselors sometimes develop treatment plans based on a client's symptoms and the assumptions (interpretations) about underlying cognitive structures. We noted that the use of interpretation takes much practice and warned against counselors haphazardly making such responses.

Positive counseling was the next skill we highlighted. We noted that solution-focused questions are often used in positive counseling and that positive counseling assumes we have choices relative to our mental, physical, and spiritual states; that we are not determined by early childhood or other factors; and that we need to be careful when labeling or diagnosing a person. We gave a website where you can assess your positivity ratio, and we identified three principles when using positive counseling, including (a) increasing positive emotion about the past, present, and future; (b) increasing engagement and absorption in "love, work, and leisure"; and (c) promoting a meaningful life. We went on to note some activities that could be integrated into practice, including strength exercises, gratitude exercises, hope and optimism exercises, drawing positives out of negatives, and other positive counseling interventions.

The last area of specialized training we included was life coaching, or just coaching. We noted that coaching spends little time examining the past or focusing on problems. Instead, it focuses on identifying goals and finding solutions, views the helping relationship as a partnership rather than a therapeutic relationship, is strength based, and is often conducted in a less structured environment than counseling. We explained that one can become a board-certified coach (BCC) through the Center for Credentialing and Education.

Key Words and Terms

A, B, and Cs

activating event

advocacy

asking the client to justify the discrepancy

assault and homicidal danger assessment tool

assessing for homicidality

assessing for suicidality

automatic thoughts

Beck, Aaron

belief about the event

board-certified coach

Center for Credentialing and Education

challenging client discrepancies

coaching

cognitive-behavioral responses

confrontation: challenge with support

consequential feelings and behaviors

core beliefs

crisis counseling

disaster counseling

discrepancy between clients' expressed and underlying feelings

discrepancy between clients' feelings and behaviors

discrepancy between clients' idealized selves and real selves

discrepancy between clients' values and behavior

drawing positives out of negatives

eight steps when dealing with a person in crisis

eight steps when responding to a disaster

Ellis, Albert

gratitude exercises

higher-level empathy

hope and optimism exercises

intermediate beliefs

interpretation

irrational thoughts

levels and types of advocacy interventions

life coaching

Multicultural and Social Justice Counseling Competencies

other positive counseling interventions

positive counseling

Post-Traumatic Stress Disorder (PTSD)

protective factors for suicide and homicide

reframing

reinforcement contingencies

risk factors for suicide and homicide

social justice

strength exercises

trauma counseling

using satire

you/but statements

Credits

Section II

Treatment Issues

The last four chapters of *Counseling and Helping Skills* focus on treatment issues. Chapter 7 focuses on case management, which encompasses a broad range of activities to ensure optimal services to clients, including providing informed consent and professional disclosure statements, assessment, developing client goals, monitoring psychotropic medications, writing notes and reports, confidentiality of records, ensuring security of client records, documenting client contact hours, termination and making referrals, conducting follow-up, and practicing time management.

Chapter 8 examines case conceptualization, diagnosis, and treatment planning. Focusing first on case conceptualization, we discuss its importance in understanding themes regarding a client's life and in exploring ideas about the causation of client problems. We examine the difference between theory-driven case conceptualization and non-theory-focused case conceptualization and highlight the biopsychosocial assessment model—a non-theory-specific model that examines the client in three domains: biological, psychological, and sociocultural. We explore this model by introducing Jake, a client we have already highlighted in the text. We note how a diagnosis is a natural outgrowth of the case conceptualization process, and we discuss some important concepts when making and reporting a DSM-5 diagnosis. We then show how such a diagnosis can be developed for Jake. The chapter also highlights how case conceptualization, along with a diagnosis, can be useful in developing treatment plans and give some examples, again using Jake. We conclude the chapter by showing how theory can be applied to the case conceptualization process.

Chapter 9 examines culturally competent counseling and starts with examining the importance of it. It next focuses on nine reasons why some diverse clients are wary of counseling. It then defines culturally competent counseling and offers three models that counselors can use in becoming culturally competent counselors, including the RESPECTFUL model, the cross-cultural and social justice counseling competencies, and an integrative model of culturally competent counseling. The last part of this chapter examines strategies for working with 11 diverse populations, including individuals from different ethnic and racial groups; individuals from diverse religious backgrounds; women; men; lesbian, gay, bisexual, transgender, and questioning individuals; the poor and the homeless; children; older persons; individuals with serious mental disorders; individuals with disabilities; and individuals who use and abuse substances.

The last chapter of the text, Chapter 10, examines ethical, legal, and professional issues. It starts by examining the purposes and limitations of ethical codes and then goes on to describe four models of ethical decision-making models, including problem-solving, moral, developmental, and social constructivist. It next examines 10 important ethical issues, including informed consent, confidentiality, privileged communication, competence, maintaining boundaries and prohibited relationships, values in the counseling relationship, cross-cultural counseling, technology in counseling, supervision, and reporting ethical violations. It then highlights how counselors perceived 77 ethical situations, and this is followed by the identification of 26 best-practice behaviors. The chapter concludes with a short discussion about the importance of malpractice insurance.

CHAPTER 7

Case Management

Learning Objectives

1. To learn about the broad range of case management activities, including the following:
   a. Informed consent and professional disclosure statements
   b. Assessment for treatment planning
   c. Developing client goals
   d. Monitoring psychotropic medications
   e. Writing notes and reports
   f. Confidentiality of records
   g. Ensuring security of records
   h. Documenting client contact hours
   i. Termination and making referrals
   j. Conducting follow-up
   k. Practicing time management

Introduction

Case management, which has been called, by some, the overall process involved in maintaining the optimal functioning of clients (Summers, 2016; Woodside & McClam, 2018), encompasses a broad range of activities, including providing informed consent and professional disclosure statements, assessment, developing client goals, monitoring psychotropic medications, writing notes and reports, confidentiality of records, ensuring security of client records, documenting client contact hours, termination and making referrals, conducting follow-up, and practicing time management. Although some of these tend to be done at specific times during the relationship, many need to be examined and reassessed throughout the relationship (see Figure 7.1). With an increased emphasis on accountability within the mental health professions, case management has become critical to the work of the counselor. Let's look at each of these activities that make up the broad area of case management.

FIGURE 7.1   Case Management Flowchart

Informed Consent and Professional Disclosure Statements

Having clients give their *informed consent* to treatment is a critical aspect of the beginning of the counseling relationship, as underscored by the ACA (2014) Code of Ethics:

> Clients have the freedom to choose whether to enter into or remain in a counseling relationship and need adequate information about the counseling process and the counselor. Counselors have an obligation to review in writing and verbally with clients the rights and responsibilities of both counselors and clients. Informed consent is an ongoing part of the counseling process, and counselors appropriately document discussions of informed consent throughout the counseling relationship. (Section A.2.a. Informed Consent)

Prior to giving informed consent, clients are often given a *professional disclosure statement* that summarizes the purposes, procedures, and nature of the counseling relationship and covers a wide net. For instance, the ACA Code of Ethics, as well as books on ethics, suggest that the following areas be addressed in such a statement (ACA, 2014; Corey, Corey, & Corey, 2019; Remley & Herlihy, 2016):

1.   Purposes, goals, techniques, and procedures of the counseling relationship
2.   Potential risks and benefits of counseling

3. The counselor's credentials, experience, and qualifications
4. The counselor's theoretical approach to counseling
5. How services will continue should the counselor become incapacitated
6. The role of technology in counseling
7. The role of diagnosis
8. How assessment procedures will be used
9. Information about fees and billing
10. Information about clients' rights to confidentiality
11. The limits to confidentiality, especially relative to harm to self or others
12. How records will be used and what rights clients have to their records
13. How clients will participate in the ongoing counseling plan
14. That clients can refuse services at any point
15. The importance of each client's unique diversity
16. The limits to boundaries in the counseling relationship
17. Agency rules that might impact the counseling relationship
18. Legal issues that might impact the counseling relationship
19. A statement about keeping promises and commitments to clients
20. Other pertinent information

Clients can be given a written or electronic copy of the professional disclosure statement and are asked to sign the statement, which acknowledges they have read and understood the statement and give their informed consent to such treatment (see Experiential Exercise 7.1).

EXPERIENTIAL EXERCISE 7.1

Informed Consent and Professional Disclosure Statements

In Chapter 2, you had a chance to write a professional disclosure statement that covered many, but not all, of the items listed. Revisit the professional disclosure statement you wrote in Experiential Exercise 2.4 and expand it to include all these items (or write a new one). In small groups, share your professional disclosure statements and offer feedback to each other on how they can be improved.

Assessment

One important function of the counselor is to conduct a variety of assessment activities, which can involve any of a number of activities, including conducting a clinical interview, the administration of tests, and informal assessment (Neukrug & Fawcett, 2015; Schwitzer & Rubin, 2015). Assessment helps to give the counselor an in-depth understanding of the client, and the information gathered can also be used in case conceptualization, which helps us understand themes and ideas about the causation of client problems, can be important in forming diagnostic impressions, and can be used in treatment planning. Case conceptualization, diagnosis, and treatment planning will be discussed further in Chapter 8.

The Clinical Interview

Probably the most important area of assessment, the *clinical interview,* allows the counselor to gather information from a broad area of the client's life. Often, this interview takes place during the initial contact with the agency and is called an *intake interview.* Completed in a manner that will allow the client to be open and honest and provide the counselor with in-depth knowledge of the client, the counseling skills discussed throughout this text are the basis for this interview.

A good clinical interview often involves gathering information from a number of areas, including demographic information, the presenting problem or reason for referral, family background, significant medical/counseling history, substance use and abuse, educational and vocational history, other pertinent information, and the mental status exam. The information gathered, along with assessment results, a diagnosis, summary and conclusions, and recommendations, are often written up in a *psychological report.* Appendix C gives a breakdown of some of the areas that would be addressed in each of these categories, while Appendix D offers an example of a psychological report. The report is usually used for treatment planning and referral purposes. As you might imagine, information-gathering questions are a staple of a good clinical interview, although I always suggest that counselors use a fair amount of listening and empathy, especially when they touch on sensitive areas in clients' lives.

Although all areas of a clinical interview are important, one area that needs special attention is the *mental status exam,* which is an assessment of the client in a number of areas, often including the following: (a) how the client presents himself or herself (appearance and behavior), (b) the client's emotional state (affect), (c) the client's ability to think clearly (thought components), and (d) the client's memory state and orientation to the world (cognition; Akiskal, 2016; Burgess, 2013).

Mental Status Exam. What follows are abbreviated definitions of the four areas assessed in a mental status exam. Appendix E gives some typical words and terms used in the mental status report. Generally, the mental status exam is highlighted in one or two paragraphs in the psychological report, an example of which is found in the psychological report in Appendix D.

Appearance and behavior. This includes observable appearance and behaviors during the clinical interview, such as manner of dress, hygiene, body posture, tics, significant nonverbal behaviors (eye contact or the lack thereof, wringing of hands, swaying), and manner of speech (e.g., stuttering, tone).

Emotional state. Here, the examiner describes the client's affect and mood. Affect includes the client's current prevailing feeling state (e.g., happy, sad, joyful, angry, depressed, etc.) and may also be reported as constricted or full, appropriate or inappropriate to content, labile, flat, blunted, exaggerated, and so forth. The client's mood, on the other hand, represents the long-term underlying emotional well-being of the client and is usually assessed through client self-report. Thus, a client may seem anxious and sad during the session (affect) and report that his or her mood has been depressed.

Thought components. The manner in which the client thinks, or thought components, are generally broken down into the content and the process of thinking. Content includes such things as whether the client has delusions, distortions of body image, hallucinations, obsessions, suicidal or homicidal ideation, and so forth. A statement about a client's thought process often includes references to circumstantiality, coherence, flight of ideas, logical thinking, intact as opposed to loose associations, organization, and tangentiality.

Cognition. Whether a client is oriented to time, place, and person (knows what time it is, where he or she is, and who he or she is) is one important aspect of cognition and should generally be included in the mental status report. Other aspects include a write-up on the client's short- and long-term memory, an evaluation of the client's knowledge base and intellectual functioning, and a statement about the client's level of insight and ability to make judgments. Experiential Exercise 7.2 gives you the opportunity to write a mental status report.

EXPERIENTIAL EXERCISE 7.2

Writing a Mental Status Report

Find a partner and have one person role-play a seriously impaired client while the other, the counselor, assesses the client's mental status. Then write a mental status report. After the first role-play, switch roles and have the second counselor assess the client and write the mental status report. Use the mental status report section of the psychological report found in Appendix D as a model. The words and terms noted in Appendix E can help you in writing your mental status report. When you have finished, discuss the following issues in class:

1. How difficult was it to assess a client's mental status?
2. What would have helped you in your assessment?
3. What questions might help you in assessing all four areas of the client's mental status?
4. What value do you see in conducting a mental status report?
5. Do you have other questions about the mental status report?

Testing

Testing involves conducting a formal assessment of the client with testing instruments that have been shown to have *test worthiness*, which means they are valid (measure what they're supposed to measure), reliable (measure accurately), cross-culturally fair, and practical for the purpose for which they are being used (Neukrug & Fawcett, 2015). In many states, counselors can give a wide variety of tests, usually with the exception of projective testing and some of the more involved cognitive ability tests (e.g., intelligence testing). However, counselors should know their state laws to determine what kind of tests they can give. Whatever tests they do give, counselors should be trained and competent in giving them (ACA, 2014).

> Counselors use only those testing and assessment services for which they have been trained and are competent. (ACA, 2014, Section E.2.a., Limits of Competence)

Testing should be given to assess gaps, gain an increased understanding of the client's issues, help with diagnosis and case conceptualization, and assist in treatment planning. Tests that are administered should match the purpose for which the client has come to counseling (ACA, 2014). For instance, I once was asked to test a person who had a dissociative identity disorder (multiple personality disorder) and who was fairly integrated (did not readily move from one personality to another). However, the purpose of the testing was to see whether she was capable of work, as she had been denied Social Security disability benefits, yet she believed she could not work. Thus, the kinds of tests I used were very different than the ones I would have used to assess for her dissociative identify disorder. Some of the many kinds of test categories include career and vocational assessment, intellectual and cognitive assessment, personality testing, achievement testing, and aptitude testing.

Informal Assessment

Informal assessment includes a wide variety of assessment procedures that require little advanced training and are aimed at providing a quick and focused assessment of a client (Neukrug & Fawcett, 2015). Although generally not as valid or reliable as tests, they can be quickly administered and can be created to focus directly on a client's presenting concern. Some of the many types of informal assessment include observation; rating scales; classification methods, such as behavior or feeling word checklists (see Appendix A); environmental assessment, such as observing a person at his or her home or workplace; records and personal documents; and performance-based assessment, such as when a person is assessed on a task in a real-life situation. Informal assessments are often counselor-made, and the number and types of instruments that one can come up with are limited only by one's imagination. Reflection Exercise 7.1 shows one type of easily developed informal assessment that one can use with a client. Can you come up with others?

REFLECTION EXERCISE 7.1

Physical Abuse Checklist

The following is an informal assessment of physical abuse by a partner. This simple behavior checklist can quickly assess if a person is physically abused. (Check any items that you have experienced from your partner in the past two weeks).

- Slaps you
- Punches you
- Hits you
- Throws things at you
- Bites you
- Pulls your hair
- Threatens you with a weapon
- Holds you down
- Pinches you

- Grabs you
- Burns you
- Drives recklessly with you in the car
- Physically prevents you from leaving
- Ties you up
- Shoves you
- Pushes you
- Picks at you
- Chokes you

* The number of weeks can be changed.

As you look at this checklist, do you think it is valid (assesses what it's supposed to assess), reliable (consistently measures what it's supposed to measure), is cross-culturally fair, and is practical to use? If you remember, these four attributes show the worthiness of the instrument.

Goal Development

The development of goals for clients is a critical aspect of most therapeutic approaches (Cooper & Law, 2018), and identifying specific goals should be a relatively easy process if the counselor has completed a thorough assessment of the client. Some general rules of thumb that a counselor should consider in goal development include the following:

1. *Goal development should be an outgrowth of the assessment process.*
2. *Goal development should be collaborative.* Goals should not be "given" to the client but jointly developed.
3. *Goals should be attainable.* If too lofty, the client will feel like a failure if goals are not met. If too simple, goals are less likely to help the client feel successful.
4. *Progress toward goals should be monitored.* Not monitoring progress can lead clients to question their counselors' ability or commitment. In addition, it can result in lack of follow-through on the part of clients. Lack of progress needs to be reviewed to determine whether goals need to be changed.
5. *Goals can be changed.* If a client is not reaching his or her goals, discuss why. Were they too difficult or too easy? Were they the wrong goals? Were they not attempted due to lack of time or motivation? After determining why they were not reached, rework the goals and try again.
6. *Develop new goals as former goals are reached.* As clients reach their goals, determine whether they are ready to work on new ones.
7. *Attainment of goals should be affirmed.* Clients work hard to reach their goals, and it is important that they are affirmed for their success.
8. *Know when to stop.* Although it is important to keep clients moving forward, also know when to encourage a client to stop. Sometimes a client has simply finished!

Documenting that progress is being made has become increasingly important as funding sources for mental health services have become scarcer (Drake & Latimer, 2012; Woodside & McClam, 2018). In fact, some funding sources today will not renew funding if documentation of attainment toward goals is not demonstrated. The simplest way to document such progress is to make a note in the client's chart. Innovative counselors can create charts and graphs to visually document client progress (see Experiential Exercise 7.3).

EXPERIENTIAL EXERCISE 7.3

Assessing Needs and Developing Goals

Part I: Spend 10 to 20 minutes interviewing another student who is role-playing a client or discussing a real situation. While interviewing your client, assess the client's needs. When the interview is near completion, write down the client's needs as you view them. After you have finished, obtain feedback from your client as to the accuracy of your assessment.

Part II: With your role-play client in Part I, spend a minimum of 10 minutes developing your client goals. The goals should be an outgrowth of your client's needs that were formulated in Part I. Make sure that the goal-setting process is collaborative and that the client is comfortable with the ones developed.

Monitoring Psychotropic Medications

The use of *psychotropic medications*, sometimes called *psychopharmacology*, has come a long way since its widespread utilization during the mid-1900s. With an increase in the types of medications available and the lessening of side effects, medications are now prescribed for almost any kind of psychological problem and, despite some challenges (see Fact Sheet 7.1), should often be considered as an adjunct to treatment.

FACT SHEET 7.1

Advantages and Disadvantages of Psychotropic Medication

Advantages of medication	*Disadvantages of medication*
• The effectiveness of medication can be examined easily.	• Only counseling can address the complexity of the human condition.
• Medications can sometimes instill hope as a person quickly begins to feel better.	• Counseling can lead to autonomy; drugs can lead to dependence.
• Medication can help motivate clients to put work into the helping relationship.	• The positive effects of medications can lessen the desire for some clients to work on their problems.
• Sometimes, the quick response of medication can reduce the likelihood of a serious mental illness (e.g., schizophrenia) occurring again.	• Targeted medications for certain mental illnesses can increase some clients' beliefs that they embody the illness for which the medicine is prescribed.
• Medication may help some people who are not helped by psychotherapy.	• Outcome research on some psychotropic medications is mixed and confusing.
• Sometimes, medications are more cost-effective than psychotherapy.	• Most psychotropic medications have side effects, and sometimes these can be serious and long lasting.
• The biological basis of some disorders means treatment by medication is crucial.	• Psychotropic medications do not solve life's problems—only the client can.

Although counselors cannot prescribe medication, they often will refer to medical professionals who can prescribe, and a working knowledge of medication can be helpful when consulting with these professionals. Therefore, counselors should know medication basics so they can intelligibly consult with medical professionals, assist clients in adhering to their medication regimes, help identify potential side effects, and have a sense of knowing whether the medication is working.

Commonly, psychotropic medications have been classified into five groups: *antipsychotics, mood-stabilizing drugs, antidepressants, antianxiety agents,* and *stimulants* (National Institute of Mental Health, 2016). The following sections provide a very brief overview of these drug groups to give you a sense of what they can do along with a few of the possible problems associated with some of them (see Experiential Exercise 7.4). Please remember, the information given here is only a small portion of what we currently know about psychotropic medications and is mostly taken from three important psychopharmacological textbooks (see Preston, O'Neal, & Talaga, 2017; Schatzberg & Nemeroff, 2017; Videbeck, 2017). If you would like more information about psychopharmacology for mental disorders, consult these books and other sources of information.

Has Medication Helped or Hurt?

As you discuss the classifications of the psychotropic medications listed in the following sections, share with the class your experience of individuals you know who have benefited from, or have been harmed by, the use of medication. If you wish, discuss your own use of medication for a mental health problem.

Antipsychotic Drugs

Antipsychotic drugs, sometimes called *neuroleptics*, are used to treat all types of psychoses and occasionally bipolar disorder, depression with psychotic features, paranoid disorder, delirium, and dementia. Today, there is a wide range of these drugs, and sometimes they can dramatically alter the course of treatment for an individual who is having an acute psychotic episode (see Fact Sheet 7.2). For instance, the quicker an individual can recover due to the use of medication, the greater the likelihood that future psychotic episodes will not occur. Although antipsychotic medications can assist an individual in living a more normal life, they are often not a cure and can have a wide range of side effects, including blood disorders, involuntary movement problems, memory problems, decreased libido, motor issues, and much more.

FACT SHEET 7.2

Some Common Antipsychotic Medications

Conventional antipsychotics		Second-generation antipsychotics	
Generic name	Trade name	Generic name	Trade name
Chlorpromazine	Thorazine	Clozapine	Clozaril
Haloperidol	Haldol	Risperidone	Risperdal
Thioridazine	Mellaril	Olanzapine	Zyprexa
Trifluoperazine	Stelazine	Quetiapine	Seroquel
Fluphenazine	Prolixin	Ziprasidone	Geodon
Perphenazine	Trilafon	Aripiprazole	Abilify
Thiothixene	Navane		
Loxapine	Loxitane		
Molindone	Moban		

Mood-Stabilizing Drugs

As far back as the 1800s, the element *lithium* was found to be helpful in treating a number of afflictions. Then, in the early 1950s, lithium was found to be an effective treatment for bipolar disorder (then called manic depression). Lithium seems to act particularly well in lessening the effects of manic symptoms. For individuals who take lithium, the level of drug in the system has to be assessed through a blood test. Too much lithium can cause severe side effects, and too little will be ineffective in treatment. Like the antipsychotics, lithium can produce a number of undesirable side effects, although they are generally viewed as less serious than those of the antipsychotic medications. For individuals who don't respond well to lithium, several anticonvulsant medications, such as Depakote, Tegretol, and some benzodiazepines (antianxiety drugs) have been helpful in treating manic episodes.

Antidepressants

Over the past 100 years, there has been a host of psychotropic drugs to help with the treatment of depression. Starting with the use of *amphetamines* in the early 1900s and later in the century with *monoamine oxidase inhibitors* (MAOIs) and then *tricyclics*, new and better drugs to treat depression were found. However, in more recent years, the *selective serotonin reuptake inhibitors* (SSRIs) have been the drug of choice and have shown more success than past medications (Hillhouse & Porter, 2015). In fact, for some, the SSRIs have been called miracle drugs due to their limited side effects and often dramatic results. Consequently, drugs such as Celexa, Luvox, Paxil, Prozac, and Zoloft have very quickly become commonplace in American society. In addition to being beneficial for depression, SSRIs also show promise in treating obsessive-compulsive disorder, panic disorder, some forms of schizophrenia, eating disorders, alcoholism, obesity, and some sleep disorders. Along with the SSRIs, a number of *atypical antidepressants* have also shown promise in the treatment of depression. Some of these include Serzone, Desyrel, Effexor, Serzone, Remeron, and Wellbutrin. Recent research shows that counseling may be as effective as these drugs, and counseling plus drugs may be slightly more effective (Qaseem, Barry, & Kansagara, 2016).

Antianxiety Medications

The use of modern-day antianxiety agents started with the discovery of Librium, which came on the market in 1960. Today, *benzodiazepines*, such as Valium, Librium, and Xanax, are frequently used in conjunction with psychotherapy for generalized anxiety disorders, as they have a calming effect on the individual. Benzodiazepines have also been shown to be helpful for insomnia and in reducing stress and the management of alcohol withdrawal. However, tolerance of and dependence on benzodiazepines can occur, and there is a potential for overdose on these medications. *Nonbenzodiazepines*, such as Buspar and Gepirone, are an alternative to the benzodiazepines.

Stimulants

Over the years, amphetamines were used—mostly unsuccessfully—as a diet aid, as an antidepressant, and to relieve the symptoms of sleepiness. However, during the 1950s, amphetamines were found to have a *paradoxical effect* in many children diagnosed with attention deficit disorder with hyperactivity (ADHD); it seemed to calm them down and help them focus. Today, the use of *stimulants* in the treatment of attention deficit disorder is widespread, with the three most common drugs being Ritalin, Cylert, and

Dexedrine. Stimulants have also been successful in treating narcolepsy and are somewhat successful in treating residual attention deficit disorder in adults.

Managing Psychotropic Medications

Psychopharmacology has come a long way since the 1950s, when the first "modern" psychotropic medications were introduced. Today, medications are used for a wide array of disorders, are more effective, and have fewer side effects. As psychological disorders become better understood, new and even more effective medications can be developed. Increasingly, counselors will be working with clients who are taking an array of psychotropic medications. When working with clients taking psychotropic medication, counselors should know the basics of such drugs, when such drugs are not being effective, and when to refer to medical professionals when a client is in need of a medication review (see Reflection Exercise 7.2).

REFLECTION EXERCISE 7.2

Diagnosis and Medication: Helpful or Problematic?

In small groups, for each of the following vignettes, consider whether you believe a diagnosis hurts or helps each person (diagnosis will be discussed in greater detail in Chapter 8). Also, discuss whether you believe medication is part of the problem or the solution to the problem.

- Joselin is in middle school and has been assessed as having a panic disorder. She can do well in school most of the time. However, a few times a week, she has severe panic attacks that end up with her leaving school and going home. They have become so intense and embarrassing for her that she now wants to be homeschooled. She has an older brother and twin younger sisters, all of whom seem to be doing well. Her father has a history of anxiety and her mother of depression, but their marriage is described as "solid." Joselin's mother and father fear that Joselin's panic disorder is "genetic" and don't know what to do. She has just begun counseling, and her counselor is suggesting she get a referral for possible antidepressant medication that also has antianxiety effects.
- John, a 35-year-old married male, has been having difficulties in his relationship with Steve (32), who, John states, constantly thinks John is cheating on him, even though he is not. Steve also has delusional thoughts about the government having the ability to hear everyone's conversation through their computers. He has "secretly" told John about this but does not want others to know, as he's afraid they'll think he is crazy. Steve comes from a family in which schizophrenia is prevalent, and John is concerned that Steve is beginning to show some tendencies toward schizophrenia. John is hopeful that he can help Steve receive treatment and medication quickly to ward off a "full-fledged schizophrenic episode."
- Eduardo, a 27-year-old single male, has been dating Elicia for 3 years. He states that Elicia has been pressuring him to get married and that he does not currently feel ready for marriage, although he says he loves her. He goes on to report that she is threatening to leave the relationship if he does not "take the next step." He describes himself as "severely depressed and anxious" and does not know what to do. He is considering going to counseling and hopes he can get some medication to help him through this difficult time in his life.

Writing Process Notes, Case Notes, and Case Reports

Client records are a critical aspect of case management and are important for several reasons (Baird, 2014; Summers, 2016):

- They help assist counselors in conceptualizing client problems and making diagnoses.
- They help determine whether clients have made progress.
- They are important when obtaining supervision.
- They assist the counselor in remembering what the client said.
- The may be used in court to show adequate client care took place.
- They are often mandated by insurance companies and government agencies to approve the treatment being given to clients.
- They are sometimes used in assessing agency effectiveness for funding agencies.

The kinds of notes or reports you write will likely depend on the agency or institution in which you work. However, three types of notes and reports typically required at agencies and institutions include psychotherapy or process notes, case notes, and case reports.

Psychotherapy or Process Notes

Psychotherapy notes, often called *process notes*, are relatively short notes written by all counselors to highlight important points and summarize every meeting a client has with the counselor. These notes are used to jog the memory of the counselor the next time he or she meets with the client. With some counselors having dozens of clients, process notes are useful and often essential.

Under the *privacy rule* of the Health Insurance Privacy and Portability Act (HIPAA), psychotherapy notes should not be viewed by an unauthorized person, and in the case of these kind of notes, clients have limited or no access to them (American Psychological Association, 2013; U.S. Department of Health and Human Services, 2017). The actual definition from HIPPA is as follows:

> … notes recorded (in any medium) by a health care provider who is a mental health professional documenting or analyzing the contents of conversation during a private counseling session or a group, joint, or family counseling session and that are separated from the rest of the individual's medical record. Psychotherapy notes excludes medication prescription and monitoring, counseling session start and stop times, the modalities and frequencies of treatment furnished, results of clinical tests, and any summary of the following items: diagnosis, functional status, the treatment plan, symptoms, prognosis, and progress to date. (Electronic Code of Federal Regulations, 2018, Section §164.501 Definitions)

Case Notes, Case Reports, Psychological Reports

Although the terms *case notes* and *case reports* are often used interchangeably, some view case reports as more involved and longer than case notes. Both case notes and case reports can include a wide variety of ways of summarizing client information. Some examples include the intake interview, highlights of a client's goals and objectives, periodic summaries of clients' progress, termination summaries, specialized reports for the courts or other agencies, transfer summaries, broad-based psychological reports, and more. In contrast to process notes, clients almost always have the right to access case notes and case reports.

Today, counselors often use sophisticated software to assist in writing case notes and case reports. Whether using such software or writing the report on your own, the minimum information found in such notes or reports usually includes the name of the client, the date, major facts noted during contact, progress made toward achieving client goals, and the counselor's signature. More involved reports may include demographic information (e.g., date of birth, address, phone number, date of interview, e-mail address), reason for report, family background, other pertinent background information (e.g., health information, vocational history, history of adjustment issues/emotional problems/mental illness), mental status, assessment results, diagnosis, and a summary, conclusions, and recommendations section (see example of a report in Appendix D).

Any written information about a client needs to be relatively objective and, as much as possible, based on observable behavior, not opinion. Remember that whatever a counselor writes could be subpoenaed by the courts, and the counselor could be held liable for his or her statements. Therefore, writing from an objective, dispassionate point of view is essential when keeping case notes. Generally, the third person point of view should be used when referring to the client. For example, it would be better to say "Family information was gathered from Jim" than "I collected family information from Jim." Any subjective information gathered from the client should be noted as such. To assist in this, begin subjective statements with phrases such as "It seems that ... ," "Jim noted that ... ," "It appears that ... ," "Jim reported that ... ," "Claire related that ... ," and "Claire recounted that ..."

When writing case notes, counselors should not be biased, portray sexist attitudes, use significant amounts of psychological jargon, or make statements expressing their own values or opinions (unless the counselor's opinions are called for, as when a court is asking for it or the counselor is making a diagnosis). Also, counselors should write the case notes or case reports so that other mental health professionals can readily understand them.

Soap Notes

One approach to writing case notes that has gained popularity over the years is called *SOAP notes* (Woodside & McClam, 2018). These notes focus on the client's **S**ubjective understanding of what the client has experienced, the counselor's **O**bjective description of what he or she understands the client's situation to be, the counselor's **A**ssessment of the client's situation, and a description of the treatment **P**lan. Using SOAP notes, Table 7.1 gives an example of how such a method is used with a depressed client. These notes are focused and easy to keep, and one can see progress over time.

Whereas SOAP notes tend to be shorter summaries of what is going on in the client's life and in counseling, a psychological report, as the one in Appendix D, is a more involved assessment of the client's life. Try writing your own psychological report using the directions in Experiential Exercise 7.5.

TABLE 7.1   SOAP Notes/Reports

Subjective: Description by client of her experiences in the world

The client describes periodic depressive episodes and notes that she feels sad much of the time and "mopes around" her house. Her sadness, she states, has been pervasive in her world, and she reports having difficulty relating to others. She notes that she has difficulty starting and completing tasks and is concerned that she is not properly parenting her children.

Objective: Description by counselor of client behaviors

The client looked dishevelled when she came to the session. She had difficulty talking and sobbed periodically during the session. The client was given a Beck Depression Inventory, which she scored a 35 on. This indicates severe depression. Behaviors described also indicate depression, including lack of sleep, loss of weight, and inability to get tasks done. This has resulted, on multiple occasions, in her children going to school without lunch and without clean clothes. Depression started after the death of her mother, which occurred approximately 8 months ago.

Assessment: Summary of counselor's thinking with evidence of assessment of client

The client describes serious depression that seems congruent with a diagnosis of major depressive disorder of DSM-5. This diagnosis is consistent with her symptoms of sadness, lack of motivation, difficulty sleeping and eating, not completing tasks, and difficulty relating to others. Behaviors and test results indicate ongoing depression.

Plan: Description of treatment plan by counselor

The treatment plan includes ongoing grief counseling regarding the death of her mother. This should start with rapport building and empathy but soon lead to defining goals so that she can attend to important issues in her life, such as attending to her children. Psychiatric consultation for possible antidepressant medication is planned within the next week. Monitoring of medication will occur during scheduled counseling sessions.

Confidentiality of Records

Today, information found in client records is protected by the HIPPA privacy rule, which sets limits and conditions on the release of information without the client's authorization (American Psychological Association, 2013; U.S. Department of Health and Human Services, 2017). However, there are some exceptions, such as when the counselor is legally liable or required to release such information by law. This *may* occur in some of the following situations: (a) when the counselor is consulting with a professional or undergoing supervision for the benefit the client, (b) in certain cases of mandatory reporting (e.g., child or spousal abuse), (c) if the client is in danger of harming self or others, (d) if the court subpoenas a client's records and the counselor is not protected by *privileged communication* (see Chapter 10), (e) if a client gives permission, in writing, to share information with others, and (f) when the counselor releases certain information to health insurance companies or funding sources that are underwriting counseling services.

In addition to protecting the privacy of client records, HIPAA gives clients rights to their health information in most instances (Remley & Herlihy, 2016). Similarly, the Freedom of Information Act of 1974 allows individuals access to records maintained by a federal agency that contain personal information about the individual (U.S. Department of Justice, 2014). Also, the Family Education Rights and Privacy Act (FERPA) assures individuals the right to access their own, and their children's, educational records (U.S. Department of Education, 2018).

On a more practical level, a client rarely asks to see his or her records. Nevertheless, if a client did make such a request, I would first attempt to talk with the client about what is in the records and try to understand why he or she wants to view the records. Sometimes a client's request to see his or her records says more about progress (or lack of progress) in counseling than a real desire to see the records. If, after talking with

Writing a Psychological Report

Using the guidelines that follow, interview a student and subsequently write a case report. When it is complete, share it with others in small groups to gain feedback or hand it in to your instructor, who will review it and give you feedback. Use Appendix D as a model.

Possible Categories for Psychological Report

1. Demographic information (e.g., date of birth, address, phone number, date of interview)
2. Reason for report
3. Family background
4. Other pertinent background information (e.g., health information, vocational history, history of adjustment issues/emotional problems/mental illness)
5. Mental status
6. Assessment results, if any
7. Diagnosis
8. Summary and conclusions
9. Recommendations
10. Signature

the client, he or she still wants to see the records, I might suggest that I write a summary of the records. If this is still unsatisfactory, it is generally the client's legal right to have access to his or her records, and I will give the client a copy of them. Finally, except in certain instances, custodial parents generally have the right to view records of their children (C. Borstein, attorney, personal communication, February 20, 2018). The ACA (2104) ethics code parallels clients' right to access their records when it says the following:

> Counselors provide reasonable access to records and copies of records when requested by competent clients. Counselors limit the access of clients to their records, or portions of their records, only when there is compelling evidence that such access would cause harm to the client. Counselors document the request of clients and the rationale for withholding some or all of the records in the files of clients. (Section B.6.e., Client Access)

> and

> When clients request access to their records, counselors provide assistance and consultation in interpreting counseling records. (Section B.6.f., Assistance with Records)

Ensuring Security of Records

> Counselors ensure that records and documentation kept in any medium are secure and that only authorized persons have access to them. (ACA, 2014, Section B.6.b, Confidentiality of Records and Documentation)

Client records need to be kept in secure places, such as locked file cabinets and password-secured computers. Any records sent electronically need to be encrypted and be HIPAA compliant. Under the *HIPPA security rule*, there must be administrative, physical, and technical safeguards in place:

> *Administrative safeguards.* Examples include having a process in place to identify risks, designating a security official, implementing a process to authorize access to information only when appropriate, providing training and supervision to workforce members, and performing periodic assessments of security policies and procedures.

> *Physical safeguards.* Examples include implementing processes and procedures to limit unauthorized access to facilities, workstations, and devices.

> *Technical safeguards.* Examples include technical policies and procedures to control access, to ensure data integrity, and to safeguard electronic transmission over a network. (Privacy Rights Clearinghouse, 2018, Section 3.c)

Clearly, counselors today need to be aware of the technological safeguards that should be put into place at the workplace, especially if they are independent practitioners. In addition, clerical help needs to understand the importance of confidentiality when working with records. In fact, many agencies have clerical staff sign statements, often legally binding, acknowledging that they understand the importance of the confidentiality of records and that they will keep all correspondences and information confidential (see Reflection Exercise 7.3).

REFLECTION EXERCISE 7.3

How Secure Are Records?

Unfortunately, counselors sometimes forget how easily client records can be misplaced or the information in them made too readily available to the public. The following true stories highlight the ways information in records can be mishandled and stress the importance of keeping records secure and confidential.

1. When working as an outpatient therapist at a mental health center, a client appropriated his paper records that had been left "lying around." Because the records were written in "psychologese," using diagnostic language, the client was understandably quite upset by what he found. He would periodically call emergency services and read his records over the phone to the emergency worker while making fun of the language used in the records.

2. While taking a class in my doctoral program, we were reviewing an intellectual test assessment of an adolescent that had been completed a number of years earlier. Suddenly, one of the students in the class yelled out, "That's me!" Apparently, although there was no identifying name on the report, he recognized it as describing him (he had been given a copy of the report previously).

REFLECTION EXERCISE 7.3—CONTINUED

3. In 2014, 4.5 million medical records, including mental health records, were hacked from Community Health Systems (CHS; Pagliery, 2014). Although CHS thought they had a secure system, they found out otherwise, and due to HIPAA, individuals could now sue CHS for breach of information.

Besides the obvious liability issues of these true scenarios, these examples show the importance of ensuring administrative, physical, and technical safeguards when securing client records.

Documentation of Contact Hours

Documentation of contact time and what occurred with clients during their counseling sessions has become increasingly important as counselors have had to respond to requirements set forth by insurance companies as well as local, state, and federal funding agencies (Summers, 2016). Every setting deals with documentation of client hours differently, and the resulting documentation is generally based on the following:

1. The kinds of issues and goals clients tend to work on in the setting
2. The expectation of the setting for the number and length of sessions
3. The expectations of the setting for the kind of case notes or records that are needed
4. Client expectations about how often and how long they will be meeting
5. The kind of case notes ethically and legally needed (e.g., process notes, case notes, SOAP notes, etc.)
6. The expectations of what will happen if a client meeting is cancelled or extended
7. The expectations of funding agencies (e.g., insurance companies, state regulatory commissions, state boards of education, etc.)
8. Laws regarding the amount of time the counselor should meet with clients

Today, most agencies and schools have some mechanism for recording client meeting times with counselors and how those meeting times are documented. As you consider the setting in which you want to work, think about the kinds of documentation that might be needed (see Experiential Exercise 7.6).

Termination and Making Referrals

Clients are terminated or referred to other professionals for numerous reasons, and this process should be as seamless as possible (Summers, 2016; Woodside & McClam, 2018). Some reasons for client termination or referral include being referred as a part of the treatment plan because the professional is leaving the agency, the professional has died, the professional feels incompetent to work with the client, and the client has reached his or her goals and is ready to move on to another form of treatment.

The ACA (2014) Code of Ethics underscores the importance of appropriate termination or referral when working with clients. The following offers situations when plans for client referral or termination should, or should not, be made.

Ways of Documenting Hours

Form groups of four or five students based on the kind of setting where you would like to work. After forming your groups, spend some time either consulting with an agency or searching the Internet for examples of the following (this assignment might take a few days):

1. The expectations regarding how often and how long clients will meet with their counselors
2. How client contact hours are documented
3. The kinds of case notes that are expected and how they are documented
4. Laws or regulations that might dictate how documentation occurs
5. How payment occurs as a result of documentation
6. What happens regarding payment if a meeting is cancelled

After your group has gathered this information, share what you found in class. Consider the different kinds of documentation that are needed as you hear from students who are interested in working in different settings than your own.

- If the counselor lacks the competence to be of "professional assistance," the client should be referred.
- When it has become clear that the client is no longer likely benefitting from counseling, the client should be referred or terminated.
- When the counselor is on vacation or ill or after the client has been terminated from counseling, plans for clients to see other counselors should be in place.
- Should a counselor die, become incapacitated, retire, or terminate practice, a plan for a client to see other counselors should have been made.
- Counselors should *not* refer a client due to values differences (e.g., political beliefs, attitudes about sexuality, etc.). Instead, counselors should respect differences and seek assistance in working with clients who have different values than themselves.

If a counselor is to make a referral, he or she should do the following:

1. Discuss the reason for making the referral with the client and obtain his or her approval.
2. Obtain, in writing, permission to discuss the client with another professional. Any information about the client (even just the client's name) should not be discussed without such permission.
3. Monitor the client's transition to the other professional to ensure appropriate continued care.
4. Assure that confidentiality of client information is maintained in the referral process (see Experiential Exercise 7.7).

EXPERIENTIAL EXERCISE 7.7

Making Referrals

Find a fellow student and have one role-play a counselor while the other role-plays a client. Choose one of the aforementioned reasons why a counselor might refer a client and role-play a situation in which such a referral is to take place. Reflect on how it feels to make a referral of a client. Share your feelings in small groups or with the class.

Conducting Follow-Up

Follow-up, another important function of case management, can be completed by a phone call, by a letter, by an elaborate survey of the client, or in other ways. It can be done a few days to a few weeks after the relationship has ended and serves many purposes (Summers, 2016). Follow-up may be required by some funding agencies to ensure that services have been adequate (how many times have you received a follow-up survey recently?). Some of the reasons for the importance of follow-up include the following:

1. It functions as a check to see whether clients would like to return for counseling or be referred to a different counselor.
2. It allows the counselor to assess whether change has been maintained.
3. It gives the counselor the opportunity to determine which counseling techniques have been most successful.
4. It offers an opportunity to reinforce client change.
5. It allows the counselor to evaluate services provided to the client.

Follow-up is one method to conduct program evaluation and ensure excellence in services being rendered. These days, follow-up is a necessary and often critical aspect of counseling services.

Practicing Time Management

With ever-increasing caseloads and demands placed on counselors, time management has become crucial to avoid burnout, compassion fatigue, and vicarious traumatization (Woodside & McClam, 2018). *Time management* strategies serve several purposes, including helping counselors ensure that all clients are seen within a reasonable period of time and assisting professionals in remembering meetings, appointment times, and other obligations. Today, there are a number of time management systems. Although this text will not delve into these different systems, suffice it to say that addressing time management concerns is paramount in today's world.

Summary

This chapter reviewed 11 important areas of case management (or the overall process involved in maintaining the optimal level of functioning for clients), including providing informed consent and professional disclosure statements, conducting assessment for treatment planning, developing client goals, monitoring psychotropic medications, writing notes and reports, confidentiality of records, ensuring security of client records, documenting client contact hours, termination and making referrals, conducting follow-up, and practicing time management.

We started by highlighting the importance of obtaining informed consent, in writing, from clients. This generally occurs by offering a client a professional disclosure statement that spells out critical areas related to the nature and limits of the helping relationship. The statement is subsequently signed to acknowledge the services the client is about to receive. We identified 20 important areas to cover when writing a professional disclosure statement.

Moving on to assessment for treatment planning, we noted that in many settings, counselors are asked to conduct a clinical interview, administer and interpret tests, and use informal assessment procedures to further understand the client. We talked about the fact that the intake interview is often the first important clinical interview the client undergoes and that the result of this interview is sometimes a psychological report. We highlighted the areas important in writing a psychological report and spent a particular amount of time examining the mental status exam, one aspect of the report that describes the client's appearance and behavior, affect, thought components, and cognition. We pointed out that assessment procedures are used in the case conceptualization process, which helps the counselor understand client themes and identify causation of problems and is used in treatment planning (to be discussed more in Chapter 8).

Relative to testing, we talked about the importance of test worthiness, which means a test is valid, reliable, cross-culturally fair, and practical. We noted that it was important to know state laws and one's own level of competence to give certain tests. Going on to informal assessment, we noted that although these assessment procedures are less valid or reliable than tests, they are sometimes useful, as they can be a quick measure of various areas of client concerns.

Moving on to a discussion on goal development, we identified eight rules of thumb in developing goals, including the idea that they should be an outgrowth of the assessment process, collaborative, attainable, monitored, changeable, developed anew when former ones are reached, affirmed when reached, and no longer developed when the client has reached an end point to counseling.

We next moved on to a discussion about monitoring client use of psychotropic medications. We pointed out advantages and disadvantages of such use and gave a quick overview of the five groups of psychotropic medications: antipsychotics, mood-stabilizing drugs, antidepressants, antianxiety agents, and stimulants. We noted that since counselors will be working with clients who are taking an array of psychotropic medications, they should know the basics of such drugs, should be aware of when such drugs are not being effective, and should know when to consult with and refer to medical professionals regarding psychotropic medication.

Knowing how to write process notes, case notes, and case reports was next discussed. We first identified a number of reasons why case notes and case reports are important. We then defined psychotherapy notes, often called process notes, as notes that are used to jog the memory of the counselor for the next time he or she sees the client. We noted that the privacy rule of HIPPA underscores the notion that others should not see client records and that in the case of psychotherapy or process notes, clients have limited access to them. We then distinguished case notes from case reports and noted that case reports tend to be a bit more involved. We also noted that psychological reports are even more involved and referred to the example of a psychological report in Appendix D. We noted that written information about clients should be relatively objective and should not portray bias, sexism, psychological jargon, or an undue amount of counselor opinion. We went on to describe SOAP notes: **S**ubjective understanding of what the client has experienced, the counselor's **O**bjective description of what he or she understands the client's situation to be, the counselor's **A**ssessment of the client's situation, and a description of the treatment **P**lan. An example of SOAP notes was given.

A discussion of confidentiality of records highlighted six areas where client records may be released without client permission. These included (a) consultation or supervision, (b) mandatory reporting, (c) if the client is in danger of harming self or others, (d) some cases of court subpoenas when the counselor is not protected by privileged communication, (e) if a client gives permission, in writing, to share information, and (f) when certain information is given to health insurance companies or funding sources that are underwriting counseling services. We noted that clients generally have the right to their health records and educational records as underscored by HIPAA, the Freedom of Information Act, and FERPA.

When talking about the security of client records, we noted that the HIPPA privacy rule suggests administrative, physical, and technical safeguards be in place. We also noted that records should be encrypted, file cabinets locked, and computer password-secured.

Relative to the documentation of contact hours, we identified eight items to consider, based on the setting in which the counselor works, when documenting client contact hours. These included such things as the kinds of issues and goals of clients, the expectation of the setting, ethical concerns, legal concerns, and more.

When discussing termination and referral, we highlighted a number of situations in which plans for client referral or termination should be in place, including when the counselor is not competent, when the client is no longer benefiting, if the counselor will be away from work for an extended period of time, and when the counselor dies. We noted that counselors should not refer due to value differences between them and their clients. We identified some things to consider when making a referral, such as gaining client approval, gaining permission from clients to talk with other professionals, monitoring the transition, and assuring confidentiality.

We talked about the importance of conducting follow-up in terms of checking to see if clients would like to come back, being able to assess whether change has been maintained, determining what techniques worked best, being able to reinforce change, and evaluating services that had been given to clients. We concluded the chapter with a brief discussion of practicing time management to avoid burnout, compassion fatigue, and vicarious traumatization.

Key Words and Terms

amphetamines

antianxiety agents

antidepressants

antipsychotic drugs

assessment for treatment planning

atypical antidepressants

benzodiazepines

case notes

case reports

client contact hour

clinical interview

conducting follow-up

confidentiality of records

documentation of contact hours

DSM-5

ensuring security of records

Family Education Rights and Privacy Act

FERPA

Freedom of Information Act of 1974

goal development

Health Insurance Portability and Accountability Act

HIPAA

HIPAA privacy rule

informed consent

intake interview

lithium

mental status exam

monitoring psychotropic medications

monoamine oxidase inhibitors

mood-stabilizing drugs

neuroleptics

nonbenzodiazepines

paradoxical effect

privacy rule

privileged communication

process notes

professional disclosure statement

progress toward client goals

psychological report

psychopharmacology

psychotherapy notes

psychotropic medications

selective serotonin reuptake inhibitors

SOAP notes

stimulants

termination and making referrals

test worthiness

testing

time management

CHAPTER 8

Case Conceptualization, Diagnosis, and Treatment Planning*

Learning Objectives

1. To define case conceptualization
2. To understand the difference between theory-specific and non-theory-specific case conceptualization
3. To describe the biological, psychological, and sociocultural domains of the biopsychosocial assessment model of case conceptualization and to demonstrate how it is implemented
4. To show how themes and ideas about causation are generated from case conceptualization
5. To provide a brief overview of the Diagnostic and Statistical Manual, 5th edition
6. To demonstrate how the case conceptualization process can be used to help determine an accurate diagnosis
7. To define the treatment planning process and show how it is developed through the case conceptualization process
8. To briefly define four schools of counseling and psychotherapy, identify well-known theories within those schools, and demonstrate how a theoretical lens can be applied to the case conceptualization process

Introduction

This chapter will examine how we come to understand our clients, make diagnoses, and formulate treatment plans. First, we will examine the *case conceptualization* process, which has to do with the methods we use to understand the client. Then we will examine how a *diagnosis* is the natural outgrowth of this process. Finally, we will look at how *treatment planning* flows out of our case conceptualization process and diagnostic formulation. Finally, we will provide a brief overview of how theory can inform our treatment plans (see Figure 8.1).

Case Conceptualization

Sometimes called *case formulation, case conceptualization* is the process the counselor uses to understand the client's situation. This process can help develop a diagnosis and form treatment strategies that can lead to successful outcomes. Zubernis & Snyder (2016) define case conceptualization in the following manner:

---

* This chapter was written by Carolyn Cullen and Ed Neukrug.

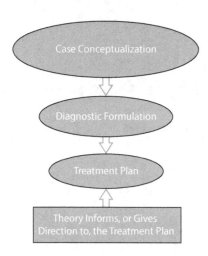

FIGURE 8.1 Case conceptualization, diagnosis, and treatment planning

Case conceptualization is the process counselors use to understand the client's symptoms, thoughts, emotions, behaviors, and personality constructs and to make sense of the client's presenting problems. Effective case conceptualization entails thinking integratively, developing and testing hypotheses, and planning treatment based on these hypotheses. (p. 41)

In order to develop a working understanding of the client's issues, the counselor must gather data, integrate it, and formulate some general ideas from which to come up with a diagnosis and develop interventions (Sperry & Sperry, 2012). This is often easier said than done and is a process that matures after years of training and reflective practice. As a new counselor, it is important to start thinking about the multiple aspects of a client's life and how knowledge of the client can help one develop strategies for change. Case conceptualization helps us move in that direction.

Theory-Specific or Non-Theory-Specific Case Conceptualization

One problem with understanding and implementing case conceptualization is the multiple models of case conceptualization that have been developed over the years and the different mechanisms they use for implementing its practice (Ridley & Jeffrey, 2017a).

> For a variety of reasons, clinicians often fall short in accomplishing [case conceptualization]. … One reason for their shortcomings is the state of crisis in formulating clinical pictures of clients, due significantly to confusing and field-wide disagreements on the theory and method of the process. … (Ridley, Jeffrey, & Roberson, 2017, 359)

Some models suggest that the case conceptualization should be completed through the lens of a counselor's particular theoretical perspective. For instance, Berman (2015) offers a case conceptualization process for no less than 10 different theoretical orientations (e.g., psychodynamic, behavioral, cognitive, emotion-focused, constructivist, and more). This approach assumes that the

> … case conceptualization approach to psychotherapy initially involves the clinician deciding on a theoretical perspective and developing a hypothesis about the factors that cause and maintain the problems to then guide a personally meaningful intervention, test the hypothesis, and revise the intervention accordingly. (Bucci, French & Berry, 2016, p. 517)

However, others note that theory-specific case conceptualization models can be particularly trying for new counselors, who are still struggling to understand their own theoretical orientations.

> Theory-specific models may also be especially difficult for new trainees, who sometimes are admonished to quickly identify a single therapeutic orientation that works for them and adhere to it unwaveringly. … (Ridley & Jeffrey, 2017b, p. 381)

One option for beginning counselors is to practice non-theory-specific case conceptualization and then apply basic counseling skills with a client when addressing the treatment plan process. This eliminates the initial need for a theoretical perspective, which many beginning counselors have not yet fully embraced. As the beginning counselor increasingly learns theory, he or she can slowly begin to view treatment goals through the particular theoretical lens he or she is embracing. In this chapter, we will present the biopsychosocial assessment model of case conceptualization. This theory-free model examines three important domains for understanding the client and developing treatment plans. However, as counselors increasingly understand and embrace theories or integrative theoretical approaches, they can start to view the knowledge gained from the biopsychosocial assessment model through their theoretical prisms.

The Biopsychosocial Assessment Model

Introduced during the 1970s to help the medical profession move to a more holistic way of understanding the person, the *biopsychosocial assessment model* today is seen a comprehensive and integrative way of approaching case conceptualization and has been adopted by the mental health professions (Meyer & Melchert, 2011). The model looks at individual client issues but also examines broader systemic concerns as well as the interplay among the three domains it gathers information about. The biopsychosocial assessment model is similar to other contemporary models of case conceptualization that stress in-depth inquiry into the individual as well as social environment issues (Ellis, Hutman, & Deihl, 2013; Zubernis, Snyder, & Neale-McFall, 2017).

As the name implies, the biopsychosocial assessment model calls for looking at three domains in the client's life: biological, psychological, and sociocultural. In a study of three different mental health clinics, Meyer and Melchert (2011) found that most therapists gather biopsychosocial assessment information routinely in the intake process. However, they also found that therapists do not always collect information in a thorough and comprehensive way. Within the biological, psychological, and sociocultural domains, Meyer and Melchert created several components based on standards put forth by researchers as well as the Joint Commission for the Accreditation of Health Care Organizations and the American Psychiatric Association. The following identifies some of the items that are looked at within each domain. Use of the clinical interview, testing, and informal assessment (already discussed in Chapter 7) can be helpful in gathering the information from the domains.

Biological Domain	Psychological Domain	Sociocultural Domain
General medical history	History of present illness	Employment
Medications	Individual psychiatric history	Legal issues
Childhood health history	Suicidal or homicidal ideation	Relationships
	Substance use history	Current living situation
	Childhood abuse history	Education history
	Mental status examination	Religion/spirituality
	Psychological traumas	Family history
	Personality styles and characteristics	Multicultural issues
	Behavioral observations	Financial resources
	Individual developmental history	Military history
		Interests/hobbies

When using the biopsychosocial assessment model, one explores the various elements of each of the domains and examines how they might interact with one another. Ultimately, themes, ideas about causation, and diagnoses will arise after such an in-depth look at the domains. Ideally, a treatment plan should emerge after examining the themes, causations, and diagnoses. After one has gained expertise in a theoretical orientation, he or she can apply that lens to the treatment plan (see Figure 8.2).

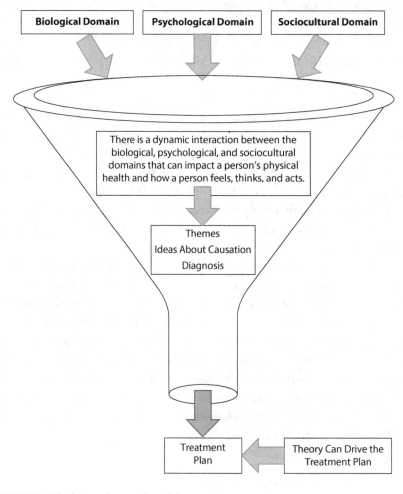

FIGURE 8.2   The biopsychosocial model

Using the Biopsychosocial Model With a Client

If you remember from previous chapters, Jake Miller is a 34-year-old married male who sought out counseling due to extreme anxiety, concerns about his children's well-being, and problems in his marriage. Jake and his family are described in some amount of detail in Appendices B and D. Read the two appendices to become reacquainted with Jake, and let's see how we would use the biopsychosocial model to understand him.

Biological domain:

- *General medical history*: No significant medical history. Currently, ongoing headaches, feeling tired much of the time, trouble sleeping, loss of weight.
- *Medications:* Currently on no medications. Took Luvox at age 23 for anxiety and mild depression after meeting Angela, who was later to become his wife.
- *Childhood health history.* No significant medical history.

Psychological domain:

- *History of present illness:* Starting about 10 weeks ago, Jake began to have extreme anxiety, problems with sleep, headaches, loss of appetite, and problems with his marriage and children. This started when his children, Luke, age 10, and Celia, age 7, accidentally knocked his car out of park and it rolled into the street.
- *Individual counseling/psychiatric history:* Saw counselors twice. First when he was 13, 3 years after an incident with his twin sister, Justine, when they moved their father's car as a "joke" but it was hit by a semi, which caused his sister to have serious cognitive impairment. Jake felt guilt and anxiety over the incident and states counseling helped. Jake was in counseling again at age 23 soon after meeting Angela, who was later to become his wife.
- *Suicidal or homicidal ideation:* None reported.
- *Substance use history.* None reported. States he is a social drinker.
- *Childhood abuse history:* None reported.
- *Mental status examination (MSE):* Jake was causally and neatly dressed for the interview. He made appropriate eye contact and was oriented to time, place, and person. He often fidgeted in his chair, moving his body back and forth during the interview. He reports feeling "anxious most of the time" and notes that he still feels guilty about the car accident with his twin sister, Justine, at the age of 10. He states he has been feeling anxious for the past 10 weeks since an incident when his children knocked his car out of park and it rolled down the driveway. He reports waking up multiple times at night just to check that everyone is in bed and safe. He notes that he has lost some weight—mostly, he believes, due to his disinterest in food as a result of his anxiety. He reports feeling tired much of the time and has ongoing headaches. At one point during the interview, when talking about the accident with Justine, he became tearful, saying, "I shouldn't have listened to her—it's all my fault." Jake's thoughts were clear, memory good, and he is above average intellectually. He has good insight and fair judgment. He reports no suicidal or homicidal ideation.
- *Psychological traumas:* At age 10, Jake was involved in an incident with his twin sister when they moved their father's car as a "joke" but it was hit by a semi, which caused Justine to have serious cognitive impairment. Jake seems to still carry evidence of this traumatic event, as noted by his current anxiety, ongoing feelings of guilt about his sister's current level of functioning, and his controlling behavior, which involves trying to ensure safety in his home with his children and wife.
- *Personality styles and characteristics*: Jake currently is showing some obsessive behaviors related to worry regarding the safety of his children and his wife. This involves asking his wife to homeschool the children, yelling at the children whenever they are involved in what he describes as "rough play," waking up at night to ensure all the doors are locked, and ensuring that the children are within visual distance of him so they won't be harmed.

- *Behavioral observations:* Jake shows visual signs of anxiety through rapid speech, yelling at the children, constantly checking on the children, and getting up at night, sometimes multiple times, to ensure the doors are locked.
- *Individual developmental history:* Jake had a normal developmental history until the age of 10, when he and his twin sister, Justine, were involved in an incident when they rolled their father's car into the street and it was hit by a semi. His sister sustained severe cognitive impairment, and this traumatic moment in his life seemed to leave him with guilt, depression, and anxiety that periodically becomes worse at stressful times in his life.

Sociocultural domain
- *Employment:* Employed as a mechanical engineer for 8 years.
- *Legal Issues:* None reported.
- *Relationships:* Describes relationship with his wife and children as currently strained since an incident in which his children accidentally rolled his car into the street. He states he is easily angered by his children, is vigilant about their safety, and has been controlling with his wife, insisting that she homeschool the children to ensure their safety. He describes his relationship with his parents and his wife's parents as "good," although notes that since the car incident when he was a child (see "psychological trauma"), his family relationship with his parents still "haunts each of them." Jake notes that his sexual relationship with his wife had been "normal" until his recent concerns regarding safety. He states they are "rarely intimate now."
- *Current living situation:* Lives with wife, Angela, and children Luke (10) and Celia (7).
- *Education history:* Attended public school until college. Jake obtained his bachelor's and master's degrees in mechanical engineering from University of Kansas. He states he did well in school, particularly in math. However, he also noted that he always "wrote poorly" and thought he was "dyslexic." He was never tested for a learning disability.
- *Religion/spirituality:* Jake states he is agnostic and that his wife, Angela, is Episcopalian, although he notes that "she is not very religious" and the family rarely, if ever, goes to church. He notes that he'd rather "believe in science" than some "unknown God."
- *Family history:* Jake has a twin sister, Justine, who sustained serious cognitive impairment when the two of them were 10 years old and they were "playing" in their father's car and tried to move it, and it was hit by a semi. Jake continues to blame himself for the accident and states the accident continues to haunt his family. Jake met his wife, Angela, in graduate school and has been married 10 years. He describes his family as having been loving and healthy until a recent incident when his son, Luke, knocked Jake's car out of park and it moved into the street. Jake's daughter, Celia, was also in the car. Jake states that since that time he has had a resurgence of anxiety and has wanted to control what everyone is doing in the family—mostly to ensure their safety. He notes that when the children are home, he constantly wants to make sure they are within visual distance. He also reports making sure that all the doors are locked at night, even waking up multiple times during the middle of the night to check. He states that whenever the children play "rough" games, he goes into a rage, yelling at them to stop it. He also notes that he has asked Angela to homeschool the children, as he is concerned that something "bad" will happen at school. This, he reports, has led to problems in his marriage. Meanwhile, Jakes states that Luke and Celia have been symptomatic

since the accident, with Luke "not listening to anyone" and Celia having ongoing stomachaches that cause her, at times, to come home from school.

- *Multicultural issues:* Jake's wife, Angela, is biracial. Her paternal grandparents are Nigerian, although her father is American and a college English professor. Angela's mother, a social worker, is White. Angela is her parents' biological daughter, and her parents also adopted two African American children: Marcus, who is 31, gay, and in a relationship, and Lillian, who is 29 and married. Jake describes his children as biracial. He reports no major concerns regarding his children and seems accepting of his brother-in-law's sexual orientation. He notes that Angela has seen herself as White while visiting Nigeria and Black in the United States. He also states that she had a "caretaking" personality growing up, especially relative to her sister, who had a congenital hip deformity. He reports that she struggles with her identity and that causes "issues" in their relationship from time to time, noting that sometimes she is "my caretaker" and other times she simply wants to be independent.
- *Financial resources:* Jake describes himself as "middle class" and reports no financial difficulties.
- *Military history:* None
- *Interests/hobbies:* Jake has recently become involved with a national association that advocates for child-safe automobiles. Jake relates this involvement back to the traumatic event he had as a child, and he believes his skill as a mechanical engineer can be useful in the development of safer cars.

Themes and Ideas About Causation With Jake

Now that we have gathered all the information from the biopsychosocial model, we can begin to come up with *themes, ideas about causation,* and a *diagnosis* for Jake. These can all be useful in our treatment planning. For instance, when reviewing the biopsychosocial information, here are some of my thoughts about Jake:

1. Jake is struggling with anxiety that seems to be related to an earlier incident in life.
2. Jake's anxiety is negatively impacting his relationships with his children and his wife.
3. Jake's early incident with his sister, Justine, was traumatic and has shaped his life in many ways.
4. Jake may be struggling with PTSD from the original accident.
5. Jake seems to continue to carry guilt from the original accident with his twin sister, Justine.
6. Jake's need to control his children and wife is negatively impacting his family.
7. Jake's family of origin still seems to be struggling with the impact of the car accident and resulting cognitive impairment sustained by Justine.
8. Jake has a number of current medical issues that seem to be related to his anxiety and worry (headaches, trouble sleeping, weight loss).
9. Jake had some success with the use of Luvox for similar symptoms when he was 23 years old.
10. Jake's children are symptomatic, with Luke not listening and Celia having ongoing stomachaches. These symptoms may be related to Jake's worry and anxiety.
11. Jake seems to have good insight, but judgement may be interfering with his relationships.
12. Jake's recent controlling attitudes may be feeding into Angela's issues relative to her own identity and her need to not be in a caretaking role.

All these are useful in determining a diagnosis and developing a treatment plan. Let's turn to an understanding of how to make a diagnosis, eventually come back to a diagnosis for Jake, and then move on to understanding how to develop our treatment plan.

Diagnosis and the DSM-5

Derived from the Greek words *dia* (apart) and *gnosis* (to perceive or to know), the term "diagnosis" refers to the process of making an assessment of an individual from an outside or objective viewpoint. An important step in treatment planning, a diagnosis is a natural outgrowth of the assessment process, which can provide valuable information for clients and counselors. Although attempts to classify mental disorders have been made since the turn of the century, it was not until 1952 that the American Psychiatric Association (APA) published the first comprehensive mental health diagnosis system called the *Diagnostic and Statistical Manual of Mental Disorders* (DSM-I; Blashfield, Keeley, Flanagan, & Miles, 2014). DSM-I was 132 pages long, had 128 diagnostic categories, and cost $3.00! In 2013, the fifth edition of the DSM was published, which is 947 pages long and contains 541 diagnoses within 21 diagnostic categories (APA, 2013; see Appendix F). The DSM-5 is the most widespread and accepted diagnostic classification system of mental disorders and has become increasingly important for a number of reasons (Neukrug & Fawcett, 2015; Schwitzer & Rubin, 2015):

- It is a means for related mental health professionals to have a common diagnostic language with which to communicate.
- It can be helpful in conceptualizing client problems.
- It can be helpful in treatment planning.
- It helps clients and counselors understand clients' mental disorders.
- It can be helpful in deciding which medications might be an aid in a person's treatment plan.

DSM-5 is used to provide diagnostic information for insurance companies so they will reimburse counselors and other mental health professionals for treatment. With close to 20% of all Americans experiencing a mental disorder in any given year and over 30% having been in counseling (Kalkbrenner & Neukrug, 2018b; National Alliance on Mental Illness, 2018a), it's not surprising that the DSM has become a critical assessment tool. In addition to providing diagnoses for mental disorders, the DSM-5 can also assist counselors in identifying what are called *psychosocial and environmental stressors* through the use of what are called *Z codes*—a classification system for these common concerns (e.g., job loss, marital problems, homelessness, relationship issues). The mental disorder codes and the Z codes parallel the same codes offered in the *International Classification of Disease (ICD)* manual used by health care providers (e.g., doctors, nurses, etc.), albeit the DSM-5 gives more involved definitions than the ICD. In addition to listing mental disorder diagnoses and Z codes, counselors are encouraged to list medical diagnoses when they have an impact on their clients' psychological functioning. Thus, a diagnosis of an individual could look this:

F32.1	Major depression, single episode, moderate
Z56.9	Problems related to employment
Z63.0	Relationship distress with spouse
M50.020	Cervical disc disorder, unspecified level

Making and Reporting Diagnoses

Besides naming a diagnosis, a number of other factors should be identified when reporting a diagnosis. These include how to list co-occurring diagnoses; whether the diagnosis has subtypes or specifiers and its severity; provisional and informal diagnoses; and "other specified disorders" and "unspecified disorders" (Neukrug & Fawcett, 2015).

Co-occurring diagnoses: With approximately eight million Americans having *co-occurring disorders* (more than one disorder), it is important to consider their ordering (Co-Occurring Disorders, 2018). Whereas the first diagnosis is called the principal diagnosis, the secondary and tertiary diagnoses should be listed in order of clinical attention. If a disorder is due to a general medical condition, the medical condition is generally listed first, followed by the disorder, often with a note such as "due to the general medical condition."

Subtypes, specifiers, and severity. Some diagnoses have *subtypes,* and it is important to identify which type the disorder is. For example, for Adjustment Disorder, one should specify if it is with depressed mood, with anxiety, with mixed anxiety and depressed mood, with disturbance of conduct, with mixed disturbance of emotions and conduct, or unspecified. Many diagnoses have *specifiers*, which further delineate the symptoms but may not be mutually exclusive (you can often have more than one specifier). For instance, for Conduct Disorder, one should specify whether it is "with limited prosocial emotions," which means that the individual must show two or more of the following: no sense of remorse or guilt, callousness and lack of empathy, being unconcerned about performance, and shallow or deficient affect. DSM also offers the counselor the ability to rate the *severity* of some diagnoses. For example, for Major Depressive Disorder, the severity could be rated as mild, moderate, or severe based on the number and types of symptoms the person has. In summary, for subtypes, the counselor chooses just one; for specifiers, the counselor picks as many that apply; and for severity, the counselor identifies the level of seriousness of the disorder.

Provisional and informal diagnoses: When making a diagnosis, a counselor will sometimes have a strong inclination that the client will meet the criteria but does not yet have enough information to firmly justify the diagnosis. In this case, a *provisional diagnosis* can be made (e.g., Provisional Disorder: Cyclothymic Disorder). Later, if the diagnosis is shown to be correct, the provisional label can be removed. Finally, a number of informal statements are sometimes made about a diagnosis, which can help clinicians understand a client. *Rule-out* is used when there is not enough information to make a diagnosis but a specific disorder might be considered (e.g., rule out Generalized Anxiety Disorder). *Traits* are used when a person does not meet a criterion but seems to have several features of the disorder (e.g., Narcissistic Personality Disorder traits). *By history* is written when a client has a history of a disorder from another agency or mental health professional that may or may not be borne out by the counselor's current experience of the client (e.g., Major Depression, by history). Finally, *self-report* is used when a client states he or she has been diagnosed in the past with a certain disorder (e.g., alcohol dependence, by self-report).

Other specified and unspecified disorders: Sometimes a person has clinically significant impairment, but it does not seem to meet the criteria for a diagnostic category. In that case, *other specified disorder* can be used to communicate why the criteria does not fit. *Unspecified disorder* is used if a counselor does not want to, or is unable to, communicate specifics of the disorder. For example, if someone has many, but not enough, of the symptoms as those listed in DSM for a panic disorder, the diagnosis could be "Other specified Panic Disorder—due to insufficient symptoms." Otherwise, the clinician could report "Unspecified Panic Disorder."

Criticism of DSM-5

DSM-5 has its critics, including those who question some of the diagnoses, believe its categorization is dehumanizing, suggest it leads to labeling, believe it is not sufficiently scientific, claim it does not account for societal factors that impact their formulation, and believe that mental disorders are relational, not in a person (Cooper, 2017; Rubin, 2018). Despite these naysayers, the DSM continues to be widely used, and courses are often taught that focus solely on the diagnostic process (see Experiential Exercise 8.1).

EXPERIENTIAL EXERCISE 8.1

Developing a Diagnosis

By referring to a DSM-5, have a student role-play one of the diagnoses without letting the rest of the class know which diagnosis he or she is attempting to mimic. The rest of the class can sit around the student and assess the student, trying to determine which diagnosis it is. When you have come up with some good guesses, answer the following questions:

1. Were you able to come up with the correct diagnosis?
2. What skills were most helpful in determining the diagnosis?
3. Were there any Z codes that would apply to this individual's situation?
4. Were there competing diagnoses, and, if so, which do you think was primary?
5. How could this diagnosis be helpful in treatment planning?
6. Might being diagnosed in this manner cause the individual any problems?

Coming Up With a Diagnosis for Jake

Now that we have an understanding of how to use the DSM-5, we can begin to look at one or more possible diagnoses with Jake. Referring to earlier in the chapter where we came up with our list of 12 themes and ideas about causation, we can begin to come up with some tentative diagnoses. For Jake, I come up with the following:

- Adjustment Disorder, with anxiety (F43.21)
- Rule out Generalized Anxiety Disorder (F41.1)
- Rule out Post-Traumatic Stress Disorder (F43.10)
- Possible spelling learning disability (F81.81)
- Relationship distress with spouse or intimate partner (Z63.0)
- Parent-child relational problem (Z62.820)
- High expressed emotion level within family (Z63.8)

Let's take a quick look at each of these:

Adjustment Disorder, with anxiety: Since Jake's symptoms started about 10 weeks ago and appear to be a response to an "identifiable stressor" (the children knocking the car out of park), Jake's symptoms would fit the "adjustment disorder" category. Since he has classic signs of anxiety (feeling anxious, loss of weight, disinterest in food, trouble sleeping, obsessive thoughts), it seems apparent that the adjustment disorder is "with anxiety."

Rule out Generalized Anxiety Disorder: In many ways, Jake meets all the symptoms necessary for a Generalized Anxiety Disorder; however, to meet the criteria for this disorder, it must occur for at least 6 months. At this point, he does not meet that criteria. Should treatment not be successful and he continues to have the same symptoms, he might later fit this category. Hopefully, treatment will be successful!

Rule out Post-Traumatic Stress Disorder: Jake has some of the symptoms of PTSD but probably does not fit all the criteria to have this disorder. For instance, he has been exposed to a traumatic situation (the original accident with his sister). He periodically does have flashbacks to the event and upsetting memories about it. He does blame himself, has difficulty sleeping, and is hypervigilant about ensuring safety. Also, his symptoms do create distress in his life. However, he also has been able to go long periods of time with relatively little anxiety. In the end, he probably does not fit this diagnosis, although elements do exist.

Possible spelling disability: Jake notes that he always has had trouble with spelling, and it impacted that aspect of his schooling. Relative to his other strengths in school, Jake could have a potential spelling disability. This can be explored further if Jake and his counselor think it will benefit his life.

Relationship distress with spouse or intimate partner: Clearly, Jake and Angela have not been getting along since the incident with his children. Their sexual relationship has diminished, and Angela is upset at Jake's controlling behavior and his need to have the children homeschooled.

Parent-child relational problem: Jake's response to his children has been to try and control their behavior. This often results in him yelling at them. They seem to have responded to his attempts at control through Celia's psychosomatic problems (stomachaches) and by Luke not listening and exhibiting acting-out behaviors at school. They also do not respond well to Jake's commands.

High expressed emotion level within family: Jake, Angela, Luke, and Celia all seem on edge. Jake is constantly trying to control everyone to ensure safety. The children are acting out at school and at home. Angela is upset as Jake attempts to control the children and push her toward homeschooling the children. The family's emotional level is high.

Conclusion

Understanding DSM-5 is not rocket science, but it does take a bit of time to learn how to use it adequately. Use of the DSM is a natural outgrowth of the case conceptualization process and can help in treatment planning. Now that we have come up with some themes, ideas about causation, and diagnoses for Jake, let's consider the treatment planning process, which would be the next step in helping Jake feel better about himself and assisting the family in feeling better about one another.

Treatment Planning

The next phase in working with clients is developing a treatment plan that addresses the case conceptualization process and the diagnoses. The treatment plan is the map of how you are going to work with your client and often includes such things as identifying the client problems, suggesting treatment modalities, goals of counseling, and how change might be measured.

> A treatment formulation follows from the diagnostic, clinical, and cultural formulations and serves as an explicit blueprint governing treatment interventions. Rather than answering the "What happened?" or "Why did it happen" questions, the treatment formulation addresses the "What can be done about it, and how?" question. (Sperry, Carlson, Sauerheber, & Sperry, 2015, p. 5)

A Four-Step Treatment Planning Model

Some have suggested that counselors should consider *four steps to treatment planning* (Neukrug & Schwitzer, 2006; Schwitzer & Rubin, 2015): (I) *defining the problems*, (II) *developing achievable goals*, (III) *deciding on treatment modality*, and (IV) *measuring change*.

In going back to our example with Jake, let's see how we can use these four goals to address our treatment plan. For instance, in defining the problems, we can use our themes, ideas for causation, and diagnostic impressions to help determine those concerns that need to be addressed. With Jake, we find the following:

I. *Defining the problems*
    1. Jake's struggle with anxiety
    2. Jake's feelings of guilt about the accident with Justine
    3. Jake's yelling at the children and attempts to control Angela
    4. Angela's sense that she is feeling controlled by Jake
    5. Jake's lack of intimacy with Angela
    6. Jake's lack of sleep, loss of weight, and headaches
    7. Luke's "not listening to anyone"
    8. Celia's stomachaches
    9. Jake's sense that his family of origin is still "haunted" by the accident
    10. Angela's lack of clarity about her identity

After we have identified our problems, it is relatively easy to convert these into achievable goals. Let's look at the goals we might develop for Jake.

II. *Developing achievable goals*
    1. Reduce Jake's anxiety
    2. Find ways to help Jake deal with his guilt
    3. Reduction in Jake yelling at children
    4. Reduction in Jake's attempts to control Angela
    5. Reduce Celia's stomachaches
    6. Help Luke "listen" better

7. Help Angela develop a strong sense of self
8. Increase Jake's ability to sleep, help him gain weight, and help him reduce his headaches
9. Restore a level of intimacy between Jake and Angela
10. Bring a sense of normalcy back to Jake's family of origin

As achievable goals are determined for Jake, we can begin to consider what treatment modality might be used to address those goals. In Jake's case, the following modalities come to mind, although all may not be implemented at once.

III. *Deciding on treatment modalities*
   1. Individual counseling focused on a reduction of Jake's anxiety and guilt
   2. Marital counseling to restore a sense of intimacy and health to Jake and Angela's relationship
   3. Family counseling with Jake and his family of origin to talk about the incident that resulted in Justine's cognitive impairment
   4. Possible individual counseling for Angela to help her sort out her sense of identity
   5. Psychiatric consultation for possible medication adjunct to assist Jake with his anxiety

Now that we know our goals and have decided our treatment modalities, measuring change is a naturally intuitive process. What follows are some of the different types of ways I came up with to measure change with Jake and his family. Do you have any other ways that you can measure change?

IV. *Measuring change*
   1. Reduction in anxiety, as measured verbally from Jake, using a scaling instrument that assesses anxiety from session to session (1 = no anxiety, 10 = extreme anxiety) and by an assessment instrument such as the Beck Anxiety Instrument (BAI)
   2. Reduction in yelling at the children and Jake's controlling behaviors (observations by Angela and children)
   3. Increase in level of intimacy between Jake and Angela (self-reports by Jake and Angela)
   4. Self-report by Jake of reduction in guilt regarding the accident
   5. Angela reporting going to counseling for her sense of self
   6. Jake's family of origin attending short-term family counseling
   7. Over time, reduction in use of medication
   8. Better sleep, increased weight, reduction in headaches (self-report or use of journal to document change)

Writing Your Treatment Plan

There is no one mechanism for *writing your treatment plan*. Some agencies or institutions might prefer that a counselor spell out all four steps, just as we did with Jake. Others may prefer a summary of Jake's situation, followed by recommendations for treatment (see Reflective Exercise 8.1).

REFLECTIVE EXERCISE 8.1

Writing a Summary and Recommendations

The following provides a summary and a list of some possible recommendations for Jake. See if there are other items you would include in the summary or additional recommendations. Make a list of any and share them in class.

Summary and Recommendations

This 34-year-old married male sought counseling due to increased anxiety, problems with sleep, loss of appetite, headaches, and problems in his marriage and with his children. Jake suggests that many of these issues stem from a history in his family of origin when he was involved in a car accident at age 10 with his twin sister, Justine. At that time, at his sister's urging, he moved his parents' car and was accidentally struck by a semi, resulting in severe cognitive impairment for his sister. He was not injured. He reports feeling guilty and responsible for the accident. He attended counseling at age 13 for continued feelings of guilt and anxiety due to the accident. He was in counseling one other time, just prior to his marriage, for feelings of being overwhelmed and closed in.

Recently, his daughter and son were involved in an incident in which they pushed his car out of park and it moved down the driveway. Jake states that this incident caused a resurgence in his anxiety. He states that since that time he has been trying to get a handle on his anxiety by keeping everyone safe in the home. He reports asking his wife to homeschool the children (which she has said no to), and he states he is constantly trying to control the family to ensure their safety.

Jake is a fairly insightful man who is experiencing guilt, anxiety, and mild depression that appears to be related to the recent incident when his children knocked his car out of park and it rolled down the driveway. This incident is reminiscent of the car accident he had with his twin sister when he was 10 and seems to have caused a resurgence of Jake's fears and anxiety. His fears about something similar happening with his children are permeating his life, and he is having difficulty controlling the resulting anxiety. He attempts to control this anxiety by controlling others around him. This has resulted in symptoms in his children and problems in his marriage.

On a positive note, Jake has a good understanding of himself, is wanting to examine his life through counseling, and is wanting to heal his family problems. He is highly educated, bright, and hopeful about making changes in his life. The following is recommended:

- Referral to a psychiatrist for possible medication to alleviate his anxiety
- Counseling, one hour weekly, to discuss past issues related to his car accident with his sister and current problems with his family
- Possible marital counseling to relieve some of the stress in his marriage
- Possible family of origin counseling to discuss ongoing feelings about the accident with Jake's sister
- Further testing for a possible learning disability in spelling, should Jake wish to pursue

Case Conceptualization Process Through a Theoretical Lens

As you increasingly become familiar with theories of counseling, you are likely to drift toward and embrace one theory, lean heavily on a theory and integrate techniques from various other theories, or integrate two or more theories into your own theoretical approach (Corey, 2019). With well over 300 theories (Neukrug, 2015; Meichenbaum & Lilienfed, 2018), choosing a theoretical approach can be a difficult task. Today, there are generally four schools of psychotherapy identified—psychodynamic, existential-humanistic, cognitive-behavioral, and postmodern—within which most theories fall (Neukrug, 2015, 2018). Presented here is a brief description of each of these schools, followed by some thoughts on how a counselor who embraces that school of thought might view Jake's situation. If the case conceptualization process was used with Jake and then viewed through a theoretical lens, more involved descriptions of how case conceptualization can be integrated with theory would be developed. The following just gives you a taste of this process.

Psychodynamic Approaches

Developed near the beginning of the 20th century but maintaining widespread popularity today, *psychodynamic approaches* vary considerably but contain some common elements. For instance, they all suggest that an unconscious and a conscious affect the functioning of the person in some deeply personal and "dynamic" ways. They all look at early child-rearing practices as being important in the development of personality. They all believe that examining the past, and the dynamic interaction of the past with conscious and unconscious factors, are important in the therapeutic process. Although these approaches have tended to be long-term, in recent years some have been adapted and used in relatively brief treatment modality formats. Some of the more popular approaches that are considered psychodynamic are *psychoanalysis*, *Jungian therapy*, *Adlerian therapy*, *attachment therapy*, and *object-relations theory*.

Jake: Those who embrace any of a number of psychodynamic approaches believe that a strong ego can withstand difficult times in life, as it knows how to find available resources to overcome life's obstacles. With Jake, something in his early childhood prevented him from developing an ego that could withstand such obstacles. This is why when his children had the incident with his car, Jake began to decompensate and develop serious anxiety with associated problems (e.g., lack of sleep, lack of eating, headaches, obsessive behaviors, need to control, etc.). The psychodynamic theorist would want to help Jake look at his early attachment to important caretakers, particularly his parents, so that he can better understand what went awry. Ultimately, Jake would need to understand some of the reasons he did not develop a strong enough ego, and through reparenting efforts with his counselor, can begin to learn new and healthier ways of functioning that can help him get through the most difficult times in life. This approach tends to be long-term, as looking at the past and developing new and healthier ways of functioning through reparenting and ego building is an arduous process.

Existential-Humanistic Approaches

Loosely based on the philosophies of *existentialism* and *phenomenology*, *existential-humanistic approaches* were particularly prevalent during the latter part of the 20th century but continue to be widely used today. Existentialism examines the kinds of choices one makes to develop meaning and purpose in life and, from a psychotherapeutic perspective, suggests that people can choose new ways of living at any point in their lives. Phenomenology is the belief that each person's reality is unique and that to understand the person, you must hear how that person has come to make sense of his or her world. These approaches tend to stress the importance of developing a trusting and "real" relationship with the counselor, focusing on the here and now, and gently challenging clients to make new choices in their lives. Although generally shorter than the psychodynamic approaches, these therapies tend to be longer than the cognitive-behavioral approaches. Some of the more well-known existential-humanistic approaches include *existential therapy*, *Gestalt therapy*, and *person-centered counseling*.

Jake: This approach views the counseling relationship as a joint journey that is based on the notion that Jake can only be understood and feel comfortable sharing his innermost thoughts through a trusting, accepting, and empathic relationship. As this relationship is developed, Jake will feel increasingly safe within the counseling relationship and be open to talking about all aspects of himself. Therefore, it is likely that he will want to talk about his feelings about the car accident with Justine, the guilt he has felt, and how it has impacted his life with Justine, his parents, his wife, and his children. He will likely examine how his anxiety and its associated behaviors have negatively affected himself and others around him. His ability to change the present by taking responsibility for the behaviors and relationship choices he has made will increasingly take precedence within the counseling relationship. Slowly, Jake will examine how he can make new choices so he can decrease his anxiety and have increasingly real and meaningful relationships with his wife, his children, Justine, and his parents (see Reflective Exercise 8.2).

REFLECTIVE EXERCISE 8.2

Jake Undergoing Existential-Humanistic Therapy

Now that you have a good sense of who Jake is and have conceptualized his life situation, consider how you might work with him from an existential-humanistic perspective. Then review the role-play of Dr. Ed Neukrug with Jake. Is his work with Jake how you would have imagined it to be? Do you think the techniques he used fit the existential-humanistic perspective? Are there clear goals for Jake, and do you think he will eventually begin to reduce his anxiety and build more effective relationships with those he loves? Share your thoughts in class.

Cognitive-Behavioral Approaches

Cognitive-behavioral approaches look at how cognitions and/or behaviors impact one's current manner of living in the world and assume that cognitions and/or behaviors have been learned and can be relearned. Although building a relationship is important in these approaches, it is seen as a way of building trust so clients will be more likely to change specific behaviors and cognitions; it is not core to the theories, as in the existential-humanistic approaches. These approaches tend to spend a limited amount of time examining the past, as they focus more on how present cognitions and behaviors affect the individual's feelings, thoughts, actions, and physiological responses. They all propose that after identifying problematic behaviors and/or cognitions, one can choose, replace, or reinforce new cognitions and behaviors that result in more effective functioning. These approaches tend to be shorter term than the psychodynamic or existential-humanistic approaches. Four of the more well-known approaches that constitute the cognitive-behavioral school became popular during the latter part of the 20th century and continue to have widespread appeal today. They include *behavior therapy*, *rational emotive behavior therapy* (REBT), *cognitive behavior therapy*, and *reality therapy*.

Jake: After building a relationship, Jake will be asked to examine his cognitions and his behaviors to see how cognitive distortions, irrational thinking, and negative core beliefs are impacting his feelings, his physiological responses (e.g., high cortisol levels, which cause stress), and his behaviors. He will also examine how his behaviors are negatively impacting others around him. Through a psychoeducational process, he will be taught how he can change his thinking and his behaviors so he can feel less anxious and act in healthier and more loving ways with Angela, his children, and his parents. He will be prescribed homework that will entail changing his irrational or faulty beliefs as well as practicing new behaviors that will help him feel better and act more loving toward those around him. Through practice and reinforcement from his counselor and those around him, he will eliminate his irrational and faulty beliefs, develop new rational and healthy core beliefs, and develop new positive behaviors (see Reflective Exercise 8.3).

REFLECTIVE EXERCISE 8.3

Jake Undergoing Cognitive Behavioral Therapy

Now that you have a good sense of who Jake is and have conceptualized his life situation, consider how you might work with him from a cognitive-behavioral perspective. Then review the role-play of Dr. Ed Neukrug with Jake. Is his work with Jake how you would have imagined it to be? Do you think the techniques he used fit the cognitive-behavioral school? Are there clear goals for Jake, and do you think he will eventually begin to reduce his anxiety and build more effective relationships with those he loves? Share your thoughts in class.

Postmodern Approaches

Narrative therapy, solution-focused brief therapy, and *relational-cultural therapy* are three relatively recent postmodern therapies and are based on the philosophies of *social constructivism* and *postmodernism*. Postmodernism suggests that no one reality holds the truth and that we should question many of the past assumptions we took for fact. Those with this philosophy even doubt many of the basic assumptions of past popular therapies that suggest that certain structures cause mental health problems (e.g., id, ego, superego, a self-actualizing tendency, core beliefs, internal locus of control, etc.). Social constructivism suggests that individuals construct meaning in their lives from the discourses they have with others and the language used in their cultures and in society. They suggest that through language, behaviors, and laws, those in power can create havoc for those whose identities are in the minority (e.g., culturally diverse clients, women, individuals with disabilities, sexual minorities, etc.). Thus, they encourage that the counseling relationship be highlighted by equality and non-pathology. Rather than harp on past problems that tend to be embedded in oppressive belief systems, postmodern approaches suggest that clients can find exceptions to their problems and develop creative solutions and new ways of understanding their world. Postmodern approaches tend to be short-term therapies, with solution-focused brief therapy being considered a particularly short-term approach, sometimes lasting fewer than five sessions.

Jake: Although postmodern approaches can be vastly different in how they work with the client, they all have the basic assumption that there is no inherent pathology "within" Jake, that Jake can develop new ways of living in the world, and that through discourse, people can change. Thus, Jake's anxiety is not seen as embedded within his personality, and counseling is seen as positive and forward moving. Since Jake's anxiety is clearly upsetting Jake and those around him, the postmodern counselor would want to understand Jake's story, or dominant problem-saturated narrative, and begin to seek solutions that will help Jake and those around him feel better. The counselor will not act like an aloof expert or know-it-all. Instead, he or she will show curiosity and be caring and humble about Jake's situation. Listening carefully to Jake's story, the postmodern counselor will help Jake explore past positive coping mechanisms and past exceptions to his current problem-dominated story (e.g., anxiety and controlling behaviors). The identification of past coping mechanisms, past exceptions to his current problems, and new positive solutions will be used to help Jake develop new narratives as he reauthors his life. Jake will begin to de-emphasize his current problem-saturated story and build new positive narratives and more helpful ways of living.

Reflective Practice: Applying Case Conceptualization, Diagnostic Formulation, and Treatment Planning

Hinkle and Dean (2016) have found role-plays can be helpful for beginning counselors to practice the cognitive complexity, reflection skills, and affective awareness required to master the skills needed in case conceptualization. Of course, one-on-one supervision can also be helpful in this process. Ellis, Hutman, and Deihl (2013) found that supervisees have varying degrees of reflective practice skills. At a basic level, the supervisee can describe therapeutic events using cause and effect. At the next level, the supervisee can examine patterns within cases. At the most advanced level, the supervisee can detect and reflect on patterns across cases in relation to self and can challenge assumptions underlying conceptualizations. Wherever counselor trainees are in this process, as they learn more about the counseling process and increasingly engage in supervision, they will get better at case conceptualization, developing a diagnosis, and formulating a treatment plan (see Experiential Exercise 8.2).

EXPERIENTIAL EXERCISE 8.2

Practicing Case Conceptualization, Making a Diagnosis, and Treatment Planning

Part 1: Angela

Throughout this chapter you have examined how Jake's situation can be examined through the case conceptualization process. In addition, using Jake as an example, we demonstrated how to form a diagnosis and develop a treatment plan. Finally, we briefly looked at how therapy might take place with Jake through approaches from the four major schools: psychodynamic, existential-humanistic, cognitive-behavioral, and postmodern.

In getting to know Jake, you also obtained a glimpse into Angela's (Jake's wife) world. Using Appendices B and D, review Angela's situation one more time. In addition, you may want to view Angela with Dr. Neukrug undergoing a psychodynamic approach to therapy and a postmodern approach to counseling. This will give you additional information about Angela and allow you to reflect on these theoretical approaches.

After you have gained knowledge about Angela, as best as you can, use the biopsychosocial assessment model to conceptualize Angela's situation. Then come up with a diagnosis using DSM-5. Finally, develop a treatment plan for Angela. Share what you came up with in small groups.

Part 2: Role-Play

In addition to, or instead of, exploring Angela's situation, do a role-play with a student, friend, or client, and use the biopsychosocial assessment model to develop your case conceptualization. Then, using DSM-5, come up with a diagnosis of your client and develop a treatment plan based on your case conceptualization and diagnosis. Finally, consider what the process might look like if your client underwent a psychodynamic, existential-humanistic, cognitive-behavioral, or postmodern approach to counseling. In small groups, share how the case conceptualization, diagnosis, and treatment planning process went and how you envisioned counseling unraveling.

Summary

This chapter examined the process of case conceptualization, making a diagnosis, and developing a treatment plan. We first noted that case conceptualization, sometimes called case formulation, is used to help a counselor better understand a client's situation. We noted that there are many models of case conceptualization, some of which view clients through a particular theoretical perspective, while others are non-theory-specific. For this chapter, we focused on the biopsychosocial assessment model, a non-theory-specific model of case conceptualization.

Focusing on the biopsychosocial assessment model, we explored its three domains, which include the biological, psychological, and sociocultural spheres. We highlighted several areas that should be explored within each and noted that there is an intimate interaction between the three domains; that is, they can impact each other, sometimes in mysterious ways. That is why this model is seen as holistic. We noted that as the counselor gains knowledge of the three spheres, he or she will begin to see themes and develop ideas about causation. In addition, we noted that knowledge gained from the domains can help the counselor develop his or her diagnostic formulation. We used Jake as an example when examining the three domains with a client, considering themes and ideas of causation, and formulating a diagnosis.

To form a diagnosis, knowledge of DSM-5 is necessary. Thus, we offered a very brief history of DSM and examined its importance in the mental health field. We highlighted a number of factors when considering reporting a diagnosis, including how to report co-occurring diagnoses; the use of subtypes, specifiers, and severity when making diagnoses; different types of provisional and informal diagnoses, such as when one uses rule-out, traits, by history, and self-report; and when a diagnosis of "other specified disorder" or "unspecified disorder" might be used. We ended this section by noting that although DSM-5 is widely used, it also has its share of critics, such as those who question some of the diagnoses, others who believe DSM use of categorization is dehumanizing and leads to labeling, some who believe it is not sufficiently scientific, some who claim it does not account for societal factors that impact their formulation, and others who believe that mental disorders are relational, not in a person. We ended this section by explaining Jake's diagnostic formulation using DSM-5.

The next part of the chapter explored a natural outgrowth of case conceptualization and diagnostic formulation—treatment planning. We offered a four-step process for treatment planning that includes defining the problems, developing achievable goals, deciding on treatment modality, and measuring change. Again, using Jake as an example, we described the four-step process. Although we highlighted the four-step process, we also noted that there is not one single mechanism for developing and writing a treatment plan and showed how simply writing a summary of a client's situation, followed by a list of recommendations, is sometimes used.

Near the end of the chapter, we examined what it would be like to view a client through a particular theoretical lens. Briefly describing the psychodynamic, existential-humanistic, cognitive-behavioral, and postmodern schools of counseling and therapy, we showed how the process of therapy might look if Jake had gone through each. This brief review of theory is a precursor to the development of a theory-driven case conceptualization process that students will develop over time as they become more familiar with different counseling theories.

The chapter concluded by encouraging you to develop a reflective practice; that is, to continually reflect on your case conceptualization process as you develop your skills as a counselor. Sometimes, we noted, this can be facilitated through supervision. We encouraged you to use Angela, Jake's wife, in considering the case conceptualization process, making a diagnosis, and developing a treatment plan. We also suggested you can role-play with a fellow student, friend, or client and practice case conceptualization, diagnostic formulation, and treatment planning.

Key Words and Terms

Adlerian therapy

attachment therapy

behavior therapy

biological domain

biopsychosocial assessment model

by history

case conceptualization

case formulation

cognitive behavior therapy

cognitive-behavioral approaches

co-occuring diagnoses

deciding on treatment modality

defining the problem

developing achievable goals

"dia"

diagnosis

Diagnostic and Statistical Manual of Mental Disorders

DSM-5

existentialism

existential-humanistic approaches

existential therapy

four steps to treatment planning

Gestalt therapy

"gnosis"

ideas about causation

informal diagnoses

Jungian therapy

measuring change

narrative therapy

object-relations theory

other specified disorder

person-centered counseling

phenomenology

postmodern approaches

postmodernism

provisional diagnoses

psychoanalysis

psychodynamic approaches

psychological domain

rational emotive behavior therapy

reality therapy

relational cultural therapy

rule-out

self-report

severity

social constructivism

sociocultural domain

solution-focused brief therapy

specifiers

subtypes

themes

traits

treatment planning

unspecified disorder

writing your treatment plan

CHAPTER 9

Culturally Competent Counseling

Learning Objectives

1. Understand the importance of being culturally competent within an increasingly diverse country
2. Underscore several reasons why some diverse clients are wary of counseling, which includes the counselor:

    a. Believing in the melting-pot myth
    b. Not having the ability to adapt the counseling relationship
    c. Lacking an understanding of social forces
    d. Having an ethnocentric world view
    e. Being ignorant of his or her unconscious bias
    f. Having an inability to understand cultural differences in the expression of symptomatology
    g. Using unreliable assessment and research instruments
    h. Not being aware of institutional discrimination
    i. Having an individualistic perspective

3. Offer a definition of culturally competent counseling and delineate the process
4. Describe three models of culturally competent counseling, including:

    a. The RESPECTFUL model
    b. The Multicultural and Social Justice Counseling Competencies
    c. An integrative model of culturally competent counseling

5. Examine strategies for counseling with a number of select populations, including the following:

    a. Individuals from different ethnic and racial groups
    b. Individuals from diverse religious backgrounds
    c. Women
    d. Men
    e. Lesbian, gay, bisexual, transgender, and questioning individuals
    f. The poor and the homeless
    g. Children
    h. Older persons
    i. Individuals with serious mental disorders
    j. Individuals with disabilities
    k. Individuals who use and abuse substances

Introduction

Every person is like all persons, like some persons, and like no other persons ...

(Kluckohn & Murray, 1953, p. 335)

This chapter offers an understanding of how to work with culturally diverse clients and highlights the importance of counselors having appropriate beliefs and attitudes, knowledge, and skills to work successfully with a wide variety of clients. The chapter first focuses on the importance of cross-cultural counseling, then identifies nine reasons why some diverse clients are wary of counseling. It then offers a definition of culturally competent counseling, which is followed by models and competencies of culturally competent counseling. It concludes by offering strategies for working with several different populations, including different ethnic and racial groups; people from diverse religious backgrounds; women; men; lesbian, gay, bisexual, transgender, and questioning (LGBTQ) individuals; those who are homeless and poor; children; older persons; individuals with serious mental disorders; individuals with disabilities; and substance users and abusers.

Why Cross-Cultural Counseling?

By the year 2043, individuals from diverse backgrounds are expected to be the majority of the population in the United States, and as you can see from Figure 9.1, in 2060, the country will look very different than it does now (U.S. Census Bureau, 2016, 2018a).

YEAR							
2016	61.3%	17.8%	13.3%	5.7%	1.3%	.2%	2.6%
2060	43%	31%	15%	8.2%	1.5%	0.30%	6.4%
	Non-Hispanic White	Hispanics	African-American	Asian	American Indian	Native Hawaiian/Other Pacific Islander	Two or More Races

FIGURE 9.1   Changes in Ethnic Composition of U.S. Over Time

These changing demographics are a function of several factors, such as higher birth rates within minority populations; most legal immigrants now being Asian, Black, Latinx, or another minority; and immigration rates being the highest in American history (U.S. Department of Homeland Security, 2018; U.S. Census Bureau, 2017b). Like past immigrants, today, many immigrants claim a strong affiliation with their cultural heritage.

Due to changing immigration patterns, increased intermarriage, and social factors, changes in the racial, ethnic, and cultural backgrounds of people in American society have transformed the religious composition of the country as well (Pew Research Center, 2018a). Although America is still decidedly Christian (about 50% Protestant and 20% Catholic), it is less so than years ago, and there are increased numbers of people of other religions, such as Muslims, Buddhists, and Hindus. In addition, close to 23% of Americans do not affiliate with any religion, and about 7% of those are atheists or agonistics.

In addition to the increasing ethnic, cultural, and religious diversity, there has been greater acceptance of diversity regarding gender identity, gender role stereotypes, gender equality, and same-sex relationships (Pew Research Center, 2018b; Szymanski & Carretta, 2019; Trepal, Wester, Notestine, & Leeth, 2019). Increasing understanding and acceptance of differences seems more the norm today, although there are clearly some who are not happy with these changes.

Changes in local, state, and federal laws have precipitated a gradual move toward acceptance of diversity in our culture and have given many Americans a heightened sensitivity to, and awareness of, the many diverse groups that make up the United States. Changing demographics in the country make it increasingly important for counselors to make sure their approaches to helping work with a wide variety of clients. Unfortunately, this has not always been the case.

Why Some Clients Are Wary of Counseling

Imagine being distrustful of counselors, confused about the counseling process, or feeling worlds apart from the counselor you were seeing. Would you want to begin, or continue in, a counseling relationship? Assuredly not. Unfortunately, this is the way it is for many clients from diverse backgrounds. In fact, when compared to Whites, culturally diverse clients are more likely to be spoken down to, find the counseling relationship less helpful, seek mental health services at lower rates, and terminate counseling prematurely (Escobar, 2012; Lo, Cheng & Howell, 2013; National Alliance on Mental Illness [NAMI], 2018a; U.S. Department of Health and Human Services, 2014; Williams, 2013). The reasons for diverse clients being distrustful of counseling is complicated and historical; however, some concerns that have been voiced over the years include the following (Hays & Erford, 2018; McAuliffe, 2019; Sue & Sue, 2016):

1. *The melting-pot myth.* For many years, most Whites saw the United States as a "melting pot," where individuals from different cultures would assimilate into the American culture. Although some assimilation occurs with people from all cultures, the history of immigration in the United States has mostly seen new immigrants from similar backgrounds living in the same communities and maintaining their unique traditions. This *cultural mosaic* has brought beauty and differences to this country. If counselors assume clients should "melt into" the greater American culture, they are likely to make clients feel as if they should be somebody other than who they are.

Example: A counselor encourages a client who lives with individuals of her own culture in a poorer section of town, to move to a "safer (and Whiter) part of town." The client feels as if she is being pushed to do something she does not want to do and to leave those with whom she is most comfortable. It leaves her feeling conflicted about her counselor.

2. *Inability to adapt the counseling relationship.* Most counseling theories were developed from a Western, White, and male perspective and emphasize individualism, expression of feelings, cause and effect, self-disclosure, and the importance of insight. Clients from some cultures, however, may not value some of these attributes and feel uncomfortable with such an approach. Despite this, some counselors find it difficult to adapt their approaches based on the cultural backgrounds of their clients, and some never even consider it.

    Example: A Vietnamese client is encouraged to talk about her feelings regarding her family's immigration to the United States, even though her posture and tone of voice suggest she is not comfortable with this. Expression of feelings is not the norm in Vietnam, and she feels embarrassed, put on the spot, and wronged when she tries to refuse.

3. *Lack of understanding of social forces.* Counselors are well trained in examining how internal forces (e.g., thoughts, unconscious factors, feelings) impact the kinds of choices made by clients. However, such a focus sometimes neglects how external forces, such as prejudice and discrimination, can impact a client.

    Example: A female client who is being paid less at her job than her male counterparts is distraught about the pay inequity. The counselor suggests: "What are you saying to yourself to make you feel so badly?" In this case, it might be better for the counselor to help the client advocate for an equitable pay raise.

4. *Ethnocentric worldview.* If a counselor assumes that clients share a similar worldview, he or she may have a negative reaction to a client who believes differently about certain subjects. The counselor may even believe that the client's reactions are indicative of emotional instability or client misunderstanding. The counselor should, instead, respect the client's worldview.

    Example: A counselor inadvertently offends a Muslim client when she says to her, "Have a wonderful Christmas." When the client responds with little enthusiasm to the counselor's salutation, the counselor shows nonverbal indignation toward the client.

5. *Ignorance of one's own unconscious bias.* Research has shown that almost all of us have some amount of unconscious bias toward certain groups. However, when a counselor makes no attempt to monitor his or her bias, it can impact clients in negative ways.

    Example: A counselor who believes he is accepting of all gender identities unconsciously believes that being transgender is against the laws of nature. When working with a transgender female, the counselor is not aware that he grimaces when the client describes the transitioning process. The client drops out of counseling.

6. *Inability to understand cultural differences in the expression of symptomatology.* Expression of symptoms can vary dramatically as a function of the cultural background of the client. A counselor who assumes that certain symptoms are indicative of pathology may not realize that the client is

simply expressing a common behavior from the client's culture. This can clearly lead to misdiagnosis and mistreatment.

Example: A Puerto Rican client presents with somatic complaints and is immediately referred to his doctor. The counselor didn't realize that somatization is a common way of showing grief in some Hispanic cultures, and in this case, it was a response to the client dearly missing his daughter, who is back in Puerto Rico.

7. *Unreliability of assessment and research instruments.* Over the years, assessment and research instruments have notoriously been culturally biased. Although they have gotten better, an effective counselor should assess the effectiveness of such instruments with all populations before using them.

Example: An African American client is given a cognitive ability test by a counselor to assess his ability at being a firefighter. Although the test predicts well for Whites, it does not do so for African Americans and should not be used in this instance. It would have been best if another form of assessment (e.g., a performance-based assessment that measures actual on-the-job performance) had been used.

8. *Institutional discrimination.* Because racism, heteronormativity, prejudice, and bias are embedded in society, they often go unrecognized and become a natural but unhealthy part of organizations and institutions.

Example: Mental health practitioners at a mental health agency consistently diagnose African American males with schizophrenia at higher rates than others. Actually, African Americans do not have higher rates of schizophrenia, but training programs and mental health centers have done a poor job at understanding how to properly conduct clinical interviews with African American males, and these clients often are misdiagnosed.

9. *Individualistic perspectives.* Whereas Whites tend to view the world from an individualistic perspective (I can pick myself up from my bootstraps), some cultural groups have historically had a collectivistic perspective, where consulting parents, elders, or wise individuals in the culture is the norm. If counselors assume a client should be the deciding force in decision-making, they may turn off a client or even upset the broader system if they push the client to make a decision without consultation with an important person within the client's cultural circle.

Example: A client who is Native American wants to consult with his elders before making an important decision regarding getting married. The counselor, however, suggests the client should make the decision on his own, as this would be a sign of maturity. The client feels confused, upset, and caught between two different cultural beliefs. Having the client consult with his elders would have been more natural and healthy in this case.

Conclusion

These nine examples highlight some reasons the counseling relationship has not been effective for many clients from diverse backgrounds. They demonstrate the need for counselors to be culturally competent and the need for greater sensitivity in counseling diverse clients. By attending to these issues and similar ones, counselors can obtain an improved understanding of diversity, be able to make better treatment plans, see a decrease in the dropout rate when counseling historically oppressed clients, and see an increase in satisfaction with the helping process. The following section offers a definition of what it is to be culturally competent. This is followed by some models and competencies counselors can use to become culturally competent.

Defining Culturally Competent Counseling

Although many definitions of *culturally competent counseling* exist, I like *McAuliffe's definition of culturally competent counseling* (2013) because it is direct and to the point. He suggests that culturally competent helping is "a consistent readiness to identify the cultural dimensions of clients' lives and a subsequent integration of culture into counseling work" (p. 6). McAuliffe (2019) and others (e.g., Hays & Erford, 2018; Ratts et al., 2015, 2016; Sue & Sue, 2016) go on to further define the process of culturally competent helping and include such things as the following:

1. Being aware of one's own attitudes and beliefs to minimize how they might negatively impact clients
2. Having the knowledge and skills to appropriately work with clients from a variety of diverse backgrounds
3. Knowing how to obtain additional knowledge and skills, including supervision, to enhance one's ability to work with a variety of clients from diverse backgrounds
4. Having the curiosity to understand individuals from various cultures and backgrounds and being able to accept differences
5. Understanding the forces of power, privilege, marginalization, and oppression
6. Being willing to advocate for clients when necessary
7. Being willing to advocate for causes when important to clients and the counseling profession
8. Understanding the intersection of various client identities (sexual, cultural, gender, etc.)
9. Understanding many of the reasons that cause clients to distrust the counseling relationship
10. Having the ability to immerse oneself in the world of another

Becoming Culturally Competent

Both the RESPECTFUL model and the Multicultural and Social Justice Counseling Competencies can help counselors be culturally competent in their work with clients. Let's look at both and then examine a model that integrates many of these ideas when working with clients from diverse backgrounds.

The RESPECTFUL Model

Touched on in Chapter 1, the RESPECTFUL model offers a pragmatic approach to working with clients in that it helps the counselor focus on 10 areas of potential differences between the client and counselor that the counselor can explore. When this model is used with caring curiosity and empathy in the counseling relationship, counselors can better understand their clients and bridge the gap that sometimes exists between clients' and counselors' cultures. This model examines the following domains (see Experiential Exercise 9.1).

R: religious/spiritual identity

E: economic class/background

S: sexual identity

P: level of psychological development

E: ethnic/racial identity

C: chronological/developmental challenges

T: various forms of trauma and other threats to one's sense of well-being

F: family background and history

U: unique physical characteristics

L: location of residence and language differences (Lewis, Lewis, Daniels, & D'Andrea, 2011, p. 54)

EXPERIENTIAL EXERCISE 9.1

Using the RESPECTFUL Model

Pair up with a student or, if completed outside of class, with a person you would like to learn more about. It would be particularly powerful if you could find someone who is of a culture with which you have little familiarity. Then, using your foundational skills and your information-gathering questions, ask the individual about the 10 dimensions of the RESPECTFUL model. When you have finished, reflect on what you have learned about the person. How might the information you gathered impact your work with this person if he or she was a client? If possible, share some of your thoughts with the class.

The Multicultural and Social Justice Counseling Competencies[1]

Originally, multicultural counseling competencies and separate social justice counseling competencies were created to assist counselors when working with diverse clients. However, in light of the intimate relationship between multicultural helping and social justice work, it was decided to combine the two into one set of competencies: The Multicultural and Social Justice Counseling Competencies (Ratts, et al., 2015, 2016). A summary of these competencies is presented here.

The Multicultural and Social Justice Counseling Competencies are sectioned off into four domains: (a) counselor self-awareness, (b) client worldview, (c) counseling relationship, and (d) counseling and advocacy interventions. Each of the first three domains are defined by attitudes and beliefs, knowledge, skills, and action. The last domain (addressed in Chapter 6 when we discussed advocacy) focuses on social justice work, particularly in the following areas: *intrapersonal, interpersonal, institutional, community, public policy,* and *international and global affairs.*

---

1   Quotes in this section are from Ratts et al., 2015.

Domain I: Counselor Self-Awareness

Attitudes and beliefs: Counselors "are aware of their social identities, social group statuses, power, privilege, oppression, strengths, limitations, assumptions, attitudes, values, beliefs, and biases" (p. 5).

Knowledge: Counselors "possess an understanding of their social identities, social group statuses, power, privilege, oppression, strengths, limitations, assumptions, attitudes, values, beliefs, and biases" (p. 5).

Skills: Counselors "possess skills that enrich their understanding of their social identities, social group statuses, power, privilege, oppression, limitations, assumptions, attitudes, values, beliefs, and biases" (p. 5).

Action: Counselors "take action to increase self-awareness of their social identities, social group statuses, power, privilege, oppression, strengths, limitations, assumptions, attitudes, values, beliefs, and biases" (p. 6; see Experiential Exercise 9.2).

EXPERIENTIAL EXERCISE 9.2

Counselors' Awareness About Privilege

Awareness of the kinds of privilege that some have is important when working with clients. It helps us understand that due to life circumstances, some clients have a much more difficult time than others. This exercise helps us examine the kinds of privilege we have had in our lives and can be done in one of two ways.

If done in a classroom: Stand in a line about 10 feet away from the instructor and face him or her. The instructor will then read each of the statements found in Appendix G, and you should simply follow the instructions (take a step back or forward for each statement). This will visually show you who has grown up with more privilege.

If done on your own: Read the statements and place a plus sign next to each statement if you were to take a step forward and a minus sign next to each statement if you were to take a step back. You can then count all your plusses and minuses and add them up (7 plusses and 5 minuses result in 2 plusses overall). Then the instructor can obtain the average score from the class, and you can compare your score to the average score.

Discussion: After the exercise is complete, students can discuss the following questions:

1. How advantageous is it to have privilege in our society?
2. Are there any disadvantages to having privilege?
3. How disadvantageous is it to not have privilege?
4. If you grew up with privilege, what would your life be like if you hadn't?
5. If you grew up with little privilege, what would your life be like if you did have privilege?
6. How might your experience of privilege impact how you do counseling?

Domain II: Client Worldview

    Attitudes and beliefs: Counselors "are aware of clients' worldview, assumptions, attitudes, values, beliefs, biases, social identities, social group statuses, and experiences with power, privilege, and oppression" (p. 6; see Reflection Exercise 9.1).

    Knowledge: Counselors "possess knowledge of clients' worldview, assumptions, attitudes, values, beliefs, biases, social identities, social group statuses, and experiences with power, privilege, and oppression" (p. 7).

    Skills: Counselors "possess skills that enrich their understanding of clients' worldview, assumptions, attitudes, values, beliefs, biases, social identities, social group statuses, and experiences with power, privilege, and oppression" (p. 7).

    Action: Counselors "take action to increase self-awareness of clients' worldview, assumptions, attitudes, values, beliefs, biases, social identities, social group statuses, and experiences with power, privilege, and oppression" (p. 8).

REFLECTION EXERCISE 9.1

Counselors' Knowledge About Clients

Read this case description, and then, based on your knowledge of visually impaired, indigent Irish Americans, consider how you might have greeted this man if he had come to your office and what kind of treatment planning you might consider. Then go on to Part 2 and read how knowledge of the visually impaired and Irish Americans could have been helpful. Discuss in class your thoughts on this case.

Part 1: "Case description: John McGowan, a 70-year-old visually impaired widower with a strong Irish heritage and culture, was brought to a clinician's office by his adult daughter after finding him disheveled, still in his pajamas, and crying over a bowl of uneaten cereal when she checked on him at noon. Between sobs, John could not convey to his daughter what had precipitated this latest incident.

When making the appointment, the daughter told the receptionist that her father had experienced other 'weepy' episodes since Thanksgiving (three months ago), but previously she had always been able to coax him out of them by playing some lighthearted Irish music. Since Thanksgiving, her father had had difficulty sleeping and seemed to have lost interest in most things that had previously given him pleasure. She added that her mother, who also strongly identified as Irish, had died suddenly of a heart attack 15 months ago. Her father had always depended on his wife to 'be his eyes' and to care for his daily needs. They had met while still in parochial high school and became engaged shortly after graduation. When John was 19, he suffered severe visual impairment from a car accident, which prevented him from completing a plumber's apprenticeship. During their subsequent 48-year marriage, his wife supported them both, and neighbors cared for their daughter during work hours. John spent his days reading Braille versions of poetry and fiction, with unrealized aspirations of being a writer. Since his wife died, he had learned to use a cane but resisted the idea of having a seeing-eye dog. As a result, he was mostly confined to his small apartment, leaving only to have a drink on Saturday night at the local bar, to attend Sunday mass, and to visit his daughter's family. He had very limited financial resources because he was no longer covered by his deceased wife's pension; however, the daughter was so concerned that she agreed to pay 'out of pocket' for her father's treatment." (Hansen, Pepitone-Arreola-Rockwell, & Greene, 2000, p. 656).

Part 2: The following is a description of how a clinician might interact with this client if he had knowledge of the visually impaired and of Irish American indigents:

"Imagine that Dr. Smith has knowledge and experience in working with visually impaired, indigent Irish Americans. With this background, she may have decided to meet initially with John alone—out of respect for the characteristically strong Irish sense of privacy. She would use the 'sighted guide technique' for greeting him in the waiting area, asking simply, 'Would you like to take my arm?' On entering her office, the clinician would inquire if John wanted a description of the space, being sure to note the possible seating options and the location of windows and lighting (because some visually impaired individuals are adversely affected by glare and illumination). She might begin the interview with factual questions regarding his current living situation, the extent of his visual impairment, and his recent medical and psychological symptoms, only later broaching the more emotion-laden topic of the death of his wife. Likely, she would consider multiple hypotheses regarding the etiology of his depression, including his unresolved grief over the death of his wife, his lack of adequate independent coping skills in her absence, the contribution of his Irish heritage to his reluctance to ask for help and to his fatalistic outlook, the isolation and depression common in visually impaired individuals, the possibility of an organically based onset, plus the real-world economic constraints impinging on his life. The culturally competent psychologist would search for a delicate balance between the need to verbalize facial or bodily gestures to compensate for John's lack of visual acuity and his traditional Irish culture's prohibition regarding overt emotional expressiveness. In keeping with the cultural mandate to avoid direct expressions of difference or conflict, the psychologist would be likely to use humor and storytelling to indirectly explore differences between herself and John" (Hansen, Pepitone-Arreola-Rockwell, & Greene, 2000, pp. 656–657).

Domain III: Counseling Relationship

    Attitudes and beliefs: Counselors "are aware of how client and counselor worldviews, assumptions, attitudes, values, beliefs, biases, social identities, social group statuses, and experiences with power, privilege, and oppression influence the counseling relationship" (p. 9).

    Knowledge: Counselors "possess knowledge of how client and counselor worldviews, assumptions, attitudes, values, beliefs, biases, social identities, social group statuses, and experiences with power, privilege, and oppression influence the counseling relationship" (p. 9).

Skills: Counselors "possess skills to engage in discussions with clients about how client and counselor worldviews, assumptions, attitudes, values, beliefs, biases, social identities, social group statuses, power, privilege, and oppression influence the counseling relationship" (p. 10).

Action: Counselors "take action to increase their understanding of how client and counselor worldviews, assumptions, attitudes, values, beliefs, biases, social identities, social group statuses, and experiences with power, privilege, and oppression influence the counseling relationship" (p. 10; see Experiential Exercise 9.3).

EXPERIENTIAL EXERCISE 9.3

Talking About Cultural Differences in the Counseling Relationship

Sometimes, no one wants to acknowledge the elephant in the room. For instance, when a client is culturally different than the counselor, both will often think about their differences but never discuss them. However, in ongoing helping relationships, it is often important to acknowledge and talk about differences to understand how the client's identity has impacted his or her life, including the relationship with the counselor. Do you possess the skills to "talk race" or other diversity issues with clients in a positive way?

Find a person, in or out of class, who in some way identifies as a person from a historically oppressed cultural group. Using the following questions or others, see if you and the person can talk openly and honestly. In class, discuss the ease you had in doing this exercise.

1. Have you experienced any bias, prejudice, or discrimination in your life?
2. When you have faced bias, prejudice, or discrimination, how did you react?
3. What kind of privilege do you think you were denied due to your class, gender, race, sexual orientation, cultural identity, or other differences?
4. What is it like to be ... (female, Black, gay, lesbian, poor, disabled, etc.)?
5. Do you think that cultural differences could influence a counseling relationship?
6. If I was your counselor, is there anything I could do to positively impact a counseling relationship with you?

Domain IV: Counseling and Advocacy Interventions

a. *Intrapersonal:* "The individual characteristics of a person such as knowledge, attitudes, behavior, self-concept, skills, and developmental history" (p. 11).

   Intrapersonal interventions: Counselors "address the intrapersonal processes that impact privileged and marginalized clients" (p. 11).

b. *Interpersonal:* "The interpersonal processes and/or groups that provide individuals with identity and support (i.e., family, friends, and peers)" (p. 12).

Interpersonal interventions: Counselors "address the interpersonal processes that affect privileged and marginalized clients" (p. 12).

c. *Institutional:* "Represents the social institutions in society such as schools, churches, community organizations" (p. 12).

   Institutional interventions: Counselors "address inequities at the institutional level" (p. 12).

d. *Community:* "The community as a whole represents the spoken and unspoken norms, values, and regulations that are embedded in society. The norms, values, and regulations of a community may either be empowering or oppressive to human growth and development" (p. 13).

   Community interventions: Counselors "address community norms, values, and regulations that impede the development of individuals, groups, and communities" (p. 13).

e. *Public policy:* "Public policy reflects the local, state, and federal laws and policies that regulate or influence client human growth and development" (p. 13) .

   Public policy interventions: Counselors "address public policy issues that impede on client development with, and on behalf of clients" (p. 13).

f. *International and global affairs:* "International and global concerns reflect the events, affairs, and policies that influence psychological health and well-being" (p. 14).

   International and global affairs interventions: Counselors "address international and global events, affairs and polices that impede on client development with, and on behalf of, clients" (p. 14; see Experiential Exercise 9.4) .

EXPERIENTIAL EXERCISE 9.4

Advocating Locally and Globally

I'm confident that the majority of students enter the helping professions to be of service to the down-trodden and those struggling with life problems. Although the helping relationship can assist clients in raising their self-esteem and in helping clients learn how to advocate for themselves, another way to help our clients is through institutional, community, public policy, and global advocacy interventions. In small groups, brainstorm ways that your group could advocate for individuals. Make a list and then share it with the class. If the energy and will is felt in the class, pick one or two of the items on the list and follow through with them.

An Integrative Model of Culturally Competent Counseling

Two models of understanding the person from a multicultural perspective are the *tripartite model of personal identity* and the *existential model of cross-cultural counseling,* both of which define ways of being in the world (Moodley & Walcott, 2010; Sue & Sue, 2013). Taking some liberty with these models, I have come up with *three spheres of experience* that define the self that all individuals embody: our individual, group, and universal experiences (see Figure 9.2). The culturally competent counselor takes into

FIGURE 9.2   Three areas of experience that define the self

account a number of important concepts when working with clients within these three spheres, including knowing and monitoring his or her biases; being curious, respectful, collaborative, and building a working alliance; not embodying any of the nine reasons for clients to be wary of counseling; learning about the client's culture and belief system (knowledge); using the RESPECTFUL model; using appropriate skills based on the client's cultural background; considering if the client has an individualistic or collectivist perspective; knowing when to be an advocate; giving full attention to the three areas of experience that define the self; and being committed to the client's well-being and the counseling process. Figure 9.3 illustrates these important concepts and demonstrates the integrative model of culturally competent counseling.

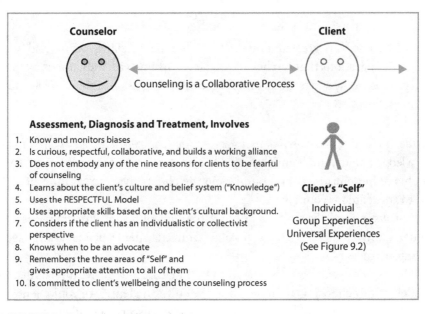

FIGURE 9.3 Culturally competent helping

Considerations When Working With Select Populations

This section of the chapter provides ideas for how to counsel select groups of diverse clients with which you might work. We hope that these groups typify the backgrounds of many clients you might work with, but if they do not, gain the knowledge and skills to work with other clients with whom you might work. Many of these suggestions are paraphrased from other work I have written (see Neukrug, 2016, 2017b) as well as current literature written about these groups (see Reflection Exercise 9.2).

REFLECTION EXERCISE 9.2

Is This You?

As you read about the following populations, consider whether you are, or have ever been, one of these individuals. If so, see if the suggestions for working with these groups make sense to you. If they don't seem to ring true, do you have other suggestions to add to those listed? Are there some that should be removed? Send them to me through the publisher's address, or e-mail me. I'll consider them for the next edition.

Counseling Individuals From Different Ethnic and Racial Groups[2]

Although cultural differences are great among African Americans, Asians, Latinx, and Native Americans, there are some broad suggestions that can be followed for working with individuals from these and other ethnic and racial groups. Some suggestions include the following (McAuliffe, 2019; McAuliffe, Grothaus, & Goméz, 2013; Sue & Sue, 2016):

1. *Embrace the multicultural counseling and social justice competencies.* Be aware of your own biases, have knowledge about your client's cultural background, gain the skills to work with your client based on his or her cultural background, help the client advocate for himself or herself, and be prepared to advocate for your client.

2. *Encourage clients to speak their own language.* Although counselors are not necessarily expected to be bilingual, knowing meaningful expressions from the client's primary language can help build the working alliance.

3. *Assess the client's cultural identity.* Use the RESPECTFUL or integrative models discussed earlier (or other model of your choosing) to understand the cultural identity of your client. Sometimes, our assumptions about a client's identity are not accurate. Discerning a client's cultural identity can help in assessing needs and making goals.

4. *Check accuracy of the client's nonverbal expression.* Nonverbal language varies across cultures, and counselors should ask their clients about their nonverbal expression when in doubt.

5. *Make use of alternate communication modes.* Some clients may be reticent to express themselves verbally because they distrust the counselor, do not understand the totality of the counseling relationship, or are fearful of speaking "incorrectly" (e.g., English is a second language). When reasonable, use acting, drawing, music sharing, storytelling, or collage making to enhance communication.

6. *Encourage clients to bring in culturally significant and personally relevant items.* Having clients bring in meaningful items (e.g., books, photographs, articles of significance, culturally meaningful items) can assist the counselor in understanding the client, the client's family, and the client's culture.

7. *Vary the helping environment.* The counseling relationship may be unfamiliar territory to a client, and sitting in a small private room might be anxiety provoking. At times, it might be smart to explore alternative helping environments to ease clients into the counseling relationship (e.g., take a walk, have a cup of coffee at a quiet restaurant, initially meet a client at his or her home if it seems appropriate).

8. *Don't jump to conclusions about clients.* Don't fall into the trap of assuming that clients will act in stereotypical ways. Many clients won't match a stereotype.

9. *Assess sociopolitical issues.* Ask the client about his or her life and sociological and/or political issues that are impacting the client.

10. *Be skillful and knowledgeable.* Show caring curiosity, use appropriate skills, have knowledge of the client's cultural background, keep your promises, and be committed.

---

2 Adapted from Richmond Calvin, "Counseling Myths Questionnaire," *Theory, Practice, and Trends in Human Services: An Introduction,* ed. Ed Neukrug, pp. 206–215. Copyright © 2012 by Cengage Learning, Inc.

Counseling Individuals From Diverse Religious Backgrounds

When working with any individual, it is important to understand his or her religious background and how it might impact the counseling relationship. Some pointers to keep in mind concerning religion and the counseling relationship include the following (Fowler, 1995; see Association for Spiritual, Ethical, and Religious Values in Counseling, n.d.; Young & Young, 2011):

1. *Embrace the multicultural counseling and social justice competencies.* Be aware of your own biases, have knowledge about your client's cultural background, gain the skills to work with your client based on his or her cultural background, help the client advocate for himself or herself, and be prepared to advocate for your client.

2. *Determine the client's religious background early in the counseling relationship.* As a basis for future treatment planning, a counselor should know the client's religious affiliation and how it might impact the counseling relationship (e.g., holidays, times for prayer, how to address individuals, issues of touch, etc.). This information can be acquired at the initial interview; however, a counselor should also be sensitive to any client who may initially resist a discussion of religion.

3. *Ask the client how important religion is in his or her life.* For some clients, religion holds little influence; for others, it is a driving force. In either case, counselors should not assume that clients know much about the intricacies of their religions, as many, even those who identify as religious, have only a rudimentary understanding of their religious traditions. Assessment of the role religion plays in a client's life can assist in goal setting and treatment planning.

4. *Assess the client's level of faith development.* Whereas low-stage faith development clients tend to be dualistic and concrete and work better with a fair amount of structure and firm goals, high-stage faith development clients see the world in complex ways, value many kinds of faith experiences, and would likely feel more comfortable in a counseling relationship that values abstract thinking and self-reflection (see Fowler, 1995).

5. *Don't make false assumptions about clients.* Be careful not to stereotype (e.g., a counselor who might falsely believe that all Jews keep a kosher home). Also, do not project your faith onto others (e.g., a Christian counselor who assumes that all people of faith are born with original sin).

6. *Educate yourself concerning your client's religious beliefs.* Counselors should know rudimentary information about the religious affiliation of clients. They can learn by taking a course or workshop, by reading, by attending a client's place of worship, and, if appropriate, by asking the client.

7. *Become familiar with holidays and traditions.* Clients are more likely to feel a sense of closeness with a counselor if they see that the counselor has gone out of his or her way to learn about the major holidays and traditions related to the client's religion. This knowledge also helps to avoid making embarrassing errors (e.g., some Muslims would not want to be offered food during the day in the month of Ramadan).

8. *Remember that religion can deeply affect a client on many levels, including unconscious ones.* Some clients who deny any religious affiliation may continue to be unconsciously driven by the basic values they were originally taught. Look at clients' actions; don't just listen to their words. For instance, a "nonpracticing Catholic" may continue to feel guilty over certain issues related to the religious beliefs with which he or she was raised.

9. *Show curiosity, be humble, and be committed.* We can't know everything about every religion, but we can show clients that we are committed to learning more and to respecting their religious orientation. This will go a long way in ensuring a solid working alliance and positive client outcomes.

Counseling Women

Several authors have suggested that due to the oppression that women face in society and as a result of their unique identity development, specific guidelines should be applied when working with them (American Psychological Association [APA], 2007; Clark, Neukrug, & Long, 2018; Pusateri & Headly, 2015). The following addresses some of these guidelines:

1. *Embrace the multicultural counseling and social justice competencies.* Be aware of your own biases, have knowledge about your client's cultural background, gain the skills to work with your client based on her cultural background, help the client advocate for herself, and be prepared to advocate for your client.

2. *Use a helping model that has been adapted for women.* Many helping theories have been based on a so-called male model of behavior. Therefore, ensure that whatever model you use, it is adapted to or amenable for women.

3. *Build an equal relationship, give up power, and demystify the counseling relationship.* Downplay the expert role and encourage women to trust themselves. Female counselors may want to use self-disclosure with female clients, but male counselors should be much more tentative about using this technique. In either case, the counselor should be viewed as an equal who is there to help, not as omnipotent.

4. *Identify ways in which client problems may be a function of sociopolitical forces.* Women are often rendered powerless by abusive men, institutional sexism (e.g., salary inequities), and gender role expectations (e.g., women must look a certain way to be considered beautiful). Help female clients see how their lives may have been impacted by these forces.

5. *Validate and legitimize angry feelings toward their predicament.* As women come to see how they have been victimized, counselors can assist them in combating feelings of powerlessness, helplessness, and low self-esteem. This can be facilitated by encouraging women to participate in consciousness-raising activities about women's issues (e.g., reading books, attending seminars, taking part in women's groups, etc.).

6. *Provide a safe environment to express feelings as clients begin to form connections with other women.* Counselors can validate feelings of fear and competition with other women that result from society's objectification of women. As these feelings dissipate, clients can move toward having a strong and special connection to other women.

7. *Promote healing through learning about women's issues.* Encourage clients to learn about women's issues, oppression of women, societal stereotypes of women, etc. This can help women understand the many barriers they have faced. Such knowledge can be soothing as a woman moves to develop a new sense of self. Counselors can also assist clients in understanding the difference between anger at a man and anger at a male-dominated system.

8. *Help clients with conflicting feelings between traditional and newly found values.* Clients may feel torn between newfound feminist beliefs and values that they may not see as congruent with those beliefs (e.g., wanting to be independent versus wanting to stay home to raise the children). Counselors should validate these contradictory feelings, acknowledge the confusion, and assist clients in fully exploring their belief systems.

9. *Facilitate an integration of client's new identity.* After women have explored their traditional and newly found values, counselors can assist them in integrating the varying, and sometimes conflicting, beliefs they choose to embrace (e.g., stay-at-home vs. working mom). This helps women feel empowered, as they come to realize that they alone decide which beliefs and ways of living they want to live out.

10. *Say goodbye.* Help women move on with their newfound identity by encouraging them to try being in the world without counseling. Counseling can always be resumed in the future if needed.

Counseling Men

> My father didn't embrace me, but I learned how to embrace him. Then, he embraced me.
>
> (Ed Neukrug)

Men in today's society are sometimes seen as not having issues because they have occupied, and continue to occupy, positions of power. Thus, they are often viewed as holding privilege. However, counselors must be aware that having power and privilege can have its own unique problems, that there are many men who are not in such positions, and that there are unique men's issues that need to be understood within the counseling relationship. A number of authors have offered ideas that can be incorporated into a set of guidelines when working with male clients (Englar-Carson, Evans, & Duffey, 2014; Evans, Duffey, & Englar-Carlson, 2013; Neukrug, Britton, & Crews, 2013; Wexler, 2009):

1. *Embrace the multicultural counseling and social justice competencies.* Be aware of your own biases, have knowledge about your client's cultural background, gain the skills to work with your client based on his cultural background, help the client advocate for himself, and be prepared to advocate for your client.

2. *Accept men where they are.* Men can often be on guard when initially entering the counseling relationship. Therefore, the counselor should accept men where they are in an effort to build trust. Once men feel safe, they tend to work hard on their issues.

3. *Don't push men to express what may be considered "softer feelings."* Some suggest that, by its very nature, the counseling relationship sets up expectations that men should express what are typically considered "female feelings" (e.g., deep sadness, feelings of incompetence, feelings of inadequacy, and feelings of closeness). However, men can often feel uncomfortable with the expression of certain feelings and are more at ease with thinking things through, problem-solving, goal setting, and the expression of some other feelings, such as anger and pride. Push a man too quickly, and he may be pushed out of the counseling relationship.

4. *Validate men's feelings and views of how they have been constrained by male gender role stereotypes.* To protect their egos, men will sometimes initially blame others or society for their problems, and early in the counseling relationship, male clients may talk about how they are constrained by gender role stereotypes and pressures in society (e.g., he must work particularly hard for his family). Validation of these views and feelings helps to build trust and establish the relationship. A counselor can accept feelings without necessarily accepting the logic behind them.

5. *Have a plan.* Structure and goal directedness are often preferred by men. Therefore, early on, the counselor should be willing to collaborate with men on a plan for the counseling relationship. Plans can be changed later if need be.

6. *Discuss developmental issues.* Although each man has his own unique issues, he will also likely be struggling with common male developmental issues. The counselor should be aware of and willing to discuss these issues (e.g., mid-life crises).

7. *Slowly encourage the expression of new feelings.* As trust is formed, men may express what are "softer," sometimes labeled "feminine," feelings (e.g., sadness, feelings of intimacy, guilt). Counselors should reinforce the expression of these newfound feelings.

8. *Explore underlying issues and reinforce new ways of understanding the world.* Expression of new feelings will lead to the emergence of underlying issues (e.g., unresolved childhood issues, feelings of inadequacy). One important yet sometimes painful issue for men is their relationship with their father. How fathers modeled, distanced themselves, and showed love can become a template for men's relationships, and men need to reflect on whether their past template works for them today.

9. *Explore behavioral change.* As men gain new insights into self, they may wish to try new ways of acting in the world. The client, in collaboration with the counselor, can identify new potential behaviors and try them out.

10. *Encourage the integration of new feelings, new ways of thinking about the world, and new behaviors into men's lifestyle.* The expression of new feelings, newly gained insights, and new ways of thinking and acting will slowly take on a life of its own and be integrated into the client's way of living. Counselors can actively reinforce these new ways of being.

11. *Encourage new male relationships.* As male clients grow, new male friendships that allow a man to freely express his feelings with another man can be encouraged. Men's groups can allow men to develop more intimate relationships with other men, feel supported, and be challenged to change.

12. *Say goodbye.* Although some men may want to continue in the counseling relationship, others will see it as time limited—a means to a goal. Thus, the counselor should be able to say goodbye and end the counseling relationship. Doing this sets the groundwork for the client to come back, if he so desires.

Counseling Lesbian, Gay, Bisexual, Transgender, and Questioning (LGBTQ) Individuals

Those who are *lesbian, gay, bisexual, transgender and questioning* (LGBTQ) have unique concerns that counselors should consider, and, admittedly, coming up with some general guidelines is a bit difficult. However, based on some research, the following offers some guidelines that can be considered for LGBTQ clients (Dragowski & Sharron-del Rio, 2016; Ritter, 2015; Sue & Sue, 2013; Szymanski & Carretta, 2019). However, always keep in mind that, whether a client is heterosexual, lesbian, gay, bisexual, transgender, or questioning, each client will have his or her unique struggles and individual path in life.

1. *Embrace the multicultural counseling and social justice competencies.* Be aware of your own biases, have knowledge about your client's cultural background, gain the skills to work with your client based on his or her cultural background, help the client advocate for himself or herself, and be prepared to advocate for your client.

2. *Know identity issues.* Be familiar with the identity development of lesbian, gay, bisexual, transgender, and questioning individuals, especially as it relates to the coming out process.

3. *Understand the differences among people who are lesbian, gay, bisexual, or transgender.* Although lumped together here, great differences exist among LGBTQ individuals. For instance, identity development for LGBTQ individuals is often considerably different.

4. *Promote an LGBTQ-friendly agency atmosphere.* Make sure that the agency atmosphere and your office is inviting to all individuals. This can be done by not having heteronormative or heterosexist materials in the office and ensuring that all forms and questionnaires are LGBTQ friendly. Of course, staff and counselors should be nonjudgmental and accepting of all individuals who come to the agency.

5. *Understand how societal oppression impacts LGBTQ clients.* Be cognizant that various forms of prejudice continue to be prevalent in society, and be sensitive to how such prejudice may impact your clients.

6. *Adopt an affirming and strength-based approach.* Affirm your clients' sexual orientation and gender identity and view all sexual identities and orientations as equally healthy.

7. *Don't jump to conclusions about lifestyle.* Don't assume that an LGBTQ client is comfortable living in what the dominant culture understands to be a lesbian, gay, bisexual, or transgender lifestyle. This lifestyle, often portrayed in movies and on TV, is not how most LGBTQ clients live their lives.

8. *Know the unique issues of LGBTQ clients.* By reading professional literature about LGBTQ individuals and becoming involved with LGBTQ groups, counselors can gain an understanding of some of the unique issues these individuals face.

9. *Know community resources.* Be aware of community resources that might be useful to LGBTQ individuals.

10. *Understand the idiosyncrasies of religion toward being LGBTQ.* Be familiar with particular religious and spiritual concerns unique to those of the LGBTQ community.

11. *Show curiosity, be humble, and be committed.* We can't know everything about all our LGBTQ clients, but we can show clients that we are committed to learn and to respect who they are. This will go a long way in ensuring a solid working alliance and positive client outcomes.

Counseling the Poor and the Homeless

With over half a million Americans experiencing homelessness every night and close to 18% of children and 13% of Americans living under the poverty level, it is critical that counselors know how to work with the poor and the homeless. Using a variety of sources, here are some general guidelines (APA, 2018; Clark, Moe, & Hays, 2017; Foss-Kelly, Generali, & Kress, 2017; U.S. Census Bureau, 2018a; U.S. Department of Housing and Urban Development, 2017; Zalaquett & Chambers, 2017):

1. *Embrace the multicultural counseling and social justice competencies.* Be aware of your own biases, have knowledge about your client's cultural background, gain the skills to work with your client based on his or her cultural background, help the client advocate for himself or herself, and be prepared to advocate for your client.

2. *Focus on social issues.* When working with individuals struggling to have their basic needs met, it is important for the counselor to focus on social issues, such as helping a person obtain food and housing, as opposed to spending an inordinate amount of time on intrapersonal issues. Don't forget the intrapersonal, but remember that basic needs should be initially addressed.

3. *Know related legal issues.* Laws, such as the McKinney-Vento Homeless Act ("History of the McKinney Act," 2015), help the homeless find housing and food and ensure that homeless children have access to public schools. Other laws assist those in poverty through housing assistance, food stamps,

medical care, and more. Counselors should know federal and state laws that might impact their work with the homeless and the poor.

4. *Know the client's racial/ethnic/cultural background.* Because a disproportionate number of the homeless and poor come from historically oppressed groups, if counselors are to connect with these clients, they may need to educate themselves about, and feel comfortable working with, clients who are culturally different from themselves.

5. *Be knowledgeable about health risks.* The homeless and the poor are at greater risk of developing AIDS, tuberculosis, and other diseases. The counselor should have knowledge of such diseases, be able to do a basic medical screening, and have referral sources available.

6. *Be prepared to deal with multiple issues.* With up to 50% of the homeless struggling with mental illness and/or substance abuse, counselors must often deal with the multiple issues of homelessness, poverty, mental illness, and chemical dependence.

7. *Know about developmental delays, and be prepared to refer.* Homeless and poor children are more likely to have delayed language and social skills, be abused, and have delayed motor development compared with other children. Counselors should know how to identify developmental delays.

8. *Know psychological effects.* Counselors should know how to respond to clients' psychological and emotional reactions to homelessness and poverty, which can include despair, depression, and a sense of hopelessness.

9. *Know resources.* Counselors should be aware of the vast number of resources available in the community and make referrals when appropriate.

10. *Identify and expand on client strengths.* Those who are poor and homeless are often stigmatized, and society's views about them sometimes become internalized. Counselors should help clients identify their strengths, use their strengths to work toward a better life, and affirm and appreciate who they are and the strengths they have.

Counseling Children

Today, approximately 20% of children have a mental health condition, 11% have a mood disorder, 10% have a conduct disorder, 8% have an anxiety disorder, and half of all lifetime cases of mental disorders start by the age of 14 (NAMI, n.d.). Like adults, children are not immune to mental disorders, poverty, disease, crisis, or trauma. Clearly, counselors need to know appropriate interventions with children. Here are a few ideas on how to work with children in counseling (Henderson & Thompson, 2016; National Institute of Mental Health, 2009; Vernon, 2009):

1. *Embrace the multicultural counseling and social justice competencies.* Be aware of your own biases, have knowledge about your client's cultural background, gain the skills to work with your client based on his or her cultural background, help the client advocate for himself or herself, and be prepared to advocate for your client.

2. *Know the limits of confidentiality.* As noted in Chapter 7, generally, parents have the right to all information about their child's counseling sessions. Rather than seeing parents as potential adversaries, counselors should work collaboratively with parents for the health of the child. Sometimes this can be tricky, but counselors must be able to balance a trusting relationship with the child and a working relationship with the parents. How this occurs will depend on the age of the child and the specific elements of the family dynamics.

3. *Know developmental theory.* Although children mature at varying rates, there are predictable stages of biological, cognitive, and moral development. If facing mental health problems, an unhealthy family, and no counseling, their passage through these stages will be tumultuous. However, if in counseling with a helper who has a keen awareness of lifespan theories, children can more easily transition through these stages in healthy and relatively untraumatic ways.

4. *Use appropriate counseling skills.* Counseling children is different from counseling adults, and counselors should generally be child centered, able to build trusting relationships, know how to use questions that offer choices for answers, use alternative modes of communication, be able to apply developmentally appropriate activities, and understand the child through his or her world, which involves friends, school, and family.

5. *Use alternative modes of communication.* Artifacts, toys, and various art supplies (e.g., dolls, children's books, clay, puppets, etc.) that are developmentally appropriate can help children communicate their concerns to the counselor. Children will project their experiences on such objects and through them communicate their life stories.

6. *Don't lead the child.* Children, especially young children, can be easily led and even develop false beliefs that are subtly given to them by their counselors. It is therefore important that sessions are child centered so that the child tells his or her true story and does not create a story that is a function of the counselor's biases.

7. *Know relevant laws.* Laws regarding confidentiality, privacy, custody, abuse, and more vary from state to state. Counselors should be familiar with them and know how they will impact their counseling relationships. Counselors are almost always mandated reporters if they suspect abuse, so they should know how to reach and consult with Child Protective Services or other authorities.

8. *Know available resources.* After an appropriate assessment is conducted, a counselor will sometimes realize that a child needs to be referred to a physician, a developmental specialist, a therapist who has a specialty in an area that the counselor is not familiar with (e.g., trauma), or another specialist. Counselors should have at hand a potential referral list when these concerns arise.

9. *Practice appropriate closure.* Children can develop close relationships with their counselors. They should know, from the outset, the process of counseling, how long it will likely take, and how it will end. When ending the relationship, it is particularly important that the counselor tend to appropriate closure activities so the child does not feel abandoned.

Counseling Older Persons

With those over the age of 65 quickly becoming 20% of the U.S. population, it is likely that counselors will increasingly be working with older individuals (U.S. Census Bureau, 2018b). To ensure that their concerns are addressed, counselors should consider the following (APA, 2014; Chatters & Zalaquett, 2013; Meyers, 2014c; Williams, 2017):

1. *Embrace the multicultural counseling and social justice competencies.* Be aware of your own biases, have knowledge about your client's cultural background, gain the skills to work with your client based on his or her cultural background, help the client advocate for himself or herself, and be prepared to advocate for your client.

2. *Adapt your counseling style.* The counselor may need to adapt the helping relationship to fit the older client's needs. For instance, use journal writing or art therapy for older persons who have difficulty hearing. For nonambulatory clients, have a session in the client's home.

3. *Build a trusting relationship.* Older persons seek counseling at lower rates than other clients, and those who do may be less trustful, having been raised during a time when counseling was much less common. Thus, counselors need to pay particular attention to building a sound relationship based on trust.

4. *Know potential sources of depression.* Depression can have many origins for an older person, including the loss of loved ones, lifestyle changes, identity confusion, and changes in health. Counselors should be capable of identifying the many potential sources of depression.

5. *Know about identity issues.* Changes in one's identity as a result of retirement, changing family roles, and changing roles in one's community can lead to feelings of depression, anxiety, or despair. Some older persons may need to redefine themselves as they no longer function in their previous roles. Counselors can assist clients in finding a new sense of meaning in their lives.

6. *Know about possible and probable health changes.* Predictable health changes can yield depression and concern for the future. Unpredictable changes can lead to loss of income and emotional problems. Counselors should be alert to potential health problems and their emotional counterparts in older persons.

7. *Have empathy for changes in interpersonal relations.* Aging brings changes in significant relationships as friends, lovers, spouses, and partners develop health problems, relocate, or pass away. Counselors should be knowledgeable about such changes and have empathy toward their clients concerning these changes.

8. *Know about physical and psychological causes of sexual dysfunction.* Counselors should be aware of the possible physical and psychological causes of sexual dysfunction in older persons and ways to ameliorate such problems. In addition, counselors should always be cognizant that regardless of age, people are always sexual beings.

9. *Be respectful, be committed, and be wise.* Most older people have lived full lives and have had an identity different than what the counselor now sees. Respect an older person's years on this earth, and be committed to and understanding of the person in his or her later stages of life.

Counseling Individuals With Serious Mental Disorders

With large percentages of Americans experiencing a serious mental disorder at some point in their lives (NAMI, 2018b), there is little doubt that as a counselor you will need to know about a broad range of psychiatric disorders, the different kinds of psychotropic medications, and the unique needs of those with serious mental illness. Specific steps that counselors can take when working with this population include the following (Crowe & Averett, 2015; Garske, 2016; Kress & Paylo, 2018):

1. *Embrace the multicultural counseling and social justice competencies.* Be aware of your own biases, have knowledge about your client's cultural background, gain the skills to work with your client based on his or her cultural background, help the client advocate for himself or herself, and be prepared to advocate for your client.

2. *Help your client understand his or her mental illness.* Many clients do not have an understanding of their illness, the usual course of the illness, and the best methods of treatment. Clients should be fully informed with up-to-date knowledge about their mental illness.

3. *Help your client work through feelings concerning his or her mental illness.* Many clients are embarrassed about their disorders and feel stigmatized as a result of societal views on mental illness. Having a nonjudgmental attitude toward clients is always critical, and sometimes support groups can help to normalize clients' views of themselves.

4. *Ensure attendance to counseling.* Because they are in denial about their illness, embarrassed, or simply do not care, clients may sometimes miss appointments. Counselors can call clients the day before their appointment, have a relative or close friend help the client get to the counselor's office, work on specific strategies to help clients remember to come in for their appointments, or find innovative ways of contacting their clients (e.g., online, home visits).

5. *Assure compliance with medication.* Clients may discontinue medication out of forgetfulness, denial about the illness, uncomfortable side effects, because they believe they won't have a relapse, or because they believe medication is not helpful. Counselors need to ensure that clients continue to take their medication, and when doubts arise about the effectiveness of medication, counselors should consider making a referral for a medication review.

6. *Assure accurate diagnosis.* Accurate diagnosis is crucial for treatment planning and the appropriate use of medication. Counselors can assure accurate diagnosis through testing, clinical interviews, interviews with others close to the client, and through appropriate use of supervision.

7. *Reevaluate the client's treatment plan, and do not give up.* The mentally ill are some of the most difficult clients to work with, and it is easy for counselors to become discouraged. Counselors need to continue to be vigilant about their work with the mentally ill, be committed to them, and continually reevaluate treatment plans.

8. *Involve the client's family.* Some families can offer great support to clients, and they can be windows into clients' psyches. Thus, it is important to assure adequate family involvement and to help families understand the implications of clients' diagnoses.

9. *Know resources.* The mentally ill are often involved with many other resources in the community (e.g., Social Security office, housing authority, support groups). It is therefore crucial that the counselor have a working knowledge of these resources.

10. *Stay positive and stay committed.* Because the mentally ill are such a difficult population to work with, counselors can become discouraged, burn out, and develop compassion fatigue. It is important for counselors to maintain their own wellness so they can stay positive and be committed to their clients.

Counseling Individuals With Disabilities

Close to 13% of Americans have a disability, and as you might guess, it increases as a function of age, with half of Americans 75 and older having a disability, one-fourth between 65 and 74, 13% between 35 and 64, around 5% to 6% of those between 5 and 34 years old, and close to 1% of those under the age of 5 (Pew Research Center, 2018). As federal laws have increasingly supported the rights to services for individuals with disabilities, counselors have taken a more active role in their treatment and rehabilitation. Observing the following treatment issues can assist counselors in providing positive services for this group (Kelsey & Smart, 2012; Marini, Graf, & Millington, 2018; Smart, 2016):

1. *Embrace the multicultural counseling and social justice competencies.* Be aware of your own biases, have knowledge about your client's cultural background, gain the skills to work with your client based on his or her cultural background, help the client advocate for himself or herself, and be prepared to advocate for your client.

2. *Have knowledge of the many disabling conditions.* Obviously, a counselor needs to obtain knowledge of various disabling conditions, and if he or she does not have the knowledge, obtain supervision, participate in continuing education, or refer the client to someone who does have such knowledge.

3. *Help the client know his or her disability.* Clients should be fully informed of their disability, the probable course of treatment, and their prognosis. Knowledge of their disability will allow them to be fully involved in the decision-making process, treatment planning, and any emotional healing that needs to take place.

4. *Assist the client through the grieving process.* Clients who become disabled will often pass through stages of grief as they accept their condition. Similar to Kubler-Ross's stages of death bereavement, clients will often experience denial, anger, negotiation, resignation, and acceptance (Kubler-Ross & Kessler, 2014). The counselor can facilitate the client's progression through these stages.

5. *Know referral resources.* Individuals with disabilities have diverse needs, and it is important that counselors are aware of community resources (e.g., physicians, social services, physical therapists, special education teachers, experts on pain management, vocational rehabilitation, and so forth).

6. *Know the law and inform clients of the law.* Being familiar with many of the laws that protect the rights of clients with disabilities will help the counselor assure that the client is receiving all necessary services and that the client is not being discriminated against. Counselors can also empower clients by helping them understand their rights under the law.

7. *Be prepared for vocational/career counseling.* When challenged with a disability, many people will face having to make a career transition. Counselors should be ready to do career/vocational counseling or refer a client to a career/vocational counselor.

8. *Include the family.* Families can offer support, assist in long-term treatment planning, and help with the emotional needs of the client. Whenever reasonable, include the family.

9. *Be an advocate.* Individuals with disabilities commonly face prejudice and discrimination. Counselors can be client advocates by knowing the law, fighting for client rights, and assisting the client in fighting for his or her rights. A client who knows his or her rights and who acts as an advocate for himself or herself will likely feel empowered.

10. *Respect and empower your clients.* Most individuals with disabilities do not continually focus on their disabilities. Counselors should avoid the overuse of labels, speak to their client's abilities, and be positive forces for their clients.

Counseling Individuals Who Use and Abuse Substances

With alarming numbers of individuals in all walks of life abusing illicit and prescription drugs, there is little question that counselors today need to know how to work with clients who may be dependent on or addicted to substances. The following guidelines offer a number of critical issues to consider when working with these individuals (Fisher & Harrison, 2018; Lewis, Dana, & Blevins, 2015; Substance Abuse and Mental Health Services Administration, 2016):

1. *Embrace the multicultural counseling and social justice competencies.* Be aware of your own biases, have knowledge about your client's cultural background, gain the skills to work with your client based on his or her cultural background, help the client advocate for himself or herself, and be prepared to advocate for your client.

2. *Assess for substance dependency and abuse.* Those who abuse substances are often private about their use; thus, a counselor would be smart to conduct a structured interview that asks about a wide range of substance abuse issues. In addition, several good assessment instruments can assess for use and abuse. The earlier you identify a potential problem, the greater the likelihood that counseling will be successful.

3. *Gain knowledge about substance abuse.* Counselors should have basic knowledge about the course of treatment for various substances. Theories of substance abuse treatment vary, and the course of treatment can change based on the type of substance being abused.

4. *Know about co-occurring disorders and abuse.* It is not unusual for a substance abuser to be abusing more than one substance and to also have a mental disorder. Counselors need to know how to address all of the client's concerns (e.g., which disorder to address immediately, how to balance the treatment of multiple disorders).

5. *Keep up on medical innovations and biological interventions.* Treatment of substance abusers can change dramatically as new medical innovations arise (e.g., use of Narcan for opioid overdose and other pharmaceutical interventions for a variety of chronic addictions). Ensure, through continuing education, that are you familiar with the most recent developments.

6. *Build a relationship and stay committed.* Although a large number of individuals who abuse substances want to stop, they may have a difficult time doing so, and it is common for substance abusers to have "slips." Counselors need to be committed to their clients' treatment, even when they falter. Knowing that a counselor is there for them, regardless of their mistakes, can help clients get back to treatment quickly.

7. *Be prepared to refer to rehabilitation facilities or hospitals.* Sometimes, hospitalization is critical to save the life of a substance abuser. Other times, rehabilitation facilities may be the only mechanism to help the abuser. Know these resources and how to refer to them.

8. *Refer to self-help groups.* Alcoholics Anonymous, Al-Anon, Narcotics Anonymous, and other self-help groups have become an important part of treatment for many substance abusers. Be aware of these resources and have them available for your clients.

9. *Focus on family support.* When in treatment, support by family can be critical to clients. When it seems helpful, consider including family members in the treatment.

10. *Stay in touch, and stay committed.* Substance abuse can be a lifelong problem, and it is important the abuser know the counselor is committed to him or her as long as necessary—even if it is over the span of several years.

Final Thoughts

This part of the chapter touched on a number of populations with which you are likely to work in your career as a counselor. However, many other populations were left out. As you do work with clients from

EXPERIENTIAL EXERCISE 9.5

Interviewing Diverse Clients

Find a person who identifies as a member of one of the populations we discussed in this chapter. Then, using the descriptions outlined in this chapter, ask the individual questions about his or her life. Add other questions, as needed, to obtain a full picture of the individual. For instance, if I was interviewing a person struggling with substance abuse, I might ask the questions that follow. When everyone in class has finished their interviews, share what you found in groups or with the larger class.

1. What kind of substances have you abused over your lifetime?
2. Are you still using?
3. If you ever stopped or are currently not using, what most helped you stop?
4. How has your substance use or abuse impacted your life?
5. Have you ever sought counseling for your substance use and/or abuse?
6. Have you ever been hospitalized or in a rehabilitation facility for your substance use and/or abuse?
7. Have you ever been to a self-help group, such as AA, for your substance use and/or abuse?
8. What kind of support have you received from your family and friends for your substance use or abuse?
9. What kind of help and commitment from a counselor would you find worthwhile if you were seeking such assistance?
10. What resources do you think would be most helpful for you in stopping your substance use or abuse?
11. Any other thoughts about your substance use or abuse that might be helpful to a counselor?

varied backgrounds, keep in mind that culturally competent counseling is "a consistent readiness to identify the cultural dimensions of clients' lives and a subsequent integration of culture into counseling work" (McAuliffe, 2013, p. 6). This implies that you have a desire to work with all clients and that you have the willingness to learn about new groups as you develop as a counselor. Always be willing to learn more, be supervised, and expand your level of competence as you take in new knowledge about ways of counseling different populations (see Experiential Exercise 9.5).

Summary

This chapter began with a look at the changing demographics in the United States and highlighted the importance of being culturally competent, given the diverse society in which we live. We then noted that diverse clients are sometimes wary of counseling for a number of reasons, including the counselor believing in the melting-pot myth, not having the ability to adapt the counseling relationship, lacking an understanding of social forces, having an ethnocentric worldview, being ignorant of his or her unconscious bias, having an inability to understand cultural differences in the expression of symptomatology, using unreliable assessment and research instruments, not being aware of institutional discrimination, and having an individualistic perspective.

The chapter went on to define culturally competent counseling. Using McAuliffe's (2013) definition, we noted it included "a consistent readiness to identify the cultural dimensions of clients' lives and a subsequent integration of culture into counseling work" (p. 6). We then identified 10 important processes that go into being a culturally competent counselor.

In the chapter, we went on to discuss the RESPECTFUL model of cross-cultural counseling, the Multicultural and Social Justice Counseling Competencies, and an integrative model of cross-cultural counseling. The integrative model combined some of the ideas from the RESPECTFUL model and the Multicultural and Social Justice Counseling Competencies. It also took some ideas from the tripartite model of personal identity and the existential model of cross-cultural counseling by defining three aspects of self in all persons: individual experiences, group experiences, and universal experiences. We noted 10 important aspects of the integrative model, which included the counselor knowing and monitoring his or her biases; being curious, respectful, and collaborative and building a working alliance; not embodying any of the nine reasons for clients to be wary of counseling; learning about the client's culture and belief system (knowledge); using the RESPECTFUL model; using appropriate skills based on the client's cultural background; considering if the client has an individualistic or collectivist perspective; knowing when to be an advocate; giving full attention to the three areas of experience that define the self; and being committed to client's well-being and the counseling process. We also pointed out that the development of goals should be a collaborative process.

The second half of the chapter examined a number of strategies for working with select populations, including individuals from different ethnic and racial groups; individuals from diverse religious backgrounds; women; men; lesbian, gay, bisexual, transgender, and questioning individuals; the homeless and the poor; children; older persons; individuals with serious mental disorders; individuals with disabilities; and, individuals who use and abuse substances. The chapter concluded by reminding you that culturally competent counselors are willing to learn more, be supervised, and expand their level of competence as they take in new knowledge about ways of counseling different populations.

Key Words and Terms

attitudes and beliefs, knowledge, skills, and action

collectivistic perspective

community advocacy

counseling children

counseling individuals from different ethnic and racial groups

counseling individuals from diverse religious backgrounds

counseling individuals who use and abuse substances

counseling individuals with disabilities

counseling individuals with serious mental disorders

counseling lesbian, gay, bisexual, transgender, and questioning individuals

counseling men

counseling older persons

counseling the poor and the homeless

counseling women

culturally competent counseling

domain I: counselor self-awareness

domain II: client worldview

domain III: counseling relationship

domain IV: counseling and advocacy interventions

ethnocentric worldview

existential model of cross-cultural counseling

group experiences

ignorance of one's unconscious bias

inability to adapt the counseling relationship

inability to understand cultural differences in expression of symptomatology

individual experiences

individualistic perspective

individuals with serious mental disorders

institutional advocacy

institutional discrimination

integrative model of culturally competent counseling

international and global affairs advocacy

interpersonal advocacy

lack of understanding of social forces

McAuliffe's definition of culturally competent helping

melting-pot myth

Multicultural and Social Justice Counseling Competencies

public policy advocacy

the Self

three spheres of experience

tripartite model of personal identity

universal experiences

unreliability of assessment and research instrument

Credits

CHAPTER 10

Ethical, Legal, and Professional Issues

Learning Objectives

1. Understand the purpose of, and limitations to, ethical codes
2. Learn about and apply four different ethical decision-making models, including problem-solving, moral, developmental, and social constructivist models
3. Examine the following ethical issues important in the work of the counselor and apply the knowledge to related vignettes:
   - Informed consent
   - Confidentiality
   - Privileged communication
   - Competence
   - Maintaining boundaries and prohibited relationships
   - Values in the counseling relationship
   - Cross-cultural counseling
   - Technology in counseling
   - Supervision
   - Reporting ethical violations
4. Reflect on 77 ethical situations to which counselors responded
5. Highlight 26 best-practice behaviors that will help ensure optimal work with clients
6. Examine the importance and cost of malpractice insurance

Introduction

In this chapter, we will first examine the purpose of, and limitations to, ethical codes and then describe four models of ethical decision-making, including problem-solving, moral, developmental, and social-constructivist models. Next, we will highlight several select ethical issues, including informed consent, confidentiality, privileged communication, competence, maintaining boundaries and prohibited relationships, values in the counseling relationship, cross-cultural counseling, technology in counseling, supervision, and reporting ethical violations. Each of these areas includes ethical vignettes for you to ponder. We provide and ask you to reflect on the results of a 77-item survey of counselor behaviors completed by more than 500 ACA members who were asked to determine whether each behavior was ethical or unethical. The chapter then offers 26 ways to provide best practice as a counselor and decrease the likelihood of being sued. If sued, however, we encourage you to have malpractice insurance, which is highlighted in the last section of the chapter. Throughout the chapter, we will be referring to ACA's (2014) Code of Ethics, but feel free to refer to the ethics code of other professional organizations if you prefer

(e.g., American Mental Health Association, American School Counselor Association, American Psychological Association, National Board for Certified Counselors, and so forth). ACA's (2014) Code of Ethics can be found at www.counseling.org/resources/aca-code-of-ethics.pdf.

Purpose of and Limitations to Ethical Codes

Ethical codes are relatively new in the helping professions, with the first code published by the American Psychological Association in 1953. ACA followed suit soon after that with its first code in 1961. ACA tends to revise its code about every 10 years, and its latest code was published in 2014 (ACA, 2014). A lot can change in 10 years. For instance, parts of codes can quickly become obsolete, and codes can sometimes not cover new, important areas. However, there are still a number of important purposes of ethical codes (Corey, Corey, & Corey, 2019; Remley & Herlihy, 2016). For instance, ethics codes do the following:

- Protect consumers from unethical and incompetent work of counselors
- Further the professional stance of the professional organization and the members they serve
- Show that a profession is grounded in a specific body of knowledge, skills, and values
- Reflect and uphold specific values and beliefs of a profession
- Offer a framework for the ethical decision-making process
- Offer some measure of defense in case one is sued (if the code was followed)

Although accomplishing all these, there are the following *limitations of ethical codes* (Corey et al., 2019; Remley & Herlihy, 2016):

- Codes do not address all issues one will face
- They cannot always be enforced
- Often, they do not bring the consumer into the code construction process
- Codes can be at odds with other methods of addressing the issue (e.g., laws)
- Sometimes codes conflict with other codes or even within the same code
- Sometimes codes conflict with the values of the professional

Ethical codes delineate the values and beliefs of a professional organization, but they are not legal documents. However, the licensing boards of some states will adopt the code, thus making them have a bit of legal clout. In fact, 18 states have adopted ACA's 2014 Code of Ethics (Shifflet, 2016). Most importantly, ethical codes can be used in the sometimes difficult ethical decision-making process. The following section describes four models of ethical decision-making, and, along with the code, the counselor can use these models in deciding on a direction when facing an ethical dilemma.

Ethical Decision-Making Models

Ethical codes are important guides in helping us make decisions, but they often don't tell us which decision to make. For instance, suppose you have a client you think *may* be suicidal; the code states:

> The general requirement that counselors keep information confidential does not apply when disclosure is required to protect clients or identified others from serious and foreseeable harm or when legal requirements demand that confidential information must be revealed. Counselors consult with other professionals when in doubt as to the validity of an exception. Additional considerations apply when addressing end-of-life issues. (Section B.2.a., Serious and foreseeable harm and legal requirements)

The code is specific, kind of—if you think there is foreseeable harm, you can consult and, if need be, break confidentiality. But what if you're still unsure after consulting? What do you do then? Four models of ethical decision-making have been developed over the years that can help you decide what decision path to go down (Cottone & Tarvydas, 2016; Levitt & Moorhead, 2013; Welfel, 2016). They include problem-solving models, moral models, developmental models, and the social constructivist perspective. Let's examine each of these.

Problem-Solving Models

This pragmatic, hands-on model has been described by several people and involves a number of common-sense steps. One model, by Corey et al. (2019), includes eight steps, and carefully navigating through them can help the counselor come up with a decision. The steps include the following:

1. Identifying the problem or dilemma
2. Identifying the potential issues involved
3. Reviewing the relevant ethical guidelines
4. Knowing the applicable laws and regulations
5. Obtaining consultation
6. Considering possible and probable courses of action
7. Enumerating the consequences of various decisions
8. Deciding on the best course of action

You can see how going through these eights steps can help a professional gain some clarity into an ethical dilemma while offering a clear-cut method of dealing with a thorny ethical issue.

Moral Models

While the problem-solving model emphasizes the pragmatic aspects of ethical decision-making, other theorists stress the role of moral principles in this process. Although not necessarily mutually exclusive with the problem-solving model, the moral model suggests that the counselor examine a number of moral principles in making a decision of ethical consequence. One well-known model by Ann Kitchener (1984, 1986; Urofsky, Engels, & Engebretson, 2008) describes the role of five moral principles in making ethical decisions and suggests counselors reflect on them when faced with thorny ethical decisions. They include (a) *autonomy,* preserving client's self-determination; (b) *beneficence,* protecting the good of others and society; (c) *nonmaleficence*, avoiding doing harm to clients and others; (d) *justice*, treating clients fairly and equally; and (e) *fidelity*, maintaining clients' trust and being committed to them. A sixth moral principle, *veracity*, is generally attributed to Meara, Schmidt, and Day (1996) and is often added to this list. Veracity has to do with being truthful and genuine with the client about the counseling relationship. Other moral models suggest that helpers should be cognizant of their character or virtues and strive to make decisions by being self-aware, compassionate, and understanding of cultural differences and by doing good and having a vision for the future (Welfel, 2016).

Developmental Models

Instead of focusing on the ethical decision-making steps or moral principles, the developmental model examines the cognitive ability of the decision maker when making ethical decisions (Lambie, Hagedor, & Ieva, 2010; Levitt & Moorhead, 2013). Those who are at lower levels of cognitive development tend to be black and white in their thinking, believe there is a right and wrong when making decisions, and tend to look for the truthful or correct response. In contrast, those who are at higher levels of cognitive development view ethical decision-making as a more complex process that is deeply self-reflective. They can see multiple ways of viewing the problem, are more flexible, and are adept at considering differing points of view. These models suggest that facilitating movement of counselor trainees and counselors toward higher-level thinking can change the manner in which they view a problem and respond to it.

For instance, let's examine two counselors. One, James, is at a lower developmental level, and the other, Georgia, is at a higher level. Both are faced with the same dilemma. James and Georgia work at a substance abuse rehab conducting group counseling. One day, a client of theirs who is addicted to crack cocaine comes in and has a negative urine screening for marijuana. The client, who has been in the clinic and clean for 36 of his 60 days, goes up to his counselor and says, "I had a pass to go home for the weekend, and while at home, a friend of mine offered me some pot. I took a couple of hits, and then realized I was screwed. I'm so sorry, and I want to stay in rehab so I can be clean of everything." The rules are that any negative screening means the client is thrown out of the clinic. James examines the ethical guidelines, reads the agency policy guidelines, and decides that the "right thing to do," and the only choice he has, is to report his client to an administrator. Georgia, however, views ethical decision-making differently. She also reads the agency policy and reviews the ethical guidelines. In addition, she uses one or more ethical decision-making models to help her decide what to do. She also consults with others to gain other points of view and only then carefully deliberates about what would be best for her client, the agency, society, and herself. After careful deliberation, she comes to a decision about how to proceed.

In this case, the conclusion is less important than the process, as Georgia has dealt with the situation in a complex and thoughtful manner, as opposed to James's somewhat hasty decision-making. In fact, although both may come to the same conclusion, I would rather work with someone like Georgia because she shows thoughtfulness and the ability to self-reflect—qualities I would want in a colleague (and a friend!). Thus, one can see that ethical decision-making can be, and perhaps should be, a complex process (see Reflection Exercise 10.1).

Ethical Decision-Making—Considering Alternatives

In small groups, brainstorm various processes you can use, and come up with different scenarios for the aforementioned ethical dilemma. Consider any decision possible (even ones that can get the counselor fired). Then discuss the consequences of them in your small groups. Share what the small group considers to be the best decision with the class.

Social Constructivist Perspective

Those who take a social constructivist perspective believe that "what is real is not an objective fact; rather, what is real evolves through interpersonal interaction and agreement as to what is 'fact'" (Cottone, 2016, p. 79). This approach assumes that ethical decision-making does not take place "in the head" of the counselor but as a social interaction between the counselor and the parties involved, which could include the client, significant others related to the client, supervisors, and a larger social context (e.g., beliefs of professionals and professional organizations). As a result, there may be more than one truth or answer to an ethical dilemma. Individuals who take on a social constructivist perspective are humble with their clients, collaborators, supervisors, and others involved in the dilemma. They believe solutions come out of dialogue and conversation. They approach all parties involved with curiosity and wonder and treat them as equals and collaborators in the decision-making process as they jointly try to find the best solution to the ethical dilemma being faced. However, best is relative, as there may be several best solutions, and, jointly, those involved need to negotiate to find a solution or solutions. This approach is not for the faint-hearted, as it requires including people in the decision-making process that are often left out (e.g., clients and people close to the clients; see Reflection Exercise 10.2).

Using Ethical Decision-Making Models

Using each of the ethical decision-making models just described, reflect on the following vignette and then share your thoughts in small groups or with the class. Show how each model can be used to help guide your decision-making process.

You work with a 15-year-old child at a mental health agency (or at a school—your choice). You have been seeing her for several months, and she has just confided with you that she is considering becoming sexually active with her boyfriend. She says her boyfriend insists that she not use birth control and that he will make sure she does not get pregnant. She is excited about being with her boyfriend sexually and is looking for your approval. You have spoken with her mother about the importance of confidentiality but also made the girl and the mother aware of the limits of confidentiality due to the girl's age. Also, in your informed consent statement, which both the girl and mother signed, you noted that you would break confidentiality if there was foreseeable danger.

Select Ethical Issues and Ethical Dilemmas

The following highlights a number of important ethical areas generally described in most codes of ethics, including informed consent, confidentiality, privileged communication, competence, maintaining boundaries and prohibited relationships, values in the counseling relationship, cross-cultural counseling, technology in counseling, supervision, and reporting ethical violations. Using the ACA (2014) Code of Ethics, we describe each area and then go on to offer several related ethical vignettes. In reviewing these issues and responding to the vignettes, consider the ethical decision-making models, and refer to the ACA (2014) Code of Ethics (www.counseling.org/knowledge-center/ethics).

Informed Consent

Already discussed in Chapter 7, *informed consent* involves the client's right to know the purpose and nature of all aspects of client involvement with the counselor and having the client give his or her consent for treatment (Corey et al., 2019; Remley & Herlihy, 2016; see Section a.2, Informed Consent in the Counseling Relationship, of ACA's 2014 Code of Ethics). We noted that clients are generally handed a *professional disclosure statement* that describes the parameters of counseling and are generally asked to sign it, acknowledging they give their informed consent for treatment. After referring to the ACA Code of Ethics statement on informed consent in Chapter 7 as well as the 20 items that tend to be highlighted in a professional disclosure statement (see p. 145 of Chapter 7), reflect on the vignettes that follow.

Ethical Vignettes Related to Informed Consent

1. After working with a client for several sessions, a counselor believes that her client has an antisocial personality disorder. In fact, the counselor is becoming increasingly nervous when working with her client and is concerned for her safety. The counselor feels as if she does not have the adequate training to work with the client, and even if she gained it, there are other professionals she knows who have more experience working with such clients. The counselor explains to the client that she would like to refer her to another counselor, at which point the client becomes livid. The client says that the counselor never explained this in the professional disclosure statement. Does the client have a point? Should the counselor refer the client? What ethical, professional, and legal issues might there be?

2. A counselor gives a written document to a family explaining the limitations of confidentiality and the general direction the family sessions will take. After reading the informed consent document, the parents sign it and bring in the family. The informed consent document is not given or described to the children, who are 8 and 5 years old. Has the counselor acted ethically, professionally, and legally? Should children be involved in reading and/or signing informed consent statements?

3. A counselor develops a four-page, single-spaced professional disclosure statement, which is often quickly read by his clients and subsequently signed. The counselor realizes that due to its length and clients' desire to start counseling, clients rarely read the document. On a few occasions, clients have even said things such as "Oh, I thought you were a doctor" (he's not), "I didn't realize it was going to cost this much," and "I didn't think this was going to be how counseling was," and one client asked the counselor what he would do if he thought the client was suicidal. The counselor questions if most of his clients ever read the professional disclosure statement, as he knows that all the items asked about were covered in it. Is there anything the

counselor can do to make sure the clients are fully informed? What ethical, professional, and legal issues are there?

4. A counselor never uses a written professional disclosure statement nor has his clients sign informed consent statements. Instead, he verbally announces what will occur in counseling and asks clients, caringly, if they understand and have any questions. Is this ethical, professional, and legal?

Confidentiality

Keeping client information confidential is one of the most important ingredients in building a trusting relationship (Milliken & Neukrug, 2009; Neukrug & Milliken, 2011) and is covered thoroughly in ACA's (2014) Code of Ethics in Section B: Confidentiality and Privacy. However, when to keep *confidentiality* can be tricky and is not always clear-cut:

> A 17-year-old client tells you that she is pregnant. Do you need to tell her parents? What if the client was 15 or 12? What if she was drinking or using cocaine while pregnant? What if she tells you she wants an abortion? What if she tells you she is suicidal because of the pregnancy?

Although most of us would agree that confidentiality is a key part of the helping relationship, it may not always be the best course. All ethical decisions are, to some degree, a judgment call, but some general guidelines can be followed when you are considering making a decision to break confidentiality (always check local laws, however, to see if there are variations). Generally, confidentiality can be broken for the following reasons:

- If a child is a minor and the law states that parents have a right to information about their child (usually, they do have such a right)
- If a client asks the counselor to break confidentiality (e.g., the counselor's testimony is needed in court)
- If a counselor is bound by the law to break confidentiality (e.g., calling Child Protective Services for suspected child abuse)
- To reveal information about a client to the counselor's supervisor—information that will help in processing the counseling relationship and will benefit the client
- When a counselor has a written agreement from his or her client to reveal information to specified sources (e.g., other mental health professionals who are working with the same client)
- If a client is in danger of harming himself or herself or someone else. This is known as *foreseeable harm* (sometimes called *duty to warn*; see Reflection Exercise 10.3, then do Experiential Exercise 10.1).

REFLECTION EXERCISE 10.3

The Tarasoff Case

The case of *Tarasoff v. Board of Regents of University of California* (1976) set a precedent for the responsibility that mental health professionals have regarding maintaining confidentiality and acting to prevent a client from harming self or others. This case involved a client who was seeing a psychologist at the University of California at Berkeley health services. The client told the psychologist that he intended to kill Tatiana

REFLECTION EXERCISE 10.3—CONTINUED

Tarasoff, his former girlfriend. After the psychologist consulted with his supervisor, the supervisor suggested that he call the campus police. Campus security subsequently questioned the client and released him, seeing no immediate likelihood of harm. The client refused to see the psychologist any longer, and 2 months later, he killed Tatiana. Tatiana's parents sued and won, with the California Supreme Court stating that the psychologist did not do all that he could to protect Tatiana. Although state laws vary on how to handle confidentiality, this case suggests that if mental health professionals believe there is foreseeable harm, they have a duty to warn individuals and must break confidentiality when the public's safety is at risk. Generally, they must do all that is reasonably possible to assure that a person is not harmed. In this case, contacting Tatiana Tarasoff may have been the prudent thing to do.

If you are faced with a situation in which you think a client is in danger of harming self or someone else, what do you believe is your responsibility? Is it enough to consult with your supervisor? What if you disagree with your supervisor's decision?

EXPERIENTIAL EXERCISE 10.1

Unanswered Questions About Tarasoff

The Tarasoff case is one of the reasons almost all ethical codes have a statement about what to do in case a professional is faced with foreseeable harm presented by a client. If you remember from earlier in the chapter, in these cases confidentiality can be broken, and consultation is recommended if a counselor is in doubt about what to do. However, the Tarasoff case leaves a lot unanswered. For instance, Donald Bersoff, former president of the American Psychological Association, gave these following scenarios to his students and received a number of varied responses to whether confidentiality should be broken (Vitelli, 2014). In small groups, consider how you would respond to the following scenarios. Share them in class.

- "The patient says he is going to go home tonight and stab his wife in the arm. Asked if he is going to kill her, he responds, 'No, I just want her to bleed a bit.'
- The patient says he is going to go home tonight and punch his wife in the jaw.
- The patient says he is going to go home tonight and just cut off the tip of her pinky (on the nondominant hand).
- The patient says he is going to go home tonight and slap his wife in the face.
- The patient says he is going to go home tonight and scream at his wife until she cries." (Vitelli, 2014, para. 11)

In addition to times when breaking confidentiality is permissible, there are times when it is clearly not. Generally, it is not appropriate under the following conditions:

- If the counselor is frustrated with a client and he or she talks to a friend or colleague about the case just to let off steam. (Note: Even if names and identifying information are not given, this is unethical.)
- When a counselor has a request from another helping professional about information on the client but the other helping professional has not obtained a signed request form from the client
- When a friend asks a counselor to tell him or her something interesting about a client with whom the counselor is working
- When breaking confidentiality will clearly cause harm to a client and does not fall into one of the categories listed earlier

Now that we have examined when one should generally keep or break confidentiality, let's look at a few ethical vignettes. You probably want to have your ACA (2014) Code of Ethics nearby.

Ethical Vignettes Related to Confidentiality

1. After working at an agency for a few months, you realize that many counselors are talking about their clients with other counselors in a cathartic manner, not as a form of consultation or supervision. Is this ethical, professional, and legal?
2. While working with a client, she expresses her concern about her grandmother, who, she states, lives by herself, is depressed, has stopped eating, and has lost a considerable amount of weight. You contact the grandmother, but she refuses services. Is there anything you can do? Can you contact the police or support services at an agency?
3. While you are talking with a 15-year-old male client, he informs you that on a recent vacation, he was sexually molested by an uncle. He asks you not to tell his parents. What do you do?
4. A 17-year-old client tells you he is having sexual relations with his 17-year-old stepsister. What do you do?
5. A client of yours tells you that sometimes when she's drinking, she gets severely depressed and thinks about killing herself. You ask her if she has a plan, and she says, "Well, sometimes I think about just doing it with that gun my husband has." One day, she calls you; she's been drinking, and she tells you she's depressed. She hangs up, saying, "I don't know what I might do." What do you do?
6. While working with a client, she reveals that sometimes she takes the belt out and "whacks my kids good 'cause they just won't shut up." Do you break confidentiality and tell Child Protective Services? Since Child Protective Services won't reveal who has made the report, do you tell your client that you reported her?
7. A client who is receiving services in your agency demands to see her case notes. In them, you have noted her diagnosis, concerns about her parenting, and other information that you have not shared with her. You try to talk to her about why she wants to see the notes, and you suggest you can offer her a summary of them, but she says she wants a copy of the actual notes. Do you have to give them to her? (See Chapter 7 if you are unsure what to do.)
8. A client you have been seeing at a crisis center comes in and asks to see records pertaining to him. These include crisis logs that have information in them about other clients as well as case notes you have made concerning his situation. How do you respond?

Privileged Communication

Whereas confidentiality is described in ethical codes as the importance of keeping client information in confidence, *privileged communication* is decreed by state legislatures and refers to information that can legally be held in confidence (remember: ethical guidelines are not legal documents!; Remley & Herlihy, 2016). The client decides what is privileged. Generally, licensed professional counselors and related licensed mental professionals, priests and ministers, lawyers, and doctors are afforded the right of privileged communication with their clients. In contrast, communication between clients and school counselors, or other types of counselors, are usually not privileged. However, privileged communication is defined differently from state to state, and you should contact your state licensing board, state board of education, or other entities to know how it may be defined in your state and to determine whether you are a covered professional (Stone, 2015). The right of therapists to hold privileged communication was solidified by a 1996 court case, *Jaffee v. Redmond* (see Reflection Exercise 10.4).

REFLECTION EXERCISE 10.4

Jaffee v. Redmond

The 1996 court ruling *Jaffee v. Redmond* upheld the right to privileged communication for licensed social workers (Remley, Herlihy, & Herlihy, 1997). In this case, a police officer named Mary Lu Redmond was chasing a man who she thought stabbed another man. During the chase, Redmond shot and killed him. The family of the man she killed sued Redmond as well as the police department and the village, alleging that Redmond had used excessive force. Upon hearing that Redmond had received counseling from a licensed social worker, the plaintiff's lawyers attempted to require the social worker to give up her records and testify at the upcoming trial. Claiming that their communications were privileged, and on advice of her lawyer, Redmond refused to hand over her records. At that point, the judge told the jurors to presume that the records were likely to be negative to Redmond's case. The jury ended up awarding $545,000 to the plaintiffs. After a series of appeals, the U.S. Supreme Court decided that the licensed therapist did indeed hold privileged communication and that the judge's instruction prejudiced the jury and was unwarranted. Since the decision described the social worker as a "therapist" and "psychotherapist," the ruling likely protects all licensed therapists in federal courts.

Since our ethics codes entrust us to keep information between ourselves and our clients confidential, under what circumstances, if any, do you think a counselor should be compelled to break confidentiality?

The ACA (2014) ethics code only addresses privilege once:

> When ordered by a court to release confidential or privileged information without a client's permission, counselors seek to obtain written, informed consent from the client or take steps to prohibit the disclosure or have it limited as narrowly as possible because of potential harm to the client or counseling relationship. (Section B.2.d, Court-Ordered Disclosure)

Now that we've discussed privileged communication, see what you can do with the following vignettes. Keep your ACA (2014) Code of Ethics nearby to help you.

Ethical Vignettes Related to Privileged Communication

1. You are working toward your license under supervision by a licensed counselor. One of your clients, a woman with two children, is in counseling partly due to anxiety about her upcoming divorce. You receive a subpoena to go to court to provide information about your client for a child custody battle the couple is having. You decide to go to court but do not reveal any information, stating, "This is confidential information; I refuse to reveal anything." Are you acting ethically, professionally, and legally?

2. A licensed counselor tells you that she was recently asked by a court to reveal information about her client, who was being sued for injuring a person while driving intoxicated. The counselor refuses to reveal any information and is cited by the judge for being in contempt of court. The counselor is appealing the case, stating that the client's communication is privileged and that she does not have to reveal such information. Does she have a point?

3. A client's husband shows up at your office demanding to know if his wife is in counseling with you. You refuse to let him know if his wife has been in a counseling relationship with you and note that, in either case, all information at your office is confidential and privileged. He tells you that he'll sue you and the rest of this "fleabag" operation and that you have no right to keep information from him. Is what you stated accurate? Can you come up with any circumstances under which he would be able to gain information about his wife?

4. A licensed counselor has been working with a client who has confessed to you that he molested a 15-year-old girl 5 years ago. You believe there is no indication that he will perpetrate another such act. You are subpoenaed by the court to testify about the incident, but your client asks you not to testify, since the relationship is privileged. Should you testify?

Competence

Counselor *competence* is consistently acknowledged as a crucial ethical concern by most professional associations, and knowing one's limits of professional knowledge and level of competence is essential for the counselor (Corey, et al., 2015; Neukrug & Milliken, 2011). If you remember from Chapter 1, Section C.2., Professional Competence, of ACA's (2014) Code of Ethics addresses several issues related to competence, including the following:

- To only practice within one's area of training and experience ("boundaries of competence")
- To only practice new specialty areas if one has gained the appropriate education, training, and supervision
- To not accept employment in areas in which one has not been properly trained
- To monitor one's effectiveness and take appropriate steps when one realizes improvement is needed
- To consult with others when one has ethical concerns
- To participate in continuing education to keep up on current trends
- To monitor oneself for physical and emotional problems and to stop counseling when one is seriously impaired
- To make appropriate plans for transfer of clients to a colleague in case of a "counselor's incapacitation, death, retirement, or termination of practice"

See how you do with the following vignettes about competence and scope of knowledge. Keep your ACA (2014) Code of Ethics nearby.

Ethical Vignettes Related to Competence

1. A counselor decides to get trained in eye movement desensitization and reprocessing (EMDR), a process sometimes used in working with clients who have PTSD. The counselor undergoes the training, which consists of two weekends and additional case consultation with an EMDR expert. After completing all requirements, the counselor receives a certificate of completion. The counselor then goes on to advertise himself as a "trained EMDR specialist" and an "expert in treating trauma." Is this ethical, professional, and legal?

2. A counselor with a master's degree in school counseling has an opportunity to take a job, at a higher salary, as a rehabilitation counselor, despite the fact that she has not had coursework in that area. She is excited about her new job. Under what circumstance, if any, would this be ethical, professional, and legal?

3. A counselor is working with a client who begins to share bizarre thoughts concerning the end of the world. The counselor has had little training in working with individuals who show psychotic tendencies but decides he can handle the situation by taking an online continuing education workshop on working with psychotic patients. He does not undergo supervision. What ethical, professional, and legal issues might the counselor have in this case?

4. A client who is taking the antidepressant Prozac tells her counselor that she is still depressed and sees no changes despite having taken the medication for 2 months. The counselor suggests to the client that she might need an increase in her dosage or may need to try a different antidepressant. She suggests the client see the psychiatrist for a consult. Is telling the client that she might need an increased dosage or a different medication ethical, professional, and legal?

5. A counselor who will be relocating in 6 months to a new part of the country lets each of his clients know about his upcoming move. He says to each of them, "If you need to continue counseling, you can go to the state licensing board website and find someone listed there to see." Is this enough? Should he be making additional accommodations for his clients? If so, what do you think he should do?

Maintaining Boundaries and Prohibited Relationships

Formerly called *dual relationships* or *multiple relationships*, this refers to maintaining appropriate boundaries between the counselor and the client to ensure that the counseling relationship maintains its professional status. There are a number of times when maintaining appropriate boundaries would be critical. Sections A.5: Prohibited Noncounseling Roles and Relationships and A.6: Managing and Maintaining Boundaries and Professional Relationships of ACA's (2014) Code of Ethics offer these suggestions about maintaining boundaries:

- "Sexual and/or romantic counselor–client interactions or relationships with current clients, their romantic partners, or their family members are prohibited."
- "Counselors are prohibited from engaging in counseling relationships with persons with whom they have had a previous sexual and/or romantic relationship."

- Counselors are prohibited from having a sexual relationship with a former client for 5 years since their professional relationship ended, and if they are considering having a sexual relationship, they have to ensure, in writing, that the relationship will not be exploitive of the former client.
- "Counselors are prohibited from engaging in counseling relationships with friends or family members with whom they have an inability to remain objective."
- Counselors should not engage in social media with clients, although clients can access a professional website of a counselor.
- Counselors should generally avoid counseling relationships with those with whom they have had any kind of previous relationship. If they do accept such clients, they should ensure proper counseling through the informed consent statement, consultation, and supervision.
- Counselors should carefully consider if they should have any interactions with their clients outside of the formal counseling relationship (e.g., attend a funeral, wedding, graduation).
- Counselors should avoid "non-professional relationships with former clients, their romantic partners, or their family members when the interaction is potentially harmful to the client."

Maintaining boundaries and avoiding prohibited relationships are central to a trusting counseling relationship. With this in mind, look at the following vignettes. Keep your ACA (2014) Code of Ethics nearby.

Ethical Vignettes Related to Maintaining Boundaries and Prohibited Relationships

1. For months, a counselor has been encouraging her client to become involved in an increased exercise regime. One day, her client shows up at her spin class. What responsibility, if any, does the counselor have in this case? Would it be ethical and professional for the counselor to stay in the spin class?
2. A counselor is recently divorced and starts to date using an online dating service. He meets a person online, and they decide to meet for dinner. He finds himself immediately attracted to the person, but while they are talking, he realizes that he counseled the person's sister. What, if anything, should he do?
3. A counselor is attracted to her client and is having sexual fantasies about him. She knows it is inappropriate to become intimately involved with him but is concerned that her thoughts are interfering with the counseling relationship. She decides to have an open discussion with him about her feelings, hoping that it will help her get beyond her feelings. Is this appropriate? Is it ethical and professional? What do you think she should do?
4. A counselor's neighbor, who the counselor does not know well, periodically discusses problems with the counselor concerning her child. At one point, the neighbor says to the counselor, "You know, you have such great insight into my child. Maybe he can see you in counseling." The counselor is in private practice and, since he hardly knows the neighbor, says that a professional counseling relationship can be arranged. Is this ethical, legal, and professional? Are there any circumstances under which this might be okay?
5. A counselor lives in a rural community where there are few counselors, and he often is approached by potential clients he knows socially but with whom he does not have in-depth relationships. Are there any circumstances under which the counselor can accept these individuals as clients?
6. A counselor is working at a crisis center that has several volunteer workers. The counselor becomes attracted to a volunteer who, 7 years prior, used to be one of his clients, but he is no longer seeing

her professionally. The counselor decides to pursue a relationship with the former client. Is this appropriate? Is this ethical? Are there any safeguards he should adhere to?

7. A client who has had difficulty becoming pregnant has seen her counselor for years. The client believes that the counselor's commitment to and care for her has helped her get through this difficult time in her life. After years of trying, the client becomes pregnant and asks the counselor to come to her baby shower. She will be very disappointed if the counselor does not come. Should the counselor go? Explain any safeguards she should use if she decides to go or not go.

Values in the Counseling Relationship

Partly the result of some recent legal cases (Kaplan, 2014; Rudow, 2013), ACA's (2014) Code of Ethics added some important sections on how the counselor's personal values were to be handled when working with clients. In particular, one case has been cited as a reason for this change (see Reflection Exercise 10.5). Two sections of the current ACA's (2014) ethics code speak to the issue of values:

> Counselors are aware of—and avoid imposing—their own values, attitudes, beliefs, and behaviors. Counselors respect the diversity of clients, trainees, and research participants and seek training in areas in which they are at risk of imposing their values onto clients, especially when the counselor's values are inconsistent with the client's goals or are discriminatory in nature. (Section A.4.b, Personal Values)

and

> Counselors refrain from referring prospective and current clients based solely on the counselor's personally held values, attitudes, beliefs, and behaviors. Counselors respect the diversity of clients and seek training in areas in which they are at risk of imposing their values onto clients, especially when the counselor's values are inconsistent with the client's goals or are discriminatory in nature. (Section A.11.b, Values Within Termination and Referral)

REFLECTION EXERCISE 10.5

Julea Ward v. Board of Regents of Eastern Michigan University (EMU)

At EMU, Julea Ward, a graduate student in counseling, discovered she would be counseling a client who had been in a same-sex relationship. Believing she could not counsel him due to her religious beliefs regarding same-sex relationships, she asked her supervisor to refer him to another counselor. After considering this request, the supervisor decided that Ms. Ward should still be able to counsel this man and scheduled an informal review of Ms. Ward. The result of this review was a statement by the program that Ms. Ward needed to learn how to set aside her religious beliefs and be open to counseling a man in a same-sex relationship. She was thus asked to complete a remediation program or have a formal hearing with the faculty. She asked for a formal hearing and was eventually dismissed from the program. Ms. Ward sued EMU, and the courts initially upheld the school's decision. However, after appeal, the suit was settled out of court. This lawsuit, and others, had the result of changing the ACA ethics code so that it now more strongly states that counselors should not refer clients due to value differences. What are your thoughts about referring clients due to value differences?

As is evidenced from ACA's Code of Ethics, clients cannot be referred due to values differences; however, they should be referred if the counselor believes he or she does not have the training or competence to work with the client. Ideally, counselors should refer clients prior to taking them on if they believe they cannot work with them due to lack of knowledge and skills: "If counselors lack the competence to be of professional assistance to clients, they avoid entering or continuing counseling relationships" (ACA, 2014, Section A.11.a). In addition, the Ethics Code, and counselors themselves, strongly condemn imposing values on clients (e.g., religious beliefs, political ideas, etc.; Neukrug & Milliken, 2011). Let's look at a number of vignettes that speak to the issue of values in the counseling relationship. Keep your ACA (2014) Code of Ethics nearby when considering your responses.

Ethical Vignettes Related to Values

1. A counselor's client is from Tanzania, where partial clitoridectomy, the partial removal of the clitoris, is sometimes practiced and viewed as an ancient ritual and rite of passage. The client, who has an 11-year-old daughter, tells the counselor that it's time for the child to observe this ritual. She sees this as an important coming-of-age ceremony for her child, and family and friends will be at the ceremony. What is the counselor's ethical, professional, and legal obligation?

2. A counselor is working with a 12-year-old child who was born a biological boy but now identifies as a girl. The parents want their child to be their son and deny she is a girl. Therefore, they insist that she not wear clothes identified as female and that she partake in what are considered to be traditionally male activities (e.g., being involved in sports and dating girls). What ethical, professional, and legal concerns does the counselor have?

3. A counselor is working with a client who is a polygamist and has three wives. This practice is against the counselor's state law, and the counselor is personally offended by it. The counselor believes the client is misogynistic and verbally abusing his wives. What ethical, professional, and legal obligations does the counselor have?

4. After working with a client for a few months, a counselor realizes the client is addicted to cocaine and has a drinking problem. The counselor has little expertise in working with clients with substance abuse. What is the counselor's ethical and professional obligation in this case? Under what circumstances, if any, should the counselor continue working with the client?

5. A light-skinned African American Muslim counselor is regularly considered White by his clients. One of his clients is racist and continually makes anti-Muslim and anti-Black racist remarks, thinking that his counselor shares similar beliefs. The counselor is irritated by his client's remarks and wonders if it is negatively impacting his work with the client. What ethical obligation does the counselor have in this case? How do you think the counselor should respond? (See Reflection Exercise 10.6.)

REFLECTION EXERCISE 10.6

Racist and Anti-Semitic Remarks by My Client

Similar to item 5 just discussed, I once had a client who regularly made racist and anti-Semitic remarks. For a few months, I listened carefully as I tried to build a relationship with him. One day, he again made an anti-Semitic remark, at which point I looked at him and said, "You know, I'm Jewish." He quickly replied, "Oh, you're different."

Do you think that what I said was appropriate? Was it ethical and professional? Do you think I should have said anything? Did I have any grounds to refer this client? Is there anything else you can think of that I could have done?

Cross-Cultural Counseling

Throughout the ACA (2014) ethics code are statements about tending to cross-cultural differences and being culturally competent with clients. What follows are short summaries of a select number of these statements and their corresponding place in the code. Those in quotes are taken directly from the code.

- Counselors communicate to clients in ways that are developmental and cross-culturally appropriate and use interpreters when necessary. They should ensure that their clients understand their informed consent statements and take into account cultural differences in application of procedures based on the client's culture. (Section A.2.c, Developmental and Cultural Sensitivity)
- Counselors should understand their own cultural identities and examine how it may impact their counseling relationships. (Section A, Introduction)
- Counselors take into account how clients' understanding of confidentiality and privacy might vary based on their cultural background and have ongoing discussions with their clients about such concerns. (Section B.1.a, Multicultural/Diversity Considerations)
- "Counselors are knowledgeable about culturally and clinically appropriate referral resources and suggest these alternatives." (Section A.11.a, Competence within Termination and Referral)
- "Counselors inform parents and legal guardians about the role of counselors and the confidential nature of the counseling relationship, consistent with current legal and custodial arrangements. Counselors are sensitive to the cultural diversity of families and respect the inherent rights and responsibilities of parents/guardians regarding the welfare of their children/charges according to law. Counselors work to establish, as appropriate, collaborative relationships with parents/guardians to best serve clients." (Section B.5.b, Responsibility to Parents and Legal Guardians)
- "Whereas multicultural counseling competency is required across all counseling specialties, counselors gain knowledge, personal awareness, sensitivity, dispositions, and skills pertinent to being a culturally competent counselor in working with a diverse client population." (Section C.2.a, Boundaries of Competence)
- Counselors do not engage in discrimination. (Section C.5., Nondiscrimination)

- "Counselors recognize that culture affects the manner in which clients' problems are defined and experienced. Clients' socioeconomic and cultural experiences are considered when diagnosing mental disorders." (Section E.5.b, Cultural Sensitivity)

As you are already aware, cross-cultural issues are central to becoming a competent counselor. Let's see how you do responding to the following vignettes that speak to this important issue. Keep your ACA (2014) Code of Ethics nearby for assistance.

Ethical Vignettes Related to Cross-Cultural Counseling

1. A counselor believes that she has not worked well with an immigrant client from Myanmar due to cross-cultural differences. Rather than referring the client, she decides to obtain supervision and read more about the client's culture. Is this ethical, professional, and legal?
2. When working at your agency, you find some of your colleagues are subtly making sexist jokes and even remarks about some clients' lack of intelligence due to their cultural backgrounds. What responsibility do you have ethically, professionally, and morally? What would you do?
3. You find members in your family making sexist and racist jokes. Do you have any ethical, professional, and/or moral obligations in this case? What would you do? Have you ever faced this situation? What did you do?
4. A counselor you work with consistently blames his clients for their problems, even though you think it is obvious that external forces, such as poverty and racism, have negatively impacted their lives. Your colleague believes every person can thrive "if they really want to." What ethical, professional, or legal obligation do you have in this case, if any?
5. A colleague you work with tells you he believes that being gay or lesbian is a choice. He says he would never treat his gay and lesbian clients like that but that he knows, deep down inside, that they can choose to be straight. Do you have any ethical, professional, and moral obligation with this counselor?
6. A friend of yours advertises that she is a Christian counselor. You discover that when clients come to see her, she encourages them to read parts of the Bible during sessions and tells clients they need to ask for repentance for their sins. Is this ethical? Is this professional? Is this legal?
7. When working with a Korean client who is not expressive of her feelings, a counselor pressures the client to express feelings. The helper tells the client, "You can only get better if you express yourself." Is this counselor acting ethically and professionally?
8. When offering a parenting workshop to individuals who are poor, you are challenged by some of the parents when you tell them that "hitting a child is never okay." They tell you that you are crazy and that sometimes a good spanking is the only thing that will get the child's attention. Do they have a point? How should you respond? What ethical, professional, and legal obligations do you have, if any?

Technology in Counseling

As you are fully aware, technology has greatly changed the manner in which some people do counseling. Counseling is now conducted online, by phone, and even by e-mail. Confidentiality concerns, privacy issues, and concerns about security of records have become paramount and have been impacted by a number of laws, including the Health Insurance Portability and Accountability Act (HIPAA), the Family Educational Rights and Privacy Act (FERPA), and the Freedom of Information Act (FOIA; see Chapter

7). The 2014 Code of Ethics, Section H: Distance Counseling, Technology, and Social Media, addresses several of these concerns which are highlighted here:

- When using technology in counseling, counselors "develop knowledge and skills regarding related technical, ethical, and legal considerations (e.g., special certifications, additional course work)."
- Counselors "understand that they may be subject to laws and regulations of both the counselor's practicing location and the client's place of residence" and ensure that clients are aware of these legal concerns.
- "Counselors ensure that their clients are aware of pertinent legal rights and limitations governing the practice of counseling across state lines or international boundaries."
- "Counselor acknowledge the limitations of maintaining the confidentiality of electronic records and transmissions. They inform clients that individuals might have authorized or unauthorized access to such records or transmissions (e.g., colleagues, supervisors, employees, information technologists.)"
- "Counselors inform clients about the inherent limits of confidentiality when using technology. Counselors urge clients to be aware of authorized and/or unauthorized access to information disclosed."
- Counselors use appropriate encryption standards relative to confidentiality and transmission of records.
- When engaged in technology with clients, counselors take steps to verify the client's identity (e.g., code words).
- Counselors make clients aware of the limitations of counseling when using technology.
- Counselors should have clearly distinguishable professional and personal social media presences, and counselors should limit access to confidential information about the counselor.

Here are a few vignettes that speak to technology in counseling. With your ACA (2014) Code of Ethics nearby, see how you might respond to them.

Ethical Vignettes Related to Technology in Counseling

1. A counselor lives 10 miles from a border state and sees clients in his office who live in the bordering state. Frequently, he engages in telephone counseling or online counseling with his clients if they can't make it into the office. Is this ethical, professional, and legal? Is there anything he should do to ensure its legality?
2. Despite the fact that a counselor fully informs all his clients about the limits of confidentiality with technology, one of his client's computers is hacked, and her estranged husband manages to hear a live broadcast of one of her counseling sessions in which she speaks of their abusive relationship. The client is outraged and tells the counselor that she is going to sue him. Did the counselor act ethically, professional, and legally? Is there anything more the counselor could have done to ensure confidentiality? Can the client sue the counselor?
3. A client is in an ongoing online instant messaging counseling relationship with a counselor. One week, at the beginning of their session, the counselor paraphrases what occurred the week before. The client insists she did not have the previous session, saying she had tried to connect but had connection problems. Apparently, her "code name" was stolen and someone else pretended to be

her. Is this counselor liable for this "mistake"? Is there anything else the counselor could have done to ensure confidentiality?

4. A counselor uses encrypted software when sending confidential information to insurance companies and other professionals. However, the encrypted software is not HIPAA approved. Are there consequences to using non-HIPAA-approved encryption? Is this ethical, professional, and legal?

5. A school counselor is concerned about one of her students and decides to ask the student to befriend her on a social media platform on which the student is active. The student does so. Is this ethical, professional, and legal? What might the consequences be of befriending her and of not befriending her?

Supervision

One method of ensuring adequate services to clients is through supervision. Supervision allows the counselor to examine his or her view of human nature, theoretical approach, ability at implementing techniques, and effectiveness with clients. Supervision should start during a counselor's training program and will often continue as long as a person is working with clients. A strong supervisory relationship that is based on trust, mutual respect, and understanding can assist counselors in taking a good look at attitudes, knowledge, and skills (Bernard & Goodyear, 2018; Corey et al., 2019). The supervisor's responsibilities are broad, and you are encouraged to read all of Section F: Supervision, Training, and Teaching, of the ACA (2014) Code of Ethics to view the many roles of the supervisor. To highlight some of the more salient roles, we find that supervisors are responsible for the following:

- Ensuring the welfare of the client
- Ensuring that supervisees inform clients that they are undergoing supervision and the limits, therefore, of confidentiality
- Ensuring appropriate boundaries are kept between the supervisee and supervisor
- Acting as gatekeepers for the profession and assisting supervisees in finding remedial assistance when needed
- Helping supervisees find counseling services, if needed, and avoiding offering counseling services to the supervisee
- Providing ongoing feedback to the supervisee about the supervisee's progress as a counselor
- Recommending the dismissal and removal from training programs, counseling settings, and credentialing processes if the individual cannot provide acceptable counseling services to the clients the individual serves

Now that we've briefly discussed some ethical concerns related to supervision, look at the following vignettes. Keep your ACA (2014) Code of ethics nearby.

Ethical Vignettes Related to Supervision

1. A counselor believes his client is suicidal, but his supervisor, after a careful review of the situation and after meeting with the client, decides otherwise. The counselor is concerned, believes there is foreseeable harm, and thinks he needs to act. What recourse, if any, does he have? What ethical, professional, and legal issues might there be?

2. After meeting with his supervisee, a supervisor is concerned that the child of a client that the supervisee is working with is being abused and believes she should report the parent to Child Protective

Services. The supervisee has doubts and is concerned that if the supervisor does report the child, it will negatively impact the supervisee's relationship with the parent. What should the supervisee do? If the supervisor does report the parent, will the parent suspect the supervise and/or the supervisor of reporting her? What ethical, professional, and legal consequences are there for reporting or for not reporting?

3. After having worked for a semester with a supervisee, a supervisor has serious doubts about the trainee's ability as a counselor. As a consequence, the supervisee has been placed in a professional development plan in her graduate program that focuses on improving her counseling skills. The supervisee disagrees with the supervisor's assessment. What recourse, if any, does the supervisee have? What ethical, professional, and legal considerations should the supervisee and the supervisor consider?

4. In his professional disclosure statement to clients, a counselor fails to tell them that he is being supervised. Is this ethical, legal, and professional?

5. Under supervision, a supervisee increasingly feels comfortable talking about her own issues, to the point that the supervisor thinks they are breaching an imaginary line between supervision and counseling. The supervisor suggests the supervisee enter counseling, and the supervisee becomes angry and feels abandoned by the supervisor. How should the supervisor respond? Has the supervisor acted ethically, legally, professionally?

Reporting Ethical Violations

Section I of the ACA (2014) Code of Ethics, Resolving Ethical Issues, helps counselors and others know how to proceed when addressing an ethical violation. Here are some highlights of that section, but you are encouraged to read the whole section.

- Whenever possible and feasible, a counselor should try to resolve ethical dilemmas with open communication and with involvement of all parties involved. Seeking consultation with colleagues and supervisors is advised, when necessary.

REFLECTION EXERCISE 10.7

Informal Resolution of an Ethical Violation

A psychologist I knew reported another psychologist to the state licensing board for writing poor assessment reports. The licensing board turned around and reprimanded the reporting psychologist for not going directly to the other psychologist and trying to resolve the issue informally.

Would you be willing to report a colleague of yours for a minor ethical violation? Are you willing to talk to your friends and family if they do something you consider to be a minor moral concern? It takes resolve to report people or to confront those we are close to. Yet it is our moral and ethical responsibility.

- If serious harm has occurred or is likely to occur, a counselor should take appropriate action, which may include "referral to state or national committees on professional ethics, voluntary national certification bodies, state licensing boards, or appropriate institutional authorities." (Section 1.2b, Reporting Ethical Violations)

- If a counselor believes another counselor has violated an ethical code, the counselor should try to address the issue informally with the other counselor, unless serious harm has occurred to a client.

Consider the following vignettes regarding reporting of unethical behavior. Keep your ACA (2014) Code of Ethics nearby.

Ethical Vignettes Related to Reporting Ethical Violations

1. A counselor has just started her PhD and is advertising herself as being a PhD candidate. She has put her name on a nameplate along with "PhD Candidate" next to it. A colleague of hers believes this is confusing to clients, as she is not anywhere near completion of her PhD. Is it ethical, professional, and legal for the friend to advertise herself as a PhD candidate? Should the colleague confront the counselor?

2. A client is possibly suicidal, and the counselor, who is being supervised, needs help assessing her suicidality. The counselor invites a colleague to help her assess the client's level of suicidality. The counselor's supervisor is not consulted and, when the supervisor finds out, tells the counselor she has broken confidentiality and committed an ethical violation. The supervisor reports her to the licensing board. Has the counselor acted appropriately? What about the supervisor?

3. A counselor suspects that a colleague has been engaging in insurance fraud. The counselor believes that this violation is so egregious that the counselor foregoes talking to him directly and reports him to the insurance company and to the licensing board. Has the counselor acted ethically, professionally, and legally?

4. A counselor strongly suspects that a colleague is having sex with a client. The counselor approaches the colleague, but he denies it. Because the counselor still has strong suspicions, she goes to the ACA ethics board. The ACA ethics board informs the counselor that the counselor's colleague is not a member and they have no jurisdiction. They suggest the counselor go to the state licensing board. Has ACA acted appropriately? What should the counselor do?

Surveying Ethical Behaviors of Counselors

In 2011, Neukrug and Milliken surveyed more than 500 members of ACA and asked these counselors to give their *perceptions of 77 counselor behaviors*. Table 10.1 lists each of those behaviors along with the percentage of ACA members who thought the behavior was ethical. Each student should make a list of five to 10 of these behaviors and then form small groups. In your groups, select a few behaviors and find the corresponding section(s) in ACA's ethical code that speak to it. Pick two or three of the items from your group list and share them in class along with the section(s) of the code that corresponds to them. What thoughts does the group and the class have on these selected behaviors?

TABLE 10.1   What Is Ethically Correct Behavior?

COUNSELOR BEHAVIOR	Percent of counselors who viewed behavior as ethical
1. Being an advocate for clients	99
2. Encouraging a client's autonomy and self-determination	98
3. Breaking confidentiality if the client is threatening harm to self	96
4. Referring a client due to interpersonal conflicts	95
5. Having clients address you by your first name	95
6. Making a diagnosis based on DSM	93
7. Using an interpreter to understand your client	89
8. Self-disclosing to a client	87
9. Counseling an undocumented worker (illegal immigrant)	87
10. Consoling your client through touch (e.g., hand on shoulder)	84
11. Publicly advocating for a controversial cause	84
12. Keeping client records on your office computer	74
13. Attending a client's formal ceremony (e.g., wedding)	72
14. Counseling a terminally ill client on end-of-life decisions, including suicide	69
15. Providing counseling over the Internet	68
16. Hugging a client	67
17. Not being a member of a professional association	66
18. Counseling a pregnant teenager without parental consent	62
19. Telling your client you are angry at him or her	62
20. Sharing confidential information with an administrative supervisor	59
21. Guaranteeing confidentiality for couples and families	58
22. Refraining from making a diagnosis to protect a client from a third party (e.g., an employer who might demote a client)	55
23. Bartering (accepting goods or services) for counseling services	53
24. While completing a dissertation, using the title PhD Candidate in clinical practice	48
25. Withholding information about a minor despite parents' request	48
26. Selling clients counseling products (e.g., books, videos, etc.)	47
27. Using techniques that are not theory- or research-based	43
28. Pressuring a client to receive needed services	43
29. Becoming sexually involved with a former client (at least 5 years after the counseling relationship ended)	43

COUNSELOR BEHAVIOR	Percent of counselors who viewed behavior as ethical
30. Not allowing clients to view your case notes about them	43
31. Referring a client unhappy with his or her homosexuality for reparative therapy	38
32. Accepting only clients who are male or clients who are female	37
33. Guaranteeing confidentiality for group members	37
34. Charging for individual counseling although seeing a family	35
35. Accepting clients only from specific cultural groups	32
36. Breaking the law to protect your client's rights	32
37. Reporting a colleague's unethical conduct without first consulting the colleague	30
38. Sharing confidential client information with a colleague	29
39. Not reporting suspected spousal abuse	29
40. Not having malpractice coverage	28
41. Counseling a client engaged in another helping relationship	27
42. Seeing a minor client without parental consent	25
43. Viewing a client's web page (e.g., Facebook) without consent	23
44. Counseling diverse clients with little cross-cultural training	22
45. Having sex with a person your client knows well	22
46. Setting your fee higher for clients with insurance	22
47. Counseling without training in the presenting problem	20
48. Not allowing clients to view their records	17
49. Trying to change your client's values	13
50. Kissing a client as a friendly gesture (e.g., greeting)	13
51. Accepting a client's decision to commit suicide	12
52. Accepting a gift from a client that's worth more than $25	12
53. Revealing confidential information if a client is deceased	11
54. Counseling a colleague with whom you work	11
55. Having a dual relationship (e.g., client is your child's teacher)	10
56. Telling your client you are attracted to him or her	10
57. Not having a transfer plan should you become incapacitated	9
58. Trying to persuade a client to not have an abortion	8
59. Treating homosexuality as a pathology	6
60. Making grandiose statements about your expertise	6
61. Giving a gift worth more than $25 to a client	5

COUNSELOR BEHAVIOR	Percent of counselors who viewed behavior as ethical
62. Keeping client records in an unlocked file cabinet	5
63. Not participating in continuing education	5
64. Engaging in a counseling relationship with a friend	5
65. Terminating the counseling relationship without warning	5
66. Not offering a professional disclosure statement	3
67. Referring a client satisfied with his/her homosexuality for reparative therapy	3
68. Lending money to your client	3
69. Sharing confidential information with a significant other	3
70. Not reporting suspected abuse of an older client	1
71. Not informing clients of legal rights (e.g., HIPAA, FERPA, confidentiality)	1
72. Stating you are licensed when you are in the process of obtaining a license	1
73. Revealing a client's record to his or her spouse without permission	<1
74. Not reporting suspected abuse of a child	<1
75. Attempting to persuade a client to adopt a religious belief	<1
76. Implying that a certification is the same as a license	<1
77. Not revealing the limits of confidentiality to your client	<1

Ensuring Best Practice as a Counselor

At this point in the chapter, you might be saying to yourself, "There are so many potential ethical concerns out there, maybe I shouldn't even go into this field." In actuality, keeping oneself safe from potential ethical violations is not so difficult. It involves knowing your ethics code, using one or more decision-making models when faced with an ethical dilemma, and using *best practices* when working with clients. Corey et al. (2019), as well as others who have written about ethics, have come up with a number of ways to ensure one is practicing ethically and legally. Here is a good list:

1. Be familiar with relevant laws
2. Don't impose your values on clients
3. Always be professional with your clients
4. Do not refer clients due to values differences
5. Keep good notes and annotate client progress
6. Don't miss your appointments with your clients
7. Be respectful, caring, and kind with your clients
8. Make sure you have a good record-keeping system
9. Know the law relative to reporting abuse in your state
10. Don't work with clients out of your area of competence
11. Ensure that your paper and electronic records are secure

12. Keep records and information about clients confidential
13. Know and be good at a theory that you use with your clients
14. Refer clients when you are not competent at working with them
15. Conduct a clinical assessment and inform clients of what you found
16. Have a professional disclosure statement and obtain informed consent
17. Ensure that clients understand what you have them sign or what you tell them
18. If you work with minors, obtain written permission from parents and guardians
19. Consult with others when needed, but make sure you get client permission to do so
20. Do not have sex with current or former clients or any close friend or relative of a client
21. Make sure that clients understand they never have to continue in the counseling relationship
22. Have the attitudes and beliefs, knowledge, and skills to work well with a wide variety of clients
23. Have appropriate boundaries and do not counsel those who are friends, relatives, or colleagues
24. Understand countertransference and how your reactions to clients can interfere with treatment
25. Inform clients about their potential diagnosis and the risks and benefits of a specific treatment plan
26. Know how to assess for lethality and how to respond if a client is in danger of harming self or others

Malpractice Insurance

Hopefully, we made you aware enough in this chapter to consider the purchase of *malpractice insurance*. In truth, counselors are not regularly sued by clients or others, but in case they are, it is prudent to obtain malpractice insurance. Lose a lawsuit without insurance, and you can be paying for the rest of your life. Currently, if you are a member of ACA and a master's student in counseling, you receive free complimentary malpractice insurance from Healthcare Providers Service Organization (HPSO, 2018). If you are a new professional, you receive a 50% discount on malpractice insurance, and professionals who spend more than $100 per year receive a 10% discount if they are a member of ACA. Although the amount you will pay will vary from state to state and is based on other considerations, if a counselor is a member of ACA, HPSO generally charges under $150 a year if working in an agency and under $300 if in private practice. Check out their website at www.hpso.com to see the benefits of malpractice insurance and how much you would have to pay.

Summary

This chapter began by examining the purpose of, and limitations to, ethical codes. We then described four models of ethical decision-making, including problem-solving, moral, developmental, and social-constructivist models. Problem-solving approaches are straightforward and have a series of steps, such as identifying the potential issues involved, reviewing the relevant ethical guidelines, knowing the applicable laws and regulations, obtaining consultation, considering possible and probable courses of action, enumerating the consequences of various decisions, and deciding on the best course of action. Moral models examine moral principles in making ethical decisions. Kitchener's moral model included autonomy: the client's self-determination; beneficence: protecting the good of others and society; nonmaleficence: avoiding doing harm to clients and others; justice: treating clients fairly and equally; and fidelity: maintaining clients' trust and being committed to them. A sixth moral principle, veracity, is generally added to this list and has to do with being truthful and genuine with clients. Developmental models examine the cognitive development of the decision-maker, and it is assumed that those with higher levels of cognitive development are more complex and self-reflective in their ethical decision-making. Finally, social constructivist models examine the narratives and multiple perspectives from all involved in the ethical decision-making process and assume there are multiple truths. Individuals from this perspective try to include all those involved in the ethical dilemma and in the decision-making process (e.g., the client, significant others in a client's life, counselor, supervisor, etc.).

The bulk of the chapter examined several select and important ethical issues including informed consent, confidentiality, privileged communication, competence, maintaining boundaries and prohibited relationships, values in the counseling relationship, cross-cultural counseling, technology in counseling, supervision, and reporting ethical violations. For each of these areas, we defined the word or term and highlighted specific parts of the ACA ethical standards where it is found. Some lawsuits that were highlighted relative to some of the ethical concerns included the Tarasoff decision and how it stressed the importance of responding to foreseeable harm and of knowing when there is a duty to warn; the Jaffee decision and how it solidified the right to privileged communication; and the Ward decision and its impact on ensuring that we do not refer clients due to values differences. Some laws we noted included the Freedom of Information Act (FOIA), the Health Insurance Portability and Accountability Act (HIPAA), and the Family Educational Rights and Privacy Act (FERPA). These laws strengthen client privacy and confidentiality, which has become especially important with the use of technology in counseling. We supplied ethical vignettes for each of the ethical areas highlighted in the chapter so that you could wrestle with the dilemma and apply your ethical decision-making models.

As the chapter neared its conclusion, we examined a survey of more than 500 ACA members' perceptions of 77 counselor behaviors to determine whether they viewed the behavior as ethical or unethical. We then asked you to judge each of the behaviors. We then highlighted 26 best-practice methods you can use to avoid unethical behavior. We noted that although few counselors get sued, it is prudent to have malpractice insurance, and we noted that one company, Healthcare Providers Service Organization (HPSO), offers such insurance through ACA.

Key Words and Terms

ACA Code of Ethics

autonomy

beneficence

best practices

competence

confidentiality

cross-cultural counseling

developmental models

dual relationships

duty to warn

ethical decision-making models

Family Educational Rights and Privacy Act (FERPA)

fidelity

foreseeable harm

Freedom of Information Act (FOIA)

Health Insurance Portability and Accountability Act (HIPAA)

Healthcare Providers Service Organization (HPSO)

informed consent

Jaffee v. Redmond

Julea Ward v. Board of Regents of Eastern Michigan

justice

Kitchener, Ann

limitations of ethical codes

maintaining boundaries and prohibited relationships

malpractice insurance

moral models

multiple relationships

nonmaleficence

perceptions of 77 counselor behaviors

privileged communication

problem-solving models

professional disclosure statement

purpose of ethical codes

reporting ethical violations

social constructivist models

supervision

Tarasoff v. Board of Regents of University of California

technology in counseling

values in the counseling relationship

veracity

Credits

Appendix A: Feeling Words Checklist

Abandoned	Enlightened	Lonely	Shocked
Adored	Enthusiastic	Lost	Shy
Aggravated	Envious	Lovable	Skeptical
Aggressive	Exasperated	Loving	Sorrowful
Angry	Excited	Lucky	Sour
Anxious	Exhilarated	Lying	Spectacular
Appreciated	Extraordinary	Magical	Stifled
Apprehensive	Exuberant	Mean	Strong
Argumentative	Failure	Mindful	Stubborn
Ashamed	Fantastic	Miraculous	Stupid
Assertive	Fearful	Miserable	Teased
Assured	Fearless	Misunderstood	Tender
Awe	Focused	Motivated	Terrific
Awesome	Forced	Neglected	Terrified
Awful	Free	Nervous	Thoughtful
Betrayed	Frigid	Obligated	Thoughtless
Bitter	Frustrated	Open	Thrilled
Bliss	Fulfilled	Oppressed	Tormented
Bold	Fun	Overwhelmed	Tranquil
Bored	Glad	Pained	Traumatized
Brilliant	Glowing	Panicked	Troubled
Brokenhearted	Gracious	Paranoid	Trusting
Burdened	Grateful	Passionate	Unaccepted
Calm	Grieving	Peaceful	Unconcerned
Capable	Guilty	Pitiful	Undesirable
Caring	Happy	Playful	Understood
Cheerful	Helpless	Pleasant	Uneasy
Comfortable	Hopeful	Pleased	Unfriendly
Concerned	Hopeless	Positive	Unfulfilled
Confident	Honored	Powerless	Unhappy
Confused	Humiliated	Precious	Unhelpful
Content	Hurt	Pressured	Unloved
Criticized	Impatient	Proud	Unsuccessful
Decisive	Impossible	Provoked	Unwanted
Dejected	Inadequate	Punished	Unworthy
Depressed	Incapable	Quiet	Uplifted
Difficult	Indecisive	Ready	Upset
Dirty	Insecure	Receptive	Useless
Disappointed	Inspired	Recognized	Valued
Discontented	Interested	Rejected	Valuable
Discouraged	Intolerant	Relaxed	Victimized
Disgusted	Invigorated	Renewed	Vindictive
Disrespected	Invincible	Repulsive	Warm
Distressed	Irresistible	Resentful	Wary
Doubtful	Irresponsible	Resilient	Weary
Drained	Irritated	Respected	Whole
Dynamic	Jealous	Restless	Wise
Eager	Joyful	Sad	Worried
Elated	Joyous	Satisfied	Worthless
Embarrassed	Jubilant	Scared	Worthy
Empowered	Kind	Selfish	Wrong
Empty	Let down	Serene	
Energized	Limitless	Shameful	

Appendix B: The Miller Family

JAKE AND ANGELA Miller recently celebrated their 10th anniversary with their friends, parents, and children. Jake's father and mother, Ted and Ann, were there, and they brought Jake's sister, Justine. Ted and Ann met in Atlanta and have been married for 42 years. Ted earned a law degree and has worked in corporate law ever since, while Ann worked as a piano teacher until her twins, Jake and Justine, were born. Jake is 34, and Angela is 33.

Angela's parents, Dexter and Evangeline, celebrated with the family. Dexter and Evangeline met in college in California 41 years ago. Dexter, whose parents are from Nigeria, is an English professor at a mid-sized private university. Evangeline worked as a social worker facilitating adoptions. Due in part to her work, Evangeline and Dexter eventually adopted two African American children when Angela was 5: Lillian, who was just an infant, and Marcus, who was 2. Angela is their only biological child. Lillian is a social worker, married, and has two children. Marcus is gay, lives with his partner, and recently left his job as a high school English teacher to pursue his PhD in literature. Angela is biracial.

Jake and Angela met in graduate school. Today, Jake works as a structural engineer, and Angela is an art teacher at an elementary school. They have two children, Luke (10) and Cecile (7). Although the family and extended family have had few mental health concerns, Jake has recently had some bouts with anxiety, which have begun to affect his relationship with his wife and children. The situation has become so difficult that it has placed a strain on Jake and Angela's relationship. In addition, their growing tensions might be contributing to problems their children recently started to experience at school.

Jake

Jake remembers having had a happy childhood until the age of 10. From what he could tell, his parents, Ted and Ann, got along well. Ann seemed to have lots of friends she saw often and was active in the community, and Ted seemed content in his work. Jake describes his childhood like this: "I don't really remember anything bad happening when I was a kid. My parents seemed like they had a lot of fun together, they got along well, teased each other—they were affectionate and all that. What stands out for me is how much fun my twin sister, Justine, and I had when we were kids. We were into everything: climbing on the roof of the house or digging holes under the shed until the floor caved in—that kind of thing. There was nothing that Justine wouldn't try. She was funny, real quick, you know, and so brave. Nothing scared her. That was before the accident.

"One day, Justine got it in her head that we would take Dad's car out of the garage and park it on the other side of the wooded area across the interstate. It was a joke for April Fool's day. We were only 10, and of course I was scared, but Justine was sure it would be a good trick, so before I knew it, we were in the car and I was driving! Justine was laughing; I remember that she had her bare feet curled up under her and, as always, no seat belt. I guess I didn't look or something, 'cause right after I pulled the car out onto the interstate, a semi hit the car and Justine went through the windshield. She was never the same. She was out for a long time, and when she finally came out of her coma, she had a serious brain injury. She had to learn to talk again and all that. When she did talk ... well, she wasn't Justine anymore." Today, Justine is cared for by her parents and is able to maintain a job at a local fast-food restaurant. However, she continues to have serious cognitive impairment. Although Jake tends to get along with her, he periodically quips at her, telling her he thinks she can do better than she's been doing.

After the accident, Jake began to have problems with anxiety. He had a hard time sleeping through the night and had nightmares. "Things changed a lot at our house. It seemed like no one ever laughed anymore, and we didn't do anything. Before the accident, my parents would come up with something spontaneous and fun, and we would get up and go! But after Justine changed, well, things at the house got real quiet, and I always felt that something bad was going to happen. I was afraid to leave the house sometimes." Jake's parents took him to a psychiatrist briefly to address the nightmares and anxiety, but they did not talk about his feelings together as a family and rarely referred to the accident.

As the years passed, Jake's anxiety lessened, and he was only occasionally disturbed by anxiety or nightmares. He seemed to move on with his life and successfully finished high school, college, and graduate school. He met and married his wife while in graduate school. Soon after he married and had children, he became involved with a national association that advocates for child-safe automobiles, "just so nothing like what happened to Justine could happen to anyone else again."

Although Jake sounds proud when describing his wife and children, in recent months he has been struggling with a number of issues. Jake notes, "We've been having problems with Luke. He's fearless, like Justine was—and always into something! He's not bad, just mischievous, but lately he's been getting in trouble at school. A couple of months ago, Luke and Cecile were playing in the car, and Luke knocked the car out of park. I was mowing the lawn and came around the corner just in time to see the car roll into the street. I felt my chest tighten; I couldn't breathe. I thought I was having a heart attack! Since the incident with the car, I am anxious all the time. I can't sleep, and when I do, I have nightmares. I have been afraid for Angela to take the car and … I guess I've been difficult to deal with." Jake is constantly checking all the locks, making sure the car is in park, and always checking on the children. He has even asked Angela to homeschool the children to make sure they are safe. He also is aware that his relationship with Angela is different: "Angela and I just seem kind of disconnected lately." Jake has also noted that his anxiety has caused him to miss work lately, and he is very concerned he will get a poor performance evaluation.

Angela

Angela is feeling at a loss. One afternoon she confided to the school counselor, "I really don't know what is happening to our family. Jake has just gotten so anxious that it is a full-time job keeping up with all his fears. He wants me to homeschool Celia and gets so angry with me for insisting Celia go to public school, and Luke just won't listen to him at all. I feel like I'm a character in one of those really bad movie-of-the-week things. Sometimes I go into the bathroom, turn on the water in the tub, and cry. I don't want to live my life this way."

When Angela was growing up, she spent the fall and spring on a university campus and spent summers in Nigeria with her father's family. She notes: "I enjoyed spending time with my grandparents, but somehow I always felt out of place. When I was in Nigeria, my cousins treated me differently because as far as they were concerned, I was White and an American, but when I was back in America, I was Black. But I really didn't feel Black, either. In fact, most of the time I felt more like a Nigerian kid than an American. You'd never catch me talking to my parents or teachers the way the kids at school talked to adults!

"No matter where we were, there was always one constant: my role as caretaker. Lillian, my adopted sister, was born with a congenital hip deformity that made walking difficult. It was my job to see to Lillian and make sure she had what she needed. I was never free to just go out and play with the other kids. I always had to stay near Lillian. I felt so trapped when I watched the other children on their bikes or playing chase. That's how I feel now, with Jake's demands. I feel trapped, watching everyone else live their lives and still, after all these years, not really knowing who I am."

Luke

Luke is 10, and he's starting fifth grade this year. Luke has been a vibrant, active little boy since day one. He is curious and bright. His mother, Angela, has delighted in his willingness to try anything. He seems to live life fully and to feel things deeply. His laughter is contagious, but when Luke is angry he can be difficult to reason with.

Luke's father spends a lot of time trying to rein Luke in: "He's like a wild horse sometimes. He can be so out of control." Luke doesn't always listen to warnings about safety—staying out of the car, for instance. If something breaks or someone is hurt, it is often Luke who is at the bottom of it. These incidents make Jake furious. Angela isn't comfortable with the way Jake yells at Luke, and lately they have been fighting over it.

Cecelia

Cecelia ("Celia") is 7 and is going to be in the second grade. Her mother explains, "Right away, we could see a difference between the two children. Celia is much more cautious than Luke—an observer. She tends to absorb whatever feeling is around her. She gets caught up in Luke's excitement, and she likes to join Luke in his adventures and pranks. Celia worries, though, and her hesitation sometimes makes Luke angry. A lot of the time, Luke and Celia start out playing together but end up in an argument."

Recently, Celia has had problems with anxiety. What began as a mild resistance to going to school has become a real problem. More and more often, her mother gets a phone call from the school nurse saying that Celia has a stomachache and wants to come home. Angela became really worried when Celia got so anxious one morning about getting on the bus to go on a field trip that she wet her pants.

Appendix C: Categories Generally Assessed in a Psychological Report

Demographic Information

Name:	DOB:
Address:	Age:
Phone:	Sex:
Ethnicity:	E-mail address:
Date of interview:	Name of interviewer:

Presenting Problem or Reason for Referral

1. Who referred the client to the agency?
2. What is the main reason the client contacted the agency?
3. Reason for assessment

Family Background

1. Significant factors from family of origin
2. Significant factors from current family
3. Some specific issues that may be mentioned are as follows: where the individual grew up, sexes and ages of siblings, whether the client came from an intact family, who were the major caretakers, important stories from childhood, sexes and ages of current children, significant others, and marital concerns

Significant Medical/Counseling History

1. Significant medical history, particularly anything related to the client's assessment (e.g., psychiatric hospitalization, heart disease leading to depression)
2. Types and dates of previous counseling

Substance Use and Abuse

1. Use or abuse of food, cigarettes, alcohol, prescription medication, or illegal drugs
2. Counseling related to use and abuse

Educational and Vocational History

1. Educational history (e.g., level of education and possibly names of institutions)
2. Vocational history and career path (names and types of jobs)

3. Satisfaction with educational level and career path
4. Significant leisure activities

Other Pertinent Information

1. Legal concerns and history of problems with the law
2. Issues related to sexuality (e.g., sexual orientation, sexual dysfunction)
3. Financial problems
4. Other concerns

Mental Status Exam

1. Appearance and behavior (e.g., dress, hygiene, posture, tics, nonverbals, manner of speech)
2. Emotional state (e.g., affect and mood)
3. Thought components (e.g., content and process: delusions, distortions of body image, hallucinations, obsessions, suicidal or homicidal ideation, circumstantiality, coherence, flights of ideas, logical thinking, intact as opposed to loose associations, organization, and tangentiality)
4. Cognitive functioning (e.g., orientation to time, place, and person; short- and long-term memory; knowledge base and intellectual functioning; insight and judgments)

Assessment Results

1. List assessment and test instruments used
2. Summarize results
3. Avoid raw scores and state results in unbiased manner
4. Consider using standardized test scores and percentiles

Diagnosis

1. DSM-5 diagnoses
2. Include other diagnoses such as medical, rehabilitation, or other salient factors

Summary and Conclusions

1. Integration of all previous information
2. Accurate, succinct, and relevant
3. No new information
4. Inferences that are logical, sound, defendable, and based on facts in the report
5. At least one paragraph that speaks to the client's strengths

Recommendations

1. Based on all the information gathered
2. Should make logical sense to reader
3. In paragraph form or as a listing
4. Usually followed by signature of examiner

Appendix D: Psychological Report

Demographic Information

Name:	Jake Miller	Ethnicity:	Caucasian
Address:	5555 Anxiety Road	DOB:	May 14, 1985
	Apprehension, KS	Email:	jake.miller@gmail.com
Phone:	316.555.5555	Marital Status:	Married
Examiner:	Edward Neukrug	Date:	January, 5, 2019

Presenting Problem/Reason for Referral

This 34-year-old married male sought out counseling due to extreme anxiety, concerns about his children's well-being, and problems in his marriage. He describes his anxiety and problems with his family as occurring about 10 weeks ago when his children, Luke (10) and Celia (7), were playing unsupervised in his car and knocked the car out of park. The car rolled, but no one was injured. He would like some help with his anxiety and hopes he can "return his family to normalcy."

Family Background

Jake notes that he met his wife, Angela, in graduate school and has been married for 10 years. They have two children, Luke (10) and Cecilia ("Celia," age 7). Jake reports that he has had bouts with anxiety over his lifetime, but it has become particularly difficult in recent months since the incident when Luke knocked Jake's car out of park and the car rolled into the street. Celia was also in the car. Although no one was injured, Jake states that this incident set off a "surge of anxiety" and reminded him of a similar incident he had with his twin sister, Justine, when he was a child.

Jake's twin sister, Justine, is intellectually disabled. He states that when they were 10, Justine wanted to play a practical joke on his parents and urged Jake to move their parents' car. Jake states that he accidentally moved the car into the roadway, where a semi hit the car and caused serious cognitive impairment for Justine. Jake was not seriously injured. Jake reports feeling guilt since that time, blaming himself for the accident. Jake states that his parents, Ted and Ann, had a good relationship until the car accident. He notes that the family was always "having fun and laughing" up to that point. However, since then, he reports "a cloud over everyone in the family." Jake notes that he struggled with anxiety and depression after the accident for a few years but eventually overcame it after seeing a counselor at the age of 13.

Jake notes that since Luke knocked the car out of park, Jake has had a resurgence of anxiety and has wanted to control what everyone is doing in the family—mostly to ensure their safety. He notes that when the children are home, he constantly wants to make sure they are within visual distance. He also reports making sure that all the doors are locked at night, even waking up several times during the middle of the night to check. He states whenever the children play "rough" games, he goes into a rage, yelling at them to stop. He also notes that he has asked Angela to homeschool the children, as he is concerned that something bad will happen at school. This, he reports, has led to problems in his marriage. Meanwhile, Jakes states that Luke and Celia have been symptomatic since the incident, with Luke "not listening to anyone" and Celia having ongoing stomachaches that cause her, at times, to come home from school.

Jake describes Angela as stubborn and not wanting to homeschool the children, which he would prefer to ensure his children's safety. He notes that Angela is biracial and the oldest of three children, with a younger brother, Marcus, who is 31 and gay, and Lillian, who is 29. Angela's siblings are both African American and adopted. Angela is her parents' only biological child. Jake states that Angela was often the caretaker in her family and struggled with her identity, as she felt White when spending the summers in Nigeria with her family and Black when back in the States living at home. Jakes reports that Angela spent an inordinate amount of time caring for her sister, who had a congenital hip deformity.

Jake's and Angela's parents are living, and they report that they have a "decent" relationship with them. However, Jake notes that issues from the past still haunt each of them, including the car accident with Jake and Angela's sense of not having a clear identity.

Significant Medical/Counseling History

Jake reports having been in counseling twice in his life. The first time was when he was 13, which he describes as beneficial and focused on his guilt over his accident. He saw the counselor for about 6 months. He states that when he was 23 and met Angela, he felt mild depression and moderate anxiety and saw a counselor. After a psychiatric consult, he was prescribed 10mg of Luvox. He states that he saw the counselor for about 9 months, and between the Luvox and the counseling, he began to feel better. He views his anxiety at that point in his life related to feeling like he would be swallowed up by the relationship and not have any control in his life. He relays no significant medical history.

Substance Use and Abuse

Jake is a social drinker. He reports no illegal or prescribed abuse of substances.

Educational and Vocational History

From K–12, Jake attended public school. He reports that he always wanted to be a mechanical engineer and was always good at math. He states he did well in school but noted that he always "wrote poorly" and wondered if he was "dyslexic." He was never tested in school for a learning disability. He attended the University of Kansas, where he obtained his bachelor's and master's degrees in engineering. He has been at his current job as a mechanical engineer for 8 years. His father, Ted, was a lawyer, and his mother, Ann, a piano teacher. He states that they always pushed him to obtain a professional degree and were happy when he became an engineer.

Other Pertinent Information

Jake states he "loves Angela" and feels as if he is the cause of many of their problems. He hopes that counseling will help "bring things back to the way they were." He notes that his sexual relationship with

Angela was "normal" until recently, when they began to argue over the children and what Jake states Angela describes as "[his] controlling personality." He reports no legal problems. Jake states he is agnostic and that his wife, Angela, is Episcopalian, although he notes that "she is not very religious" and the family rarely, if ever, goes to church. He says he'd rather "believe in science" than some "unknown God."

Mental Status

Jake was casually and neatly dressed for the interview. He made appropriate eye contact. He was oriented to time, place, and person. He often fidgeted in his chair, moving his body back and forth during the interview. He reports feeling "anxious most of the time" and notes that he still feels guilty about the situation with Justine. He states he has been feeling anxious for the past 10 weeks since the incident with his children moving his car. He reports waking up multiple times at night just to check that everyone is in bed and safe. He notes that he has lost some weight—mostly, he believes, due to his disinterest in food as a result of his anxiety. He reports feeling tired much of the time and has ongoing headaches. At one point during the interview, when talking about the accident with Justine, he became tearful, saying, "I shouldn't have listened to her—it's all my fault." Jake relates his current anxiety to the car accident with Justine and the resulting trauma he experienced from it. Jake's thoughts were clear and his memory good, and he is above average intellectually. He has good insight and fair judgment. He reports no suicidal or homicidal ideation.

Assessment Results

The following assessment procedures were administered: the 16PF, the WRAT-5, the Kinetic Family Drawing, a sentence completion, the Beck Depression Inventory-II (BDI-II), the Beck Anxiety Inventory (BAI), the trauma history questionnaire, and the Substance Abuse Subtle Screening Inventory (SASSI).

On the BDI-II, Jake's score of 14 shows mild to no depression. On the BAI, he scored a 36, which shows severe anxiety. Anxiety and feelings of frustration and guilt were evidenced in his sentence completion, such as when he noted, "I see myself as responsible for the accident" and when he stated, "I get angry when I can't make things the way I want them to be," and "The thing I'm most afraid to talk about is the accident." Sadness was noted when he stated, "I feel the saddest when I "think about the accident." When asked to draw a picture of his family all doing something together, Jake drew them having a picnic. His family was all sitting at a table, Angela and Jake on opposite sides and the two kids sitting very close to one another and closer to Angela. Notably, a fence circumscribed the table, as if to keep everyone inside and safe. There were no smiles on anyone's faces, and the distance between Angela and Jake seemed significant.

On the 16PF, Jake had significantly high scores on the following: *rule consciousness*, meaning he is conscientious, moralistic, staid, and rule bound; *perfectionism*, which means he has strong willpower and likes to exert control; and *tension*, meaning he is tense, driven, and frustrated. He received low scores on *traditional*, meaning he is conservative in his ideas and respects tradition, and on *practical*, which means he is down to earth and conventional. On the global scores, which is a conglomeration of a number of the 16 factors, he scored high on *anxiety, tough-mindedness*, and *self-control*. Jake's Holland code was an REI, which fits his current occupation of engineer. He showed no evidence of substance abuse on the SASSI.

On the trauma history questionnaire, Jake identified three items to which he answered "yes," including Item 5: Have you ever had a serious accident at work, in a car, or somewhere else?, Item 10: Have you ever been in any other situation in which you feared you might be killed or seriously injured?, and Item 11: Have you ever seen someone seriously injured or killed? All items referred back to the time when Justine and Jake pushed their parents' car out of park and the car was struck by a semi. Current symptoms of anxiety and subsequent concern about wanting to ensure the safety of his family were noted on the BAI, the sentence completion, the KFD, and 16PF and may be related to this early trauma he experienced.

On the WRAT-5, Jake scored at the 92nd percentile in math, 75th percentile in reading, 70th percentile in sentence comprehension, and 35th percentile in spelling. His reading composite score was at the 72nd percentile. These results indicate a possible learning disability in spelling.

Diagnosis

- Adjustment Disorder, with anxiety (F43.21)
- Rule out Generalized Anxiety Disorder (F41.1)
- Rule out Post-Traumatic Stress Disorder (F43.10)
- Possible spelling learning disability (F81.81)
- Relationship distress with spouse or intimate partner (Z63.0)
- Parent-child relational problem (Z62.820)
- High expressed emotion level within family (Z63.8)

Summary and Recommendations

This 34-year-old married male sought counseling due to increased anxiety, problems with sleep, ongoing headaches, loss of appetite, and problems in his marriage and with his children. He relates many of these issues stemming from a history in his family of origin when he was involved in a car accident at age 10 with his twin sister. At that time, at his sister's urging, he moved his parents' car and was accidentally struck by a semi, resulting in severe cognitive impairment for his sister. He was not injured. He reports feeling guilty and responsible for the accident. He attended counseling at age 13 for continued feelings of guilt and anxiety due to the accident. He was in counseling one other time, just prior to his marriage, for feelings of being overwhelmed and closed in.

Recently, his daughter and son were involved in an incident in which they pushed his car out of park and it moved down the driveway. Jake states that this incident caused a resurgence in his anxiety. He states that since that time he has been trying to get a handle on his anxiety by keeping everyone safe in the home. He reports asking his wife to homeschool the children (which she has said no to), and he states he is constantly trying to control the family to ensure their safety.

Evidence of anxiety, need to control, feelings of perfectionism, and tough-mindedness are evidenced throughout his clinical interview. He self-reports anxiety, which is confirmed by the BAI and by the 16PF. Other tests, such as his KFD and the 16PF, reveal a need to control his family and ensure that they are safe. The KFD also indicates distance from his wife and children. Some feelings of sadness and guilt, mostly related to the accident when he was a child, were noted during the clinical interview and on the sentence completion. Jake sees a relationship between the car accident he had with his twin sister, Justine, when he was 10 and his current anxiety.

Jake is a fairly insightful man who is experiencing guilt, anxiety, and mild to no depression that appears to be related to the car accident he had with his twin sister when he was 10. His fears about something similar happening with his children are permeating his life, and he is having difficulty controlling the resulting anxiety. He attempts to control this anxiety by controlling others around him. This has resulted in symptoms in his children and problems in his marriage.

On a positive note, Jake has a good understanding of himself, is wanting to examine his life through counseling, and is wanting to resolve the problems in his family. He is highly educated, bright, and hopeful about making changes in his life.

Recommendations

- Referral to a psychiatrist for possible medication to alleviate his anxiety
- Counseling, one hour a week, to discuss past issues related to his car accident with his sister and current problems with his family
- Possible marital counseling to relieve some of the stress in his marriage
- Further testing for a possible learning disability in spelling, should Jake wish to pursue that

Edward Neukrug

Signature

Appendix E: Common Words and Terms Used in the Mental Status Exam

Term	Definition or Description
APPEARANCE AND BEHAVIOR	
Appearance	Appropriate or baseline, eccentric or odd, abnormal movement or gait, good or poor grooming or hygiene
Eye contact	Good or poor
Speech	Within normal limits, loud, soft, pressured, hesitant
Appropriate or inappropriate	Appropriate or inappropriate to mood (e.g., laughing while talking of recent death)
EMOTIONAL STATE (AFFECT)	
Full and reactive	Full range of emotions correctly associated with the conversation
Labile	Uncontrollable crying or laughing
Blunted	Reduced expression of emotional intensity
Flat	No or very little expression of emotional intensity
Euthymic	Normal mood
EMOTIONAL STATE (MOOD)	
Depressed	Sad, dysphoric, discontent
Euphoric	Extreme happiness or joy
Anxious	Worried
Anhedonic	Unable to derive pleasure from previously enjoyable activities
Angry/hostile	Annoyed, irritated, irate, etc.
Alexithymic	Unable to describe mood
THOUGHT COMPONENTS (CONTENT)	
Hallucinations	False perception of reality: may be auditory, visual, tactile (touch), olfactory (smell), or taste
Ideas of reference	Misinterpreting casual and external events as being related to self (e.g., newspaper headlines, TV stories, or song lyrics are about the client)
Delusions	False belief (e.g., "satellites are tracking me"); may be grandiose, persecutory (to be harmed), somatic (physical symptom with no medical condition), erotic
Derealization	External world seems unreal (e.g., watching it like a movie)
Depersonalization	Feeling detached from self (e.g., "I'm living in a dream")

Term	Definition or Description
Suicidality and homicidality	Ranges from none to ideation, plan, means, preparation, rehearsal, and intent
Logical and organized	Normal state in which one's thoughts are rational and structured

THOUGHT COMPONENTS (PROCESS)

Term	Definition or Description
Poverty	Lack of verbal content or brief responses
Blocking	Difficulty with or inability to complete statements
Clang	Emphasis on using words that rhyme together rather than on meaning
Echolalia	"Echoing" client's own speech or your speech; repeating
Flight of ideas	Rapid thoughts almost incoherent
Perseveration	Thoughts keep returning to the same idea
Circumstantial	Explanations are long and often irrelevant but eventually get to the point
Tangential	Responses never get to the point of the question
Loose	Thoughts have little or no association to the conversation or to each other
Redirectable	Responses may get off track but you can direct them back to the topic

COGNITION

Term	Definition or Description
Orientation	Knows who they are, where they are, and date
Memory	Ability to remember events from recent, immediate, and long term
Insight	Ability to recognize his or her mental illness; good, limited, or none
Judgment	Ability to make sound decisions; good, fair, or poor

Appendix F: Overview of DSM-5 Diagnostic Categories

T HE FOLLOWING OFFERS a brief description of the DSM diagnostic categories and is summarized from DSM-5 (APA, 2013a). Please refer to the DSM-5 for an in-depth review of each disorder:

Neurodevelopmental disorders. This group of disorders typically refers to those that manifest during early development, although diagnoses are sometimes not assigned until adulthood. Examples of neurodevelopmental disorders include intellectual disabilities, communication disorders, autism spectrum disorders (incorporating the former categories of autistic disorder, Asperger's disorder, childhood disintegrative disorder, and pervasive developmental disorder), ADHD, specific learning disorders, motor disorders, and other neurodevelopmental disorders.

Schizophrenia spectrum and other psychotic disorders. The disorders that belong to this section all have one feature in common: psychotic symptoms; that is, delusions, hallucinations, grossly disorganized or abnormal motor behavior, and/or negative symptoms. The disorders include schizotypal personality disorder (which is listed again and explained more comprehensively in the category of personality disorders in the DSM-5), delusional disorder, brief psychotic disorder, schizophreniform disorder, schizophrenia, schizoaffective disorder, substance/medication-induced psychotic disorder, psychotic disorder due to another medical condition, and catatonic disorder.

Bipolar and related disorders. The disorders in this category refer to disturbances in mood in which the client cycles through stages of mania or mania and depression. Both children and adults can be diagnosed with bipolar disorder, and the clinician can work to identify the pattern of mood presentation, such as rapid cycling, which is more often observed in children. These disorders include bipolar I, bipolar II, cyclothymic disorder, substance/medication-induced, bipolar and related disorder due to another medical condition, and other specified or unspecified bipolar and related disorders.

Depressive disorders. Previously grouped into the broader category of "mood disorders" in the DSM-IV-TR, these disorders describe conditions in which depressed mood is the overarching concern. They include disruptive mood dysregulation disorder, major depressive disorder, persistent depressive disorder (also known as dysthymia), and premenstrual dysphoric disorder.

Anxiety disorders. There are a wide range of anxiety disorders, which can be diagnosed by identifying a general or specific cause of unease or fear. This anxiety or fear is considered clinically significant when it is excessive and persistent over time. Examples of anxiety disorders that typically manifest earlier in development include separation anxiety and selective mutism. Other examples of anxiety disorders are specific phobia, social anxiety disorder (also known as social phobia), panic disorder, and generalized anxiety disorder.

Obsessive-compulsive and related disorders. Disorders in this category all involve obsessive thoughts and compulsive behaviors that are uncontrollable, and the client feels compelled to perform them. Diagnoses in this category include obsessive-compulsive disorder, body dysmorphic disorder, hoarding disorder, trichotillomania (or hair-pulling disorder), and excoriation (or skin-picking) disorder.

Trauma-and stressor-related disorders. A new category for DSM-5, trauma and stress disorders emphasize the pervasive impact that life events can have on an individual's emotional and physical well-being. Diagnoses include reactive attachment disorder, disinhibited social engagement disorder, post-traumatic stress disorder, acute stress disorder, and adjustment disorders.

Dissociative disorders. These disorders indicate a temporary or prolonged disruption to consciousness that can cause an individual to misinterpret identity, surroundings, and memories. Diagnoses include dissociative identity disorder (formerly known as multiple personality disorder), dissociative amnesia, depersonalization/derealization disorder, and other specified and unspecified dissociative disorders.

Somatic symptom and related disorders. Somatic symptom disorders were previously referred to as "somatoform disorders" and are characterized by the experiencing of a physical symptom without evidence of a physical cause, thus suggesting a psychological cause. Somatic symptom disorders include somatic symptom disorder, illness anxiety disorder (formerly hypochondriasis), conversion (or functional neurological symptom) disorder, psychological factors affecting other medical conditions, and factitious disorder.

Feeding and eating disorders. This group of disorders describes clients who have severe concerns about the amount or type of food they eat to the point where serious health problems, or even death, can result from their eating behaviors. Examples include avoidant/restrictive food intake disorder, anorexia nervosa, bulimia nervosa, binge eating disorder, pica, and rumination disorder.

Elimination disorders. These disorders can manifest at any point in a person's life, although they are typically diagnosed in early childhood or adolescence. They include enuresis, which is the inappropriate elimination of urine, and encopresis, which is the inappropriate elimination of feces. These behaviors may or may not be intentional.

Sleep-wake disorders. This category refers to disorders where one's sleep patterns are severely impacted, and they often co-occur with other disorders (e.g., depression or anxiety). Some examples include insomnia disorder, hypersomnolence disorder, restless legs syndrome, narcolepsy, and nightmare disorder. A number of sleep-wake disorders involve variations in breathing, such as sleep-related hypoventilation, obstructive sleep apnea hypopnea, or central sleep apnea. See the DSM-5 for the full listing and descriptions of these disorders.

Sexual dysfunctions. These disorders are related to problems that disrupt sexual functioning or one's ability to experience sexual pleasure. They occur across sexes and include delayed ejaculation, erectile disorder, female orgasmic disorder, and premature (or early) ejaculation disorder, among others.

Gender dysphoria. Formerly termed "gender identity disorder," this category includes those individuals who experience significant distress with the sex they were born and with associated gender roles. This diagnosis has been separated from the category of sexual disorders, as it is now accepted that gender dysphoria does not relate to a person's sexual attractions.

Disruptive, impulse control, and conduct disorders. These disorders are characterized by socially unacceptable or otherwise disruptive and harmful behaviors that are outside of the individual's control. Generally more common in males than in females and often first seen in childhood, they include oppositional defiant disorder, conduct disorder, intermittent explosive disorder, antisocial personality disorder (which is also coded in the category of personality disorders), kleptomania, and pyromania.

Substance-related and addictive disorders. Substance use disorders include disruptions in functioning as the result of a craving or strong urge. Often caused by prescribed and illicit drugs or exposure to toxins, with these disorders, the brain's reward system pathways are activated when the substance is taken (or in the case of gambling disorder, when the behavior is being performed). Some common substances include alcohol, caffeine, nicotine, cannabis, opioids, inhalants, amphetamines, phencyclidine (PCP), sedatives, hypnotics, or anxiolytics. Substance use disorders are further designated with the following terms: intoxication, withdrawal, induced, or unspecified.

Neurocognitive disorders. These disorders are diagnosed when one's decline in cognitive functioning is significantly different from the past and is usually the result of a medical condition (e.g., Parkinson's or Alzheimer's disease), the use of a substance/medication, or traumatic brain injury, among other phenomena. Examples of neurocognitive disorders (NCD) include delirium and several types of major and mild NCDs, such as frontotemporal NCD, NCD due to Parkinson's disease, NCD due to HIV infection, NCD due to Alzheimer's disease, substance- or medication-induced NCD, and vascular NCD, among others.

Personality disorders. The 10 personality disorders in DSM-5 all involve a pattern of experiences and behaviors that are persistent, inflexible, and deviate from one's cultural expectations. Usually, this pattern emerges in adolescence or early adulthood and causes severe distress in one's interpersonal relationships. The personality disorders are grouped into the three following clusters, which are based on similar behaviors:

- Cluster A: Paranoid, schizoid, and schizotypal. These individuals seem bizarre or unusual in their behaviors and interpersonal relations.
- Cluster B: Antisocial, borderline, histrionic, and narcissistic. These individuals seem overly emotional, are melodramatic, or are unpredictable in their behaviors and interpersonal relations.
- Cluster C: Avoidant, dependent, and obsessive-compulsive (not to be confused with obsessive-compulsive disorder). These individuals tend to appear anxious, worried, or fretful in their behaviors.

Paraphilic disorders. These disorders are diagnosed when the client is sexually aroused in circumstances that deviate from traditional sexual stimuli *and* when such behaviors result in harm or significant emotional distress. The disorders include exhibitionistic disorder, voyeuristic disorder, frotteuristic disorder, sexual sadism and sexual masochism disorders, fetishistic disorder, transvestic disorder, pedophilic disorder, and other specified and unspecified paraphilic disorders.

Other mental disorders. This diagnostic category includes mental disorders that did not fall within one of the previously mentioned groups and do not have unifying characteristics. Examples include other specified mental disorders due to another medical condition, unspecified mental disorders due to another medical condition, other specified mental disorders, and unspecified mental disorders.

Medication-induced movement disorders and other adverse effects of medications. These disorders are the result of adverse and severe side effects of medications, although a causal link cannot always be shown. Some of these disorders include neuroleptic-induced parkinsonism, neuroleptic malignant syndrome, medication-induced dystonia, medication-induced acute akathisia, tardive dyskinesia, tardive akathisia, medication-induced postural tremor, other medication-induced movement disorder, antidepressant discontinuation syndrome, and other adverse effects of medication.

Other conditions that may be a focus of clinical assessment. This category ends with a description of concerns that could be clinically significant, such as abuse/neglect; relational problems; psychosocial, personal, and environmental concerns; educational/occupational problems; housing and economic problems; and problems related to the legal system. These conditions, which are not considered mental disorders, are listed Z codes and correspond to ICD-10.

In addition to these categories, the DSM-5 offers other *specified* and *unspecified disorders* that can be used when a provider believes an individual's impairment in functioning or distress is clinically significant but does not meet the specific diagnostic criteria in that category. The "other specified" should be used when the clinician wants to communicate specifically why the criteria do not fit. The "unspecified disorder" should be used when he or she does not wish, or is unable, to communicate specifics. For example, if someone appeared to have significant panic attacks but only had three of the four required criteria, the diagnosis could be "Other Specified Panic Disorder—due to insufficient symptoms." Otherwise, the clinician would report "Unspecified Panic Disorder."

Appendix G: Privilege Exercise

1. If your ancestors were forced to come to the U.S., not by choice, take one step back.
2. If your primary ethnic identity is American, take one step forward.
3. If you were ever called names because of your race, class, ethnicity, gender, or sexual orientation, take one step back.
4. If there were people of color who worked in your childhood household as housekeepers, gardeners, etc., take one step forward.
5. If you were ever ashamed or embarrassed of your clothes, house, car, etc., take one step back.
6. If your parents were professionals (doctors, lawyers, etc.), take one step forward.
7. If you were raised in an area where there was prostitution, drug activity, etc., take one step back.
8. If you ever tried to change your appearance, mannerisms, or behavior to avoid being judged or ridiculed, take one step back.
9. If you studied the culture of your ancestors in elementary school, take one step forward.
10. If you went to school speaking a language other than English, take one step back.
11. If there were more than 50 books in your house when you grew up, take one step forward.
12. If you ever had to skip a meal or were hungry because there was not enough money to buy food when you were growing up, take one step back.
13. If you were taken to art galleries or plays by your parents during childhood, take one step forward.
14. If one of your parents was unemployed or laid off, not by choice, take one step back.
15. If you attended private school or summer camp, take one step forward.
16. If your family ever had to move because they could not afford the rent, take one step back.
17. If you were told that you were beautiful, smart, and capable by your parents, take one step forward.
18. If you were ever discouraged from academics or jobs because of race, class, ethnicity, gender, or sexual orientation, take one step back.
19. If you were encouraged to attend college by your parents, take one step forward.
20. If you were raised in a single-parent household, take one step back.
21. If your family owned the house where you grew up, take one step forward.
22. If you saw members of your race, ethnic group, gender, or sexual orientation portrayed on television in degrading roles, take one step back.
23. If you were ever offered a good job because of your association with a friend or family member, take one step forward.
24. If you were ever denied employment because of your race, ethnicity, gender, or sexual orientation, take one step back.
25. If you were paid less or treated unfairly because of race, ethnicity, gender, or sexual orientation, take one step back.
26. If you were ever accused of cheating or lying because of your race, ethnicity, gender, or sexual orientation, take one step back.
27. If you ever inherited money or property, take one step forward.
28. If you had to rely primarily on public transportation, take one step back.

29. If you were ever stopped or questioned by the police because of your race, ethnicity, gender, or sexual orientation, take one step back.

30. If you were ever afraid of violence because of your race, ethnicity, gender, or sexual orientation, take one step back.

31. If you were generally able to avoid places that were dangerous, take one step forward.

32. If you were ever uncomfortable about a joke related to your race, ethnicity, gender, or sexual orientation but felt unsafe to confront the situation, take one step back.

33. If you were ever the victim of violence related to your race, ethnicity, gender, or sexual orientation, take one step back.

34. If your parents did not grow up in the United States, take one step back.

35. If your parents told you that you could be anything you wanted to be, take one step forward.

Glossary

A

A, B, and Cs. Based on rational emotive behavior therapy (REBT), a *cognitive theory* to helping developed by *Albert Ellis* where A is the *activating event*, B is the *belief about the event*, and C is the *consequential feelings and behaviors*.

ACA Code of Ethics. The ethical code for the American Counseling Association.

Acceptance. Respecting people's ideals, thoughts, and emotions unconditionally. Also called *unconditional positive regard*. One of the nine *characteristics of the effective counselor*.

Activating event. A stimulus or incident that leads to one's *belief about an event*. *Irrational thoughts* or beliefs result in negative consequences (feelings and/or behavior), while rational beliefs result in positive feelings and functional behaviors. See also *A, B, and Cs*. A component of *Albert Ellis's cognitive theory*.

Active listening. A deliberate and focused process by which the counselor attempts to establish *empathy* with a client by *reflecting feelings* and *content* of a client's statements.

Additive empathy. Also called *advanced empathy* and based on the *Carkhuff scale*, empathy that is beyond a level 3 response.

Adlerian therapy. A *psychodynamic approach* to counseling.

Advanced empathy. Empathic responses that help clients gain self-awareness by reflecting deeper feelings that were not directly stated by the client or by helping a person see a situation in a new way. Some of the ways one can show advanced empathy include the following: *reflecting nonverbal behaviors, reflecting deeper feelings, pointing out conflictual feelings or thoughts, using visual imagery, using analogies, using metaphors, using targeted self-disclosure, reflecting tactile responses, using media*, and *using discursive responses*.

Advice giving. The process by which the counselor offers his or her expert opinion in hopes that the client will follow up on the suggestions. Advice giving should be used sparingly, as there is the potential that the client will develop a dependent relationship on the counselor and could end up relying on the counselor for problem-solving. Contrast with *information giving* and *offering alternatives*.

Advocacy. One aspect of *social justice* work that involves a counselor directly or indirectly taking active steps to heal a societal wound and promote the welfare of his or her client. Levels of counselor intervention when practicing advocacy include intrapersonal, interpersonal, institutional, community, public policy, and international and global affairs (From Domain IV: Counseling and Advocacy Interventions of the *Multicultural and Social Justice Counseling Competencies*).

Affirmation. The process by which a counselor reinforces a client's actions, feelings, or behaviors by giving a genuine positive response to a client's way of being in the world. Contrast with *encouragement* and *support*.

Amphetamines. A type of *stimulant* or medication used to treat individuals living with Attention Deficit Disorder with Hyperactivity (ADHD).

Antianxiety agents. A classification of medications used primarily to treat individuals living with Generalized Anxiety Disorder (GAD) or related anxiety disorders.

Antidepressants. A classification of medications used primarily to treat individuals living with depressive and anxiety disorders. See also *selective serotonin reuptake inhibitors* (SSRIs).

Antipsychotic drugs. Sometimes referred to as *neuroleptics*, they are generally used to treat psychoses, bipolar disorder, depression with psychotic features, paranoid disorder, delirium, and dementia.

Asking the client to justify the discrepancy. One method of challenging discrepancies.

Assault and homicidal danger assessment tool: An instrument that can be used to assess for potential harm to another person.

Assessing for homicidality: The process used to determine if a client is at danger of harming another person. Involves 10 steps, some of which include using the *assault and homicidal danger assessment tool* and assessing for risk and protective factors.

Assessing for suicidality. The process for evaluating if clients are posing an imminent danger to themselves, including but not limited to the degree to which the client has developed a plan, has the means to carry out the plan, is prepared to implement the plan, has rehearsed the plan, and has acted on the plan. Also includes examining for risk and protective factors.

Assessment for treatment planning. A type of client assessment that involves multiple ways of understanding client concerns and can include (a) conducting a clinical interview, (b) administering tests, and (c) doing informal assessment. An aspect of *case management*.

Attachment therapy. A *psychodynamic approach* to counseling.

Attire or dress. The overt and covert norms within an agency regarding the style of dress for counselors and for other employees. Counselors should take into account how their attire or dress impacts their clients.

Attitude and beliefs, knowledge, skills, and actions. See the *Multicultural and Social Justice Counseling Competencies*.

Atypical antidepressants. *Antidepressants* that do not fit within the existing categories.

Automatic thoughts. Fleeting thoughts that we have all day long about how we are interacting in the world. Used in *Beck's cognitive-behavioral approach*.

Autonomy. Based on *Kitchener's moral model of ethical decision-making*, this involves empowering the client's sense of self-determination, independence, and self-sufficiency.

B

Basic empathy. Any of a number of responses that reflect back the obvious feelings and content that a person is experiencing. A level 3 on the *Carkhuff scale*.

Beck, Aaron. Individual who developed *cognitive behavior therapy*.

Behavior therapy. A type of *cognitive-behavioral approach* to counseling.

Behavioral rehearsal. See *modeling*.

Being committed. An important *foundational skill* related to *being egalitarian and positive*.

Being egalitarian and positive. A series of *foundational skills* including *honoring and respecting the client, showing caring curiosity, delimiting power and developing an equal relationship, non-pathologizing,* and *being committed*.

Belief about the event. The patterns of cognitions (rational or irrational beliefs) that one has about an *activating event*.

Belief in one's theory. This quality is important if one is to be good at *delivering one's theoretical approach* and is related to the nine *characteristics of the effective counselor*.

Beneficence. Based on *Kitchener's moral model of ethical decision-making*, this involves protecting the good of others and of society.

Benzodiazepines. A type of *anti-anxiety medication* that has an elevated risk for tolerance, dependence, and overdose if not taken properly.

Best practices. Suggestions for practicing as a counselor that will reduce the counselor's risk of being sued.

Biological domain. One of the three domains of the *biopsychosocial assessment model* of *case conceptualization*.

Biopsychosocial assessment model. A case conceptualization model that examines the *biological, psychological, and sociocultural domains* to determine themes and ideas about causation regarding clients' problems and helps to identify a diagnosis and treatment plan.

Board-certified coach. A credential that is offered through the *Center for Credentialing and Education* for *coaching*.

Body positioning. How the counselor situates his or her body while working with a client. One of the most important *nonverbal behaviors* that clients initially observe.

By history. Used when a client has a history of a disorder from another agency or mental health professional, which may or may not be borne out by the counselor's current experience of the client.

C

Caring curiosity: Counselors who have a genuine interest in getting to know their clients and are comfortable inquiring about a client's life while simultaneously honoring and respecting the person. A *foundational skill*.

Caring habits. Counselors who develop tendencies of interacting with their clients that involve using language that is supportive, encouraging, accepting, trusting, and respectful and does not use language that is *toxic* and will pathologize, diagnose, blame, or criticize.

Carkhuff scale. A five-point scale developed by *Robert Carkhuff* and based on *Carl Rogers's* definition of empathy. The scale has been used in the training of counselors to assist them in learning empathy. Level 3 responses are seen as accurately reflecting the client's affect and content. Responses below level 3 are seen as *subtractive*, while responses above level 3 are seen as *additive empathy*.

Carkhuff, Robert. Developed a five-point scale to measure the ability to make an empathic response. See *Carkhuff scale*.

Case conceptualization. The process used by counselors to make sense out of clients' symptoms, thoughts, affect, behaviors, and personality and used in the development of diagnosis and treatment planning. Also called *case formulation*.

Case formulation. See *case conceptualization*.

Case notes. A wide variety of ways of documenting and summarizing clients' information, including the *intake interview*, periodic summaries of clients' progress, termination summaries, specialized reports for the courts or other agencies, and more. Also referred to as *case reports*, they are sometimes seen as longer versions of case notes. Generally, clients have the right to see case notes and case reports. Contrast with *process notes*. See also *SOAP notes/reports*.

Case reports. See *case notes*.

Center for Credentialing and Education. The professional organization that offers a certification for *coaching*.

Challenging client discrepancies. See *confrontation: challenge with support*.

Characteristics of the effective counselor. Nine characteristics important for counselors to embody if they are to be effective. Six are part of building the *working alliance: empathy, genuineness, acceptance, wellness, cultural sensitivity,* and the *it factor*. Three are part of *delivering one's theoretical approach: competence, cognitive complexity,* and *belief in one's theory*.

CHASE LOVE. An acronym to help remember *nonverbal behaviors*, standing for: **C**ross-cultural concerns, **H**ead nodding, **A**ttire, personal **S**pace (proxemics), **E**ye contact, **L**eaning forward and open body posture, **O**ffice atmosphere, **V**oice intonation, and facial **E**xpression.

Choice theory. Developed by *William Glasser*, along with *reality therapy*. Amongst other things, these theories suggest people, including counselors, should use *caring habits*.

Client contact hours. The amount of time that counselors provide treatment to their clients.

Client-centered. A nondirective approach to counseling in which counselors allow clients to take the lead in the

direction of their sessions. Contrast with the *helper-centered* approach.

Clinical interview. This important interview allows the counselor to gather information from a broad area of the client's life. Often, this interview takes place during the initial contact with the agency and is called an *intake interview*.

Closed questions. Questions that can be answered with a *yes/no, forced choice,* or *focused-question format* type of response. These questions tend to limit the number of choices being offered to clients.

Coaching. An approach to helping that relies on a short-term, focused helping relationship in which the coach uses solution-focused questions to identify one or more issues to focus on. The coach collaboratively sets goals, affirms and encourages the client to work on goals, and helps to ensure continued follow-up after goals have been reached to ensure maintenance of goals. In coaching, little time is devoted to examining the past or focusing on in-depth problems.

Cognitive-behavioral approaches: Any of a number of approaches that examine how cognitions and/or behaviors impact one's feelings, behaviors, and physiology. Some of the more popular approaches are *behavior therapy, rational emotive behavior therapy (REBT), cognitive behavior therapy,* and *reality therapy*. Two well-known approaches were developed by Aaron Beck and Albert Ellis.

Cognitive-behavioral responses. Responses that focus on cognitions and behaviors. Two well-known approaches, *cognitive behavior therapy* and *rational emotive behavior therapy,* were developed, respectively, by *Aaron Beck* and *Albert Ellis*.

Cognitive behavior therapy. A well-known *cognitive-behavioral approach* developed by *Aaron Beck*. This approach focuses on *automatic thoughts, intermediate thoughts,* and *core beliefs.*

Cognitive complexity. The ability to understand the world in complex and multifaceted ways and to be more *relativistic* rather than *dualistic*. See *William Perry*. One of the nine *characteristics of the effective counselor.*

Collaboration. The purposeful practice of making time to talk with your client about progress being made thus far in the counseling relationship.

Collectivistic perspective. Clients who tend to defer more to parents, wise people in their culture, or others in the decision-making process.

Common factors. Factors underlying all therapeutic approaches that seem to be related to positive client outcomes. See *working alliance* and *delivering one's theoretical approach.*

Commonly used skills. Skills often used after the working alliance has been formed that push the client toward increased awareness and identified goals. Includes *advanced empathy; affirmation giving; encouragement and support; offering alternatives; information giving and advice giving; modeling; self-disclosure;* and *collaboration.*

Community advocacy. See *advocacy.*

Compassion fatigue. The process by which a counselor becomes emotionally exhausted from hearing client concerns. Can result in ineffective work and an inability to feel *empathy* with clients. Also called *vicarious traumatization.*

Competence. Relative to the ACA code, this has to do with knowing one's limits of professional knowledge, level of ability, and professional capabilities. It also has to do with being knowledgeable about the most recent professional research and trends and being able to apply them with clients. One of the nine *characteristics of the effective counselor.*

Conducting follow-up. The process by which a counselor contacts a client after the counseling relationship has ended. An aspect of *case management* that can be completed by a phone call, by a letter, by an elaborate survey of clients, or in other ways.

Confidentiality. The ethical guideline that emphasizes discretion regarding the release of client information. It is driven by knowledge of ethical, professional, and legal issues regarding when such information can be breached. Confidentiality concerns, privacy issues, and concerns about security of records have become paramount and have been impacted by a number of laws, including the *Health Insurance Portability and Accountability Act* (HIPAA), the *Family Educational Rights and Privacy Act* (FERPA), and the *Freedom of Information Act* (FOIA). Also see *foreseeable harm.*

Confidentiality of records. Keeping clients' information in secured places, such as locked file cabinets and password-secured computers. Related to the *HIPAA Privacy Rule.* Some exceptions to confidentially of records include when the counselor is consulting with a professional or undergoing supervision for the benefit the client; in certain cases of mandatory reporting (e.g., child or spousal abuse); if the client is in danger of harming self or others; if the court subpoenas a client's records and the counselor is not protected by *privileged communication*; if a client gives permission, in writing, to share information with others; and when giving certain information to health insurance companies or funding sources that are underwriting counseling services. Clients generally have access to all their records except *process notes,* sometimes called *psychotherapy notes.*

Confrontation: challenge with support. The process by which a counselor assists a client in gaining self-awareness about a *discrepancy between a client's values and behaviors, feelings and behaviors, idealized self and real self,* and *expressed feelings and underlying feelings.* Ways of confrontation include *you/but statements, inviting the client to justify the discrepancy, reframing, using satire,* and *using higher-level empathy.*

Congruence. See *genuineness.*

Consequential feelings and behaviors. A concept from *cognitive-behavioral approaches* to counseling that involves the emotions and actions that are influenced by one's *automatic thoughts* or *irrational thoughts or beliefs* about an *activating event.*

Considerations when working with select populations. The importance of focusing on specific concerns when working with select populations, including children; individuals from different ethnic and racial groups; individuals from diverse religious backgrounds; individuals who use and abuse substances; individuals with disabilities; individuals with serious mental disorders; lesbian, gay, bisexual, transgender, and questioning individuals; men; older persons; the poor and the homeless; and women. See Chapter 9 for specifics.

Content self-disclosure. The counselor's revelation of some personal information in an effort to enhance the helping relationship. See *self-disclosure.*

Co-occuring diagnoses. When making a diagnosis, when there is more than one mental disorder. The one that seems to be prominent should be listed first.

Coping questions. Questions that identify behaviors that the client has successfully used in the past to deal with his or her problems. One type of *solution-focused question.*

Core beliefs. Deep-rooted beliefs or opinions about self that impact *intermediate beliefs* and *automatic thoughts.* A concept from *Aaron Beck's cognitive-behavioral approach.*

Countertransference. The process in which the counselor's own issues interfere with effectively helping his or her clients. The unconscious transferring of thoughts, feelings, and attitudes onto the client.

Crisis counseling. Specialized ways of working with a client who is dealing with an event or situation that is perceived as so intolerable that it prevents the person from being able to use his or her usual coping mechanisms and resources and results in cognitive, affective, and behavioral problems. Often a onetime event, most people are able to regain some semblance of balance within 6 to 8 weeks following the crisis.

Cross-cultural counseling. Counseling individuals from any of a variety of diverse backgrounds. Counselors should demonstrate *culturally competent counseling*.

Cultural mosaic. Understanding that individuals from diverse cultures, especially new immigrants, are often comfortable living in communities with individuals who are similar to them. Brings diversity and uniqueness to the larger culture.

Cultural sensitivity. Being sensitive to diverse cultural groups and having the knowledge, attitudes and beliefs, and skills to work effectively with them. One of the nine *characteristics of the effective counselor*. Also see *culturally competent counseling*.

Culturally competent counseling. The ability and readiness of a counselor to understand the cultural identity of a client and to be cognizant of how the client's cultural heritage as well as the counselor's attitudes and beliefs, knowledge, and skills may impact the counseling relationship.

D

Deciding on treatment modality. One of the *four steps to treatment planning*.

Defining the problem. One of the *four steps to treatment planning*.

Delimiting power and developing an equal relationship. The process by which a counselor shows his or her client respect and joins with the client to form an equitable relationship. An important foundational skill related to *being egalitarian and positive*.

Delivering one's theoretical approach: Part of the *common factors* that contribute to positive outcomes in counseling. Includes *competence, cognitive complexity,* and *belief in one's theory*.

Developing achievable goals. One of the *four steps to treatment planning*.

Developmental models of ethical decision-making. Approaches to making ethical decisions that emphasize how one's cognitive ability impacts a counselor's ethical decision-making process. Higher-level thinkers are more complex and *relativistic*. Lower-order thinkers are more black and white and *dualistic*.

Dia. Means "apart" in Greek. Part of the word *diagnosis*.

Diagnosis. Determining a type of mental disorder through the *Diagnostic and Statistical Manual,* fifth edition.

Diagnostic and Statistical Manual, fifth edition. This edition, published in 2013, details the different types of mental disorders and is used for diagnostic purposes. Contains 21 diagnostic categories and 541 mental disorder diagnoses. Also see *co-occurring diagnoses; subtypes, specifiers,* and *severity; provisional and informal diagnoses;* and *other specified and unspecified disorders*.

Disaster counseling. Specialized ways of working with clients who have experienced a disaster. The early origins of the word means unfavorable ("dis") position of the stars ("astrum"). A disaster is the consequence of some type of major social disruption that often results in injury and death as well as property destruction throughout a community. Disasters can be human-generated or natural.

Discrepancy between client's expressed and underlying feelings. When a client's expressed feelings do not match his or her underlying feelings. Important for the process of *confrontation: challenge with support*.

Discrepancy between client's feelings and behaviors. When a client's feelings do not match his or behaviors. Important for the process of *confrontation: challenge with support*.

Discrepancy between client's idealized self and real self. When a client's perceived sense of self is not his or her actual self. Important for the process of *confrontation: challenge with support*.

Discrepancy between client's values and behavior. When a client's values do not match his or her behaviors. Important for the process of *confrontation: challenge with support*.

Diverse clients are wary of counseling. Nine reasons why some diverse clients are wary of counseling, including the counselor (a) believing in the *melting-pot myth*, (b) having the inability to adapt the counseling relationship, (c) having a lack of understanding of social forces, (d) having an *ethnocentric worldview*, (e) being ignorant of his or her unconscious bias, (f) having an inability to understand cultural differences in the expression of symptomatology, (g) using unreliable assessment and research instruments, (h) not being aware of institutional discrimination, and (i) having an *individualistic perspective.*

Documentation of contact hours. A measure of time, in hours, that counselors provide treatment to their clients. Part of *case management.*

Domains I through IV of Multicultural and Social Justice Counseling Competencies. Domains focused on in the competencies that include Domain I: Counselor self-awareness, Domain II: Client worldview, Domain III: Counseling relationship, and Domain IV: Counseling and advocacy interventions.

Drawing positives out of negatives. An exercise used in *positive counseling.*

DSM-5. See *Diagnostic and Statistical Manual,* fifth edition.

Dual and multiple relationships. A professional helping relationship in which there exists potential ethical conflicts because there are multiple roles between the counselor and the client, such as when a potential or actual client is also a neighbor or colleague or when a counselor goes to a personal celebration or activity sponsored by a client (wedding, funeral, etc.).

Dual relationships. See *dual and multiple relationships.*

Dualistic. A perspective in which one views the world in terms of black-and-white thinking, concreteness, rigidity, oversimplification, stereotyping, self-protectiveness, and authoritarianism.

Duty to warn. See *foreseeable harm.*

E

Eight steps when dealing with a person in crisis. (1) Establish rapport, (2) let individuals tell the story, (3) identify major problem(s), (4) assess for safety issues, (5) help individuals deal with their feelings, (6) explore alternatives with individuals, (7) develop an action plan, and (8) make referrals if ongoing services are needed.

Eight steps when responding to a disaster. (1) Contact and engagement, (2) safety and comfort, (3) stabilization, (4) information gathering, (5) practical assistance, (6) connection with social supports, (7) information on coping, and (8) linkage and collaborative services.

Ellis, Albert. Developed a cognitive approach to therapy called *rational emotive behavior therapy* (REBT), highlighting the impact that thoughts have on behaviors, feelings, and physiology. See *A, B, and Cs* and *irrational thoughts.*

Emotional intelligence. The ability to monitor one's emotions and knowing the appropriate time to share one's feelings and thoughts.

Empathy. Derived from the German word *einfühlung*, empathy has become a core counseling skill. Popularized by Carl Rogers, empathy is viewed as the ability to understand another person's feelings and situation in the world. Empathic responses are often viewed as *basic empathy* or *advanced empathy.* The *Carkhuff scale* operationalized this important concept. One of the nine *characteristics of the effective counselor.*

Encouragement. This skill focuses on inspiring a client toward reaching specific goals. Contrast with *affirmation* and *support.*

Ensuring security of records. An ethical responsibility of all counselors, whether using paper or electronic records. Has become particularly important with passage of *HIPAA.*

Essential skills. Skills that slowly nudge the client toward the self-examination process. Crucial near the beginning of the relationship, they are regularly revisited in the counseling relationship. They include *silence and pause time, listening skills, reflecting feelings, reflecting content, paraphrasing,* and *basic empathy.*

Ethical decision-making. The process of acting on an ethical dilemma. See *ethical decision-making models.*

Ethical decision-making models. Any of a number of models that assist counselors in making difficult ethical decisions. Include *developmental models, moral models, problem-solving models,* and the *social constructionist perspective.*

Ethnocentric worldview. One of nine reasons why *diverse clients are wary of counseling.*

Evaluative questions. Questions that are intended to assess whether clients' behaviors have been productive toward reaching their goals. One type of *solution-focused question.*

Evidence-based practice (EBP). Ensuring positive outcomes by the counselor (a) knowing the best available research-proven treatments, (b) using his or her clinical expertise to understand the client's situation and choosing the most effective treatments for it, and (c) taking into account the client's personal preferences, values, and cultural background when picking treatments. Contrast with *common factors.*

Exception-seeking questions. Questions that identify times in the client's life when he or she has not had the problem and that focus on what the client was doing during those times. One type of *solution-focused question.*

Existential model of cross-cultural counseling. This model, along with the *tripartite model of personal identity,* is used to create an *integrative model of culturally competent counseling,* which examines *three spheres of experience (individual, group,* and *universal experiences).* These all are part of *the Self.*

Existential therapy. An *existential-humanistic approach* to counseling.

Existential-humanistic approaches. Loosely based on the philosophies of *existentialism* and *phenomenology,* existential-humanistic approaches were particularly prevalent during the latter part of the 20th century but continue to be widely used today. Existentialism examines the kinds of choices one makes to develop meaning and purpose in life and, from a psychotherapeutic perspective, suggests that people can choose new ways of living at any point in their lives. Phenomenology is the belief that each person's reality is unique and that to understand the person, you must hear how that person has come to make sense of his or her world. These approaches tend to focus on developing a trusting and real relationship with the counselor, focusing on the here and now, and gently challenging clients to make new choices in their lives. Although generally shorter-term than the *psychodynamic approaches,* these therapies tend to be longer-term than the *cognitive-behavioral approaches* or *postmodern approaches.* Some of the more well-known *existential-humanistic approaches* are *existential therapy, Gestalt therapy,* and *person-centered counseling.*

Existentialism. A philosophy that is part of the *existential-humanistic approach* to counseling that examines the kinds of choices one makes to develop meaning and purpose in life and, from a psychotherapeutic perspective, suggests that people can choose new ways of living at any point in their lives.

Eye contact. A *nonverbal behavior* related to the ability of the counselor to appropriately engage a person through direct contact with their eyes. Impacted by cross-cultural differences.

F

Facial expressions. A *nonverbal behavior* related to a wide range of facial gestures made by a counselor and intended to foster the helping relationship.

Family Education Rights and Privacy Act (FERPA). A federal law that, in part, assures individuals and parents of children, the right to access their educational records.

FERPA. See *Family Education Rights and Privacy Act.*

Fidelity. Based on *Kitchener's* moral model of *ethical decision-making,* this involves maintaining clients' trust and being committed to them.

Focused-question format. Questions that focus on information that is needed.

Forced-choice format. Questions that give the client a minimum of options when responding.

Foreseeable harm. Sometimes referred to as *duty to warn,* the ethical and sometimes legal obligation of a professional to take action and breach *confidentiality* if a client is in danger of harming himself or herself or someone else.

Formula empathic responses. Structured empathic responses that are typically made by beginning counselors and use a "You feel (enter feeling word) because (enter content)" structure.

Foundational skills. Initial skills used to form a strong relationship. Include *nonverbal behaviors* of office atmosphere, attire or dress, eye contact and facial expressions, body positioning and head nodding, proxemics (personal space), touch, and voice intonation; and *being egalitarian and positive* by honoring and respecting the client, showing caring curiosity, delimiting power and developing an equal relationship, being non-pathologizing, and being committed. (See specific definitions of each).

Four steps to treatment planning. Include (a) *defining the problems,* (b) *developing achievable goals,* (c) *deciding on treatment modality,* and (d) *measuring change.*

Freedom of Information Act (FOIA) of 1974. Allows individuals access to records maintained by a federal agency that contain personal information about the individual. Most states have similar laws.

G

Genuineness. The quality of expressing one's true feelings. Being congruent or in sync with one's feelings, thoughts, and behaviors. Popularized by Carl Rogers and listed as one of his three core conditions of helping, along with *empathy* and *unconditional positive regard.* One of the nine *characteristics of the effective counselor.* Sometimes called *congruence, realness,* or *transparency.*

Gestalt therapy. A type of *existential-humanistic approach* to counseling.

Glasser, William. Founder of *reality therapy* and *choice theory.* Suggests counselors use *caring habits.*

"Gnosis." Means to perceive or know in Greek. Part of the word *diagnosis.*

Goal development. Critical for most counseling approaches, it should be an outgrowth of assessment, be collaborative, be attainable, be monitored, be changeable, be able to develop new ones as old ones are reached, and be affirmed by the counselor. The counselor should also know when to stop goal development.

Good listening. An active process in which the counselor talks minimally, concentrates on what is being said, does not interrupt or give advice, hears the speaker's content and affect, and uses good nonverbal behaviors to show that he or she is understanding the client.

Gratitude exercises. An exercise showing thankfulness that is used in *positive counseling.*

Group experiences. One of the *three spheres of experience* that make up *the Self* of the *integrative model of cultural competent counseling.* Also see *individual experiences* and *universal experiences.*

H

Head nodding. A type of *nonverbal behavior* that shows the counselor is listening to the client.

Health Insurance Portability and Accountability Act (HIPAA). A federal law that, in part, ensures the privacy of client records by restricting the amount of information that can be shared without the client's consent and allows clients to have access to their records. Also see *privacy rule.*

Helper-centered. In contrast to being *client-centered,* when the counselor directs the session.

Higher-level empathy. See *advanced empathic responses.*

Hindrances to effective listening. Factors that prevent or interfere with one's ability to listen effectively, such as preconceived notions, anticipatory reaction, cognitive distractions, personal issues, emotional responses, and distractions.

HIPAA. See *Health Insurance Portability and Accountability Act.*

HIPAA privacy rule. See *Privacy Rule.*

Hope exercises. An exercise expressing optimism and used in *positive counseling.*

Honoring and respecting. An important *foundational skill* related to *being egalitarian and positive.*

I

ICD. See *International Classification of Disease (ICD).*

Ideas about causation. Related to the case conceptualization process, these are the hypotheses that occur after a counselor has gained information from a client based on his or her case conceptualization model. Also see *biopsychosocial assessment model of case conceptualization.*

Ignorance of one's unconscious bias. One of nine reasons why *diverse clients are wary of counseling.*

Imitation. See *modeling.*

Immediacy. See *process self-disclosure.*

Inability to adapt to the counseling relationship. One of nine reasons why *diverse clients are wary of counseling.*

Inability to understand cultural differences in the expression of symptomatology. One of nine reasons why *diverse clients are wary of counseling.*

Inadvertent modeling. A type of modeling in which new behaviors are learned from the counselor in a passive way as the counselor demonstrates basic counseling skills toward the client. See *modeling.*

Individual experiences. One of the *three spheres of experience* that make up *the Self* of the integrative model of cultural competent counseling. Also see *group experiences* and *universal experiences.*

Individualistic perspective. Clients who tend to focus on an individual identity and seek answers to problems from self as opposed to outside groups, such as the family or culture. Assuming clients have an individualistic perspective is one of nine reasons why *diverse clients are wary of counseling.* See also *collectivist perspective.*

Indivisible self model. A *wellness* model that has individuals assess five factors: the creative self, the coping self, the social self, the essential self, and the physical self.

Informal diagnoses. See *provisional and informal diagnoses.*

Information-gathering questions. Questions that are intended to gather information that the counselor believes will help solve the client's problems or address the client's concerns. These questions tend to be helper-centered. Includes *open questions, closed questions, tentative questions,* and *why questions.*

Information giving. The process by which a counselor offers the client important, objective information of which the client is likely unaware. Contrast with *advice giving* and *offering alternatives.*

Informed consent. The acknowledgement by a client that he or she understands the nature and general limits of the helping relationship. Often signed after the client has read a *professional disclosure statement.*

Institutional advocacy. See *advocacy.*

Institutional discrimination. One of nine reasons why *diverse clients are wary of counseling.*

Intake interview. The client's initial contact with the agency, which must be completed in a manner that will allow the client to be open and honest with the counselor so that understanding of client issues is clear and comprehensive.

Integrative model of culturally competent counseling. A model that combines ideas from the *existential model of cross-cultural counseling* and the *tripartite model of personal identity,* which examines *three spheres of experience (individual, group,* and *universal experiences).* These all are parts of *the Self.*

Intentional modeling. A type of modeling in which the counselor deliberately demonstrates a behavior for the client so he or she will view, practice, learn, and adopt the new behavior. Clients can also choose behaviors of others with the intention of viewing, practicing, learning, and adopting those behaviors.

Intermediate beliefs. Attitudes, rules, and assumptions we make based on our *core beliefs* that impact the development of our *automatic thoughts.* Based on *Aaron Beck's* theory of cognitive therapy.

International and global affairs advocacy. See *advocacy.*

International Classification of Disease. A diagnostic manual used by health care providers, now in its 10th edition (*ICD-10*).

It identifies medical diagnoses and includes classifications from the *DSM-5,* although it does not describe them in the detail found in *DSM-5.*

Interpersonal advocacy. See *advocacy.*

Interpretation. When a counselor assumes that there is some meaning behind the client's statements that are not directly related to what the client is saying. The counselor's assumptions, which are based on hypothesizing and are related to a theoretical model the counselor holds, may or may not be correct. Often, *psychodynamic approaches* to counseling use this approach.

Intrapersonal advocacy. See *advocacy.*

Irrational thoughts. Patterns of thought, or cognitions, that are illogical and are often related to the subsequent development of negative emotions and dysfunctional behaviors. Based on *Albert Ellis's* theory of *rational emotive behavior therapy (REBT).*

It factor. The unique characteristics of a counselor that contribute to special ways of working with and ultimately building alliances with their clients. One of the nine *characteristics of the effective counselor.*

J

Jaffee v. Redmond. A court ruling that upheld the right of *privileged communication* for licensed social workers and likely can be applied to most licensed counselors and therapists but not to those who are not licensed (e.g., human service professionals).

Julea Ward v. Board of Regents of Eastern Michigan. Due to her religious beliefs, Julea Ward, a graduate student in counseling, refused to work with a client who had been in a same-sex relationship. Ward was eventually dismissed from her graduate program in counseling for her unwillingness to work with a client with different values and beliefs. She subsequently sued the program and the university. Eventually, the case was settled out of court. This case was one reason the *American Counseling Association* now has a stronger statement about the importance of counselors being able to counsel all clients, even when their values and beliefs vary dramatically from those of the client's.

Jungian therapy. A type of *psychodynamic approach* to counseling.

Justice. Based on *Kitchener's* moral model of *ethical decision-making,* this involves treating clients fairly and equally.

K

Kitchener, Karen. Developed a *moral model of ethical decision-making.*

L

Lack of understanding of social forces. One of nine reasons why *diverse clients are wary of counseling.*

LGBTQ. Lesbian, gay, bisexual, transgender, and questioning (LGBTQ) individuals.

Life-coaching. See *coaching.*

Limitations of ethical codes. Instances in which ethical codes are limited due to the following: some issues cannot be handled with a code, difficulties in enforcing codes, lack of public involvement in the code-construction process, issues addressed by codes being handled in other ways (e.g., the courts), conflicts within a code or between related codes, and conflicts between a code and the values of the professional.

Listening. The process by which one directs his or her attention to hearing a message from another person.

Lithium. An element discovered in the 1800s that was later found to be effective for the treatment of bipolar disorder.

M

Maintaining boundaries and prohibited relationships. See *dual and multiple relationships* and *sexual relationships with clients.*

Making referrals. See *termination* and *making referrals.*

Malpractice insurance. Insurance that protects a counselor in case he or she is sued. Some malpractice insurance policies are offered by *ACA,* sometimes at a discount. Also see *best practices.*

McAuliffe's definition of culturally competent helping. The perspective that culturally competent helping is "a consistent readiness to identify the cultural dimensions of clients' lives and a subsequent integration of culture into counseling work" (2013, p. 6).

Measuring change. One of the *four steps to treatment planning.*

Melting-pot myth. Belief by some that all individuals should "melt" into the larger culture. One of nine reasons why *diverse clients are wary of counseling.* Contrast with cultural mosaic.

Mental status exam. An informal assessment the counselor uses to assess a client in four areas, including (a) how the client presents himself or herself (appearance and behavior), (b) the client's affect and mood (emotional state), (c) the client's ability to think clearly (thought components), and (d) the client's memory state and orientation to the world (cognition).

Mental status report. A one- or two-paragraph statement by the counselor about the findings from a *mental status exam.*

Metaphors and analogies. Using symbols, allegories, and logical analysis to make a comparison between a client's current situation and an external event. An *advanced empathic response.*

Miracle question. A type of *preferred-goals question* focused on quickly identifying where the client wants to be in the future that helps the client get to his or her desired goals. Often put in a framework that asks "If you were to wake up in the morning and find your world to be what you want it to be, what would that look like?" See *solution-focused questions.*

Modeling. The subtle or deliberate ways in which the counselor or others can demonstrate new behaviors for the client so that the client can practice, learn, and adopt those behaviors. Also called *social learning, imitation,* or *behavioral rehearsal.* See *inadvertent* and *intentional modeling.*

Monitoring psychotropic medications. An important aspect of *case management* in which a counselor monitors any medications the client is taking related to his or her problems or mental disorders.

Monoamine oxidase inhibitors. An older classification of medications used to treat depressive and anxiety disorders. Sometimes still used today.

Mood-stabilizing drugs. A group of *psychotropic medications* used to treat bipolar disorder.

Moral models of ethical decision-making. *Ethical decision-making models* that emphasize the role of moral principles in making ethical decisions. One such model, by *Kitchener,* suggests examining the following moral principles: *autonomy, beneficence, nonmaleficence, justice,* and *fidelity. Veracity* was added later.

Multicultural and Social Justice Counseling Competencies. Having appropriate attitudes and beliefs, knowledge, and skills when working with nondominant clients. Areas of proficiency to assist counselors when working with diverse clients include four domains: (a) counselor self-awareness, (b) client worldview, (c) counseling relationship, and (d) counseling and advocacy intervention. Competencies have been endorsed by *ACA.*

Multicultural counseling. See *cross-cultural counseling.*

Multiple realities. The ability to identify multiple origins that lead to the present moment. Also speaks to varying perspectives a person or persons can have about a situation.

Multiple relationships. See *dual and multiple relationships.*

N

Narrative therapy. A *postmodern approach* to helping that suggests reality is a social construction and that each person's reality is maintained through his or her narrative or language discourse.

Natural empathic responses. Reflecting a client's affect and content while using a natural tone and fluid response.

Neuroleptics. See *antipsychotics.*

Nine characteristics of the effective counselor. See *characteristics of the effective counselor.*

Nonbenzodiazepines. Medications that have similar therapeutic effects as *benzodiazepines;* however, these medications have different chemical properties.

Nondogmatic. Closely related to being *nonjudgmental,* this refers to individuals who do not push their views onto others and are open to understanding the views of others, open to feedback, and even open to changing their perceptions of the world after hearing other points of view. Such individuals are relatively free of biases and can accept people in their differences, regardless of dissimilar cultural heritage, values, or beliefs.

Nonjudgmental. See *nondogmatic.*

Nonmaleficence. Based on *Kitchener's* moral model of *ethical decision-making,* this involves avoiding doing harm to clients and others.

Non-pathologizing. The process by which a counselor meets with a client and treats him or her respectfully in a holistic fashion. Clients are perceived as living with mental health issues as opposed to having mental health issues. An important foundational skill related to *being egalitarian and positive.*

Nonverbal behaviors. Communication that is not verbal, such as one's *office atmosphere, attire and dress, eye contact and facial expressions, proxemics (personal space), touch,* and *voice intonation.*

O

Object-relations theory. A type of *psychodynamic* approach to counseling.

Offering alternatives. When the counselor suggests to the client that there may be a variety of ways to address a problem and provides possible options from which the client can choose. Contrast with *advice giving* and *information giving.*

Office atmosphere. The mood or feel of a counselor's office. Providing an office space that is quiet, comfortable, and safe and where confidentiality can be ensured. A type of *nonverbal behavior.*

Open questions. Questions that enable clients to have a wide range of responses and encourages more than a *yes/no, forced-choice response,* or *focused-question format.*

Other positive counseling interventions. Exercises used in *positive counseling.*

Other specified disorder. When a person has a clinically significant impairment but does not seem to meet the criteria for a diagnostic category. In that case, "other specified disorder" can be used to describe why the criteria does not fit. Also see *unspecified disorder.*

P

Paradoxical effect. The unexpected result of *stimulants.* Instead of making a person overexcited, they calm down and help to focus some people who have attention deficit disorder with hyperactivity (ADHD).

Paraphrasing. A helping skill that involves the counselor reflecting the general feelings and content of what the client has said by using words and phrases similar to the client's.

Pathologizing. The process by which a counselor sees a client and treats that person as if he or she has a problem. Sometimes related to the process of giving or reinforcing a *DSM-5* diagnosis.

Perceptions of 77 behaviors. A study of counselors that examined their beliefs about 77 counselor behaviors. See Chapter 10 on ethical, professional, and legal issues for the full list of behaviors.

Perry, William. An adult development theorist who emphasized the learning process and cognitive development of college students. He researched college students and showed how they tend to move from *dualism* to *relativism* while in college.

Personal space. See *proxemics*.

Person-centered counseling. Developed by *Carl Rogers*, this is an *existential-humanistic approach* to counseling.

Phenomenology. The belief that each person's reality is unique and that to understand the person, you must hear how that person has come to make sense of his or her world.

Pointing out conflicting feelings or thoughts. A type of *advanced empathy* whereby the counselor makes a client aware of discrepancies between his or her feelings and thoughts.

Positive counseling. Assumes we have choices in our lives relative to our mental, physical, and spiritual states; we are not determined by early childhood or other factors; and that we need to be careful when labeling or diagnosing a person, as such labels can result in negative attributions, or self-statements, by professionals or by the clients themselves. Some principles of positive counseling include increasing positive emotions, increasing engagement in life work and leisure, and promoting a meaningful life. Some activities to help with this process include *strength exercises, gratitude exercises, hope and optimism exercises, drawing positives out of negatives,* and *other positive counseling interventions.*

Postmodern approaches. Based on postmodernism and social constructivism, these approaches suggest no one reality holds the truth and we should question past assumptions we took for fact (e.g., id, ego, superego, a self-actualizing tendency, core beliefs, internal locus of control, etc.). These approaches suggest that individuals construct meaning from the discourses they have with others and the language used in culture and in society. Through language, behaviors, and laws, those in power can create havoc for those who are in the minority. The counseling relationship tends to be positive and is highlighted by equality and non-pathology. Rather than harp on past problems that are embedded in oppressive belief systems, postmodern approaches suggest clients can find exceptions to their problems and develop creative solutions and new ways of understanding their world. Some approaches include *narrative therapy, solution-focused brief therapy,* and *relational-cultural therapy.*

Postmodern therapies. Those that have a postmodern approach to therapy, including *narrative therapy, solution-focused brief therapy,* and *relational-cultural therapy.* See *postmodern approaches.*

Postmodernism. Beyond modernism. Questioning of much that has come before. No one reality holds the truth. See *postmodern approaches.*

Post-Traumatic Stress Disorder (PTSD). A client's response to trauma that involves reliving aspects of the traumatic event and experiencing distress that is significant enough to interfere with his or her ability to function.

Preferred-goals questions. Questions that assess what the client is hoping his or future will look like. See also *miracle question.* One type of *solution-focused question.*

Preparing for listening. Refers to a variety of strategies counselors can use to increase the chances that they will listen to their clients effectively, including calming oneself down, not talking and not interrupting, showing interest, not jumping to conclusions, actively listening, concentrating on feelings, concentrating on content, maintaining eye contact, having an open body posture, being sensitive to personal space, and not asking questions.

Privacy rule. As defined by *HIPPA*, the limits and conditions of release of information about clients. The privacy rule notes that *process notes* or *psychotherapy notes* are not available to clients but almost all other records are.

Privileged communication. The legal right of a professional to keep information confidential if the client does not want information revealed. This legal right is determined by states and, relative to mental health professionals, generally only includes licensed counselors and other licensed therapists. See *Jaffee v. Redmond.*

Problem-solving models of ethical decision-making. A pragmatic, hands-on approach to resolving ethical dilemmas that involves following a series of eight steps.

Process notes. Written notes that are often one to three paragraphs long and used to assist the counselor in remembering salient points of a session. Clients typically do not have a right to see these as per the *privacy rule* of the *Health Insurance Portability and Accountability Act (HIPAA).* Also called *psychotherapy notes.*

Process self-disclosure. Similar to the concept of *immediacy,* this involves the counselor sharing with the client his or her moment-to-moment experience of self in relation to the client. See also *self-disclosure.*

Professional disclosure statement. An informational document about the counselor and the counseling relationship that helps the client know what is about to occur, explains the process of the counseling relationship, and provides a broad range of information about counseling, services offered, and ethical considerations. See Chapters 2 and 7 for lists of items typically placed in a professional disclosure statement. Often used when obtaining *informed consent* from clients.

Protective factors. Influences in clients' lives that guard against the likelihood of the client committing suicide or homicide.

Provisional and informal diagnoses. Any of a number of diagnoses that may be questionable, not fully formed, or not fully verifiable. They include *provisional, rule-out, traits, by history,* and *self-report.*

Proxemics. The *personal space* between the counselor and the client. A type of *nonverbal behavior.*

Psychoanalysis. A type of *psychodynamic approach* to therapy.

Psychodynamic approaches. Developed near the beginning of the 20th century but maintaining widespread popularity today, these approaches vary considerably but contain some common elements. For instance, they all suggest that an unconscious and a conscious affect the functioning of the person in some deeply personal and dynamic ways. They all look at early child-rearing practices as being important in the development of personality. They all believe that examining the past and the dynamic interaction of the past with conscious and unconscious factors are important in the therapeutic process. Although these approaches have tended to be long-term, in recent years some have been adapted and used in relatively brief treatment modality formats. Some of the more popular approaches are *psychoanalysis, Jungian therapy, Adlerian therapy, attachment therapy,* and *object-relations theory.*

Psychological domain. One of the three domains of the *biopsychosocial assessment model* of *case conceptualization.*

Psychological report. A report based on a broad range of information gathered that usually results in a diagnosis, summary, and recommendations. See Appendix C for what typically goes into the report.

Psychopharmacology. The scientific study and practice of using medications to treat an array of disorders. Sometimes called *psychotropic medications.*

Psychosocial and environmental stressors. Sources of client distress that are common concerns (e.g., job loss, marital problems, homelessness, relationship issues) and are assessed through the use of *Z codes* in *DSM-5.*

Psychotherapy notes. See *process notes.*

Psychotropic medications. See *psychopharmacology.*

Public policy advocacy. See *advocacy.*

Purpose of ethical codes. Including, but not limited to, protecting consumers, furthering professionalism, denoting a body of knowledge, asserting a professional identity, reflecting a profession's underlying values and suggested behaviors, offering a framework for *ethical decision-making,* and offering a measure of defense in case one is sued.

R

Rational emotive behavior therapy. Developed by *Albert Ellis,* a type of *cognitive-behavioral therapy* that examines *irrational thoughts* and uses the *A, B,* and *Cs* in working with clients.

Reality therapy. A theoretical framework developed by *William Glasser* that suggests we are born with five needs: survival, love and belonging, power, freedom, and fun, which can be satisfied only in the present. Glasser suggested that counselors, and all of us, should develop *caring habits.* Also related to Glasser's *choice theory.*

Realness. See *genuineness.*

Reflecting deeper feelings. A type of *advanced empathy* whereby the counselor reflects the client's underlying feelings that the client might not be aware of.

Reflecting nonverbal behaviors. A type of *advanced empathy* with which the counselor reflects the *nonverbal behaviors* the client is showing.

Reflecting tactile responses. A type of *advanced empathy* whereby the counselor reflects a visceral feeling he or she is having that is assumed to reflect something the client is experiencing. Used to show deep understanding.

Reflection of content. The process by which a counselor repeats back to the client specific statements that the client has made using the same or slightly different words.

Reflection of feeling. The process by which a counselor repeats back to the client specific feelings that the client has expressed using the same feeling word or a feeling word that is very similar to the one that the client used.

Reframing. A type of *confrontation* in which the counselor offers the client an alternative way of viewing his or her situation, followed by a discussion of this new reality.

Relational cultural therapy. A *postmodern approach* to counseling.

Relativistic. A complex form of thinking through which one has the capacity to observe *multiple realities,* is sensitive to context, and understands there are many ways to view the world.

Reporting ethical violations. An ethical responsibility to first speak to the counselor if another counselor believes the first counselor is acting unethically. If a resolution is not found or if the violation is particularly egregious, the counselor should go to the respective organization or person (professional organization, licensing board, counselor's supervisor, etc.).

RESPECTFUL counseling model. An acronym that speaks to the ingredients needed by the culturally competent mental health professional. Includes understanding **r**eligion, **e**conomic class, **s**exual identity, **p**sychological development, **e**thnicity, **c**hronological/developmental challenges, **t**rauma, **f**amily history, **u**nique physical traits, and **l**anguage.

Risk factors. Influences in a client's life that increase the likelihood of the client committing suicide or homicide.

Rogers, Carl. One of the founders of the field of humanistic counseling and education, Rogers developed *person-centered counseling.* Proponent of the importance of *empathy, congruence (genuineness),* and *unconditional positive regard* in the helping relationship.

Rule-out. Used when there is not enough information to make a diagnosis but a specific disorder might be considered.

S

Scaling questions. Questions used to rate how the client is feeling and to see if the client has made progress. Often range from 1 ("the worst I ever felt") to 10 ("the best I ever felt"). A type of *solution-focused question.*

Selective serotonin reuptake inhibitors (SSRIs). Antidepressant medications that are the most commonly used medications for treating depressive disorders. Also used for some anxiety disorders.

Self-disclosure. A helping skill by which the counselor reveals a part of his or her personal life to communicate to the client an understanding about the client's experience. Self-disclosure should be done carefully and only when a counselor is trying to show the client that the client was understood or when the counselor wants to model new behavior for the client. See *content self-disclosure* and *process self-disclosure.*

Self-report. Used when a client states he or she has been diagnosed in the past with a certain disorder.

Severity. See *subtypes, specifiers, and severity.*

Sexual relationships with clients. Having a sexual relationship with a client or former client. It is among the most damaging of all ethical violations, and virtually all helping professions have issued prohibitions against them. See also *dual and multiple relationships.*

Silence and pause time. A helping skill in which a counselor is intentionally quiet during a session to allow the client the opportunity to reflect on what he or she has been saying while also allowing the counselor to process the session and formulate his or her next response. Silent and pause time varies cross-culturally as a function of the background of the client.

SOAP notes. One approach to writing case notes that has gained popularity over the years; stands for subjective, objective, assessment, and plan.

Social constructionist models of ethical decision-making. A perspective to *ethical decision-making* that involves the belief that solutions to problems occur through dialogue between clients, counselors, and others (e.g., supervisors and others in the client's world) and not necessarily the result of reading an ethics code or from some single decision-making process.

Social constructivism. This philosophy suggests that individuals construct meaning in their lives from the discourses they have with others and the language that is used in their culture and in society. It also assumes that through language, behaviors, and laws, those in power can create havoc for those whose identities are in the minority (e.g., culturally diverse clients, women, individuals with disabilities, sexual minorities, etc.).

Social justice. Impacting the broader system (e.g., agencies, cities, country) to affect positive change for clients. See *advocacy.*

Social learning. See *modeling.*

Sociocultural domain. One of the three domains of the *biopsychosocial assessment model* of *case conceptualization.*

Solution-focused brief therapy. A type of *postmodern approach* to counseling.

Solution-focused questions. Questions that are focused on quickly identifying what behaviors have worked in a client's life, determining where the client wants to be in the future, and helping the client get to his or her desired goals. Include *preferred-goals questions, evaluative questions, coping questions, exception-seeking questions, solution-oriented questions,* and *scaling questions.*

Solution-oriented questions. Questions that broadly asks the client how the client's life would be if the problem did not exist. One type of *solution-focused question.*

Specialized skills. Skills that may be critical in some counseling relationships. Include *advocacy; assessing for lethality (e.g., suicidality and homicidality); crisis, disaster, and trauma counseling; confrontation: challenge with support; cognitive-behavioral responses; interpretation; positive counseling;* and *coaching.*

Specifiers. See *subtypes, specifiers, and severity.*

Stimulants. Any of a number of medications often used with Attention Deficit Disorder with Hyperactivity (ADHD). During the 1950s, stimulants (amphetamines) were found to have a *paradoxical effect* in children with hyperactivity.

Strength exercises. An exercise that stresses positive attributes of the client and is used in *positive counseling.*

Subtractive empathy. Empathy below a 3.0 on the *Carkhuff scale.*

Subtypes, specifiers, and severity. In *DSM-5,* some diagnoses have *subtypes,* and it is important to identify which type the disorder is. Many diagnoses have *specifiers,* which further delineate the symptoms but may not be mutually exclusive (you can often have more than one specifier). DSM also offers the counselor the ability to rate the *severity* of some diagnoses.

Suicide. See *assessing for suicidality,*

Supervision. The process by which a counselor is mentored by a more experienced professional, which allows the counselor to examine his or her view of human nature, theoretical approach, ability at implementation of techniques, and, ultimately, effectiveness with clients.

Support. A general term that acknowledges that one role of the counselor is to have the client feel as if there is someone in his or her life the client can rely on for aid and assistance and to promote his or her general well-being. Contrast with *affirmation* and *encouragement.*

T

Tactile responses. See *reflecting tactile cues.*

Tarasoff v. Board of Regents of University of California. The landmark court case that set a precedent for the responsibility that mental health professionals have regarding breaking confidentiality to prevent a client from harming self or others. Suggests that professionals must act in ways to ensure that clients will not harm self or others. See *foreseeable harm.*

Technology in counseling. Relative to ethics, the varied concerns related to Section H of the ACA Code of Ethics, which covers distance counseling, technology, and social media.

Tentative questions. Questions asked in a gentle manner that often allow for a large range of responses from the client.

Termination and making referrals. The process of ending the relationship and/or referring clients to other professionals. The ACA (2014) code is very specific about the importance of appropriate termination and referral when working with clients.

Test worthiness. Ensuring a test is worthwhile because it has good validity (assesses what it's supposed to assess), good reliability (assesses what it's supposed to assess consistently), is cross-culturally fair, and is practical.

Testing. The formal assessment of a client with an instrument that has been shown to have *test worthiness.*

The Self. This *existential model of cross-cultural counseling,* along with the *tripartite model of personal identity,* is used to create an *integrative model of culturally competent counseling,* which examines *three spheres of experience* (*individual, group,* and *universal experiences*). These three spheres all are parts of *the Self.*

Themes. The resulting patterns that a counselor notices after completing *case conceptualization,* such as when one uses the *biopsychosocial assessment model.* Useful in *diagnosis* and *treatment planning.*

Thick descriptions. Individuals who can describe their lives with some amount of complexity. They tend to be *relativistic* and can identify multiple origins that led them to where they are today, see different points of view, and understand multiple perspectives of situations.

Thin descriptions. Individuals who describe their lives with little complexity. They have a tendency to think in simple, *dualistic,* and black-and-white ways and typically adhere to a narrow perspective of reality.

Three spheres of experience. The *individual, group,* and *cultural spheres.* Related to the *integrative model of culturally competent counseling.*

Time management. Strategies that help mental health professionals ensure appropriate services and avoid burnout. Includes ensuring that all clients are seen within a reasonable period of time and remembering meetings, appointment times, and other obligations.

Touch. A *nonverbal behavior* that involves physical contact between a counselor and a client. Traditionally, counselors have been taught to rarely touch clients. However, some appropriate touch may be natural and enriching to the counseling relationship. Research suggests that cross-cultural differences exist in the ways that clients perceive and respond to touch and other *nonverbal behaviors.*

Toxic behaviors. Behaviors and attitudes that are detrimental to another person's well-being and are sometimes responsible for fostering low self-esteem (e.g., being critical, disapproving, disbelieving, scolding, threatening, discounting, ridiculing, or punishing).

Traits. Used when a person does not meet a criterion of *DSM-5* but seems to have several features of the disorder

Transparency. See *genuineness.*

Trauma counseling. Specialized ways of working with individuals who have experienced trauma. Often, trauma leads to a diminished sense of self, loss of dignity, and cognitive, affective, and behavioral problems. The person's usual way of dealing with stress does not work effectively. Trauma can be a onetime event, which usually leaves detailed memories, or an ongoing series of events that may lead to dissociation, denial, and internal rage. Examples of trauma include rape, assault, abuse, being a witness to a horrendous event, and more.

Treatment planning. The process of developing a plan for treatment. Often the result of *assessment* and the *case conceptualization* process.

Tricyclics. An older classification of medications that are used to treat depressive and anxiety disorders. Sometimes still used today.

Tripartite model of personal identity. This model, along with the *existential model of cross-cultural counseling,* is used to create an *integrative model of culturally competent counseling,* which examines *three spheres of experience (individual, group,* and *universal experiences).* These all are parts of *the Self.*

U

Unconditional positive regard. See *acceptance.*

Universal experiences. One of the *three spheres of experience* that makes up *the Self* of the *integrative model of cultural competent counseling.* Also see *group experiences* and *universal experiences.*

Unreliability of assessment and research instruments. One of nine reasons why *diverse clients are wary of counseling.*

Unspecified disorder. When a person has a clinically significant impairment but the counselor does not want to, or is unable to, communicate specifics of the disorder, "unspecified disorder" may be used. Also see *other specified disorder.*

Using analogies. A type of *advanced empathy* whereby the counselor uses an analogy that comes into his or her mind to show the client deep understanding.

Using discursive responses. Discursive responses. A type of *advanced empathy* whereby the counselor reflects something historical in the life or culture of the client that is related to what the client is experiencing in the present.

Using higher-level empathy. One method of *confrontation: challenge with support.* See *advanced empathy.*

Using media. A type of *advanced empathy* whereby the counselor uses media (e.g., movie, book, etc.) that mimics the client's situation and is a mechanism for showing the client deep understanding.

Using metaphors. A type of *advanced empathy* whereby the counselor uses a metaphor that comes into his or her mind to show the client deep understanding.

Using satire. One method of *confrontation: challenge with support.* See *advanced empathy.*

Using targeted self-disclosure. A type of *advanced empathy* whereby the counselor reveals something about self that comes into his or her mind to show the client deep understanding.

Using visual imagery. A type of *advanced empathy* whereby the counselor uses a visual image that comes into his or her mind to show the client deep understanding.

V

Values in the counseling relationship. The ethical responsibility of counselors to ensure that their values or biases are not imposed on their clients.

Veracity. Based on *moral models of ethical decision-making*, this involves being truthful and genuine within the helping relationship.

Vicarious traumatization. See *compassion fatigue.*

Voice intonation. A *nonverbal behavior* related to the pitch, tone, and volume of a counselor's voice.

W

Wellness. A wide range of activities that can be used to ensure self-care and provide optimal services to clients. A few of the many self-care activities include personal counseling, support groups, eating healthy, meditation, prayer, exercise, hobbies, journaling, and reading. One of the nine *characteristics of the effective counselor.*

Why questions. A question that seeks a deep, thoughtful response but often results in defensiveness on the part of the client.

Working alliance. The establishment of a trusting and strong relationship between a counselor and a client that is typically related to six of the nine *characteristics of the effective counselor,* including *empathy, genuineness, acceptance, wellness, cultural sensitivity,* and the *it factor.*

Writing your treatment plan. The manner in which one writes up the client's plan of treatment. There is no one way, although some suggest using the *four steps to treatment planning.*

Y

Yes/no closed questions. A type of *information-gathering question* that requires a specific yes-or-no response.

You/but statements. A type of *confrontation: challenge with support.*

Z

Z codes. A classification system for environmental and psychosocial stressors. Used in *DSM-5.*

References

Akiskal, H. S. (2016). The mental status examination. In S. H. Fatemi & P. J. Clayton (Eds.), *The medical basis of psychiatry* (pp. 3–16). New York, NY: Springer.

American Counseling Association (ACA) (2014). *Code of ethics.* Retrieved from http://www.counseling.org/resources/aca-code-of-ethics.pdf

American Counseling Association. (2011a). *Fact sheet # 6: Suicide assessment.* Retrieved from https://www.counseling.org/docs/trauma-disaster/fact-sheet-6—suicide-assessment.pdf?sfvrsn=2

American Counseling Association. (2011b). *Fact sheet # 7: Terms to know.* Retrieved from https://www.counseling.org/docs/trauma-disaster/fact-sheet-7—terms-to-know.pdf?sfvrsn=af3e0017_2

American Counseling Association. (2011c). *Fact sheet # 11: Crisis counseling.* Retrieved from http://www.counseling.org/docs/trauma-disaster/fact-sheet-10—10n1-crisis-counseling.pdf?sfvrsn=2

American Psychiatric Association. (2013). *Diagnostic and statistical manual of mental disorders* (5th ed.). Arlington, VA: Author.

American Psychological Association. (2005). *Policy statement on evidence-based practice in psychology.* Retrieved from http://www.apa.org/practice/guidelines/evidence-based-statement.aspx

American Psychological Association. (2007). *Guidelines for psychological practice with girls and women.* Washington DC: Author.

American Psychological Association. (2013). *HIPAA: What you need to know: The privacy rule—A primer for psychologists.* Retrieved from http://apapracticecentral.org/business/hipaa/hippa-privacy-primer.pdf

American Psychological Association. (2014). *Guidelines for psychological practice with older adults.* Retrieved from http://www.apa.org/pubs/journals/features/older-adults.pdf

American Psychological Association. (2018). *Health and homelessness.* Retrieved from http://www.apa.org/pi/ses/resources/publications/homelessness-health.aspx

Anderson, S. K. (2012, May 10). To give or not to give advice. *Psychology Today.* Retrieved from https://www.psychologytoday.com/blog/the-ethical-therapist/201205/give-or-not-give-advice

Association for Spiritual, Ethical, and Religious Values in Counseling (n.d.). *Spiritual competencies.* Retrieved from http://aservic.org/?page_id=133

Baird, B. N. (2014). *A guide for the helping professions* (7th ed.). New York, NY: Routledge.

Baker, S. B. (2012, December 1). A new view of evidence-based practice. *Counseling Today.* Retrieved from http://ct.counseling.org/2012/12/a-new-view-of-evidence-based-practice/

Bannink, F. (2015). *101 solution-focused questions for help with trauma.* New York, NY: W. W. Norton.

Bayne, H., & Neukrug, E. (2017). Metaphors for empathy: Getting into character. In S. E. Stewart-Spencer & C. J. Dean, (Eds.), *Metaphors and therapy: Enhancing clinical supervision and education* (pp. 80–88). Baton Rouge, LA: Independent Therapy Ink.

Bedi, R. P. (2006). Concept mapping the client's perspective on counseling alliance formation. *Journal of Counseling Psychology, 53*(1), 26–35.

Berman, P. S. (2014). Case conceptualization and treatment planning: Integrating theory with clinical practice (3rd ed.). Thousand Oaks, CA: SAGE.

Bernard, J. M., & Goodyear, R. (2018). *Fundamentals of clinical supervision* (6th ed.). Boston, MA: Pearson.

Beutler, L. E. (2014). Welcome to the party, but … . *Psychotherapy, 51*(4), 496–499. doi:10.1037/a0036540

Bishop, A. (2015). Freudian psychoanalysis. In E. Neukrug (Ed.), *The SAGE encyclopedia of theory in counseling and psychotherapy* (Vol. 1) (pp. 436–441). Thousand Oaks, CA: SAGE.

Blashfield, R. K., Keeley, J. W., Flanagan, E. H., & Miles, S. R. (2104). The cycle of classification: DSM-1 through DSM-5. *Annual Review of Clinical Psychology, 10,* 25–51. doi:10.1146/annurev-clinpsy-032813-153639

Bloomgarden, A., & Mennuti, R. B. (2009). Therapist self-disclosure: Beyond the taboo. In A. Bloomgarden & R. B. Mennuti (Eds.), *Psychotherapist revealed: Therapists speak about self-disclosure in psychotherapy* (pp. 3–16). New York, NY: Taylor and Francis.

Bolier, L., Haverman, M., Westerhof, G. J., Riber, H., Smit, F., & Bohlmeijer, E. (2013). Positive psychology interventions: A meta-analysis of randomized controlled studies. *BMC Public Health, 13.* doi:10.1186/1471-2458-13-119. Retrieved from http://www.ncbi.nlm.nih.gov/pmc/articles/PMC3599475/

Brownlee, E., (2016). How do counsellors view and practice self-care? *Healthcare Counselling & Psychotherapy Journal, 16*(2), 15–17.

Brymer, M., Jacobs, A., Layne, C., Pynoos, R., Ruzek, J., Steinberg, A., … & Watson, P. (2006). *Psychological first aid: Field operations guide* (2nd ed.). Durham, NC: National Child Traumatic Stress Network and National Center for PTSD.

Bucci, S., French, L. & Berry, K. (2016). Measures assessing the quality of case conceptualization: A systematic review. *Journal of Clinical Psychology, 72*(6), 517–533. doi:10.1002/jclp.22280

Burgess, W. (2013). *Mental status examination: 52 challenging cases.* CreateSpace Independent Publishing Platform.

Bussey, K. (2015). Social cognitive theory. In E. Neukrug (Ed.), *The SAGE encyclopedia of theory in counseling and psychotherapy* (Vol. 2, pp. 938–942). Thousand Oaks, CA: SAGE.

Calmes, S. A., Piazza, N. J., & Laux, J. M. (2013). The use of touch in counseling: An ethical decision-making model. *Counseling and Values, 58*(1), 59–68. doi:10.1002/j.2161-007X.2013.00025.x

Carkhuff, R. R. (2009). *The art of helping in the twenty-first century* (9th ed.). Amherst, MA: Human Resource Development Press.

Center for Credentialing in Education. (2016). *Board certified coach.* Retrieved from http://www.cce-global.org/Credentialing/BCC/Requirements

Centers for Disease Control and Prevention. (2017). *Suicide: Risk and protective factors.* Retrieved from http://www.cdc.gov/violenceprevention/suicide/riskprotectivefactors.html

Centers for Disease Control and Prevention. (2018). *Suicide rising across the U.S.* Retrieved from https://www.cdc.gov/vitalsigns/suicide/index.html

Chatters, S., & Zalaquett, C. (2013). Dispelling the myths of aging. *Counseling Today, 55*(12), 46–51.

Ciarrochi, J., & Mayer, J. D. (Eds.). (2007). *Applying emotional intelligence: A practitioners' guide.* New York, NY: Psychology Press.

Clark, M., Moe, J., & Hays, D. G. (2017). The relationship between counselors' multicultural counseling competence and poverty beliefs. *Counselor Education and Supervision, 56*(4), 259–273. doi:10.1002/ceas.12084

Clark, M., Neukrug, E., & Long, S. M. (2018). Relational cultural therapy. In E. S. Neukrug (Ed.), *Counseling theory and practice* (2nd ed., pp. 482–519). San Diego, CA: Cognella.

Co-Occurring Disorders. (2018, January 25). *Psychology Today.* Retrieved from https://www.psychologytoday.com/us/conditions/co-occurring-disorders

Commonwealth of Virginia Knowledge Center. (2016). *Department of Behaviors Health and Development Services: Assessing the risk of serious harm to self, module 10.* Retrieved from https://covkc.virginia.gov/Kview/CustomCodeBehind/Customization/Login/COV_Login.aspx

Conason, A. (2017, May 5). Should therapists self-disclose? The impact of therapist self-disclosure in eating disorder treatment. *Psychology Today.* Retrieved from https://www.psychologytoday.com/us/blog/eating-mindfully/201705/should-therapists-self-disclose

Cooper, M., & Law, D. (Eds.). (2018). *Working with goals in psychotherapy and counseling.* Oxford, UK: Oxford University Press.

Cooper, R. (2017). Diagnostic and statistical manual of mental disorders (DSM). *Knowledge Organization, 44*(8), 668–676.

Corey, G. (2019). *The art of integrative counseling* (4th ed.). Alexandria, VA: American Counseling Association.

Corey, G., Corey, M. S., & Corey, C. (2019). *Issues and ethics in the helping professions* (10th ed.). Boston, MA: Cengage Learning.

Cormier, S., Nurius, P. S., & Osborn, C. J. (2013). *Interviewing and change strategies for helpers* (7th ed.). Belmont, CA: Cengage.

Cottone, R. R., & Tarvydas, V. (2016). *Ethics and decision-making in counseling* (4th ed.). New York, NY: Springer.

Crowe, A. & Averett, P. (2015). Attitudes of mental health professionals toward mental illness: A deeper understanding. *Journal of Mental Health Counseling, 37*(1), 47–62.

Daniels, V. (2015). Humanistic psychoanalysis of Erich Fromm. In E. Neukrug (Ed.), *The SAGE encyclopedia of theory in counseling and psychotherapy* (Vol. 1, pp. 518–524). Thousand Oaks, CA: SAGE.

De Jong, P., & Berg, I. K. (2013). *Interviewing for solutions* (4th ed.). Belmont, CA: Cengage.

De Shazer, S. (1988). *Clues: Investigating solutions in brief therapy.* New York, NY: W. W. Norton & Company.

De Shazer, S., Dolan, Y., Korman, H., Trepper, T., McCollum, E., & Berg, I. K. (2007). *More than miracles: The state of the art of solution-focused brief therapy.* New York, NY: Routledge

Dean, L. (2015). Motivational interviewing. In E. Neukrug (Ed.), *The SAGE encyclopedia of theory in counseling and psychotherapy* (Vol. 1, pp. 668–672). Thousand Oaks, CA: SAGE.

Dragowski, E. A., & Sharron-del Rio, M. R. (2016). Reflective clinical practice with people of marginalized sexual identities. In P. B. Persen, W. J. Lonner, J. G. Draguns, J. E. Trimble, & M. R. Scharron-del Rio (Eds.), *Counseling across cultures* (7th ed. pp. 273–296). Thousand Oaks, CA: SAGE.

Drake, R. E., & Latimer, E. (2012). Lessons learned in developing community mental health care in North America. *World Psychiatry, 11*(1), 47–51.

Duan, C., Knox, S., & Hill, C. E. (2018). Advice giving in psychotherapy. In E. L. MacGeorge & L. M. Van Swol (Eds.). *The Oxford handbook of advice* (pp. 175–197). New York, NY: Oxford University Press.

Egan, G., & Reese, R. J. (2019). *The skilled helper: A problem-management and opportunity-development approach to helping* (11th ed.). Belmont, CA: Cengage.

Electronic Code of Federal Regulations. (2018). *45 CFR 164.501.* Retrieved from https://www.ecfr.gov/cgi-bin/retrieveECFR?gp=1&SID=fbe09e6471954ba39d6ad71f838af9a9&ty=HTML&h=L&mc=true&r=PART&n=pt45.1.164

Elliot, R., Bohart, A. C., Watson, J. C., & Greenberg, L. S. (2011). Empathy. *Psychotherapy, 48*(1), 43–49. doi:10.1037/a0022187

Elliot, R., Bohart, A.C., Watson, J.C., & Murphy, D. (2018). *Therapist empathy and client outcome: An updated meta-analysis.* Retrieved from https://www.researchgate.net/publication/324562138_Therapist_Empathy_and_Client_Outcome_An_Updated_Meta-analysis

Ellis, A., & MacLaren, C. (2005). *Rational emotive behavior therapy: A therapist's guide* (2nd ed.). Atascadero, CA: Impact.

Ellis, D. J. (2015). Rational emotive behavior therapy. In E. Neukrug (Ed.), *The SAGE encyclopedia of theory in counseling and psychotherapy* (Vol. 1, pp. 848–853). Thousand Oaks, CA: SAGE.

Ellis, M. V., Hutman, H., & Deihl, L. M. (2013). Chalkboard case conceptualization: A method for integrating clinical data. *Training and Education in Professional Psychology, 7*(4), 246–256. doi:10.1037/a0034132

Englar-Carlson, M., Evans, M. P., & Duffey, T. (2014). *A counselor's guide to working with men.* Alexandria, VA: American Counseling Association.

Escobar, J. I. (2012). Taking issue: Diagnostic bias: Racial and cultural issues. *Psychiatric Services.* Retrieved from http://ps.psychiatryonline.org/doi/pdf/10.1176/appi.ps.20120p847

Evans, M. P., Duffey, T., & Englar-Carlson, M. (2013). Introduction to the special issue: Men in counseling [Special Issue]. *Journal of Counseling and Development, 91*(4), 387–389. doi:10.1002/j.1556-6676.2013.00108.x

Federal Emergency Management Agency. (2015). *Crisis counseling assistance and training program.* Retrieved from http://www.fema.gov/recovery-directorate/crisis-counseling-assistance-training-program#1

Fisher, G. L., & Harrison, T. C. (2018). *Substance abuse: Information for school counselors, social workers, therapists and counselors* (6th ed.). Boston, MA: Pearson.

Flynn, T. (2013). *University of Phoenix survey reveals 38 percent of individuals who seek mental health counseling experience barriers.* Retrieved from http://www.phoenix.edu/news/releases/2013/05/university-of-phoenix-survey-reveals-38-percent-of-individuals-who-seek-mental-health-counseling-experience-barriers.html

Foss-Kelly, L. L., Generali, M. M., & Kress, V. E. (2017). Counseling strategies for empowering people living in poverty: The I-CARE model. *Journal of Multicultural Counseling and Development, 45*(3), 201–213. doi:10.1002/jmcd.12074

Fowler, J. W. (1995). *Stages of faith: The psychology of human development and the quest for meaning*. New York, NY: Harper & Row.

Frank, M. G., Maroulis, A., & Griffin, D. (2013). The voice. In D. Matsumoto, M. G. Frank, & H. S. Hwang (Eds.), *Nonverbal communication: Science and applications* (pp. 53–74). Thousand Oaks, CA: SAGE.

Franklin, C., Trepper, T. S., Gingerich, W. J., & McCollum, E. E. (2012). *Solution-focused brief therapy: A handbook of evidence-based practice*. New York, NY: Oxford University Press.

Gallagher, B. J., & Street, J. (2012). *The sociology of mental illness* (5th ed., revised). Cornwall-on-Hudson, NY: Sloan Educational Publishing.

Garske, G. G. (2016). Psychiatric disability: A biopsychosocial challenge. In I. Marini & M. A. Stebnicki (Eds.), *The professional counselor's desk reference* (2nd ed., pp. 423–428). New York, NY: Springer.

Gaskin, C. (2014). *The effectiveness of psychoanalysis and psychoanalytic psychotherapy: A literature review of recent international and Australian research*. Melbourne, AU: PACFA.

Gelso, C. (2009). The real relationship in a postmodern world: Theoretical and empirical explorations. *Psychotherapy Research, 19*(3), 253–264. doi:10.1080/10503300802389242

Gelso, C. J., Kelley, F. A., Fuertes, J. N., Marmarosh, C., Holmes, S. E., Costa, C., & Hancock, G. R. (2005). Measuring the real relationship in psychotherapy: Initial validation of the therapist form. *Journal of Counseling Psychology, 52*(4), 640–649. doi:10.1037/0022-0167.52.4.640

Giddens, J. M., Sheehan, K. H., & Sheehan, D. V. (2014). The Columbia-suicide severity rating scale (C–SSRS): Has the "gold standard" become a liability? *Innovations in Clinical Neuroscience, 11*(9-10), 66–80.

Glasser, W. (2013). *Take charge of your life: How to get what you need with choice theory psychology*. Bloomington, IN: Iuniverse Inc.

Glasser, W., & Glasser, C. (2007). *Eights lessons for a happier marriage*. New York, NY: HarperCollins.

Gold, J. M. (208). Rethinking client resistance: A narrative approach to integrating resistance into the relationship building stage of counseling. *Journal of Humanistic Counseling, Education, and Development, 47*(1), 65–70. doi:0.1002/j.2161-1939.2008.tb00047.x

Gompertz, K. (1960). The relation of empathy to effective communication. *Journalism Quarterly, 37*(4), 533–546.

Granello, D. H. (2010). Cognitive complexity among practicing counselors: How thinking changes with experience. *Journal of Counseling & Development, 88*(1), 92–100.

Hann, B., Hedden, S. L., Libari, R., Copello, E. A. P., & Kroutil, L. A. (2014). *Receipt of services for behavioral health problems: Results from the 2014 national survey on drug use and health*. Retrieved from https://www.samhsa.gov/data/sites/default/files/NSDUH-DR-FRR3-2014/NSDUH-DR-FRR3-2014/NSDUH-DR-FRR3-2014.htm

Hansen, J. T. (2006). Counseling theories within a postmodernist epistemology: New roles for theories in counseling practice. *Journal of Counseling and Development, 84*(3), 291–297.

Hansen, N. D., Pepitone-Arreola-Rockwell, F., & Greene, A. F. (2000). Multicultural competence: Criteria and case examples. *Professional Psychology: Research and Practice, 31*(6), 652–660. doi:10.1037//0735-702831.6.652

Harrison, K. (2013). Counselling psychology and power: Considering therapy and beyond. *Counseling Psychology Review, 28*(2), 107–117.

Hatzenbuehler, M. L., Keyes, K. M., Narrow, W. E., Grant, B. F., &, Hasin, D. S. (2008). Racial/ethnic disparities in service utilization for individuals with co-occurring mental health and substance use disorders in the general population: Results from the national epidemiologic survey on alcohol and related conditions. *Journal of Clinical Psychiatry, 69*(7), 1112–1121.

Hays, D., & Erford, B. T. (2018). *Developing multicultural counseling competence: A systems approach* (3rd ed.). New York, NY: Pearson Education.

Healthcare Providers Service Organization. (2018). *Home page*. Retrieved from www.hpso.com

Henderson, D. A., & Thompson, C. L., (2016). *Counseling children* (9th ed.). Boston, MA: Cengage.

Hill, C. E. (2014). *Helping skills: Facilitating exploration, insight, and action* (4th ed.). Washington DC: American Psychological Association.

Hillhouse, T. M., & Porter, J. H. (2015). A brief history of the development of antidepressant drugs: From monoamines to glutamate. *Experimental Clinical Psychopharmacology, 32*(2), 1–21. doi:10.1037/a0038550.

Hilsenroth, M. (Ed.). (2014). Common factors (Special section). *Psychotherapy, 51*(4), 467–524.

Hinkle, M. S., & Dean, L. M. (2017). Creativity in teaching case conceptualization skills: Role-play to show the interconnectedness of domains. *Journal of Creativity in Mental Health, 12*(3), 388–401.

History of the McKinney Act. (2018). *William and Mary School of Education Project Hope—Virginia.* Retrieved from http://education. wm.edu/centers/hope/resources/mckinneyact/

Hoff, L. A., Hallisey, B. J., & Hoff, M. (2009). *People in crisis: Clinical and diversity perspectives* (6th ed.). New York, NY: Routledge.

Howes, R. (2012, February 13). Eye contact in therapy, Part I: Why can't I look at my therapist? *Psychology Today.* Retrieved from https://www.psychologytoday.com/blog/in-therapy/201202/eye-contact-in-therapy-part-i

Ivey, A. E., Ivey, M. B., & Zalaquett, C. P. (2016). *Essentials of intentional interviewing: Counseling in a multicultural world* (3rd ed.). Boston, MA: Cengage.

James, R. K., & Gilliland, B. E. (2013). *Crisis intervention strategies* (7th ed.). Belmont, CA: Brooks Cole.

Jansson, B. S. (2016). *Social welfare policy and advocacy: Advancing social justice through 8 policy sectors.* Thousand Oaks, CA: SAGE.

Jayakar, P. (2003). *J. Krishnamurti: A biography.* New York, NY: Penguin Books.

Jensen, M. J., McAuliffe, G. J., & Say, R. (2015). Developmental level as a predictor of counseling skills. *Journal of Counselor Preparation and Supervision, 7*(1). Retrieved from https://repository.wcsu.edu/cgi/viewcontent.cgi?referer=&httpsredir=1&article=1065&context=jcps

Juhnke, G. A., Granello, P. F., & Lebron-Striker, M. (2007). Is path warm? A suicide assessment mnemonic for counselors. In *Professional Counseling Digest.* Alexandria, VA: American Counseling Association.

Kahn, M. (2001). *Between therapist and client: The new relationship* (revised ed.). New York, NY: W. H. Freeman/Owl.

Kalkbrenner, M., & Neukrug, E. (2018a). *Confirming the factor structure of the revised FSV scale.* Manuscript submitted for publication.

Kalkbrenner, M., & Neukrug, E. (2018b). *Confirming the factor structure of the revised FSV Scale: Appraising barriers to counseling by the American public.* Manuscript submitted for publication.

Kalkbrenner, M., Neukrug, E., & Griffith, S. A. (in press). Barriers to counselors seeking counseling: Cross validation and predictive validity of the fit, stigma, & value (FSV) scale. *Journal of Mental Health Counseling.*

Kanel, K. (2018). *A guide to crisis intervention* (6th ed.). Samford, CT: Cengage.

Kaplan, D. M. (2014). Ethical implications of a critical legal case for the counseling profession: *Ward v. Wilbanks. Journal of Counseling and Development, 92*(2), 142–146. doi:10.1002/j.1556-6676.2014.00140.x

Kelsey, D., & Smart, J. F. (2012). Social justice, disability, and rehabilitation education. *Rehabilitation Research, Policy, and Education, 26*(2–3), 229–239. doi:10.1891/216866612X664970

Kenny, C. (2011). *The power of silence: Silent communication in daily life.* New York, NY: Routledge.

Kernberg, O. F. (2006). The pressing need to increase research in and on psychoanalysis. *International Journal of Psychoanalysis, 87*(4), 919–926.

Kinnier, R. T., Hofsess, C., Pongratz, R., & Lambert, C. (2009). Attributions and affirmations for overcoming anxiety and depression. *Psychology & Psychotherapy: Theory, Research, & Practice, 82*(2), 153–169. doi:10.1348/147608308X389418

Kirschenbaum, H. (2015). Values clarification. In E. Neukrug (Ed.), *The SAGE encyclopedia of theory in counseling and psychotherapy* (Vol. 2, pp. 1035–1038). Thousand Oaks, CA: SAGE.

Kitchener, K. S. (1986). Teaching applied ethics in counselor education: An integration of psychological processes and philosophical analysis. *Journal of Counseling and Development, 64*(5), 306–311. doi:10.1177/0011000084123005

Kitchener, K. S. (1984). Intuition, critical evaluation and ethical principles: The foundation for ethical decisions in counseling psychology. *The Counseling Psychologist, 12*(3), 43–45. doi:10.1177/0011000084123005

Kluckhohn, C., & Murray, H. A. (1953). Personality formation: The determinants. In C. Kluckhohn, H. A. Murray, & D. M. Schneider (Eds.), *Personality in nature, society, and culture* (pp. 53–67). New York, NY: Alfred A. Knopf.

Knapp, M. L., Hall, J. A., & Horgan, T. G. (2014). *Nonverbal communication in human interaction* (8th ed.). Belmont, CA: Cengage.

Kress, V. E., & Paylo, M. J. (2018). *Treating those with mental disorders: A comprehensive approach to case conceptualization and treatment* (2nd ed.). Boston, MA: Pearson.

Kubler-Ross, E., & Kessler, D. (2014). *On grief and grieving.* New York, NY: Scribner.

Labardee, L., Williams, P., & Hodges, S. (2012, November 1). Counselors who coach. *Counseling Today.* Retrieved from http://ct.counseling.org/2012/11/counselors-who-coach

Lambie, G. W., Hagedor, W. B., & Ieva, K. P. (2010). Social-cognitive development, ethical and legal knowledge, and ethical decision-making of counselor education students. *Counselor Education and Supervision, 49*(4), 228–246. doi:10.1002/j.1556-6978.2010.tb00100.x

Laska, K. M., Gurman, A. S., & Wampold, B. E. (2014). Expanding the lens of evidence-based practice in psychotherapy: A common factors perspective. *Psychotherapy, 51*(4), 467–481.

Levitt, D. H., & Moorhead, H. J. H. (2013). Moral development. In D. H. Levitt & H. J. H. Moorhead (Eds), *Values and ethics in counseling: Real-life ethical decision-making* (pp. 7–18). New York, NY: Routledge.

Lewis, J. A., Dana, R. Q., & Blevins, G. A. (2015). *Substance abuse counseling.* Belmont, CA: Cengage.

Lewis, J. A., Lewis, M. D., Daniels, J. A., & D'Andrea, M. J. (2011). *Community counseling: A multicultural-social justice perspective* (4th ed.). Belmont, CA: Cengage.

Ley, D. L. (2014, February 12). Life coaches and mental illness. *Psychology Today.* Retrieved from https://www.psychologytoday.com/blog/women-who-stray/201402/life-coaches-and-mental-illness

Littell, F. H. (1986). Forward. In H. G. Locke (Ed.), *Exile in the fatherland: Martin Niemöller's letters from Moabit prison* (p. viii). Grand Rapids, MI: William B. Eerdman's Publishing.

Little, S. (2018). Listening in the dark: A response to "noise and silence in analytic talk." *Journal of Contemporary Psychoanalysis, 54*(2). doi:10.1080/00107530.2018.1458580.

Lively, K. J. (2014, March 12). Affirmations: The why, what, and how, and what if? *Psychology Today.* Retrieved from https://www.psychologytoday.com/us/blog/smart-relationships/201403/affirmations-the-why-what-how-and-what-if

Lo, C., Cheng, T., & Howell, R. (2013). Access to and utilization of health services as pathway to racial disparities in serious mental illness. *Community Mental Health Journal, 50*(3), 251–257. doi:10.1007/s10597-013-9593-7

Lopez, S. J., Pedrotti, J. T., & Snyder, C. R. (2015). *Positive psychology: The scientific and practical explorations of human strength* (3rd ed.). Thousand Oaks, CA: SAGE.

Marini, I., Graf, N. M., & Millington, M. J. (2018) *Psychosocial aspects of disability: Insider perspectives and strategies for counselors* (2nd ed.). New York, NY: Springer.

Mariska, M. A., & Harrawood, L. K. (2013). Understanding the unsaid: Enhancing multicultural competence through nonverbal awareness. *VISTAS Online.* Retrieved from https://www.counseling.org/docs/default-source/vistas/understanding-the-unsaid-enhancing-multicultural.pdf?sfvrsn=933ee334_11

Martin, G., & Pear, J. (2015). *Behavior modification: What it is and how to do it* (10th ed.). New York, NY: Routledge.

Matsumoto, D., & Hwang, H. S. (2013a). Facial expressions. In D. Matsumoto, M. G. Frank, & H. S. Hwang (Eds.), *Nonverbal communication: Science and applications* (pp. 15–52). Thousand Oaks, CA: SAGE.

Matsumoto, D., & Hwang, H. S. (2013b). Body gestures. In D. Matsumoto, M. G. Frank, & H. S. Hwang (Eds.), *Nonverbal communication: Science and applications* (pp. 75–96). Thousand Oaks, CA: SAGE.

Matsumoto, D., & Hwang, H. S. (2013c). Cultural influences of nonverbal behavior. In D. Matsumoto, M. G. Frank, & H. S. Hwang (Eds.), *Nonverbal communication: Science and applications* (pp. 97–120). Thousand Oaks, CA: SAGE.

Matsumoto, D., Frank, M. G., & Hwang, H. S. (Eds.). (2013). *Nonverbal communication: Science and applications.* Thousand Oaks, CA: SAGE.

Mayorga, M., Devries, S., & Wardle, E. (2015). The practice of self-care among counseling students. *Journal on Educational Psychology, 8*(3), 21–28.

McAuliffe, G. (2013). Culture and diversity defined. In G. McAuliffe (Ed.), *Culturally alert counseling: A comprehensive introduction* (2nd ed.) (pp. 3–20). Thousand Oaks, CA: SAGE.

McAuliffe, G. (2019). *Culturally alert counseling: A comprehensive introduction* (3rd ed.). Thousand Oaks, CA: SAGE. Manuscript in preparation.

McAuliffe, G. J. (Ed.). (2019). *Positive counseling: A guide to promoting clients' strengths and growth.* San Diego: Cognella Academic Publishing.

McAuliffe, G., Grothaus, T., & Goméz, E. (2013). Conceptualizing race and racism. In G. McAuliffe (Ed.), *Culturally alert counseling: A comprehensive introduction* (2nd ed., pp. 89–124). Thousand Oaks, CA: SAGE.

Meara, N. M., Schmidt, L. D., & Day, J. D. (1996). Principles and virtues: A foundation for ethical decisions, policies, and character. *The Counseling Psychologist, 24*(1), 4–77. doi:10.1177/0011000096241002

Meichenbaum, D. & Lilienfeld, S. O. (2018). How to spot hype in the field of psychotherapy: A 19-Item Checklist. *Professional Psychology: Research and Practice, 49*(1), 22–30. doi:10.1037/pro0000172

Meyer, L., & Melchert, T. P. (2011). Examining the content of mental health intake assessments from a biopsychosocial perspective. *Journal of Psychotherapy Integration, 21*(1), 70–89. doi:10.1037/a0022907

Myers, L. (2014a, April 18). Connecting with clients. *Counseling Today.* Retrieved from https://ct.counseling.org/2014/08/connecting-with-clients/

Meyers, L. (2014b, April 23). Advocacy in action. *Counseling Today.* Retrieved from https://ct.counseling.org/2014/04/advocacy-in-action/

Meyers, L. (2104c, March 24). Ages and stages. *Counseling Today.* Retrieved from https://ct.counseling.org/2014/03/ages-and-stages/

Meyers, L. (2017, July 25). Lending a helping hand in disaster's wake. *Counseling Today.* Retrieved form https://ct.counseling.org/tag/topic-ct-trauma-and-disaster/

Milliken, T., & Neukrug, E. (2009). Perceptions of ethical behaviors of human service professionals. *Human Service Education, 29*, 35–48.

Montague, K. T., Cassidy, R. R., & Liles, R. G. (2016). Counselor training in suicide assessment, prevention, and management. *VISTAS Online.* Retrieved from https://www.counseling.org/docs/default-source/vistas/article_65d15528f16116603abcacff0000bee5e7.pdf?sfvrsn=4f43482c_6

Moodley, R., & Walcott, R. (Eds.). (2010). *Counseling across and beyond cultures: Exploring the work of Clemmont E. Vontress in clinical practice.* Toronto, CA: University of Toronto Press.

Murphy, S. N. (2013, September 1). Attending to countertransference. *Counseling Today.* Retrieved from http://ct.counseling.org/2013/09/attending-to-countertransference/

Myers, J. E., & Sweeney, T. J. (2008). Wellness counseling: The evidence base for practice. *Journal of Counseling and Development, 86*(4), 482–493. doi:10.1002/j.1556-6678.2008.tb00536.x

Nakash, O, & Saguy, T. (2015). Social identities of clients and therapists during the mental health intake predict diagnostic accuracy. *Social Psychological and Personality Science, 66*(6), 710–717. doi:10.1177/1948550615576003

Nassar, J. L., & Devlin, A. (2011). Impressions of psychotherapists' offices. *Journal of Counseling Psychology, 58*(3), 310–320. doi:10.1037/a0023887

National Alliance on Mental Illness. (2018a). *African American mental health.* Retrieved from https://www.nami.org/Find-Support/Diverse-Communities/African-Americans

National Alliance on Mental Illness. (2018b). *Mental health by the numbers.* Retrieved from https://www.nami.org/Learn-More/Mental-Health-By-the-Numbers.

National Alliance on Mental Illness. (n.d.) *Mental health facts: Children and teens.* Retrieved from https://www.nami.org/getattachment/Learn-More/Mental-Health-by-the-Numbers/childrenmhfacts.pdf

National Institute of Mental Health. (2016). *Mental health medications.* Retrieved from https://www.nimh.nih.gov/health/topics/mental-health-medications/index.shtml

National Institute of Mental Health. (2009). *Treatment of children with mental illness: Frequently asked questions about the treatment of mental illness in children.* Retrieved from https://www.nimh.nih.gov/health/publications/treatment-of-children-with-mental-illness-fact-sheet/nimh-treatment-children-mental-illness-faq_34669.pdf

Neukrug, E. (Ed.). (2015). *The SAGE encyclopedia of theory in counseling and psychotherapy* (Vols. 1-2). Thousand Oaks, CA: SAGE.

Neukrug, E. (2016). *The world of the counselor.* Boston, MA: Cengage.

Neukrug, E. (2017a, February 2). Creative and novel approaches to empathy. *Counseling Today.* Retrieved from http://ct.counseling.org/2017/02/creative-novel-approaches-empathy/

Neukrug, E. (2017b). *Skills and techniques for human service professionals: Counseling environment, helping skills, treatment issues.* Norfolk, VA: Counseling Books Etc.

Neukrug, E. (2017c). *Theory, practice, and trends in human services: An introduction* (6th ed.). Boston, MA: Cengage.

Neukrug, E. (2018). *Counseling theory and practice* (2nd ed.). Sorrento Valley, CA: Cognella.

Neukrug, E., Bayne, H., Dean-Nganga, L., & Pusateri, C. (2012). Creative and novel approaches to empathy: A neo-Rogerian perspective. *Journal of Mental Health Counseling, 35*(1), 29–42.

Neukrug, E., Britton, B., & Crews, C. (2013). Common health-related concerns of men and their implications for counselors. *Journal of Counseling and Development, 91*(4), 390–397.

Neukrug, E., & Ellis, D. (2015). Albert Ellis. In E. Neukrug (Ed.), *The SAGE encyclopedia of theory in counseling and psychotherapy* (Vol. 1, pp. 333–336). Thousand Oaks, CA: SAGE.

Neukrug, E., & Fawcett, R. (2015). *Essentials of testing and assessment: A practical guide for counselors, social workers, and psychologists* (3rd ed.). Belmont, CA: Cengage.

Neukrug, E., & Milliken, T. (2011). Counselors' perceptions of ethical behaviors. *Journal of Counseling and Development, 89*(2), 206–216. 10.1002/j.1556-6678.2011.tb00079.x

Neukrug, E. S. & Schwitzer, A. M. (2006). *Skills and tools for today's counselor and psychotherapists: From natural helping to professional counseling.* Belmont, CA: Brooks/Cole.

Nevid, J. S. (2015, December 28). Asking the what and how questions, not the why questions. *Psychology Today.* Retrieved from https://www.psychologytoday.com/us/blog/the-minute-therapist/201512/asking-the-what-and-how-questions-not-the-why-questions

Nichols, M. P. (2009). *The lost art of listening* (2nd ed.). New York, NY: Guildford.

Norcross, J. C. (Ed.). (2011). *Psychotherapy relationships that work: Evidence-based responsiveness.* New York, NY: Oxford University Press.

Norcross, J. C. (2010). The therapeutic relationship. In B. L. Duncan, S. D. Miller, B. E. Wampold, & M. A. Hubble (Eds.), *The heart and soul of change* (2nd ed., pp. 113–141). Washington DC: American Psychological Association.

Pagliery, J. (2014, August 18). Hospital network hacked, 4.5 million records stolen. *CNN Money.* Retrieved from http://money.cnn.com/2014/08/18/technology/security/hospital-chs-hack/index.html

Perry, W. G. (1970). *Forms of intellectual and ethical development in the college years: A scheme.* New York, NY: Holt, Rinehart, & Winston.

Pew Research Center. (2018a). *Religious landscape study.* Retrieved from http://www.pewforum.org/religious-landscape-study/

Pew Research Center. (2018b). *LGBT in changing times.* Retrieved from http://www.pewresearch.org/packages/lgbt-in-changing-times/

Pew Research Center (2018c). *7 facts about Americans with disabilities.* Retrieved from http://www.pewresearch.org/fact-tank/2017/07/27/7-facts-about-americans-with-disabilities/

Phillips, L. (2018, March 1). The high cost of human-made disasters. *Counseling Today.* Retrieved from https://ct.counseling.org/2018/03/high-cost-human-made-disasters/

Pickersgill, M. D. (2013). Debating DSM-5: Diagnosis and the sociology of critique. *Journal of Medical Ethics, 40*(8), 521–525. doi:10.1136/medethics-2013-101762

Pisani, A. R., Murrie, D. C., & Silverman, M. M. (2015, December 14). Reformulating suicide risk formulation: From prediction to prevention. *Academic Psychiatry,* 1–7. Retrieved from http://link.springer.com/article/10.1007%2Fs40596-015-0434-6

Poa, E., & Kass, J. S. (2015). Managing outpatients with suicidal or homicidal ideation. *Continuum: Lifelong Learning in Neurology, 21*(3), 838–843. doi:10.1212/01.CON.0000466671.87229.c7

Ponton, R. F., & Sauerheber, J. D. (2014). Supervisee countertransference: A holistic supervision approach. *Counselor Education and Supervision, 53*(4), 254–267. doi:10.1002/j.1556-6978.2014.00061.x

Preston, J. D., O'Neal, J. H., & Talaga, M. C. (2017. *Handbook of clinical psychopharmacology for therapists* (8th ed.). Oakland, CA: New Harbinger.

Privacy Rights Clearinghouse. (2018). *Protecting health information: The HIPAA security and breach notification rules.* Retrieved from https://www.privacyrights.org/consumer-guides/protecting-health-information-hipaa-security-and-breach-notification-rules

Pusateri, C. G. & Headley, J. A. (2015). Feminist therapy. In E. Neukrug (Ed.), *The SAGE encyclopedia of theory in counseling and psychotherapy* (Vol. 1, pp. 414–418). Thousand Oaks, CA: SAGE.

Qaseem, A., Barry, M. J., & Kansagara, D. (2016). Nonpharmacologic versus pharmacologic treatment of adult patients with major depressive disorder: A clinical practice guideline from the American college of physicians. *Annals of Internal Medicine Intern Medicine, 164*(5), 350–359. doi:10.7326/M15-2570

Rankin, L. (2013). *Mind over medicine: Scientific proof that you can heal yourself.* Carlsbad, CA: Hay House.

Ratts, M. J., Singh, A. A., Nassar-McMillan, S., Butler, S. K., & McCullough, J. R. (2016). Multicultural and Social Justice Counseling Competencies: Guidelines for the counseling profession. *Journal of Multicultural Counseling and Development, 44*(1), 28–48. doi:10.1002/jmcd.12035

Ratts, M. J., Singh, A. A., Nassar-McMillan, S., Butler, S. K., & McCullough, J. R. (2015). Multicultural and Social Justice Counseling Competencies: Guidelines for the counseling profession. Retrieved from https://www.counseling.org/docs/default-source/competencies/multicultural-and-social-justice-counseling-competencies.pdf?sfvrsn=20

Remley, T. P., & Herlihy, B. (2016). *Ethical, legal, and professional issues in counseling* (5th ed.). Boston, MA: Pearson

Remley, T. P., Herlihy, B., & Herlihy, S. B. (1997). The U.S. Supreme Court decision in *Jaffe v. Redmond:* Implications for counselors. *Journal of Counseling and Development, 75*(3), 213–218.

Resnick, P. J. (2011). Suicide risk assessment. *Psychiatric Times.* Retrieved from http://www.psychiatrictimes.com/suicide/suicide-risk-assessment

Resnick, R. (2015). Gestalt therapy. In E. Neukrug (Ed.), *The SAGE encyclopedia of theory in counseling and psychotherapy* (Vol. 1, pp. 456–461). Thousand Oaks, CA: SAGE.

Rice, R. (2015a). Cognitive-behavioral therapy. In E. Neukrug (Ed.), *The SAGE encyclopedia of theory in counseling and psychotherapy* (Vol 1, pp. 194–199). Thousand Oaks, CA: SAGE.

Rice, R. (2015b). Narrative therapy. In E. Neukrug (Ed.), *The SAGE encyclopedia of theory in counseling and psychotherapy* (Vol. 1, pp. 695–700). Thousand Oaks, CA: SAGE.

Ridley, C. R., & Jeffrey, C. E. (2017a). Thematic mapping in case conceptualization: An introduction to the special section. *Journal of Clinical Psychology, 73*(4), 353–358. doi:10.1002/jclp.22353

Ridley, C. R., & Jeffrey, C. E. (2017b). The conceptual framework of thematic mapping in case conceptualization. *Journal of Clinical Psychology, 73*(4), 376–392. doi:10.1002/jclp.22355

Ridley, C. R., Jeffrey, C. E., & Roberson III, R. B. (2017). Case mis-conceptualization in psychological treatment: An enduring clinical problem. *Journal of Clinical Psychology, 73*(4), 376–392. doi:10.1002/jclp.22354

Ritter, K. (2015). Sexual minority affirmative therapy. In E. Neukrug (Ed.), *The SAGE encyclopedia of theory in counseling and psychotherapy* (Vol. 2, pp. 928–931). Thousand Oaks, CA: SAGE.

Rogers, C. R. (1980). *A way of being.* Boston, MA: Houghton Mifflin.

Rogers, C. R. (1970). *Carl Rogers on encounter groups.* New York, NY: Harper & Row.

Rogers, C. R. (1961). Ellen West and loneliness. In H. Kirschenbaum & V. L. Henderson (Eds.), *The Carl Rogers reader* (pp. 157–167). Boston, MA: Houghton Mifflin.

Rogers, C. R. (1959). A theory of therapy, personality and interpersonal relationships as developed in the client-centered framework. In S. Koch (Ed.), *Psychology: A study of science, Vol. 3, Formulations of the person and the social context* (pp. 184–256). New York, NY: McGraw-Hill.

Rogers, C. R. (1957). The necessary and sufficient conditions of therapeutic personality change. *Journal of Consulting Psychology, 21*(2), 95–103. doi:10.1037/h0045357

Rogers, C. R. (1942). *Counseling and psychotherapy: New concepts in practice.* Boston, MA: Houghton-Mifflin.

Rubin, J. (2018). The classification and statistical manual of mental health concerns: A proposed practical scientific alternative to the DSM and ICD. *Journal of Humanistic Psychology, 58*(1), 93–114. doi:10.1177/0022167817718079

Rudow, H. (2013, January 9). Resolution of EMU case confirms ACA code of ethics, counseling profession's stance against client discrimination. *Counseling Today.* Retrieved from http://ct.counseling.org/2013/01/resolution-of-emu-case-confirms-aca-code-of-ethics-counseling-professions-stance-against-client-discrimination/

Ruini, C. (2017). *Positive psychology in the clinical domains.* Cham, Switzerland: Springer International Publishing.

Sacket, C., Lawson, G., & Burge, P. L. (2012). Meaningful experiences in the counseling process. *Professional Counselor, 2*(3), 208–225. doi:10.15241/css.2.3.208

Schatzberg, A. F., & Nemeroff, C. B. (Eds.). (2017). *Textbook of psychopharmacology* (5th ed.). Washington DC: American Psychiatric Press.

Schwitzer, A. M., & Rubin, L. C. (2015). *Diagnosis and treatment planning skills: A popular culture casebook approach* (2nd ed.). Thousand Oaks, CA: SAGE.

Scott, A. T. (2014). The after effects of Hurricane Katrina in children. *Journal of Human Services, 34*(1), 174–178.

Scott, C. L., & Resnick, P. J. (2005). Violence risk assessment in persons with mental illness. *Aggression and Violent Behavior, 11*(6), 598–611. doi:10.1016/j.avb.2005.12.003

Segal, J., Johnson, W., Miller-Knight, W., Prince, S., Anderson, K., Sonnenberg, J., ... & Dale, H. (2011). Dilemmas: A dress code for counselors. *Therapy Today, 22*(9), 28–31.

Shallcross, L. (2011, March). Breaking away from the pack. *Counseling Today, 53*(9), 28–36.

Sheff, E. A. (2016). Therapy, counseling, or coaching—oh my! *Psychology Today.* Retrieved from https://www.psychologytoday.com/us/blog/the-polyamorists-next-door/201612/therapy-counseling-or-coaching-oh-my

Shifflet, E. T. (2016). *Licensure requirements for professional counselors: A state-by-state report* (2016 ed.). Alexandria, VA: American Counseling Association.

Simonds L., & Spokes N. (2017). Therapist self-disclosure and the therapeutic alliance in the treatment of eating problems. *Eating Disorders, 25*(2), 151–164.

Simpson, L. V., Abadie, J. M., & Seyler, C. D. (2015). Opening doors and holding them open for others. A tribute to disability rights advocate Charles Tubre (1941–2014). *Rehabilitation Counseling Bulletin, 59*(2), 121–124. doi:10.1177/0034355215602021

Smart, J. (2016). *Counseling individuals with disabilities.* In I. Marini & M. A. Stebnicki (Eds.), *The professional counselor's desk reference* (2nd ed.) (pp. 417–422). New York, NY: Springer.

Sommer, R. (2007). *Personal space: The behavioral basis of design.* Bristol, UK: Bosko Books.

Sommers-Flanagan, J., & Sommers-Flanagan, R. (2017). *Clinical interviewing* (6th ed.). Hoboken, NJ: John Wiley & Sons.

Sperry, L. (2016). Teaching the competency of family case conceptualizations. *Family Journal, 24*(3), 279–282. doi:10.1177/1066480716648315

Sperry, L., Carlson, J., Sauerheber, J. D., & Sperry, J. (2015). *Psychopathology and psychotherapy: DSM-5 diagnosis, case conceptualization, and treatment* (3rd ed.). New York, NY: Routledge.

Sperry, L., & Sperry, J., (2012). *Case conceptualization: Mastering this competency with ease and confidence.* New York, NY: Routledge.

Stone, C. (2015, July 1). School counseling is a state-by-state practice. *ASCA School Counselor.* Retrieved from https://www.schoolcounselor.org/magazine/blogs/july-august-2015/school-counseling-is-a-state-by-state-practice

Strong, T., & Zeman, D. (2010). Dialogic considerations of confrontation as a counseling activity: An examination of Allen Ivey's use of confronting as a microskill. *Journal of Counseling & Development, 88*(3), 332–339.

Stuntzner, S., & Hartley, M. T. (2014). Disability and the counseling relationship: What counselors need to know. *VISTAS Online.* Retrieved from https://www.counseling.org/docs/default-source/vistas/article_09.pdf?sfvrsn=157ccf7c_12

Substance Abuse and Mental Health Services Administration. (2018). *Home page.* Retrieved from http://www.samhsa.gov/

Substance Abuse and Mental Health Services Administration (2017). *Suicide prevention.* Retrieved from https://www.samhsa.gov/suicide-prevention

Sue, D. W., & Sue, D. (2016). *Counseling the culturally diverse* (7th ed.). Hoboken, NJ: John Wiley and Sons.

Suicide Prevention Resource Center. *Risk and protective factors*. Retrieved from https://www.sprc.org/about-suicide/risk-protective-factors

Summers, N. (2016). *Fundamentals of case management: Skills for the human services*. Boston, MA: Cengage.

Sung, K., & Dunkle, R. (2009). How social workers demonstrate respect for elderly clients. *Journal of Gerontological Social Work, 52*(3), 250–260. doi:10.1080/01634370802609247

Szymanski, D. & Carretta, R. F. (2013). Counseling lesbian, gay, bisexual, and transgendered clients. In G. J. McAuliffe (Ed.), *Culturally alert counseling: A comprehensive introduction* (2nd ed.) (pp. 415–452). Thousand Oaks, CA: SAGE.

Tarasoff et al. v. Regents of University of California, 529 P.2d 553 (Calif. 1974), vacated, reheard en banc, and affirmed 551 P.2d 334 (1976).

Terni, P. (2015). Solution-focus: Bringing positive psychology into the conversation. *International Journal of Solution Focused Practices, 3*(1), 8–16. doi:10.14335/ijsfp.v3i1.25

Thompson, R. A. (2016). *Counseling techniques: Improving relationships with others, ourselves, our families, and our environment* (3rd ed.). New York, NY: Routledge.

Trepal, H. C., Wester, K. L., Notestine, L., & Leeth, C. (2013). Counseling men and women: Considering gender and sex in therapy. In G. McAuliffe (Ed.), *Culturally alert counseling: A comprehensive introduction* (2nd ed.) (pp. 383–415). Thousand Oaks, CA: SAGE.

Trepper, T. S., McCollum, E. E., De Jong, P., Korman, H., Gingerich, W. J., & Franklin, C. (2014). Solution-focused therapy treatment manual for working with individuals. In J. S. Kim (Ed.), *Solution-focused brief therapy: A multicultural approach* (pp. 14–31). Thousand Oaks, CA: SAGE.

U.S. Census Bureau (2016). *U.S. Census Bureau projections show a slower growing, older, more diverse nation a half century from now*. Retrieved from http://www.census.gov/newsroom/releases/archives/population/cb12-243.html

U.S. Census Bureau (2017a). *Quick facts: United States*. Retrieved from https://www.census.gov/quickfacts/fact/table/US/PST045216

U.S. Census Bureau (2017b). *We are a changing nation: A series of population trends*. Retrieved from https://www.census.gov/library/stories/2017/08/changing-nation-demographic-trends.html

U.S. Census Bureau (2018a). *Income and poverty in the United States: 2016*. Retrieved from https://www.census.gov/library/publications/2017/demo/p60-259.html

U.S. Census Bureau. (2018b). *Older people projected to outnumber children for first time in U.S. history*. Retrieved from https://www.census.gov/newsroom/press-releases/2018/cb18-41-population-projections.htm

U.S. Department of Education. (2018). *Family Educational Rights and Privacy Act (FERPA)*. Retrieved from https://www2.ed.gov/policy/gen/guid/fpco/ferpa/index.html?

U. S. Department of Health and Human Services. (2014). *Improving cultural competence: A treatment improvement protocol*. Rockville, MD: Substance Abuse and Mental Health Services Administration.

U.S. Department of Health and Human Services. (2017). *HIPPA for professionals*. Retrieved from https://www.hhs.gov/hipaa/for-professionals/index.html

U.S. Department of Homeland Security. (2018). *Legal immigration and adjustment of status report fiscal year 2017, quarter 4*. Retrieved from https://www.dhs.gov/immigration-statistics/special-reports/legal-immigration#File_end

U.S. Department of Housing and Urban Development (2017). *The 2017 annual homeless assessment report (AHAR) to Congress*. Retrieved from https://www.hudexchange.info/resources/documents/2017-AHAR-Part-1.pdf

U.S. Department of Justice. (2014). *Freedom of Information Act guide: 2004 Edition*. Retrieved from http://www.usdoj.gov/oip/introduc.htm

Urofsky, R. I., Engels, D. W., & Engebretson, K. (2008). Kitchener's principle ethics: Implications for counseling practice and research. *Counseling and Values, 53*(1), 67–78. doi: https://doi.org/10.1002/j.2161-007X.2009.tb00114.x

van Nuys, D. (2017). *An interview with William and Carleen Glasser on happier marriages*. Retrieved from https://www.gracepointwellness.org/289-relationship-problems/article/13566-wise-counsel-interview-transcript-an-interview-with-william-and-carlene-glasser-on-happier-marriages

Vernon, A. (2009). *Counseling children and adolescents* (4th ed.). Denver, CO: Love Publishing.

Videbeck, S. L. (2017). *Psychiatric mental health nursing* (7th ed.). Philadelphia: Wolters Kluwer.

Vitelli, R. (2014, July 28). Revisiting Tarasoff: Should therapists breach confidentiality over a patient's violent threat? *Psychology Today.* Retrieved from https://www.psychologytoday.com/us/blog/media-spotlight/201407/revisiting-tarasoff

Wampold, B. E. (2010a). *The basics of psychotherapy: An introduction to theory and practice.* Washington DC: American Psychological Association.

Wampold, B. E. (2010b). The research evidence for common factors models: A historically situated perspective. In B. L. Duncan, S. D. Miller, B. E. Wampold, & M. A. Hubble (Eds.), *The heart and soul of change* (2nd ed.) (pp. 49–82). Washington DC: American Psychological Association.

Wampold, B. E., & Budge, S. L. (2012). The relationship—and its relationship to the common and specific factors in psychotherapy. *Counseling Psychologist, 40*(4), 601–623. doi:10.1177/0011000011432709

Wampold, B. E., & Imel, Z. E. (2015). *The great psychotherapy debate: The evidence for what makes psychotherapy work* (2nd ed.). New York, NY: Routledge.

Watzlawick, P., Beavin, J. H., & Jackson, D. D. (1967). *Pragmatics of human communication: A study of interactional patterns, pathologies, and paradoxes.* New York, NY: Norton

Week Staff. (2010, May 5). Growing up Sarah Silverman. *The Week.* Retrieved from http://theweek.com/articles/494693/growing-sarah-silverman

Weishaar, M. E. (2015). Aaron T. Beck. In E. Neukrug (Ed.), *The SAGE encyclopedia of theory in counseling and psychotherapy* (Vol. 1, pp. 87–89). Thousand Oaks, CA: SAGE.

Welfel, E. R. (2016). *Ethics in counseling and psychotherapy: Standards, research, and emerging issues* (6th ed.). Boston, MA: Cengage.

Wexler, D. B. (2009). *Men in therapy: New approaches for effective treatment.* New York, NY: W. W. Norton.

Whitfield, N., & Kanter, D. (2014). Helpers in distress: Preventing secondary trauma. *Reclaiming Children and Youth, 22*(4), 59–61.

Williams, A. (2017). *Helping relationships with older adults: From theory to practice.* Thousand Oaks, CA: SAGE.

Williams, S. (2013). *Mental health service utilization among African American emerging adults.* (Unpublished doctoral dissertation). Washington University, St. Louis, MO.

Wong, J. Y. (2015). The psychology of encouragement: Theory, research, and applications. *The Counseling Psychologist, 43*(2) 178–216. doi:10.1177/0011000014545091

Woodside, M. R., & McClam, T. (2018). *Generalist case management: A method of human service delivery* (5th ed.). Boston, MA: Cengage.

World Health Organization. (2018). *Global health workforce, finances remain low for mental health.* Retrieved from http://www.who.int/mediacentre/news/notes/2015/finances-mental-health/en/

Wubbolding, R. E. (2015). Reality therapy. In E. Neukrug (Ed.), *The SAGE encyclopedia of theory in counseling and psychotherapy* (Vol. 2, pp. 856–860). Thousand Oaks, CA: SAGE.

Young, C. S., & Young, J. S. (2011). *Integrating spirituality and religion into counseling: A guide to competent practice* (2nd ed.). Alexandria, VA: American Counseling Association.

Zalaquett, C. P., & Chambers, A. L. (2017). Counseling individuals living in poverty: Introduction to the special issue. *Journal of Multicultural Counseling and Development, 45*(3), 152–161. doi:10.1002/jmcd.12071

Zubernis, L., & Snyder, M. (2016). *Case conceptualization and effective interventions: Assessing and treating mental, emotional, and behavioral disorders.* Thousand Oaks, CA: SAGE.

Zubernis, L., Snyder, M., & Neale-McFall, C. (2017). Case conceptualization: Improving understanding and treatment with the temporal/contextual model. *Journal of Mental Health Counseling, 39*(3), 181–194. doi:10.17744/mehc.39.3.01

Zur, O. (2007). *Boundaries in psychotherapy: Ethical and clinical explorations.* Washington, DC: American Psychological Association.

Zuroff, D. C., Kelly, A. C., Leybman, M. J., Blatt, S. J., & Wampold, B. E. (2010). Between-therapist and within-therapist differences in the quality of the therapeutic relationship: Effects on maladjustment and self-critical perfectionism. *Journal of Clinical Psychology, 66*(7), 681–697. doi:10.1002/jclp.20683

Author Index

Subject Index

A

A, B, and Cs, 128–129

acceptance, as counselor characteristic, 9–11

activating event, 128

active listening, 55

additive empathy, 53, 67

Adlerian therapy, 177

administrative safeguards, 156

advanced empathy, 53, 63, 66, 67–74
 analogies, usage of, 69
 discursive responses, usage of, 71
 media, usage of, 70
 metaphors, usage of, 69
 pointing out conflicting feelings/thoughts, 68
 reflecting deeper feelings, 68
 reflecting nonverbal behaviors, 67
 responses, 71–73
 tactile responses, 70
 targeted self-disclosure, 70–71
 visual imagery, 69

advice giving, 66, 80–81

advocacy, 111–116
 community, 112–113, 195
 institutional, 112–113, 195
 international and global affairs, 112, 113
 interpersonal, 112–113, 194–195
 interventions, levels and types of, 112–115
 intrapersonal, 112–113, 194
 public policy, 112–113, 195

affirmation, 66, 74–77

American Counseling Association (ACA)
 Code of Ethics, 9, 15. *See* Code of Ethics (ACA)
 crisis counseling goals, 122

American Psychiatric Association (APA), 170

amphetamines, 150

analogies, usage of, 69

antianxiety medications, 150

antidepressants, 150

antipsychotic drugs, 149

anxiety disorders, 254

appearance, and mental status exam, 144

assault and homicidal danger assessment tool, 118–119

assessment
 clinical interview, 143–144
 informal, 146
 needs, 147
 of physical abuse, 146
 testing, 145
 unreliability of, 188–189

attachment therapy, 177

attire/dresses, counselor, 26

atypical antidepressants, 150

automatic thoughts, 127

autonomy, 215

B

basic empathy, 53, 54, 67

Beck, Aaron, 127–129

behavioral rehearsal, 82

behavior, and mental status exam, 144

behavior therapy, 179

being committed, 40

belief about the event, 128

belief in one's theory, 18–19

benzodiazepines, 150

biological domain, 165, 167

biopsychosocial assessment model, 165–171
 biological domain, 165, 167
 psychological domain, 165, 167–168
 sociocultural domain, 165, 168–170

bipolar disorders, 254

board-certified coach (BCC), 135

body positioning, 28–29

by history, 171

C

caring curiosity, 35–36

caring habits, 39

Carkhuff, Robert, 53

Carkhuff scale, 53
 advanced empathic responses on, 67–68

case conceptualization/formulation, 163–171
 biopsychosocial assessment model, 165–171
 cognitive-behavioral approaches, 178–180
 defined, 163
 existential-humanistic approaches, 177–178
 postmodern approaches, 179–180
 psychodynamic approaches, 177–178
 theory/non-theory specific, 164–165

case management, 141–164
 assessment. *See* assessment
 case notes, 152–153
 case reports, 152–153
 client records. *See* client records
 documentation of contact hours, 157–158
 flowchart, 142
 follow-up, 159
 goal development, 147–149
 informed consent, 142–143
 professional disclosure statements, 142–143
 psychological reports, 152–153
 psychotherapy/process notes, 152
 psychotropic medications, monitoring. *See* psychotropic medications
 SOAP notes, 153–154
 termination and making referrals, 157–158
 time management strategies, 159

case notes, 152–153

case reports, 152–153

Center for Credentialing and Education (CCE), 135

characteristics, of counselors, 5–22, 24–25
 acceptance, 9
 belief in one's theory, 18
 cognitive complexity, 15–17
 competence, 15–17

About the Author

Raised in New York City, Dr. Ed Neukrug obtained his B.A. in psychology from SUNY Binghamton, his M.S. in counseling from Miami University of Ohio, and his doctorate in counselor education from the University of Cincinnati. After teaching and directing a graduate program in counseling at Notre Dame College in New Hampshire, he accepted a position at Old Dominion University in Norfolk, Virginia, where he is currently a professor of counseling and former chair of the Department of Educational Leadership and Counseling.

In addition to teaching, Dr. Neukrug has worked as a counselor at a crisis center, a substance abuse counselor, an outpatient therapist at a mental health center, an associate school psychologist, a school counselor, and a private practice psychologist and licensed professional counselor. Dr. Neukrug has held a variety of positions in local, regional, and national professional associations in counseling and human services.

Dr. Neukrug has written dozens of articles and chapters in books and has written or edited 11 books. In addition to *Counseling and Helping Skills,* his books include: *The World of the Counselor; Experiencing the World of the Counselor: A Workbook for Counselor Educators and Students; Counseling Theory and Practice; Essentials of Testing and Assessment for Counselors, Social Workers, and Psychologists; A Brief Orientation to Counseling: Professional Identity, History, and Standards; Skills and Tools for Today's Counselors and Psychotherapists; Theory, Practice and Trends in Human Services: An Introduction to An Emerging Profession; Skills and Techniques for Human Service Professionals;* and, *The Dictionary of Counseling and Human Services.* He is editor of the two-volume SAGE *Encyclopedia of Theory in Counseling and Psychotherapy.*

In addition to his books, Dr. Neukrug has been developing an interactive and animated website entitled "Great Therapists of the Twentieth Century." If you get a chance, visit the site, which can be found on his web page at www.odu.edu/~eneukrug.

Dr. Neukrug is married to Kristina, a former school counselor who is currently developing counseling-related workbooks and activities for mental health professionals. They have two children, Hannah and Emma. If you are interested in their books and counseling-related activities, visit www.counselingbooksetc.com.